SEB COE

RUNNING MY LIFE

SEB COE

RUNNING MY LIFE

THE AUTOBIOGRAPHY

HODDER &
STOUGHTON

First published in Great Britain in 2012 by Hodder & Stoughton
An Hachette UK company

1

A CIP catalogue record for this title is available from the British Library

Hardback ISBN 978 1 444 73252 8
Trade Paperback ISBN 978 1 444 73102 6
Ebook ISBN 978 1 444 73104 0

Typeset by Hewer Text UK Ltd, Edinburgh
Printed and bound by CPI Group (UK) Ltd, Croydon CR0 4YY

Hodder & Stoughton policy is to use papers that are natural, renewable
and recyclable products and made from wood grown in sustainable forests.
The logging and manufacturing processes are expected to conform to the
environmental regulations of the country of origin.

Hodder & Stoughton Ltd
338 Euston Road
London NW1 3BH

www.hodder.co.uk

To all the extraordinary people at the London 2012 organising committee who joined me on this journey, I dedicate this book. I can honestly say that I have never worked with a more focused or passionate group of people. It's quite possible that I never will again.

CONTENTS

ACKNOWLEDGEMENTS

I have been tempted to write this book several times since my career on the track came to an end over twenty years ago. But I have always been incurably inquisitive and perhaps instinctively I felt something equally interesting lay just around the corner. And it did, though quite how interesting I could never have predicted.

Until now I wasn't prepared to draw the line but even I recognise that, while there is still plenty of life to be lived, little I will go on to do could match these last few years.

I would like to thank all those who have helped along the way.

I will forever be grateful to my father for so many reasons obvious and less obvious. I would not have been in a position to have chronicled the ups and downs of the journey without him. And my mother who kept me grounded and who crucially made me realise that life wasn't just running around in circles.

My siblings who put up with it all. Just when they thought I'd slotted neatly back into the fold I became a Conservative MP.

William Hague whose sound judgements and unflappability I absorbed by osmosis, instincts that became a crucial ingredient over the last decade.

My aunt Sheila and cousin Jupiter for their much appreciated help with family history.

Caroline Michel who pestered me for years to write this.

Roddy Bloomfield, the doyen of sports editors, for his avuncular interest in everything to do with this book and all at Hodder for being such nice people.

Susie Black, for chivvying and encouraging me in this enterprise.

Nicola Milan, Susie's successor at LOCOG who, although not involved with this book, has seen me through the day job with unfailing good humour.

Carole whose patient proof reading and occasional raised eyebrow has been invaluable.

And of course my children, Maddy, Harry, Peter and Alice who are a constant source of pleasure to me.

Photographic Acknowledgements

THE author and publisher would like to thank the following for permission to reproduce photographs:

AFP/Getty, Back Page Images/Rex Features, Bettman/Corbis, Ben Birchall/ LOCOG/PA, Brian Bould/Associated Newspapers/Rex Features, Paul Childs/ Livepic/Action Images, Colorsport, Andrew Cowie/Colorsport, Gerry Cranham/ Offside, David Crump/Daily Mail/Rex Features, Bob Dear/AP/PA, Tony Duffy/ Getty, L'Equipe/Offside, Mike Floyd/Associated Newspapers/Rex Features, Mike Forster/Daily Mail/Rex Features, Andrew Fosker/Rex Features, Monty Fresco/ Daily Mail/Rex Features, Getty Images, John Gichigi/Getty, Rupert Hartley/Getty, Hugh Hastings/Chelsea FC/Getty, Scott Heavey/Getty, Qi Heng/Zuma Press/ Action Images, Roland Hoskins/Associated Newspapers/Rex Features, Paul Kitagaki/Zuma Press/Action Images, Adrees Latif/Reuters/Action Images, Toby Melville/Reuters/Action Images, Mirrorpix, Jeff Mitchell/Getty, The Packet Series, Peter Parks/Reuters/Action Images, Parliamentary Recording Unit, Sergey Ponomarev/AP/PA, Steve Powell/Getty, Press Association Images, Rex Features, Martin Rickett/Getty, Stefan Rousseau/PA, Stefan Rousseau/Reuters/Action Images, Julian Simmonds/Rex Features, Sipa Press/Rex Features, Sporting Pictures/ Action Images, SSPL/Getty, Rob Taggart/Reuters/Action Images, Bob Thomas/ Getty, Witters/Offside.

All other photographs are from private collections.

1

BEGINNINGS

ONE of my most treasured possessions is a portrait my father painted of me when I was eight. It's in front of me now: a solemn little boy in a pudding-basin haircut, checked shirt and incongruous knitted tie. It's good. And faced by the steady gaze of my eight-year-old self, I am reminded just how extraordinary my father was. He taught himself to paint and to sculpt and did it, like everything he turned his hand to, with aplomb. And of course a few years later he applied himself to a much less likely challenge than painting a portrait of his son, namely turning that same son into the fastest middle-distance runner of his generation.

Peter Coe was always going to make something of his life. An only child, he used to say that he couldn't have imagined there being a fourth mouth to feed in the household. It definitely made him more single-minded than he might otherwise have been, and possibly more selfish, as he had nobody else to worry about. It helped that he was ferociously intelligent. A working-class boy – my grandfather was a carpenter and my grandmother worked as a cleaner – he won a scholarship to Westminster, one of the most prestigious schools in the country. Unsurprisingly, it proved somewhat of a culture shock for a 13 year old fresh out of a West London elementary, and he left after only a few weeks, but was then offered a similar scholarship at a school in Wandsworth. At Emanuel the pupils were the sons of doctors and teachers rather than judges and cabinet ministers, plus a good leavening of scholarship boys like my father. It might not have been the hothouse that Westminster was, but he thrived there, developing his love of engineering as well as learning the German that would stand him in good stead as a prisoner of war.

From this distance, it's hard to imagine what an élite education must have meant to my grandparents, who had barely had an education at all. My grandfather, Percy, was one of seven children – born in 1893 in World's End, Chelsea, within a stone's throw of the Thames – while my grandmother, Violet, was five years younger, a true cockney who took her first breath in a nursing home (she would recount with some pride) just off the Mile End Road. She was the product of a rather more flamboyant background. My great-grandfather, Harry Newbold, was a professional gambler – at one time he did racing tips for the *Daily Express* – although the Newbolds were basically music-hall entertainers. Harry and his elder daughter Rose had a tumbling act, Harry being a contortionist, while Violet and May were dancers.

Around the time my father was born Violet was charring for a family in west London, while still living in the East End. 'It would make more sense if you moved a bit closer,' her employer, Gladys Minson, argued. 'Of course it would,' retorted Violet, 'if we weren't already living in one room in Whitechapel . . .' The Minsons' radical solution was to buy the house next door, and 1 Brecon Road, Fulham – £300 in 1920 – was given to my grandparents outright. They lived there for the rest of their lives.

It was a typical mid-Victorian London terraced house of yellowish brick with a rectangular bay on the ground floor and flat fronted above. In recent years Brecon Road has been gentrified – trees lining the pavement and nowhere to park. But when I first knew it in the late fifties and early sixties, it was still working-class Fulham, with girls skipping and playing hopscotch, and boys careering down the streets on trolleys made from pram wheels. The house itself hadn't changed since my dad grew up there. There was no front garden to speak of. One stride and you were at the front door. It was a classic two-up, two down, with the kitchen/bathroom at the back and a privy in the garden next to the pond – all that remained of the Anderson Shelter dug by my grandfather at the outbreak of war. In fact the house lost a chunk at the back during the bombing, though no one was hurt.

In the summer of 1939 my father had just finished three years at the Regent Street Poly studying mathematics and mechanical engineering. His first inclination had been to go to medical school, but there was no way that kind of money could be found. I never learnt what he hoped to do once he qualified – perhaps even he didn't know – because on 3 September everything changed when Chamberlain declared war on Germany. Although prepared to defend his homeland, he was far from being a monarchist, so, to avoid swearing allegiance to the crown, he signed up for the Merchant Navy. He would serve his country but not the king.

The spring of 1941 found him working on the Blue Funnel Line's *A D Huff*, a small freighter that was shipping newsprint and pit props over from Canada. That February it was on its return voyage to Halifax, Nova Scotia, when, 600 miles west of Newfoundland, it was shelled by a German battle cruiser, the *Gneisenau*, and sank within minutes, its ballast being rubble from the bombing of Coventry . . .

Five weeks after the ship went down, Violet had a visit from Blue Funnel's chaplain, who informed her that her son was missing, presumed dead. She refused to believe it. Even though a memorial ceremony was arranged for the bereaved, she would have none of it. Her son had not been drowned, she insisted. He would be back. Friends and neighbours tried to persuade her to accept the reality, but she remained steadfast in her belief that he was still alive. Five months later her faith was vindicated. Not only had Peter survived, but he was back in Britain unscathed, having just disembarked at

Greenock on the Clyde, where the home fleet was based. His account of what had happened on the night of 22 February 1941 was the first news the allies had had concerning the *A D Huff*'s fate. As the ship sank, the crew had taken to lifeboats and some had leapt into the sea. All were subsequently picked up by the *Gneisenau*, the destroyer that had just sunk them. Transferred to a German troop carrier, they eventually disembarked at La Rochelle. Then, after a few days in a holding camp (a former French Foreign Legion barracks) they were transported north-east by rail – in ordinary passenger carriages with the seats removed – to the notorious Stalag XB on the North Sea coast near Bremen. Outside Aachen, across the French/German border, twenty seamen jumped clear of the moving train. Most were quickly picked up, but my father and the Canadian bosun escaped, splitting up once it became too dangerous to travel together. While Eddy Shackleton turned south for Marseille, Peter headed west, crossing the Pyrenees into Spain where he was interned in the notorious camp for foreign nationals at Miranda de Ebro. Released later the same summer, he arrived in Scotland, on 14 August 1941, shortly to be united with his indomitable mother.

He was without doubt a chip off the maternal block. Even when I knew her – and my grandmother was already 60 when I was born – Violet Coe was a force to be reckoned with. As she lived until she was 97, I was fortunate enough to know her very well. Politically, she was a paradox. On one level she was an unreconstructed old Tory – a framed photograph of Winston Churchill had pride of place on the mantelpiece – but socially she was liberal, playing the piano in the local boozer, the Half Way House. I remember my sisters saying, 'God, Nana, you do know that while you're playing the piano, they're all trading drugs out the back . . .' and all she said was, 'Oh well, dear.' It was still her local in 1980 when I won the 1500 metres at the Moscow Olympics and she won Fulham Grandmother of the Year!

My grandparents had little in common, and I'm guessing that their marriage was based more on expediency than anything else, not least because they were married barely a month before Peter was born (though this didn't emerge till much later). While Violet would never have said it out loud, in her quieter moments she might have admitted that Percy wasn't the challenge she needed. On a day-to-day level she was obviously much more 'worldly wise' than he was. Another phrase she used – of other people – was 'sharp as ninepence' but if it applied to anyone, it applied to her. She taught her son to read when he was only three. Not surprisingly, he absolutely adored her, and wherever we were living, Christmas in Fulham was a fixed point on the family calendar.

Although my father would escape into the country whenever he got the chance, he was quintessentially a Londoner, and one way and another that part of London became as important to me as it was to him.

Spiritually, this run-down corner of the metropolis is where I feel most at home, and when alone in London with nothing more pressing to do, I'm likely to be found nursing a coffee on Fulham Broadway, or as I still call it, Walham Green. Even though it changed its name in 1952 – four years before I was born – neither my grandparents nor my father, nor anyone else of that generation who lived within its few square miles, ever called it anything else.

I was the first of my parents' four children and, although born at Queen Charlotte's in Hammersmith, I have no memory of where we lived before moving to the West Midlands. My early recollections of London are of holidays spent with my grandmother. A noisy Irish family, the O'Connors, backed on to them, and I used to mess around with the daughter, whose name, shamefully, I have forgotten. About three years older than me and many times more street smart, we always gravitated to Fulham's spinal cord, the North End Road market – still one of the great street markets of London

– where we would generally make nuisances of ourselves. She would goad me to take ever greater risks, which mainly involved nicking apples. Mercifully, I could run fast enough to escape some lug of a stall holder who would have hung me up on a meat hook if he'd half the chance.

Now that I'm a parent several times over, it strikes me that Violet was remarkably relaxed about it all, giving me *carte blanche* to roam the neighbourhood unchecked, barely seeing me from one meal to the next. But then she'd lived among these people all her life and trusted to her instinct that no great harm would come to me, not least because everyone knew exactly who I was.

My other grandmother, Vera, came from a very different background. Her mother, my great-grandmother – whom I can just remember – came from a family of wealthy industrialists in Cheshire. As a young girl, she had been swept off her feet by a dashing, Irish-born artist, Edwin Swan. His elder brother Cuthbert was also an artist, specialising in animal paintings, one of which hangs on the wall next to my father's portrait of me. Another brother was a doctor in Ballyragget in County Kilkenny. In the next generation, Vera's sister Pauline became a nun and then, when told she had no vocation, joined the army and fought in Belgium during the war. Vera's brother Michael became a writer, while her other brother John was a GP in Holland Park, and also the doctor for HM Prison, Wandsworth. He was with one of the first British medical teams to go into Belsen in April 1945. My mother became particularly fond of her Uncle John, and it was he who gave her a lifelong love of cricket. She would tell me how he took her to watch the Fifth Test at The Oval just a few weeks before I was born in 1956 (Australia v. England, match drawn).

Edwin Swan was an accomplished portrait painter, a Royal Academician and well respected in artistic circles. His pictures still come up at auction even today, and he made enough money from it not to have to do anything else. Both Granny and my mum always said that my Swan great-grandfather is the single person I most resemble – and not just in a purely physical sense, but even down to mannerisms and general outlook on life. Sadly, we never met as he died, aged 82, two years before I was born.

Slight and long-limbed, his elder daughter Vera became a professional dancer – my sister Miranda and I are evidently cut from the same tree – and ultimately this is how she met my grandfather. She began to do Indian dancing, with a company run by Uday Shankar, Ravi Shankar's older brother, who toured America and England during the twenties promoting his version of modern Indian dance. Vera and Uday became romantically involved, but – for all the Swans' bohemian lifestyle and their own unconventional marriage – her parents didn't approve. Vera was under 21 and was persuaded to call it off. She then toured in America with Anna Pavlova's company, which included 'Oriental Impressions' choreographed by Uday. Although marriage to Uday had been thwarted, on Vera's return to London she met another Indian, Sardari Lal, a law student. They were married in August 1927 in St Pancras Registry Office. The family could do nothing about it as she was now 22, my grandfather being a year younger.

My mother – Tina Angela Lal (always known as Angela) was born two years later, in December 1929, in Golders Green, her sister Sheila being eighteen months older.

Apparently, Sardari was the black sheep of the Lal family – a reputation he maintained throughout his life. At some point the money sent to him by his landowner father either stopped or ran out and with nothing to live on – and two small girls to look after – my grandparents took passage to India.

Vera's position cannot have been easy. As an English woman married to an Indian – a 'native' – she was shunned by Delhi's English community. The same held true of the Indian community;

the Lal family would have nothing to do with her. Two of Sardari's brothers were the only members of his family who ever visited them. The local Protestant school refused to accept her daughters as pupils because they were of mixed parentage. She had better luck with the Catholics and Sheila and Angela were enrolled in the Jesus and Mary Convent in Delhi. Vera's only friends were women in the same situation as she was, and as a couple they mainly socialised with journalists.

How did my grandmother cope in this unexpected environment? What was my grandfather's family like? What was their history? All I know is that they were landowners in the Punjab. In 2011, I was approached by the BBC for their genealogy programme *Who Do You Think You Are?* and said that I hoped to find out more about my Indian heritage. Sadly, without the detailed records available in Europe and America, they ground to a halt. I could so easily have asked my grandmother when she was alive, but I didn't – too buried in competition at the time to concern myself with family history. Or perhaps I was simply unimaginative.

By the summer of 1937 the gilt was peeling off the gingerbread. Vera had had a miscarriage – a boy – and Sardari had taken it very badly and turned to drink. She made her escape first by going to Simla to escape the heat. There, with the help of Sydney Jacobson, later Lord Jacobson, who was then deputy editor of *The Statesman* in Calcutta, she returned to England. It can't have been an easy decision, and confirms the strong-willed nature of the women in my family.

She went back to Golders Green, where she and Sardari had lived as newlyweds. It's hard to imagine what it must have been like for the two girls, transported to a world of privet hedges and grey skies, far from the heat, the exotic food and indulgent ayahs that had been all they'd really known. The nuns had arranged for the girls to go to their sister convent in Willesden, but within eighteen months they were uprooted again, among the first evacuees to leave London. They were sent to Northampton and didn't return until the war had ended.

Their first billet was with what my mother described as 'a fairly ordinary family'. Her abiding memory was of the dad hogging the fire and spitting into it all day. Not only was it damp and cold but my mother, already an avid reader, now found herself in a house without books. They were there for two years. Then the two sisters were separated, Angela being re-assigned to a family called Harris who owned a second-hand bookshop. After that, she and Sheila would only meet up at school.

John and Gwen Harris were kindly, imaginative and cultured. They had a son, also John, who was slightly older, and he and Angela became lasting friends. Most importantly, John Harris was interested in the theatre – he eventually became head of drama at Hull University and a specialist on masques and the Commedia dell'Arte – and I'm guessing that those couple of years she spent with the Harrises, surrounded by books, and putting on plays, proved a huge influence, not least in her decision to train as an actress. In fact, although her career would prove short, the theatre became her great and abiding love, and on her return to London she was accepted at RADA while Sheila went to a secretarial college in Kensington.

During the war Vera had stayed in London, working as a nursing auxiliary, and had already met the man she would live with for the next forty-five years until he died. Bill Williams was a BBC announcer, kind and gentle, although I didn't get to know him until many years later because my mother and my grandmother didn't speak until I was about 12. Vera had not approved of my mother's marriage.

As for my Indian grandfather, in 1939 he had bought the Marina Hotel in the centre of Delhi, its owners – two Italian brothers – having been interned as enemy aliens at the outbreak of war. I never met him, although there are still a few people around who did, and by all accounts he sailed quite close to the wind, with fingers in all sorts of dubious pies. Luckily, his best friend appears to have been Ashwini Kumar, who went on to become director general of the Border Security Force and something of a guardian angel. I discovered this quite by chance when we met a few years ago. In 1973 he became the IOC member for India, and went on to serve as vice-president from 1983–7.

Vera made a trip back to India in the early fifties, when she stayed for three months. My mother never did, although I know she would have liked to. It was one of the last things she told me before she died – and this when she could barely eat or swallow. It doesn't surprise me. After all, it was her home until she was eight.

Sheila returned there almost immediately after the war. In 1950 she married the Indian deputy High Commissioner in London whom she had met while working as a secretary there – in secret because Vera didn't approve. There was a considerable age differ-ence. Samar Sen – known as Tinoo – was 35, my aunt 21, just old enough to marry without parental consent. Cultured, elegant and witty, she always looked more obviously Indian than Angela and, looking back, I realise I have only ever seen her wearing a sari.

Her husband's story is fascinating. He was one of the earliest intake into the Indian Civil Service and studied at Oxford in the late thirties. A propaganda film was even made of him as a young district commissioner, the Raj having decided they needed to show they were giving local people positions of responsibility. After the London posting where he met Sheila, he went to the Lebanon, Jordan and Kuwait and was High Commissioner in Australia before going to the United Nations in New York, and then to Pakistan and Sweden. I remember writing a history essay during my first term at university, vaguely listening to the radio at the same time, when the news came through that the Indian High Commissioner to Bangladesh had been shot leaving the residency in Dhaka.

For a moment I didn't make the connection, but slowly the words sank in and I realised they were talking about my uncle. Within minutes I was down the corridor pumping coins into the payphone. He had been shot in the shoulder and back, and, although serious, he survived. This was shortly after Bangladesh had split from (west) Pakistan, and Pakistan's generals were still trying to destabilise the newly independent country. It was basically a kidnap/assassination attempt gone wrong, instigated by the long hand of the Pakistan Intelligence Agency. My uncle was targeted because he had played an important role in building up world opinion in favour of an independent east Pakistan – Bangladesh. Four of the terrorists were killed in the attack, and my uncle never completely recovered, although he continued working at the UN on internal tribunals well into his eighties.

As for my own parents – Angela and Peter – the engineer and the actress met at a party. It was the spring of 1953. The old king had died but the new queen had not yet been crowned. In a couple of months Everest would be conquered but it would be another year before the four-minute mile was broken. The age difference was strangely similar to that of Sheila and Tinoo. At 35 my father was twelve years older than his 23-year-old bride. To make things even more complicated, he had been married before and had a child. Although Vera had hardly been the epitome of moral probity herself, she refused to attend the wedding. Peter Coe was divorced, and that was enough. My parents married in 1954. Sheila was there, as well as the sisters' Uncle Michael, the writer. But not her mother.

I don't know why my father's first marriage foundered. He had courted a local girl and they had married soon after the war. Perhaps it had all been too rushed, propelled by his generation's need to make up for lost time. He never spoke about what had gone wrong but I do know that he fought tooth and nail for custody of his daughter – an unusual action even today – which suggests that it was more than simple incompatibility. He was intensely loyal, and took his responsibilities very seriously, so there's no doubt he had reasons.

As an only child himself, he always knew he wanted a large family, and although little was said, I know he took the effective loss of his daughter very hard. Later in life, he told me that although by then he had been happily married to my mother for over fifty years, not a day went by without him thinking about the failure of his first marriage.

I suspect that part of my mother's appeal was that she came from an entirely different background and had no connection with this unhappy part of his life. She was certainly not involved in the break-up.

Although he was a Fulham boy from the wrong side of the tracks and she was Kensington and RADA via Delhi, they were strangely compatible, each providing what the other lacked. He was a grown-up, solid and reassuring, a do-er to her dreamer. He was also something of a loner, while she was glamorous and gregarious and he always claimed that she socialised him. There is little doubt that her family considered that she could have done better for herself. I remember my father telling me how, on being advised that her intended was a mechanical engineer, one of my mother's uncles said, 'Oh I see. So you work with your hands?' I shudder to think what he could have said a few years later. As it was he had to bite his tongue since he was still trying to get my mother over the line.

As Peter's career progressed, his job became increasingly about managing people and managing problems, but he was always happiest when ranged over a drawing board or hands-on in an engineering workshop; and if work didn't provide the necessary practical application, then he would find something that did. He was never taught to paint; he just bought some oils and set to.

Although my mother was always seen as the cultured one, in fact it was my dad who introduced her to painting. He was the ultimate autodidact – what he didn't know about thirties and forties French cinema, for example, wasn't worth knowing. At home, if some recondite *film noir* with sub-titles was up against say, *The Guns of Navarone*, we hadn't a chance, and he would be genuinely shocked that we weren't as enamoured of these black-and-white Gallic masterpieces as he was. Coming from the background he did there were inevitably gaps in his education, and I know that my mother introduced him to classical music and opera, and he eventually developed a profound appreciation.

Once I was on the way, my parents moved to a rented flat in Highgate. I have a vague memory of sitting on my dad's shoulders and walking in what I imagine must have been Parliament Hill Fields, or perhaps Hampstead. When I was barely a year old, my father was appointed as production director of one of the world's largest fishing-tackle companies, Allcocks in Redditch, south of Birmingham. Samuel Allcock started making hooks here in the 18th century, and by the 19th century this otherwise unexceptional town had become the international hub of the fishing-tackle industry. At the start, they rented in Redditch itself, and my elder sister Miranda was born in Bromsgrove Hospital eighteen months after me.

The first house they owned was in Alcester, ten minutes south of Redditch, which had the great advantage, as far as my mother was concerned, of being only eight miles from Stratford-upon-Avon. Leaving London had been bad enough, but the pill was sweetened by her proximity to Shakespeare's birthplace, and more importantly the Shakespeare Memorial Theatre. It turned out that Shakespeare was quite a common name in the area. There was even a rival fishing tackle company called Norris Shakespeare in Redditch, which eventually gobbled up Allcocks.

Until his introduction to the world of rods and reels, my father had never been fishing in his life. But from then on he became an obsessive, setting up on the banks of the Avon at Hillborough in Warwickshire nearly every Saturday. Sometimes I'd go with him. Then, as now, I found it hard to sit still, and while he'd be absorbed in pondering the development of the split reel, or the prospect of landing a barbel, I would wander off.

My ability to fall asleep anywhere, at any time, is legendary, and it's a knack I've had since I was quite small. On this particular autumn afternoon, shortly after my fourth birthday, my father roused himself sufficiently to notice I wasn't around. Panic-stricken, he spent the next hour shouting my name, searching the shallows, wading down the river, dreading what he might find, terrified of having to face my mother, who was heavily pregnant and resting at home.

Eventually he went back to the car . . . and there I was, fast asleep. Sadly, there would be no happy ending for my mother's third baby. My brother was stillborn on 31 December 1960. Understandably, my parents never did anything on New Year's Eve again. Although it was never sombre, nonetheless any kind of celebration was clearly out of the question.

My first school was at Dunnington, just across the county boundary into Worcestershire, and I started there a week or so before my fifth birthday. It was tiny with two classrooms and twenty-one pupils. The headmistress was Mrs Rawlinson, who lived in the schoolhouse adjoining it. Every morning my father would drop me off on his way to work, and on one occasion he got talking to her husband. On discovering that he taught art at Stratford High School for Girls, my father told him how he was painting my portrait. I'm guessing that Mr Rawlinson's heart must have sunk but he offered to take a look nonetheless. It wasn't a wasted journey. I can still remember that first time he came over, and how pleasantly shocked he was by what he saw, having expected little better than painting by numbers. A few years older than my parents, William Rawlinson was an extremely talented wood engraver, with an international reputation. He had been in North Africa as an official war artist with the RAF, and his drawings of ground crews at work are now in the Imperial War Museum. He and my father became great friends and remained so until Bill's death in 1993. I am lucky enough to own one of his engravings – a sublime view of Rome and the Trinità dei Monti – which he gave me when I came back from Italy in 1980, just before I went to Moscow; and four years later, after the Los Angeles Games, he presented me with my own ex-libris book plates with details of my medals and records incorporated in the design – an example both of his artistry and his thoughtfulness. I owe something equally valuable – if less obvious – to his wife, which is my handwriting. To Patricia Rawlinson, handwriting was an art form, and happily I stayed with her long enough to make it stick.

As we only had one car – I don't think my mother even drove back then – I would get a lift back from school with a local farming family, the Edkins. Although the names of the individual Edkins, junior and senior, have long gone from my memory, I remember that car as if it was yesterday, a cream Morris Traveller with peeling wood panelling down the side and an interior that smelt of manure, milk and kerosene. Every afternoon I'd be set down at the crossroads to walk home. Actually, of course, I'd run. And those few hundred yards, with the noise of the Edkins' car grinding through the gears as it pulled away, are the first memories I have of running. For me, it was as natural as breathing, something I didn't have to think about. I used to run everywhere, and never got out of breath. And I really could run before I could walk, at least that was what my parents used to say. I certainly have a memory of running alongside my pushchair. It just felt the most comfortable thing to do.

Over the next few years, until we moved to Sheffield in 1968, hardly a weekend went by without us going for a drive into the northern Cotswolds, the area between Stratford-upon-Avon, Chipping Campden and Shipston on Stour. My father didn't enjoy being at the wheel but he loved walking and taking the car was the only way to get into 'real' countryside. The lanes he took us down – marked only on OS maps – would regularly cross open farm-land where five-bar gates tended to block the way. My job was to run ahead, open the gate, wait for the car to go through, close the gate and then head off on to the next one. Looking back, of course, it was classic interval training, because I'd run two or three hundred yards alongside the car, then open the gate, pause to recover my equilibrium, close the gate, pick my way across the cattle grid – and then I'd be off again. While my parents consid-ered my routine hilarious, I thought it entirely natural. Occasionally, they'd say, 'Don't you want to hop in the car now, Seb?' and I'd say, 'No thanks!'

My father's walks were not about parking the car and ambling 200 yards from some lay-by to admire the view. These were route marches. They'd start immediately we'd finished Sunday lunch – in those days about 2.00 p.m. – and it wasn't unusual on a winter's evening still to be out at six, trying desperately to locate the car with the aid of a fading torch. Then it would be back home for a bath, because my father had an unerring affinity with mud. You'd think he could divine it, and it was a rare afternoon if we – and, just as importantly, the car – managed to avoid it, even in high summer.

We moved house, into Stratford-upon-Avon itself, when my mother became pregnant again, this time with my brother Nick, who was born in Snitterfield, just north of the town in 1962, in the same nursing home where Emma would be born eighteen months later. Our new house was literally new, a classic sixties design with a garden front and back on a purpose-built estate located on the far side of the bridge that marks the southern boundary of the town, the original ford that gave the town its name.

For my mother this was bliss. One way and another she knew everyone at the theatre – or if she didn't at the beginning she soon did – and we were always having people to stay, either members of the RSC or fellow actors up to see a show.

As for me, my new school – Bridgetown Primary – was barely 200 yards away so naturally I ran. On Saturdays I would run into the town for my weekly comic and sweets, stopping only to hand over the money before haring back again without breaking sweat. I would run errands for my mother, but on the condition she would time me. Although I had a bike by this stage, it hardly got used. Much easier to run; it would take me no longer and I wouldn't have to bother about where to leave it.

Looking back, it's clear that my father would have liked me to take up cycling. Before the war he'd been a member of the famous south London club, the Herne Hill Wheelers. The Herne Hill Velodrome, built in 1891, is one of the oldest in the world. It hosted the cycling component of the 1948 Olympics and for several years, before the new Olympic Park Velodrome was opened, it was the only cycle track in London. Bradley Wiggins started cycling there when he was 12.

My father continued to enjoy cycling long after he'd given it up himself. One of the most evocative sounds in the world, he said, was the gentle click and purr of a bike when gears, rider and machine are in perfect harmony. He loved the visual aesthetic, the perfect alignment of body and frame. Of course he missed getting out there, feeling the road under the wheels and the wind in his ears, but he derived genuine pleasure from watching it, particularly the Tour de France. By the time he retired Channel 4 had it all sewn up and for the duration of the race – three weeks – he would hunker down and accept no invitation to go out.

There are some advantages to being a successful athlete and one was being able to introduce him to one of his cycling heroes, Eddy Merckx, who dominated the Tour during the sixties and seventies in the way that Lance Armstrong did in the nineties.

What my father most admired, I think, was the dogged nature of what they do. Three weeks, six hours a day in the saddle – that was something he understood. In his youth he thought nothing of cycling to Brighton and back again to Fulham in time for Sunday lunch. When I moved to the North Downs on the Surrey/Sussex border, his whole frame of reference was cycling, because these were the roads he'd taken on the Brighton run. He knew every short cut, every bend, every steep hill. But while the landscape further out remained much the same, when we drove to Heathrow along the old A4, he'd say, 'Of course, when I rode down here, it was all cornfields.'

2

APPRENTICE

I no longer remember how or when my eleven-plus results came through, whether they were sent to our parents by post, or whether they were read out in front of the class or even the entire school. All I do know is that it was sometime in the early summer of 1968 and I had managed to do what most of my mates hadn't, which was to fail.

The eleven-plus exam was the post-war generation's passport to a grammar school and thus to the kind of education my parents had mapped out for me: O-levels, A-levels, university. Unless you were on the borderline between pass and fail, there were no second goes, re-sits or appeals. Failure was a one-way ticket into dead-end street, kicked out at 15 with a handful of CSEs at the end of it if you were lucky. Or so it was then believed. Even if the finer ramifications were lost on us, we all understood that it was a watershed. Heroes one way, numbskulls the other.

So what happened? I was certainly capable of passing – my teachers were as perplexed at my failure as everyone else. And it wasn't as if we hadn't done practice runs – verbal and non-verbal reasoning tests, arithmetic papers and essays marked out the weeks and even months preceding the exam.

Although non-selective schools had begun to be introduced in Britain – and with Labour in power since 1966 it had become government policy – comprehensive education wouldn't reach Warwickshire for another ten years. Until then the system remained as stratified as Neapolitan ice-cream.

At the top was Stratford Grammar who had the pick of the high achievers. Next came Alcester Grammar. After that, marginal failures might be slid into Kineton School, a short bus ride away. The rest ended up at the Hugh Clopton Secondary Modern. I remember observing other parents' reactions that summer. Those whose offspring had made it into the 'right' school were understandably happy. Those whose children had performed as abysmally as I had intended to educate their kids privately if at all possible. I fondly imagined that this would also be my fate.

'No, Seb. Absolutely not. You're going to Hugh Clopton's,' my father bluntly informed me; nor did he offer any sweeteners. There was no, 'You'll come through. You'll be all right,' even though I was clearly not thick. I've often wondered why he did it. Although he had been a committed communist in the thirties when fascism was the foe, I suspect it was less principle than pragmatism. Peter Coe had four children and wasn't about to squander hard-earned cash on the one who had messed up.

Looking back, it was the best thing that could have happened. If I had ended up at a third-rate public school – and, make no mistake, no one else would have had me at that juncture – I would never have gone on to do what I've done, never in a million years.

Naturally, I didn't see it like that at the time. Not one of my circle of friends went anywhere other than Stratford Grammar. As for their parents, they were stupefied. 'But surely you can't let Seb go to Clopton's?' Oh yes they could. They were absolutely brutal about it.

At heart, like any 11 year old, I wanted my parents to be proud of me, particularly my dad. He had outwitted the Nazis, he had survived the frozen deep, he had helped win the war! Failing the eleven-plus, I now saw, was not the way to go.

Many years later in a piece for the *Daily Telegraph* I wrote, 'The seeds of reincarnation so often lie in adversity.' I was referring specifically to my non-selection for the 1988 Olympics in Seoul, but

perhaps my ignominious eleven-plus result had a similarly galva-
nising effect. I may not consciously have realised it, but a chance to
re-burnish the image was about to present itself.

The one area in which there were no complaints was sport and, if
asked what I wanted to be when I grew up, I would have replied
footballer. Perhaps every boy in the country would have said the
same thing following England's World Cup victory the previous
year. Yet while I was good enough to play both for my school and
Stratford Schools, I wasn't stand-out good.

Like every other junior school, Bridgetown Primary had its
sports day, where, in addition to the usual novelty events, such as
the three-legged race and the egg-and-spoon race, they had proper
sprints. Not that we were taught how to run any more than we were
taught how to balance a tennis ball on a wooden spoon; sports day
at primary level was about end-of-term fun. But running was what
I loved beyond anything else, and the faster I ran the more exhilarating it felt. Until that afternoon I'd only ever raced against my
dad's car and I wouldn't have been surprised to find a gate halfway
down the track. The combination of natural ability and determination is hard to beat at any age, and that afternoon I won every race
I went in for.

My victories led to my being entered for the next level up:
Stratford primary schools, where I won both the long jump and the
60 yards dash. A week or so later it was the turn of the South
Warwickshire primary schools, and I can still remember running in
Solihull and getting third place in the 60 yards. At 11 years old, I
was the quickest in the school, quickest in the town, and in the top
three of a large proportion of a largish county. But if anyone had
suggested I might make a career at it, I'd have laughed, as would
everyone around me. Running as a career did not exist. But a footballer . . . Although the wages weren't in the stratospheric range
they are today, football had been professional since 1885. Not that

money would have come into it. I was obsessed by football, always was and always will be.

Whatever small success I achieved that summer was forgotten by the time I started at Hugh Clopton's in September 1968. This was a classic secondary modern in that there was nothing modern about it, but harked back to the era of vocational training. Warwickshire being a largely rural county, most jobs for educational failures like me were related to farming or market gardening, so our days were spent labouring in the school's vegetable patch. We dug the ground, planted potatoes, potted, weeded and watered. The staff had clearly thrown in the towel (or perhaps that should be trowel) on anything remotely academic.

The only indoor subject I remember with any clarity was woodwork, where our first project was crafting a dibber, a pointed stick for making holes in the ground in which to plant the aforementioned tubers . . . Other than bringing home a finely turned dibber, my productivity was zero, although it's fair to say that I could spot a dodgy King Edward's from twenty feet along with the best of them.

An innate sense that I shouldn't really be there – even the guy who took us for football had a wooden leg – was confirmed one day by the history teacher. 'What on earth are you doing here?' he said, after I'd handed in a piece of work. I loved history and had probably done something half decent. In fact, my handing in anything at all would have been enough to provoke the shocked look on his face, as this was a rare occurrence.

Moving house is said to be the third most traumatic experience in life after bereavement and divorce. And for a newly turned 12 year old, the prospect of losing your friends and having to start all over again is clearly pretty disastrous. Unless, that is, you're at a school you hate and where you have nothing in common with anyone. So when I heard that we were moving to Yorkshire, I was near delirious with excitement. I remember running to Stratford town library and poring over all the available maps, and generally hoovering up everything I could find about Sheffield. I knew that my father was going to be running a cutlery factory and that cutlery was what had made Sheffield famous throughout the world. He told me his job was to 'turn it around', which he said meant, 'we may not be there for more than four or five years, maybe shorter. It just depends how long it takes me.' That was fine by me – I envisaged the future largely in terms of birthdays, Christmas and the football season.

Our new home was 37 Marlborough Road in Broomhill, a well-heeled area of Sheffield that took its character from the nearby university. Built of local mill-stone grit, it was a rambling Victorian house on three storeys with gardens front and back, attached to its neighbour by a garage.

John Betjeman wrote about Broomhill with obvious affection in his poem 'An Edwardian Sunday', which ends 'this hill-shadowed city of razors and knives'. And hills are everywhere in Sheffield, rising up between the many streams that descend from the High Peaks in the west. Fifteen of them connect to make the city's five major rivers – the Sheaf, the Rivelin, the Loxley and the Porter – all tributaries of the largest, the River Don. These are the watercourses that drove the mill wheels that transformed Sheffield into an industrial powerhouse in the 18th and 19th centuries, and which in turn brought my father here. And, although I was not to know it when I first arrived, these hills, formed by these rivers, would prove the ultimate endurance training ground. There are 78 public parks in Sheffield and the far west of the city actually falls within the boundary of the Peak District National Park. It is perfectly possible to run from the centre of town right up on to the moors without seeing a car.

We left Stratford towards the end of the autumn term so I had my last day at Hugh Clopton's on the Friday, and the following Monday started at Tapton Secondary Modern, an eight-minute uphill trot from Marlborough Road.

For the first time I found myself living in a metropolis, and it's fair to say it was something of a culture shock. Tapton itself was huge, having been amalgamated from three smaller schools in 1960, and as a result it was very mixed socially. For every kid who lived in leafy Broomhill or further west in Fulwood and beyond, there were two from the depressed inner city, either 19th-century back-to-backs or tower blocks. There would be no gardening here. Sheffield was an industrial city, a manufacturing city, and Tapton reflected this. They took their technical drawing very seriously. They took their metalwork seriously – we didn't sit there making ornamental napkin rings; at 14 and 15 we were using lathes to make small steam engines. Maths was serious. English was serious. Languages were serious. Geography and history were deadly serious. As for the teachers, they were highly competent. And while you didn't have to like them, you had to respect them. When a teacher came into the classroom you stood up. When the headmaster came in you practically genuflected. In short, you messed around at your peril.

Discipline was maintained via the threat of corporal punishment, a sword of Damocles that hung over our adolescent heads by the finest of hairs. It could take the form of instant justice – an art teacher once slung a bunch of keys at me – but more often it was ritualised, when you'd be hauled out in front of the class to be 'caned' or 'slippered', that is given six strokes on the hand with a bamboo stick or a rubber-soled plimsoll kept in the classroom for the purpose. More serious transgressions resulted in a visit to the headmaster. I was caned by him on several occasions, always justified I have to say. One master – or should that be mistress – of the art of corporal punishment was a former nun who taught us religious instruction. She had an unusual delivery, wheeling her arm straight up and over before plunging downwards, an action reminiscent of the great England test bowler Alec Bedser.

One day she called me out to the front for the expected (and doubtless merited) punishment, but as I prepared, palm outstretched, and watched her arm whip back in that idiosyncratic fashion, I thought, 'She's going to take my hand off!' So at the last moment I pulled away, and said, 'Steady on, Miss!' The titters from the back did nothing to improve her humour and with a face like thunder she packed me off to the deputy head.

Cyril May was known to be mahogany hard and his weapon of choice was unique, as befitted his status and reputation – a car aerial. I could only imagine what scars that would leave, and as I made my way down to his study I was overcome with terror. Why hadn't I just let her do her worst and get it over with? Mercifully, when I knocked on his door there was no reply and I spent the next forty minutes keeping my head down, praying no one would wonder what I was doing out of class. I never darkened his door again and so never discovered where the car aerial sat on the scale of pain. However, I subsequently got to know Cyril well and he turned out to be an exceptional guy. Government whips are so called because, like a huntsman, they whip the hounds in order to keep them straying from the pack. And Cyril May had that role in Tapton. In effect, he was the school whip, and he did the job brilliantly and in large measure was responsible for making Tapton what it was.

As for 'Steady on, Miss!', I was never allowed to forget it. And unpleasant though being caned was at the time, once the deed was done, that was it. The great plus of this system was that nobody informed your parents.

Sport was part and parcel of the Tapton ethos. We had PE at least every other day and the facilities were good. That first winter all I really did was play football and occasionally even rugby under the friendly eye of our teacher Mr O'Keefe, who was obviously pleased to have someone in the class who didn't need to be cajoled into the team – any team! Historically, good athletes tend not to be good ball players, but I may be the exception that proves the rule. I could kick, I could catch, I could throw, I could run with the ball. I was co-ordinated. I was even passable at cricket – that summer I played for the school – and with my family and friends I played tennis eventually up to a decent level.

The XIX Olympiad had been held in Mexico City the previous October, when we were still living in Stratford. In 1968, staying up till two in the morning wasn't an option, at least for the Coe family, although on the night of 15 October, an astonishing three and a half million people did just that, because not one but two British athletes had made the 400m hurdles final. Their chances of a place on the rostrum were next to impossible as both David Hemery and John Sherwood had the lowest times of any of the eight qualifiers. But the next morning, we woke to the news that the next-to-impossible had happened. David Hemery had won gold, and John Sherwood had taken bronze. Later that week, John's wife Sheila would take silver in the long jump, and together with Lillian Board, who won silver in the women's 400m, they were the only British track and field medallists that year.

John Sherwood went on to become an inspirational PE teacher in Sheffield. He knew that if British track and field were to have a future, it was imperative to get kids excited about the sport. A Yorkshireman born and bred, he was living proof that the Olympic dream wasn't just for the élite and, as nothing succeeds like success, he asked the BBC for a copy of the broadcast to take round local schools. So one morning the following spring, the whole of Tapton crammed into the sports hall and sat cross-legged on the floor to watch the men's 400m hurdles final. The 16mm film, complete with David Coleman's commentary, was already laced through the school's projector when John started to speak. Even though the screen was reasonably large, the film was so grainy it was hard to make out individual runners. We knew that Sherwood was in lane 8 and Hemery in lane 6, and as the starter held the pistol above his head, there wasn't a fidget or a cough. Even though we already knew the outcome, the atmosphere was electric. Then, with David Coleman's hysteria mounting by the second, we watched spellbound as Hemery took the lead, and crossed the line to win by over seven metres!

Coleman famously then said, 'Who cares who came third!' The answer was several hundred Tapton boys and about a million other people in Sheffield – a faux pas that Coleman has never lived down. However, it was an astonishing performance, and the hall erupted. The race had lasted less than 50 seconds – Hemery running it in 48.12, a new world record, Sherwood less than a second behind – but it was the most exciting 50 seconds of my life. As we clustered around our new Olympic hero, I remember thinking, 'That could be me . . .'

The timing couldn't have been more propitious. A few weeks later came my first sports day at Tapton. This time there were no novelty races to detract from the main business at hand, and we had a full quota of events: sprints, long jump, high jump and hurdles. True to form I put my name down for everything in my age group, and in a few events I was put up a year or two as well – not that I looked older than my age, far from it. Although one of the oldest in my class, I was still a puny little thing with the body of a child, albeit with the legs of a man. Even so, to the accompaniment of cheers from my friends – and the incredulity of both parents and staff – I won everything I went in for. And if I could pinpoint a moment when my father began to sit up and take notice, it was then. It was as if he had been plotting my success on a sheet of graph paper and the trajectory had just taken a sharp upward turn. My mother, on the other hand, was deeply embarrassed. 'Don't you think you could just lose something, darling?' she would regularly plead. The answer was, 'No.'

We had now been in Sheffield for the best part of a year. My father always believed in getting to know his workforce, and one afternoon he was talking to a cutler who had recently arrived in Britain following the Soviet invasion of Czechoslovakia the previous August. In the course of their conversation this new employee told my father that he was an athletics coach in his spare time, and that he was now helping out at a local club, the Hallamshire Harriers. My father no doubt mentioned that he had a 13-year-old son who was into running and had the potential perhaps to go further, and this guy probably said, 'So why don't you bring him along?'

What my father didn't know was that I had already been making my own forays in that direction. After showing us the film, John Sherwood had explained that he and his wife were members of Sheffield United Harriers AC and that the club were always on the lookout for new blood, so if any of us were interested, we should go down and take a look. A couple of friends and I decided to investigate, but confusing the names, turned up at the rival club, the Hallamshire Harriers instead. Based at the municipal track in Hillsborough, beside Sheffield Wednesday's football ground, I'd had no real idea that places like this existed. Now here it was! Somewhere I could do what I enjoyed doing most in the world! After that first visit, I went several more times just to watch, and tentatively joined in a few training sessions. So when my father told me that he knew someone who had a connection there, the die was cast. I was enrolled as a junior and Hubert Scheiber became my first coach.

Hubert was a gentle guy and softly spoken. In Czechoslovakia he had coached the discus to a fairly high standard. Now he took a small group of athletes for a number of field events, and with his help I began to find my way around. I did long jump and hurdling as well as running, and I even turned out occasionally for the high jump when the club needed points.

I started competing immediately, with training sessions twice a week from 6.00 p.m. till 7.30 p.m. on Tuesdays and Thursdays. In addition, every Sunday morning the whole club – juniors and seniors – would go on a run under the watchful eye of a cluster of club coaches including Sam Smith, Fred Lewis, Malcolm Dowthwaite and Malcolm Grace, most of them former competitors themselves.

Harriers are traditionally cross-country runners – the name derives from hare coursing where men would run alongside hounds wherever the chase would lead them – and while the club had spread into many other areas of track and field, particularly road running, cross-country remained at the core of its DNA. The format was simple. Starting from the club, we'd head up into the hills and onto the moor. Half a dozen cars would leave with us and at four to six miles the juniors would be picked up and bundled into track-suits to keep warm while the rest of the field ploughed on. Even from the beginning I rarely dropped out, and by the time I was 14, wherever they led, I followed. I could run all day with these guys. I was like the Duracell Bunny.

I loved everything about it – the physical sensation, the act of putting one foot in front of the other and covering the ground effortlessly and reasonably quickly, and also, if I'm being honest, winning the approval of the older and more seasoned athletes. And in running through that amazing landscape, I was discovering some of the most extraordinary scenery in England – if not the world – in the most exhilarating and unforgettable way imaginable.

Cross-country running was literally the making of me, and it saddens me that it's now so overlooked. You are using every part of your body. It's hard and it's tough. You've got to maintain balance, you've got to be able to navigate and to think ahead, you've got to watch your feet. You may be running on a track that's the width of a table, or across terrain that is little more than peat bog, making split-second decisions every step of the way. Your brain never switches off. It's both physical and mental. It's the supreme all-round conditioner and if you can deal with what's thrown at you on a tough cross-country course, you can deal with anything.

An hour spent running across moorland in the depths of a Yorkshire winter was as testing as anything I have ever done since. There were days when I would be drenched through to the skin, rain lashing my face, wind biting my ears, fingers numb with cold in spite of gloves, when even my eyelashes had iced up.

One route I used to take started at a pub called the Yorkshire Bridge on the banks of the Ladybower Reservoir, just over the county border into Derbyshire. From there a narrow road leads back into Sheffield, 12 miles, uphill all the way, over some of the most exposed country in England. In the summer the colours of the heather are dazzling, and you can't imagine wanting to be anywhere else. But in winter it's like a moonscape, when the wind whips in from the east and the cold stabs your face like flying ice, and all you're doing is grinding it out, mile after mile after mile. I must have done that run a hundred times, perhaps even more, but if at 15 or 16, you know that you've mastered that, what else is there to fear?

For the best part of a year after I joined the Hallamshire Harriers, my father was just another parent hostage to their children's sporting activities, ferrying and cheering when required. He had little knowledge of athletics – nor, as far as I'm aware, any real interest. Although he did occasionally talk about having gone to White City when he was young, he had certainly never run himself. Then, as the months went by, he began turning up to training sessions, in part prompted by my mother, worried by what seemed my near-obsessive behaviour. 'I mean, what on earth does he do down there?' It was a perfectly reasonable question, because the truth is that I was hardly ever at home. On Saturday mornings I'd run for the school and sometimes run for the club the same afternoon – two cross-country races in a day is unheard of now. I'd be home for *Match of the Day* and barely twelve hours later I'd be back down at the club for the Sunday run, and then there were the training sessions on Tuesdays and Thursdays . . .

Although Hallamshire Harriers had been founded in 1896, like many other athletics clubs, it had no physical infrastructure. The track was owned by the council and you'd pay sixpence (2½p) or a shilling (5p) to the old groundsman to use it. As for changing, we had the municipal changing room, classic 1950s spartan, with its permanent aroma of Domestos suffused with socks, and the still evocative smell of the old-fashioned embrocation Ellimans Rub, or the homemade liniment favoured by the older members of the club, a mixture of olive oil and umber. Shortly after I joined, however, the committee decided we should build a clubhouse of our own. It wouldn't need to be elaborate, and they'd realised there were enough skills among the members – glaziers, joiners, heating engineers, floor layers – to build it 'in house'. My dad, who was now a regular presence, offered to do the design work. The land was a disused car park next to the track, which they leased from the council. The main builder was Malcolm Grace, who by chance my dad employed at the factory on a job-by-job basis. Then it was down to fundraising. Labour might come free, but materials didn't. The commitment of everyone involved was extraordinary. For a while it seemed that, once the day shifts were over, nobody did anything but work on the clubhouse. The result was basically a glorified hut, but well designed and well built and boasting a particularly fine Ruberoid floor. I remember it going down; we all stood around and marvelled, watching it being poured in its molten form. The clubhouse was, above all, immensely practical, giving us somewhere to change and shower. Walls and shelves were used to chronicle our history and were soon packed with trophies and photographs of former athletes who had made it to the top, such as Ernie Harper, who won Olympic silver in the marathon in 1936. Our club president, Joe Williams, had run in the last cross-country race ever held in an Olympic Games, in Paris in 1924. It had happened to coincide with a heat wave, and athletes were passing out all over the place; that spelled its death knell. Our current star, Trevor Wright, was one of the top distance runners in the country. He went on to win a silver medal in the European marathon championship in 1971 in Helsinki. The clubhouse had a little kitchen and was soon a social focus, somewhere for the old boys to talk about days gone by, and for us young 'uns to hang out.

There was rarely a conflict of interest between running for the school and running for the club, although the nomenclature was confusing. At school I started as a 'boy' and at 15 became a 'senior'. At club level I started as a 'colt' and at 15 I was a 'junior'. Then, as now, it was not uncommon for PE teachers to belong to the local athletics club and so they would act as a bridge, encouraging talented kids to join, giving them access to coaching. This was the case with the Hallamshire, where a couple of Tapton's PE staff were members. By this route, and the fact that by the time I reached the third year, my name was appearing in the local press and *Athletics Weekly*, other teachers were beginning to know about my life outside school. 'Ah yes, Coe, the Runner,' they'd say, and built into this new identity was the sense that 'Coe the Runner' shouldn't be allowed to get above himself.

As chance would have it, my class tutor that year, David Jackson, was also a runner. As a schoolboy he had competed for Derbyshire Schools at cross country, and had been a more-than-useful 800m runner, so I think he saw me as a bit of a kindred spirit. He had started by teaching PE, having trained at Loughborough, but he was now head of geography, and largely because of him geography became my favourite subject. The fascination I had always had for maps now had focus. I can still look at maps all day; at that stage of my life they were the closest I could get to an understanding of places I could only dream of visiting. I could explore the world through my imagination while studying a map. Like all the best teachers, David Jackson made his subject come alive. Sadly, I can't say the same about religious instruction, which he also taught that year. One day, early on in the term, he took me to one side at the beginning of the class.

'So, what's your mileage looking like this week?'

'Well, Sir,' I said, 'I'm a bit down actually.'

Lowering his voice and barely moving his lips he looked at me and said, 'OK off you go.' And I thought, did I hear right? Is this a set-up? Am I seriously going to slope off out of this classroom, get into my kit and do a few miles round the school playing fields, only to have him say, 'Hah, you fell for it!'

'Well, what are you waiting for?'

'You mean . . . really, Sir?'

'Yes, yes. Off you go.'

I never had to sit through an RI lesson again. I would turn up, he'd give me the nod and that would be it. He was basically intimating that he saw no point in teaching it anyway, which given he was an atheist was hardly surprising.

When he believed in his subject, however, he was committed. At the beginning of the fourth year we were faced with an impossible choice. The timetable dictated either French or geography. To give up the only language I was doing was mad, according to my parents. But I adored geography. There were ten of us faced with this dilemma and a group of parents decided to lobby the head. The compromise David Jackson suggested was an example of his dedication. He promised to get us through O-level in one year. The French department weren't convinced they could match this, but in the same spirit offered to give us extra lessons in the second year instead of morning assembly. So ten of us started our O-level year with geography already in the bag.

For the best part of a year my dad watched me run and watched me train and said nothing. He had spent his life assessing situations and people, and he knew I had talent. What he didn't know was how far that talent could go because he had no yardstick. He had come to athletics with a completely open mind. But much of what he heard made no sense to him. He began asking very basic questions, such as why, if the objective is to run fast and short, are you doing all this mileage? And slowly, and with forensic analysis, he set out to discover what could be achieved if the raw materials were properly harnessed. If that makes me sound like a guinea pig, I was a more than willing one.

3

COACH

DAVID Hemery's and John Sherwood's triumph over hurdles in Mexico was particularly heartening given the absence of British track success elsewhere. Since Roger Bannister's myth-shattering run of 1954, when he blazed through the four-minute barrier with Chris Chataway and Chris Brasher as pacemakers, nobody had really scaled those heights again. We had won only minor medals at middle-distance championships, although, thanks to the generally spare build of British runners, middle distance was still considered our natural home.

The mile was now dominated by Jim Ryun, a college boy from Kansas, who had broken the world record twice, first in 1966 and then in 1967. The 800m was in the ownership of New Zealander Peter Snell, who won three Olympic gold medals in 1960 and 1964, and two Commonwealth golds in 1962, not forgetting the five world records he also set, six if you include the 4 x 1 mile relay with the national team.

Peter Snell was trained in New Zealand by Arthur Lydiard, a former marathon runner who believed that extreme fitness was achieved by running extreme distances. He became a legendary coach, and his theory was that to run a world-class 800m time you had to run a hundred miles a week. And in the face of Snell's undented success – he retired at the peak of his career in 1965 – the coaching fraternity had happily accepted the nostrum.

My father didn't buy into this hegemony. His instinctive view was that long slow running turned you into a long slow runner. If my aim, he said, was to compete at 5000m when I was 21, followed by marathons at 30, then fine. But if I saw myself as a middle-distance runner, the hundred-miles-a-week regime alone had to be cast aside. And so, without the question ever really being asked or answered, it was tacitly agreed that my coaching would henceforth be in my father's hands. But while the focus shifted from the club to him, we remained firmly attached to the Hallamshire.

Ours was never a conventional coach–athlete relationship; it clearly couldn't be. But in the end I believe it was something far greater. It was a partnership. Inevitably, there were fractious moments when we didn't see eye to eye, but these stand-offs were always short-lived. Again without it really being discussed, we fashioned a way of working together that was separate from our relationship as father and son. At home he was Dad. At the track – or out training – he was Peter. While he called me Seb – both at home and out training – when he referred to me in public, it was never 'my son', it was 'my athlete', at least once I started racing. It was his way of distancing himself. I know that to outsiders this seemed extremely odd, and people would often try to make capital out of it. Obviously, it was a mechanism, but it worked. Did the fact that I was his son affect the way he coached me? In that he had a greater knowledge of me than is usually the case, then yes. But he never pulled rank as my father.

Did he put pressure on me to let him take charge? I don't think so, because even then, I instinctively knew that my old man knew what he was talking about. Nearing 50 by the time we started, he had over thirty years' experience of going into new situations, taking them by the throat and making them work. Each company he had been involved with had presented different problems – different materials, techniques, end products, markets, different everything. He would go in, shake things up, keep what worked and re-think the rest. That was what he did, and he was good at it.

Yes, he took risks but they were calculated risks. An example: he didn't jump from that train in 1941 just because an opportunity happened to present itself. While prisoners of the German navy, my father and the crew had been well treated. But the transit camp in La Rochelle had sounded loud warning bells. Once on board that train, moving inexorably across France towards the Baltic coast, he would have waited and watched, observing the guards, calculating speeds and distances, assessing dangers and opportunities, so that when the moment came he knew what had to be done. He could so easily have been caught – eighteen others who jumped at the same time were recaptured immediately. But while luck must certainly have played a part, psychologically he would have been exceptionally well prepared. This was a man who knew what stresses and privations the body could withstand. He was a cyclist, still the world's most gruelling sport, while only weeks before he had hung on in freezing water off Newfoundland for twenty minutes before he was picked up by the *Gneisenau*.

If my father's defining characteristic was stubborn determination (or as even he might put it, bloody-mindedness), it was countered by an innate pragmatism, and he approached my athletics career as he would any other project that, as production manager, he needed to turn around. Had he been sitting in his office, charged with transforming a butcher's cleaver into a scalpel – and turning it into the brand leader while he was about it – his methodology would have been the same. He'd have dissected the problem into its component parts. He'd have been working out production levels, working out what the inputs were, working out what specialist knowledge was required.

So starting with his long-term goal – to see me selected for the 1980 Olympics – his thinking went something like: 'This is the current world record over such-and-such a distance. If we accept that the optimum age for peak performance is 23 to 24, where does Seb need to be at age 18 to hit this target?'

The engineer in my father saw the human body as a machine with strengths and weaknesses that would need to be addressed before performance could improve, because natural ability only gets you so far.

What is it that makes you run harder and longer? There's the ability to run long distances and there's the ability to run quickly. Are there different systems that you need to energise? What loads do you need to apply in training to adapt and stress those systems? And how do you maximise that at race level to run strong and fast and at super-human pace? There is no point running your lungs out if you can't sustain it and the race ends in vomit-inducing failure. You are trying to find the anaerobic threshold, the optimum level at which you can sustain a pace and cross the finish line in one piece and ahead of your rivals.

Even in the late sixties, physiology in relation to exercise was a relatively new specialisation. The generally accepted father of sports science was Woldemar Gerschler, a German. He coached Rudolf Harbig who, in 1939, set an extraordinary new world record for the 800m, winning the race with an astonishing final sprint, beating Sydney Wooderson's time of the previous year by a full three seconds. It was a record that remained unbroken for sixteen years and a time that would win races in the United Kingdom today. Harbig set two further world records at 400m and 1000m before being sent to the Eastern Front where he died in 1941, the same year my father walked across France to freedom.

Gerschler's central theory was that it's not the running itself that strengthens the cardiovascular system, but the recovery effort. Nor was he the only one expounding this hypothesis. In the course of his research my father had come across a Swedish sports physiologist, Per-Olof Astrand, who was saying much the same thing: quality not quantity. Now a generation later, he put theory into practice. There would be no more meaningless mileage or pavement pounding. Instead, I would do less mileage overall, but at a faster pace, and in parallel there would be punishing speed-endurance sessions mixed with interval training. Typically, this would include running 40 x 200m with only a 30-second recovery period between each. Alternatively, I'd do 6 x 800m with equally ludicrous recovery times. Like most athletes with a daily training schedule, I would usually start from the house and by sheer chance our garden backed on to a section of the university sports field – basically, a grass lacrosse pitch and, on the far side, an all-weather area where people played anything from five-a-side football to tennis and hockey. The great advantage for me was that in the winter it was floodlit so I didn't have to train in the dark.

But Sheffield's hills were like a siren call to my father, and the three-and-a-half-mile gentle climb of the Rivelin Valley Road became as familiar to me as our garden path. I would run the prescribed 6 x 800m spending each 30-second recovery period hovering momentarily behind my father's Cortina estate. Luckily, this road is one of the most beautiful in Sheffield, loud with bird-song most of the year, and at its most vibrant on early summer mornings. The bubbling river with its succession of saturnine pools are a permanent reminder that this was the genesis of Sheffield's industrial heritage. Now the domain of fishermen and walkers, nothing remains of the mills that once towered over its banks, throbbing with noise and fervid life. For the next twenty years, two hour-long sessions per day, such as these, would become my default schedule and, in addition, of course, there were still my cross-country runs.

My father's radical re-think in relation to my training was regarded with some unease at the club. As a colt I was already winning races – in cross-country I was rarely out of the top three. And now this 'amateur', who freely acknowledged that he knew nothing about the sport, was challenging their long-held orthodoxies. In fact, of course, the amateur tag was as far removed from my father's character as can be imagined. He was utterly professional. If I trained, he came with me. There was no 'you run along and we'll discuss it later'. If he sent me out in the snow on Christmas Day, he came too, not least to make sure that I took as few risks as possible on roads that became increasingly treacherous as the thermometer plunged.

The more he learnt, the more he wanted to learn, and he would go down any avenue, however unpromising. Inevitably, some would prove blind alleys, but even they were part of the process, adding to his total sum of knowledge.

My father had one great advantage over most other coaches – who, practically without exception, were all former runners – in that he brooked no specious or imagined thresholds simply because it was the commonly held belief, or had been personally experienced. And while he discounted nothing out of hand, set-in-stone dogma and old wives' tales got very short shrift. If it made no scientific sense, it was consigned to the bin.

He didn't set out to kick over the traces, he simply wanted to reach his target in the most efficient way possible. Peter Coe was an engineer, not a DIY handyman, and tinkering at the edges wasn't in his nature. This would be a back to the drawing board, root and branch re-think, not least because he understood that to run a world-class 800m time you run 80 per cent of the distance without enough oxygen.

By early 1971, in spite of the nay-sayers, my father's training routine was beginning to pay dividends. That spring I won the Yorkshire colts cross-country title followed by the Yorkshire schoolboys cross-country. I was now 14 and rival club and school coaches concluded that I must be clocking up a monstrous number of miles every week. How else could my speed and consistency be explained? It was around this time that the idea emerged of my father being a tyrant, a reputation that stuck to him like chewing gum throughout my career.

Raw talent will only take you so far, and moving beyond it is never going to be comfortable. As my coach, Peter's job was to get the best out of me, which he undoubtedly did, sometimes pushing me to the limit. But this was what I wanted to do, and if I needed someone to remind me that success wouldn't be handed to me gift-wrapped under the Christmas tree, so be it. But it was always my choice. Crucially – and wisely – at this stage of my career, it was my father who stopped me from going to the well one too many times.

As a result of my win in the Yorkshire Schoolboys in February, I was selected for the English Schools cross-country in March. The English Schools Athletics Association has been the garden of many young competitors. Steve Ovett, Steve Cram, Tessa Sanderson, Daley Thompson – we all did English Schools, and it remains the springboard for many aspiring athletes. Over the next three years I would represent Yorkshire five times, twice in the cross-country in the spring and three times at the track and field championships later in the year.

That first English Schools meet – my first national competition – was in Luton. We travelled by coach and, after a three-hour journey, arrived around mid-afternoon, when we were taken straight to a community centre to be parcelled out to those who had offered us hospitality. Like everything else in British sport, the English Schools is underpinned by volunteers, and with over a thousand adolescent boys to accommodate, vetting of the host families was probably not a priority. There were literally hundreds of us milling around that afternoon, all looking slightly dazed and lost. It's the closest I've got to understanding how my mother must have felt when she was evacuated to Northampton.

Three of the eight of us selected to represent Yorkshire were from Sheffield, and while we were at different schools, we knew each other from the Hallamshire and had therefore been billeted together. The couple on whom we'd been landed hadn't a clue what to do with three teenage cross-country runners. 'Have you had your tea?' our host said the moment we got through the front door, in what was clearly a child-free household.

'No,' three breaking voices chorused. Apart from a sandwich on the M1 we'd had nothing since breakfast. It was then about five o'clock, the time when we would normally be getting back from school, and my personal routine was to have a glass of orange juice and a chocolate biscuit before going back out to train. Then it would be home for supper, homework and bed. So we were each handed a cup of tea and one slice of cake and the television was switched on.

As afternoon drifted into evening, we gradually realised that nothing was happening in the kitchen – no reassuring clatter of pans, and above all no tantalising smells. Finally, it dawned on us that we'd be getting nothing more to eat that night. This would be bad enough for any teenage boy, but we had a three-mile run to do the next day, the biggest race of our young lives.

'I'm starving,' I muttered to the others, 'and if I don't eat soon, I'm going to die. We can't just do nothing. They must have fish and chip shops, even down here!'

Saying we were off for a stroll, we made our escape, hot-footed it to a chippy a few streets away and, pooling our cash, bought what we could, not all of it sensible. In terms of pre-race preparation, a good night's sleep is top of the list. Yet there I was in a strange bed, with a stomach full of chips, under-cooked batter and Tizer. As I lay there desperately trying to drift off, all I could think about was the two bus-loads of supporters that the school had organised, convinced that I was going to win. I came twenty-first.

The field and track championships the following summer were even worse. That year they were held at Crystal Palace and I got billeted out to a greengrocer and his wife in Streatham, a big south

London family, so thankfully supper was plentiful and healthy. But at 5.00 a.m. I woke with a start as metal blinds began rattling up a few feet below my window, followed by vans arriving and crates being thrown on the pavement accompanied by cheery south-London banter. This time I was running 1500m and this time I came last.

My catastrophic performance wasn't hard to analyse. How could I possibly be physically and mentally fresh, Peter said, with all that crashing about when I was meant to be asleep? And it remains true that while the volunteering ethos is great in principle, billeting young athletes with strangers who have no idea of what your routine should be before an important race was a recipe for disaster.

The following spring the English Schools cross-country was at Hillingdon, west London. I can't remember now what the accommodation arrangements were, which suggests that I got a decent meal and a decent night's sleep. By then I had moved up a group, so in fact I was running against boys who were a year older than me. I can't say I noticed the rangy guy who came second, and I don't imagine he paid much attention to the stripling who came ninth. His name was Steve Ovett and it was the first time our paths had crossed. This was hardly surprising. Firstly, he came from the south; secondly, he was a year my senior; and thirdly, while he focused on the sprint end of the spectrum, I was running longer distances.

Pub quiz aficionados will know that that cross-country in Hillingdon in 1972 was the only time Steve Ovett and I ran against each other on English soil until the late eighties. The name of the winner is the answer to that other great pub teaser: who was the first person to beat Coe and Ovett in the same race? The wrong answer is Olaf Beyer in Prague in 1978. The correct answer is Kirk Dumpleton at that cross-country meet when we were still juniors, and Kirk and I would later be fellow students at Loughborough.

The final nail in the coffin of the English Schools was going to

Washington, County Durham. It was the summer of 1972. I ran in the 3000m and could manage only seventeenth. This time there hadn't been a problem about either sleeping or eating, but I had started my warm-up much too early. A well-known coach in the North East, Gordon Surtees of the British Milers Club, who had became a close friend of my father's, didn't mince his words. 'I knew he was going to run like a sewer,' he said the next time they met. 'He seemed to spend the whole bloody day warming up.' When you're young and eager, there's the tendency to run the race ten times before the starter even lifts his pistol. Rule number one: you have to stay fresh.

Important though my running was, academic success was still my father's *sine qua non*. He believed in developing what he called 'the whole person' and the following summer I had GCEs to contend with, my parents snapping at my heels like a couple of Jack Russells. Just as I could never use the 'homework' excuse when it came to training, I couldn't use the 'training' excuse when it came to revision. A repetition of my eleven-plus performance was not to be countenanced.

On my first day at Tapton five years earlier, I'd been given a quick assessment and put in the top stream. There were about thirty of us in the class, and it was immediately apparent that we were all academically able. The only thing we were bad at, it seemed, was passing exams. Virtually all of us – girls and boys – went on to higher education. Of my five best friends, one got a first in physics and became a professor. Another got a first in maths, two got degrees in English while the fifth is one of the biggest independent estate agents in Sheffield. And these are the ones I know about. By chance, in 2009, as chairman of LOCOG, I bumped into another Tapton success story. I was about to meet the English MD of Gymnova, the company who supplied all the gymnastic equipment for London 2012. I stretched out my hand, smiled, then stared – short dark hair, glasses, a keen, eager-looking, slightly crooked smile . . . The last time I saw that face, I realised, was forty years ago, disappearing up a rock face, or vanishing down a cave in the Peak District.

'Colin?' I said. 'Colin Boothroyd?'

'The very same . . .'

Yet another educational failure who, like me, somehow made it off the scrap heap.

If asked now whether I'd rather go back to the grammar-school system, with all its hard justice, the answer is probably yes, because our teachers were ambitious for us, and I know that Colin and I, and all those others, got a far better education at Tapton than most kids now enjoy in your 'bog standard' comprehensive. As for our charismatic geography teacher and athletic atheist David Jackson, he was one of those teachers you wish every child could have access to. We stayed in touch and last spoke a few days before he died in 2011. David was an assiduous correspondent right to the end. In the early days, letters of congratulation or commiseration would be waiting for me whenever I got back from a championship, putting both success and failure into perspective. These missives were always beautifully crafted and well judged, often written on Donald McGill style saucy postcards, which went down particularly well in the House of Commons. He will be missed.

However much Tapton benefited from the grammar school ethos, it was still a secondary modern and to move any further up the educational ladder I'd have to transfer to a sixth form in another school, and that needed GCEs. In the meantime, there would be no let up in my training. As my father's mantra had it: 'You can do it. One helps the other.'

My O-levels were at the end of May/early June. The results wouldn't be through till late August, but before then it was English

Schools time again. I was down to run the 3000m – the same as the previous year. I had just won at the Yorkshire Schools at that distance, so there was no reason to think I shouldn't do well.

However, this time my father was taking no chances. Yes, I had done well in Hillingdon cross-country, but every other English Schools I'd competed in had been disastrous. The whole thing was too hit and miss, he said. There were too many variables. So he made a policy decision: instead of travelling with the team, he would take me there himself. That year the meet was only two hours away, at Bebington Oval in Cheshire, which eight years later would stand in for the 1924 Olympic stadium in Paris in *Chariots of Fire*. 'We'll set off early, get there in good time. I can supervise your warm-up, you'll do the race and then we'll come home.'

The idea that anyone supervised anything at an English Schools championship was wishful thinking on his part. We were left entirely to our own devices, and as it lasted two days we'd always be queuing up for this, waiting to do that and generally hanging around the stadium doing nothing hour after hour and getting extremely bored.

The organisers were far from happy when he gave them the news. 'But this isn't what we normally do . . . We like the team to travel together.'

'Well, that's fine,' my father said. 'The rest of them can do that, but not Seb. Listen, we don't need to do the Schools. We've got the Clubs. And when he runs the Yorkshires or the Northern Counties, we go there and back on the same day, and that suits us. And when I'm not there, the club looks after him. The Schools is the only meet where that doesn't happen. Please don't misunderstand me. We like the English Schools and while I applaud your commitment and would like to support it, this simply isn't working.'

The 3000m was scheduled for the second day. I had one of my mother's wonderful home-cooked meals the night before, followed by a good night's sleep in my own familiar bed. We didn't even go into the stadium beforehand, but found a café nearby and had a cup of tea. Then I gently warmed up, checked in and ran. We were back home by 8.00 p.m. and I was down at the youth club with my mates half an hour later. Running was a bit of a mystery to most of my friends – football was our sport – and so I probably didn't even tell them where I'd been, or that I'd won, let alone by ten metres.

We were lucky, I think, to have learnt the lesson so early, albeit on the fifth occasion. Our experience in Cheshire that day reinforced my father's every instinct that in life you make your own luck. As he so often said: 'You just can't afford to play with too many variables at the same time.'

Bebington was the first time that we rubbed up against the establishment but it would not be the last.

4

GETTING THERE

My last race in 1973 was at Rotherham on 15 September. It had been a good summer. After Bebington, I'd gone on to win the 1500m at the AAA Youth Championships. The Amateur Athletics Association is the oldest governing body in the world, and 'the three As', as they were known, were considered to be Britain's national championships. They were the logical next step for a young athlete after the English Schools because, from junior level upwards, they were used as trials for international selection.

So while the track season might have come to a close, training continued throughout the following autumn and winter, and I still enjoyed my long runs with the Hallamshire on Sundays. It never failed to lift my spirits to be up on the moors, in company or on my own. The remoteness and the solitude were a necessary antidote to the pressure of a life split between school and training. Whatever frustrations I might feel on the track – which could leave me physically and emotionally drained – disappeared once I was crunching my way across the frozen landscape of the moors, where the only signs of life were the tracks of hare and deer.

Once November arrived Sheffield seemed perpetually shrouded in darkness, the skies so leaden it was hard to tell what time of day it was. Roads were either lethal with fallen leaves or lethal with rain or ice. In addition to the usual winter hazards, I now found myself running in the headlights of the family Cortina since street lights could no longer be relied upon. They were either dimmed to half their normal brightness or extinguished completely, thanks to the three-day week.

During the 1970s the British economy seemed to have lost its way. Unemployment had increased to levels reminiscent of the 1930s. Inflation was rising as fast as a spring tide, fuelled by spiralling pay settlements as wages struggled to keep pace with prices. Already at a post-war high of 7 per cent in 1970, by 1974 inflation would reach 16 per cent. In 1971, in an attempt to curb the unions' inflationary claims, the Heath government passed the Industrial Relations Act, but its very rigidity made it unworkable. With pay rises capped, when the National Union of Mineworkers demanded an increase of 25 per cent, confrontation was inevitable.

As pits went dark, miners' union leaders turned their focus to the coal-dependent economy, blockading power stations and steel works to prevent oil being brought in, bussing 'flying' pickets hundreds of miles if necessary. Barely a day went by without another union being sucked into the vortex. Often unofficial and unsanctioned, these rolling strikes became virtually continual: railways, emergency services, the car industry, British Steel, and of course the docks, historically always a focus of discontent because of its casual employment structure.

My interest in politics didn't begin with the three-day week but it sharpened my focus, and I sensed even then that this was a defining moment. It was perhaps easier for me to see the consequences of an increasingly public-sector-based economy, living where we did. If I'd come from the south, where manufacturing industry played a lesser role in daily life, perhaps I wouldn't have been so aware of what was happening. But in Sheffield the drudgery of municipal socialism was on the doorstep.

Politics was part of who we were as a family. Even as a boy I had kept a scrapbook, a kind of political diary with headlines pasted in cut from newspapers. My first political memory is of my parents being very exercised by the Vietnam war. I have a clear image of Angus Maude – Stratford's Tory MP – standing on our doorstep in

1966 with my mother confronting him on the subject and giving him very short shrift. This was in the run-up to the general election called by the then prime minister Harold Wilson, and I can still remember my parents' excitement when Labour got back in with a vastly increased majority.

My mother was really a Jo-Grimond Liberal, but she was also a classic tactical voter, who would support Labour to keep out the Tories. And while my father had been a member of the Communist party in the thirties, by the mid-to-late sixties he would have described himself as a Labour supporter. He inched further to the right throughout his life, but whether he ever voted Conservative is a matter of debate. There were some values he considered immutable, however, and although clearly 'management' in the eyes of his workforce, he always remained close to his trade-union instincts, warts and all. In his twenties, as a member of the Amalgamated Engineering Union, he'd been a young official. He'd taught at, and helped organise, the Workers Educational Association in west London, so he understood them and they in turn respected him and knew they couldn't pull the wool over his eyes when it came to negotiation. He'd been there and he'd done it from the other side.

With such divergent and strongly held views – polarised to a degree approaching absurdity if you included my grandmother in Fulham, who was a full-blown Alf-Garnett Tory – political debate around the Coe kitchen table could get heated. Everything was discussed, voices were raised or not raised, but it was always vocal and always strong.

For over two hundred years Sheffield had been the centre of cutlery manufacture for the Empire, if not the world. Silver plating had been invented there, and stainless steel. It was an extraordinary crucible of innovation and expertise – a Silicon Valley for the 18th and 19th centuries – but by the seventies it was in unmasked decline. Whole areas of the city's industrial core lay abandoned, literally marked out for demolition. Seven out of ten people were now employed in the public sector. While its communities were still weathering the storm, all around them staple industries were dying, and nobody seemed to have much idea about how to replace them, in part because of the growing and erroneous belief that over the long haul the country's burgeoning financial-services sector would somehow see us through.

Echoes of a prosperous past were there if you listened for them. On a still summer's evening sound travels, and I would drift off to sleep to the thump, thump, thump of a large steelworks, probably Dunford Hadfields or Firth Brown on the other side of town. But while foundries continued to work round the clock, cheap labour in emerging markets was slowly but surely strangling our manufacturing base, and with it centuries-old communities.

My father's factory typified the kind of business at risk of going under. It had been bought for a knock-down price by property tycoon Gerald Ronson, who had been smart enough to see that the brand still had potential and then smart enough to put my father in to turn it around. The nub of the problem was cheap imports wholesaling at prices Sheffield cutlers couldn't match. Materials alone cost more than the Hong Kong or Korean finished product. So the sector as a whole – in trouble and losing money – had panicked, and gone downmarket. But although my dad had no background in sales or marketing – he was very much a production man – he took the alternative route, a decision that would eventually turn George Butler into a highly profitable company and a brand, albeit under different ownership, that's alive today.

It can't have been easy. Peter Coe, a Londoner parachuted into a core Sheffield business, telling them what to do, laying people off, bringing others in, telling those who remained that they either accepted massive changes or they wouldn't be in business. There was nothing inherently wrong with the brand. George Butler wasn't failing because of what it produced, but how it was produced. The manufacturing process itself was inefficient, largely through the use of antiquated machinery. When my father first arrived, production practices had changed little over thirty years. So why not just drop a bomb on the place, he said, and make it easy? Because that's what they were looking at: commercial suicide. Alternatively, cultivate a market that appreciated quality and good design and you at least stood a chance of life after Taiwan.

So they did, and in a shrinking market George Butler succeeded in holding on to a portfolio of quality contracts, including Harrods and House of Fraser. They even supplied Downing Street and Buckingham Palace, and I remember a specially commissioned canteen of cutlery presented by the Boy Scouts Association to the great football legend Stanley Matthews. The most bizarre commission, though, was for the Sultan of Brunei, who ordered a set of silver-plated utensils for eating monkey brains. A marketing concept far ahead of its time was a range of cooks' knives my father designed with the American restaurateur Robert Carrier, arguably England's original celebrity chef. There's still a set in my kitchen today, knives that I assembled myself the last time I worked at the factory in the summer of 1976, a rare – and never to be repeated – example of S.N. Coe craftsmanship.

I started at the factory the summer before my O-level year, and worked there every year subsequently until I left school. It was a wonderful rabbit warren of a building, an archetypal northern factory: big old gates, tiny stairwells, raw brick, and offices partitioned by plasterboard. The most salubrious part was the showroom, but my dad's end of the business was banging the stuff out. I'd been a regular visitor ever since we'd arrived in Sheffield.

The great advantage of having a father involved in engineering was that my technical-drawing homework was always perfect, but when it came to metalwork, he threw up his hands. I remember bringing home a candelabra – an exercise in learning how to work steel – and he couldn't believe it. 'You're all living in the dark ages,' he said. 'You want to come down to the factory and make it there.' So I did. This was on machinery he'd designed himself, so inevitably this candelabra came back looking like something out of the Design Museum designed by David Mellor. Naturally, this did not go down well in the metalwork annexe at school, but in his view the days of standing over a vice with a file were over, so why not teach us to use current equipment? If Tapton's finest were hoping to go into engineering, he said, they had better get used to modern methods. It wasn't about helping me to cheat; it was about introducing me to the world as it now was, a world of computerised lathes, not metal bashing.

Over those three summers I mainly worked in the press shop where, among other things, I learnt to haft a blade – hence the Carrier knives. Haft means handle, originally for a sword, and a hafted knife is one made in two pieces. While the blade would probably be steel, the handle could be anything from electro-plated nickel silver – otherwise known as EPNS or Sheffield Plate – up to solid silver. This is very much the expensive end of the cutlery spectrum, and where the company was by then firmly positioned, thanks to the old man. We had to tip our hat occasionally to mass production, however. I remember a particularly productive fortnight when we bashed out 64,000 corn-on-the-cob spears. This may have been the last summer I worked there because I remember my brother Nick – then only about 14 but who had nevertheless been roped in – sitting upright at the fly press next to me fast asleep. Don't know what health and safety would say about that today – actually I do, not to mention the NSPCC.

By the time I left school I could have held down probably three or four jobs in George Butler's. I thoroughly enjoyed it, and not only because I had no trouble getting days off for my running commitments. I relished being in the factory. I relished being part of an organisation. I was the proverbial fly on the wall – invisible to both the staff and my father – and by osmosis learnt about the importance of people management, budget control, planning and looking ahead. If I hadn't realised it before, I came to appreciate just how smart my father was. Of course, I should have recognised it through the training programme, but in some strange way I took that for granted.

That first miners' strike in 1971 marked the beginnings of the slow but inexorable erosion of Britain's coal stocks, and in the spring of 1972 selective power cuts began. The crunch came with the Yom Kippur war in October 1973, when Egypt went into Israeli-occupied Sinai to reclaim territory taken in 1967. Oil prices rocketed, going from $11 a barrel in 1970 to $55 a barrel by the beginning of December, an increase of 500 per cent in less than four years. Far from exercising restraint at this juncture, the miners escalated their demands. As their leadership put it, 'Why can't you pay us for coal what you are willing to pay Arabs for oil?' The miners were now demanding a pay rise of 31 per cent and launched an overtime ban that cut coal production by a third. This soon became an official strike.

On 12 December, Edward Heath declared a state of emergency, the main thrust of which was limiting commercial use of electricity to three consecutive days a week from midnight on New Year's Eve. Only shops were exempt, and non-essential shops would have power only in the morning or afternoon.

I remember my father valiantly attempting to mitigate the damage, somehow contriving to get as much out of the factory in three days as he previously had from six. It wasn't a question of taking up the slack because there was no slack, although he wasn't averse to stretching the rules – I remember him bringing people in on Sundays. If that's what it took to keep the place afloat, he'd do it. Productivity ran in his veins.

Domestic electricity supply was also restricted and rolling power cuts, lasting between six and nine hours, dominated our lives for the whole of that January and February. This being Britain, there was inevitably an absurdist side to it. One government minister advised people to brush their teeth in the dark to save on lighting, and I remember my dad rigging up a car battery with a long flex and a bulb dangling over the kitchen table so we could do our homework and see to eat. As my mother pointedly remarked it took a national emergency to get him to do things at home. He could fix anything if he wanted to, but it was never top priority. He only snapped into action when she said, 'Right Peter, I'll get an engineer in.' Whether it was the washing machine, a dripping tap or an extra telephone extension, it would get done only once my mother had threatened to 'bring in an engineer'.

At the factory, my father was hands-on to a fault. On one occasion, I remember, he climbed up onto a roof to install an extractor fan, lost his footing and fell twenty feet into a gully. Needless to say, my mother was decidedly unimpressed when she collected him from the hospital. He was back at work the following day.

In February 1974, Edward Heath called a panic election, under the banner 'Who Governs Britain?' If he'd been hoping for a sympathy vote supportive of the beleaguered prime minister from an electorate frustrated by the 'bullyboy tactics' of the NUM, he was disappointed. On 1 March 1974 Harold Wilson was returned to Downing Street for what would be his third term of office, albeit at the head of a minority government.

Meanwhile, I was gearing up for the summer track season and the auguries were good, with a timed training run of 1m 55 at 800m – a personal best. But I had begun to notice a nagging pain in my leg, and X-rays soon revealed a stress fracture in my shin. Stress fractures are hairline cracks caused by tired muscles no longer able to absorb repetitive stress when the foot hits the road, and are not unusual in young, growing athletes. The only cure is complete rest. No running, no training. My father was adamant: there could be no risk of re-injury. It would be a full year before I would run in competition again. For a while it all felt very odd – without training and everything connected with it, I seemed to have lost a huge part of my day.

I was now 18 and two terms into my first year in the sixth form at Abbeydale Grange School where I had moved after leaving Tapton the previous summer. Although Abbeydale was by then a full-blown comprehensive, its previous identity as a grammar school was still there in its character, and I had no problems settling in. It was, however, further away from Marlborough Road than Tapton had been, in the valley of the River Sheaf, south of the city. Until the discovery of the stress fracture, I had always run to and from my new school. Now, for the first time in my life, I discovered the joys of waiting for a bus.

The timing could have been worse. With A-levels looming, there was no alternative but to knuckle down. My first choice for the next stage of my education was Loughborough University of Technology. Not only was the course exactly what I wanted, but you couldn't come up through track and field without knowing of its illustrious history from the sixties onwards. But unlike the practice of some American universities, acceptance was based on academic criteria only. Over the next two years I was offered places at a cluster of US universities, based solely on my lap times. For many young athletes in Britain, this was a very enticing option, offering world-class facilities, full medical support and a whole raft of scholarships. My own situation was somewhat different. It wasn't as if I was in a coaching desert. Nor was athletics my sole focus.

In the meantime, my father had his own research mapped out.

Sport was now a weapon in the cold war and the medals table was dominated by the eastern bloc, particularly East Germany and the Soviet Union itself. The general assumption was that the east was awash with drugs. Nothing was known for sure, but whisper piled upon conjecture lost nothing in the retelling, the majority refusing to believe that anything good came out of that regime. But it did. The smart money knew that it wasn't all down to chemical enhancers, and that included my father. If he thought you knew something that would help him in his search for the perfect training programme, that was good enough for him. Drugs might be part of the story, he would argue, but they weren't the whole story, and in reality the principles of coaching in the east were very good. They were great researchers and really pushed the boundaries in terms of sport science. In due course, Peter managed to obtain both Russian and East German training manuals, had them translated by a linguist friend at the university, and then just buried himself in them. Once you got beyond the introduction extolling the virtues of the political system, he said, there were nuggets on every page. But these were just two among the plethora of information-containing envelopes that would thump on our doormat from across the world, whether from US universities or from New Zealand. He devoured everything that came his way.

With unexpected time on my hands I, too, found my gaze shifting, in my case from athletics to politics. Developments following the Conservative defeat in February showed the party in near meltdown. Among the acres of newsprint on the subject, I'd found voices prepared to question the apparent consensus that the best any government could do was to manage our inexorable decline.

In spite of successive post-war Conservative administrations, industries that had been nationalised immediately by the Attlee Labour government were still nationalised, and it seemed that the policy of state intervention, with its high levels of public expenditure, now had cross-party consensus. However, among the general atmosphere of pointless hand-wringing, two people appeared to be offering an alternative vision.

Margaret Thatcher and Keith Joseph – whose views were toxic to most people I knew – were convinced that subsidising loss-making, publicly owned industry, bailing them out with huge dollops of tax payers' money, only shored up the status quo, and would certainly not deliver what the nation now expected. The NHS had been set up ostensibly to control contagious diseases but was rapidly being outrun by technological innovation. By the mid seventies these were beginning to be seen as an entitlement. But you were never going to fund keyhole surgery and hip replacements at this level from the profits of British Leyland. Margaret Thatcher and Keith Joseph were opening a front on the post-war political consensus known to the more erudite scribblers of the time as 'Butskellism' (after the Tory Rab Butler and Labour Hugh Gaitskell). It was not simply a full-frontal on socialism. It was a political *mea culpa*.

Meanwhile, Harold Wilson called another election that October. Having made peace with the miners, he hoped to get re-elected with an enhanced majority. The gamble paid off, but only just. Labour was returned with a majority of three.

Heath's position was now unsustainable. He had led the party to two successive defeats, and his term in office had been pretty disastrous by any estimation. In that era, no mechanism was in place to force him to resign, but nevertheless possible successors were setting out their stalls. Chief among them was Keith Joseph, MP for Leeds North, an outspoken critic of Heath's handling of the economy. However, his campaign was effectively derailed on 19 October, just nine days after the election. Towards the end of a wide-ranging speech in Birmingham, he raised the issue of an escalation in pregnancies among women in the lowest socio-economic groups. 'Single parents . . . are now producing a third of all births,' young women, he said, who were unfit to take on the responsibilities of parenthood. 'The balance of our population, our human stock, is threatened.' It wasn't the first time he had proffered these views, but the sound bite would prove terminal to his chances. Even when delivered in the measured terms of a seasoned politician, it was bound to be incendiary; these were the fifty pound notes of journalistic currency.

As for the party's reaction, to the previous cries of disloyalty were now added those of political naivety. He couldn't survive. Within a month he had withdrawn from the leadership contest, but not before persuading his campaign manager, Margaret Thatcher, MP for Finchley, to stand in his place. She wasn't much liked in the House of Commons, nor in the wider Tory Party, and there was a feeling that, come the vote, Heath could still win by default. So, over the next six months, her erstwhile mentor delivered speech after speech up and down the country, acting as her lightning conductor, advancing radical social and monetary policies in a country still adhering to Keynesian orthodoxy.

In February 1975 Margaret Thatcher was duly elected leader of the Conservative Party. She had won with a majority that gave her an incontestable mandate for change, her victory presaging a new direction, a new-minted confidence.

I resumed gentle training in September 1974. Back in the world of athletics, I was aware of a degree of optimism that had been missing earlier in the year. At the European Championships in Rome the previous month, we'd got a sack load of medals. Brendan Foster had won gold in the 5000m, Ian Thompson gold in the marathon, Alan Pascoe gold in the 400m hurdles and 4 x 400m relay, which paved the way for his outstanding career in sports marketing.

Overall, Britain had come third in the medal table with a total of eleven, including silver for Steve Ovett in the 800m, when he was beaten by Luciano Šušanj, a seasoned and wily campaigner from Yugoslavia.

The enforced break appeared to have done me no great harm. In

March 1975 I won the 1500m junior indoor championships at RAF Cosford, the only indoor track in the whole of Britain at that point. Then it was back to revising, but once my A levels were over in June, I began competing at meets around Sheffield and the north. The focus that summer was the AAA junior championships at the end of July at Kirkby, north of Liverpool, and the chance of being selected to represent my country at the European Junior Championships in Athens, which was obviously a very big deal.

Athletics clubs across the world operate under the umbrella of a national federation, and Hallamshire Harriers was no exception. As one of Yorkshire's top junior middle-distance runners, I was selected by the British Athletics Federation for a three-nation match at Warley in the Black Country: GB, France and Spain. Unfortunately, the way things were scheduled, the date fell just three days after the all-important AAA meet in Kirkby. All went to plan. I won the 1500m in Kirkby in a personal best time of 3m 47.1 and with it a place in the British team for Athens. But it came at a cost: blisters. The prospect of running three days later at Warley on painful, suppurating feet was neither pleasant nor sensible, particularly given the European Championships were only three weeks away.

My father immediately contacted the federation. In effect I was injured, he said. Running on badly blistered feet wasn't clever, and the last thing the federation would want would be to jeopardise something as important as my first international championship. So he asked if I could be excused the Warley meet.

The answer was blunt. If I refused to compete at Warley, I wouldn't be going to Athens. So what do you do? This was my first experience of the obduracy and short termism that marked so much of the federation at the time. It wouldn't be my last.

I didn't listen in to the conversation my old man had with them, so I don't know what he said, or how he said it. I do know that he could be brusque to the point of rudeness and often well beyond.

But be that as it may. I was lucky. I ran and I won – with some pain – although my feet were still tender when I set off for Athens, in spite of the application of formaldehyde, straight out of the Hallamshire Harriers' book of changing-room remedies.

When I attempt to explain to my children what life was like in terms of travel back then, I don't get very far. They have been crawling around airplane cabins since they were babies. In the seventies, although package holidays to the Costa del Sol or coach trips to Yugoslavia existed, foreign travel was still largely for the well off. For most people in Britain, going on holiday still meant a week at the seaside or the Lakes. That flight to Athens was the first time I had ever been in a plane, or even gone abroad. The whole business was immensely exciting – the airport, the seat belts, taxiing down the runway, that extraordinary surge of power before taking off, looking down on the clouds. And as for Athens, it was amazing! Stepping on to the tarmac was like opening an oven door, the heat at a level I could never have imagined. But I loved it – and still do. I was so relaxed that, before the final, I nodded off in an empty changing room for an hour's sleep, and woke up with just twenty minutes to spare! The race was won by Finnish athlete Ari Paunonen, but in chasing him, I sliced four seconds off my personal best, and came third, bringing home a European Championship bronze medal. I was on my way.

As a footnote, thirty-seven years later I was back in Greece for the lighting of the flame at Olympia – the start of the torch relay that would end at the Olympic Stadium in London. As I watched the ceremony, a journalist asked me if I had ever been to Olympia before and I suddenly remembered that I had. After that race in 1975, I'd had two days to kill before the flight back to England with the rest of the team. Olympia – invoked in opening ceremonies as the cradle of the Games – was one of the few places in Greece I'd heard of, so I'd made enquiries, taken the train and headed off there.

It was completely empty, just this ancient competitive arena – very different from that May morning in 2012 when a bevy of high priestesses drifted down the hill towards me, bearing the flame and a burning torch.

I started at Loughborough University the following October, 1975. Freshers week is traditionally the time when university clubs and societies set out their wares and the structure of your extra-curricular student life begins to take shape. Obviously, I signed up for the athletics club and the cross-country club, but I also joined the Loughborough Students Conservative Association. Shortly afterwards, I was elected treasurer, although there was hardly a queue for the post. However, it was down to the treasurer to organise speakers and this for me was a huge attraction.

Where better to start than Sir Keith Joseph? I never imagined for one moment that he would accept, but he did. His profile then couldn't have been much higher. Memorably described as the free marketeers' John the Baptist, he was Margaret Thatcher's right-hand man, in overall charge of policy and research. With Heath's blessing, he had founded the Centre for Policy Studies, a 'think tank', ostensibly to investigate how capitalism worked in Europe, particularly in Germany. In fact, the CPR would go a long way to formulate those policies that eventually became known as 'Thatcherism' but owed their genesis to Keith Joseph and his credo that an economy declines as its wealth-producing sector shrinks.

It's probably fair to say that students' political affiliations lean rather more to the left than to the right, and certainly in 1976 Loughborough Conservatives were in a distinct minority. Mindful of this, and aware of Keith Joseph's infelicitous 'eugenics' speech the previous year, the university authorities tried to get the meeting stopped.

Although under no little pressure from the vice-chancellor's office, shored up by the local constabulary, we stood our ground. It would be disrespectful to withdraw the invitation, I insisted. Sir Keith Joseph was a baronet, a former cabinet minister and shadow home secretary. 'So, no. You do not dis-invite this man.'

The day duly arrived. The police were clearly expecting trouble, and there was a large uniformed presence around the campus from early that morning. By the time we were due to start, the gym was packed, and people were hanging off the wall bars.

As the person responsible for inviting the latter-day seer, I had been deputed to do the meet and greet, but it was a very nervous 19 year old who shepherded the instantly recognisable figure along the walkway from the car park, obliged to run the gauntlet of baying students lining the path. Whistles, cat calls and general shouting rose in a crescendo as we came in, and I remember thinking, 'What have I done?'

Derided by the press as 'the mad monk', he struck me as a distinctly vulnerable figure. There was something inherently disarming about this late middle-aged, cerebral man, facing such animosity without a sign of rancour. He talked about enterprise and initiative and the entrepreneurs who were society's wealth creators. Overall, it was more like listening to a quirky Oxford don expounding theories on moral philosophy than a tub-thumping politician. By the time we were halfway through, the atmosphere had changed from hostility to gentle acquiescence due, in large measure, to the candour of his answers and his obvious honesty. He also had a disarming tendency to encase his face in his hands for what seemed an interminable pause before answering.

I learnt one lesson that day I would never forget: don't talk down to the young or try to modify your message. There is no such thing as policy fashioned specifically for them. People become engaged with politics because they hear something that excites them, they hear something that frames things in a different way. And that's what Keith Joseph and Margaret Thatcher did for me. At some fundamental level I understood that there had to be a paradigm shift in the way we did business in this country. And there was. But my adopted city, and others like it, would pay a very high price in its wake.

Clearly, with Peter now 60 miles away up the M1, I needed someone to monitor my training, and that person was George Gandy. A lecturer in bio-mechanics, George combined his academic role with that of head track coach. He was hewn from solid Geordie rock, with firm and often fixed views about the way things had to be done. In other words, not so dissimilar to my old man, and in fact they had already been in touch as there was little George didn't know about conditioning and weight training.

Strange to relate, bio-mechanics is closely related to engineering in that it relies on traditional engineering science to analyse biological systems. But on a day-to-day level George was a great believer in listening to your body, and not taking risks. No matter how efficient the blood/oxygen ratio, athletes remain hostage to their bones and musculature. To continue the machine analogy, the body is a complex series of levers, hinges and pivots operated by muscles and tendons. Or as inventor Buckminster Fuller memorably put it: 'Man is a self-balancing, 28-jointed, adapter-base bi-ped and electro-chemical reduction plant, integral with the segregated stowages of special energy extracts in storage batteries for subsequent activation of thousands of hydraulic and pneumatic pumps, with motors attached . . .'

What determines how fast you can go is the length of your stride, how powerfully you can push into that stride, and the rate of your stride, i.e. how fast you can get your legs to pump.

The foot alone has 26 bones, 33 joints, 107 ligaments, 19 muscles and 19 tendons. And while on one level the body is extremely strong, it is also extremely fragile, and the difference between the two is often related to balance. If your left side is stronger than your right, it's not simply that you don't want your muscles out of kilter, but it's a diagnosis in itself, showing that you're running asymmetrically. This impinges on posture and balance and potentially can manifest itself from the neck down, shoulders, lower back and even displacement of hips. As for your knees, everything depends on how your feet hit the ground. The experience of the stress fracture in early 1974 taught me one very important lesson. At the first hint that something is wrong, stop and investigate. Never train through pain or illness. You can't 'run it off' as the old boys would tell you. There is always a price to pay for every injury, and a reason.

Injury is the athlete's greatest fear. Not only can it lose you a race, it can lose you a year, at worst a career. Even small injuries accumulate and remain as weaknesses, and while you can learn to compensate, you are never totally free of them.

Training is not about running quicker, it's about running smarter, about understanding optimal pace levels that challenge or enhance specific systems. Only run at paces that will achieve the physiological adaptations you seek. By running faster than you need in training you run a higher risk of injury.

Under George's guidance I began circuit training and weight training, working on upper-body strength and hamstring strength in addition to winter speed work. And while Loughborough didn't have Sheffield's hills, or the beauty of the moors to entice me up on them, it did have something else – training partners who would become friends for life.

5

FRIENDS AND RIVALS

IT makes you wonder if there was something in the water, but for a while it seemed as if everyone around me was called Steve. There was Steve Ovett and later Steve Cram; Steve Lacy and Steve Scott, American milers; and Steve Crabb, an Enfield boy I sometimes used as an unofficial pacemaker. But the most important Steve in my life has been Steve Mitchell, training partner and friend since the moment we met nearly forty years ago in my first year at Loughborough. Steve is a few years older than I am so he'd actually graduated by the time I arrived, although he was still a member of the university athletics set-up.

Our first encounter was at the annual cross-country club dinner in the spring of 1976. The background music was the usual mix of Abba, Rod Stewart and Hot Chocolate, but towards the end of the evening it abruptly changed and the melancholy jazz standard *I Can't Get Started* began to weave its magic, delivering me from disco hell straight back to the jazz age. As a first-year I was still in awe of most of the faces around me, but when I spotted the guy responsible for this cultural shift, I headed over.

'I . . .'

'You got a problem?'

'God, no, it's fantastic!'

'Oh, good. I've had a gutful of that crap.'

'Bunny Berigan,' I said. He still looked a bit wary, but nodded approvingly. And that, to quote Humphrey Bogart, was the start of a beautiful friendship.

Mitchell and I started training together almost immediately. He had been a junior international steeplechaser, and still competed, but was now working as a teacher in the town. I ended up sharing his extraordinary house – of which more later – although not until I, too, had graduated.

As for the virtuoso trumpet player who recorded *I Can't Get Started* in 1937, Bunny Berigan is a name only true jazz aficionados will be familiar with. In fact, I've never been a great trad fan, having grown up listening to quite sophisticated jazz, which is what was played on the family record player at home and has been an important part of my life ever since. The first recording I consciously remember hearing was *History of a Boy Scout* by Dave Brubeck. Even then – and I could only have been about seven as we were still living in Alcester – I knew I'd heard something quite intoxicating. Brubeck was a classically trained white guy who broke all the rules, his melodies labyrinths of cross-rhythms and quirky time signatures. Looking back, this was an advanced level entry, although from the fifties onwards Brubeck was many Americans' introduction to jazz thanks to the concert tours he made around college campuses.

My introduction to more mainstream jazz came later, when a trip back to Fulham wasn't complete without a visit to New Merlin's Cave in Clerkenwell at Sunday lunchtime. This was a uniquely English institution, an unlikely mix of old jazzers, children, grannies, pies and pints. Presiding over this mish-mash of 20th-century Londoners was the inimitable George Melly with John Chilton's Feetwarmers, playing heart-warming, bass-slapping, toe-tapping jazz in a fug of cigarette smoke that you could barely see through. Bursts of raucous laughter suggested that it was replete with double entendres and less salubrious references, which I never got.

This was not great jazz, but for sheer exuberance it had no match. With his red hat, spiv ties and tipster suits, George Melly was even then a figure of myth and legend, and I developed a taste for live jazz that would never be dimmed.

Through Steve Mitchell I met another seminal figure in my life, another jazz aficionado, Malcolm Williams. Malcolm had been a mature student at Loughborough at the same time as Mitchell, and by the time I arrived he was teaching PE at Daneford, a tough comprehensive in Tower Hamlets in east London, alma mater of boxer John H. Stracey and Arsenal and England footballer Charlie George.

Sport was everything to Malcolm, but it's probably fair to say that, in all other respects, he and I had little in common, not background, not age and certainly not politics. He would have defined himself back then as Labour, but scratch the surface and economically he was a Marxist. When it came to social issues, however, he was further to the right than my grandmother. Capital punishment? Most certainly. As for gay marriage and ages of consent . . . As he would say, 'Don't get me started . . .' Malcolm was great company, a very funny man but also quietly observing of life, in all its inequities and absurdities.

The third member of the trio who would become my *de facto* support team in the years to come was Sean Butler. A Liverpudlian from Toxteth, Sean arrived in Loughborough when I was in my third year and, like me, ended up living in Steve Mitchell's house. Down to earth and unflinchingly loyal, he must have covered thousands of miles with me over the years, both in Britain and overseas, for parcels of training before races. I know of no other set of people who would have given such space to my quirkiness, although it took me a good many years to appreciate it.

In terms of British achievement, the glow of optimism delivered by our athletes at the European Championships in Rome in 1974 proved a false dawn. Britain's performance in the Montreal Olympics in 1976 was a complete washout. All the expectations we'd had were dashed through injury and under-performance, and we actually came joint bottom in the athletics medals table. The only medal in track and field was a solitary bronze for Brendan Foster in the 10,000m while Daley Thompson – still a junior – came eighteenth, although a year earlier he'd won the AAA Junior 100m and decathlon title.

I had competed in the Olympic selection trials at Crystal Palace two months earlier. However, they clashed with my end-of-year exams, so I only just made it on time, resulting in yet another spat between my dad and the authorities. I ran well – improving again on my personal best for the distance. Unfortunately, I got knocked out of the heat, but stayed around to watch the final, which was won by Steve Ovett. This race became notorious as the first time he gave the wave, which then became his trademark, when he crossed the line. It earned him no plaudits among the athletics fraternity. But the group I was sitting with – a posse of Loughborough students competing in the trials – took particular exception to it, not because he was being arrogant and cocky, although that's how the British press saw it, but because we read it as a direct snub to David Moorcroft, whom he cruised past on his way to victory. Moorcroft was a Loughborough alumnus, one of us. Blood was thicker than water.

Later he said that he was waving to his father, who had a heart condition, to tell him he could stop worrying. Whatever the reason, we just got used to it. Compared with what now routinely takes place at the beginning of the 100m when Usain Bolt is running, this was the foothills of the athletics cabaret.

Failing to be selected for Montreal had far-reaching consequences, as I'll explain. I took little comfort from the fact that my heat was the faster of the two, and that even placed seventh, my time was better than Ovett's. When it comes to championship racing, however, times are irrelevant. It's crossing the line first that matters. So Steve was selected for both the 800m and 1500m for his

Olympic debut at Montreal. And although he made the final, he was outrun and outmanoeuvred. In fairness, he was racing against Alberto Juantorena – middle name 'Danger'. I kid you not. Also, he was drawn in lane 8 in the 800m – the worst possible place in an Olympic final – and they were playing with new lane-changing rules[1], subsequently abandoned. As for the 1500m, he ran out of petrol having run hard in the 800m. But he was still only twenty and just reaching the finals was no mean feat.

One of the engines driving the recovery of middle-distance running from the sixties onwards was the British Milers Club, run by an eccentric character called Frank Horwill. What Frank did in raising both the profile and the standard of our home-grown talent cannot be overestimated. A great plus was that the BMC covered the whole of the country, so you never had to travel very far. The guy in charge of the north west was a wonderful old coach, Eddie Powell, who struck up a great friendship with my father, not least because he knew what Peter was talking about. As Stretford, where he was based, was only a click across the Pennines, we would go to meets there frequently and early August 1977 saw us heading off for my third race there that season. The first had been a 1500m, followed by a mile, and now I was doing the 800m. I'd last raced at the distance three weeks before at Loughborough with a personal best of 1m 50.7.

I won, and easily, with a time of 1m 47.7 – three whole seconds quicker than at Loughborough. From being a good county-stand-ard runner when I'd arrived that morning, I'd set off back across the Pennines with a time that propelled me to the fringes of interna-tional competition.

I'll never forget that drive across the snake pass – the moors a rich purple in the late evening sunshine – sitting in companionable

---

[1] The international 800m had a two-turn stagger – at 220m – between 1974 and 1976.

silence with my father. Not till we reached the Snake Inn did he even speak. 'I think we might just have found your distance.'

Fate hangs by a thread. If I had run that time, and shown that form, three weeks earlier at the Olympic selection meeting at Crystal Palace, it would have been enough to get me the third spot on the team. And if I'd gone to Montreal – even if I'd not survived the first round – the experience I'd have gained would have been beyond price, and Moscow would have been very different.

I spent the rest of that summer competing in the north and for the first time in a year managed to get in some uninterrupted and concentrated training. Much as I was enjoying Loughborough, it was great to be home, running around the Derwent Reservoirs and across to Stocksbridge through moorland purple with heather, revelling in the freedom and the beauty around me, and of course it was back to the familiar repetitions along the Rivelin Valley Road and my father as ringmaster.

That summer also marked the beginning of my friendship with Brendan Foster, then promoting athletics meets at Gateshead Stadium. We had met at an awards dinner at Vaux Breweries in Sunderland. Their drays were a common sight in the North East until they closed in 1999. Although this was my first year as a senior athlete, Brendan generously put me in races against John Walker and David Moorcroft – gods as far as I was concerned. Brendan was a very big figure in the sport, and tremendously popular with the public, even beyond his native Tyneside. As an Olympic bronze and European gold medallist and world-record holder, he'd become something of a media hero. And when it came to pulling in the punters, he was 'canny', a PR wizard before the term existed. World-class athletes were Gateshead's big draw, but an unknown 18 year old offered something a bit different. While I could hardly claim to be a Geordie, I was at least a northerner by adoption, a home-grown David to the middle-distance Goliaths that would regularly burn up the Gateshead track. It was a case of 'Who's this skinny kid from Sheffield, prepared to run toe to toe with an Olympic champion? He doesn't appear to be scared of anything!' And basically I wasn't. I was happy to go off and run from the front, because running against the best in the world was a great opportunity, something a rookie like me was unlikely to experience anywhere else at this stage of my career.

That meet of the British Milers Club at Stretford was a turning point. From now on I would focus on the 800m, 1500m and the mile. These last two are versions of the same race – a historical and cultural anomaly. There's no real difference in the way that they're run. However, the 800m – the metric equivalent of the half mile – is a different matter and, as far as I am concerned, the most taxing. It needs the leg speed of a world-class 400m runner, but the stamina of a good 5000m runner.

Above all, the 800m demands a tactical acumen that no other distance calls upon, and is the closest you get to playing chess at 15 or 16 mph. As in chess, you're trying to stay one or sometimes two moves ahead of the opposition, the difference being that in an 800m you have more than one opponent. What if the space you've carved out for yourself is suddenly gobbled up? Part of the skill is always having an escape route. If you get boxed in, the business end of the race has probably already escaped you. Nor is this thinking done at leisure. At a world-class pace, an 800m race is run at 17 mph, which equals 26 feet/second, and you may have eight or nine athletes fighting over a space no bigger than two lengths of the average dining-room table. You have to be able to run in traffic and manoeuvre.

You really require a highly tuned on-board computer because the need to make decisions comes at you thicker and faster than at any other distance. When to hold back, when to accelerate, where to go. Judgement about distance is crucial and it's hard to calculate exactly how far ahead the leader is when there are five other guys in-between. And unlike the 1500m, where you can recover mid-race from a misjudgement, at 800m it tends to be terminal, as I know to my cost.

The 800m starts in lanes, but after 110m you face a free-for-all as the athletes break and bolt for the inside. While your starting lane is important, it's not as critical as the lane draw in the 200m, for example, where statistically lanes 3, 4 and 5 throw up most of the winners.

In the 800m, an inside lane gives you the advantage of seeing the whole field, but the risk is that when they do break at 110m, you get engulfed. If you're drawn in lane 8, as Ovett found in Montreal, you are in essence running blind. Go off too gently and you'll spend the rest of the race chasing the field – a heavy price to pay for not expending energy too early. The middle lanes give you a greater peripheral view, but you still have to keep your wits about you at the break.

If they're being honest, few middle-distance runners naturally gravitate to front running – although, of course, front running is in itself a tactic, a fact overlooked by people who disparage it as the only option for those who don't have the change of pace. It's true that being out there on your own does demand both enormous self-confidence and supreme conditioning. Luckily, I actually enjoyed running from the front. I liked having a clear track in front of me and enjoyed controlling the tone and the style of the race. But I also had a good turn of speed, so if necessary I was happy to sit in with the field, knowing that I had the ability to shift through the gears if it was called upon at any point in the race.

Pace judgement is a crucial asset. At the height of my career, if my father said, 'OK, go out and run 400 metres in 62 seconds,' I could pretty much guarantee to be within no more than a few tenths either side, and probably closer. But under most racing conditions, time is the last thing you'll be thinking about. The lap times, or 'splits' as they're known, are called out from the side of the track, but are often inaudible or in a foreign language and therefore useless, and when they appear digitally, they can be masked by officials. The exception is a world-record attempt, when the whole field is obsessed with split times.

For every middle-distance runner worth the name, the sub-four-minute mile is a rite of passage, and at the end of August 1976 an opportunity presented itself at Crystal Palace. Ten days earlier I'd run 4m 1.7 at Gateshead, coming in third behind the world-record holder, John Walker. To lose those additional two seconds – somewhere in the region of fifteen yards – I knew I would have to extend myself, and decided I had nothing to learn by hanging back among the pack. So, after talking it through with my father, I decided to run from the front right from the start. At the Commonwealth Games in 1974, in the final of the 1500m, the Tanzanian Filbert Bayi had done just that. It was an astonishing race – he not only won, but broke both the Commonwealth and world records.

Unless you were pacemaking for somebody else, running from the front was not common back then. But, being slight, jockeying for position in the middle of the pack was something I never relished. I knew it would mean going for broke, but I decided it was worth the punt.

In races longer than 800m, while you're given a position to start with, you can cross to the inside as soon as you like, and so it risks being a bit of a scrum. I avoided that by going straight to the front, led for three laps, then got engulfed by the field, which wasn't a surprise. Then, entering the final straight I got a second wind and was taught a tactical lesson by Branislav Manilowski, the barrel-chested Polish steeplechase champion from Montreal. With about 150 yards to go, I went to ease him out of the way when, without breaking stride, he buried his elbow in my ribcage so sharply that I could feel the effect for weeks afterwards. Following the race, and clearly in considerable pain, I related the story to some of those who had later breezed past me, who just laughed, saying, 'Well, you won't do that again!' Certainly not against him. He had a reputation for taking no prisoners.

It pays to be brave. Even though I came in seventh, pushing the pace from the start had done the trick and with a time of 3m 58.4 I had joined the élite club of sub-four minute milers. But elated as I was, my time was still nearly ten seconds slower than John Walker's world record.

That autumn, back in Loughborough, I worked on building up my body strength and conditioning. This was now embedded in my weekly programme and, under George Gandy's guidance, I had become quite a confident weightlifter, lifting many times my own body weight. I was also training with sprinters on the synthetic track at the Harvey Hadden sports complex in Nottingham. We'd set off twice a week in a beaten-up university minibus, George at the wheel. While George had a great many skills, it's fair to say that driving wasn't among them and we'd draw lots not to have to sit in the front passenger seat.

Unbelievably, while Loughborough was a powerhouse of excellence, having already produced a cluster of national and international athletes, we were still running on cinders and without floodlights. As the nights closed in, George would edge his Volvo estate as close as he could to the track and put on his headlights so at least we could see coming down the finishing straight.

At the beginning of January 1977, at the end of the Christmas holidays before heading back to Loughborough, I was included in a group of distance runners earmarked for a week's warm weather training in Gibraltar. While the climate was certainly mild, it's hard to see what else it had to offer. Some of the more suspicious among the older heads suggested that the hotel, the Caleta Palace, had to be owned by somebody who knew somebody in the federation, there being no other reason to go there.

That week I covered something over 100 miles. Seven-and-a-half miles every morning and seven and a half every evening around the perimeter road, half of it in a tunnel, and we probably came home paler than we went out. Brendan was there as well as Ian Stewart, who had taken the 5000m bronze in Munich. It gave me a crucial insight into just how serious these guys were. All of us are now retired, but we still laugh about that week whenever we meet up. Appalling though it now seems, to break the monotony we would run holding a batch of small pebbles, the aim being to see how many Gibraltar apes we could hit at full flow, for which we had points and a league table. Ian Stewart, I remember, came out significantly ahead.

Later that month I won my first senior title, the 800m UK indoor championship at RAF Cosford. Next came a UK v. Germany meet in Dortmund and another 800m, in which I beat the 1500 Olympic bronze medallist Paul-Heinz Wellmann, setting a new Commonwealth record in the process. That was the first time I crossed paths with Daley Thompson, who was making his indoor debut. I can't now remember what event he was competing in – it was a way of keeping his hand in since he needed to be master of ten events for the decathlon. We were only a small team and when it came to handing out the numbers, I was given 007. This big guy who I'd never met immediately came over.

'That's my number,' Daley said.

'Well, it might be, but I'm wearing it today.'

The start of a lifelong friendship.

Two weeks later, in a match against France at Cosford, I chipped another tenth of a second off my own record.

The next date on the international calendar was the European Indoor Championships in San Sebastián in March 1977. This was my third trip abroad, and far bigger than anything I had done before. Again, it was a very small team and we were accompanied by the then chairman of the AAA, the gentle and softly spoken Robert Stinson. As an undergraduate he had competed for Oxford University and I would later replace him as British representative on the IAAF (International Association of Athletics Federations) when he eventually retired in 2003. Just before the final, I asked him to hold my track shoes, while I warmed up. He still had an air of dreaming spires about him, and when I returned to claim them, he was nowhere to be seen. I looked wildly around, having visions of running my first big international in my road shoes. I eventually found him watching the skiing on a TV monitor that was attached like a limpet to the ceiling of a corridor. After handing over my shoes, he accompanied me to the end of the tunnel, where a mêlée of coaches were giving last-minute instructions to their athletes in a babel of languages. So I turned expecting him to give me 'one for the Gipper' – last-minute words of wisdom and inspiration. Instead, he looked at me benignly and said, 'Well, bye-bye then.'

As at Crystal Palace, I decided to run from the front, but I had learnt my lesson and this time I didn't fade or lose the lead. When I broke the tape, I could barely believe what I had done. I was now the holder of a European title! Not only that, I had set a new UK indoor record. I wasn't the only British success story that day. Mary Stewart, Ian Stewart's sister, won the 1500m, and Jane Colebrook won the women's 800m, equalling the world record. Three British gold medallists in the space of forty minutes! The press couldn't get enough of us. Having come home from Montreal with nothing, here were a new generation of British athletes, bouncing back, breaking records and actually winning medals!

Ten days later the euphoria was put into perspective when I strained my Achilles tendon and had to take three months off from competitive racing.

By July, I was back in the fray. In spite of my injury I had been selected for the Europa Cup final in Helsinki, my first senior outdoor international.

The 800m at international level is not for the faint-hearted and in Helsinki I learnt another lesson in rough-housing. I'd been bunched in the middle of the pack, moved wide off the final bend, and was in the process of overtaking West German Willi Wülbeck, and gaining on the others. I was feeling good and thought I might even be onto something, but before I knew what had happened I found myself heading off the track almost at right angles. While attempting to overtake Wülbeck I had been unceremoniously shoved in the back. Although I managed to reorientate myself sufficiently to grab fourth place, Wülbeck went on to win. I finished the race with blood trickling down both legs, my shins badly spiked. An appeal was lodged but not upheld. How times have changed! An infringement like that today would almost certainly have cost Wülbeck the race and possibly an even stronger reprimand. Unsurprisingly, when my dad heard the track judges' verdict, he exploded on a scale that Alex Ferguson would have been proud of.

While Steve Ovett and I had still never run against each other on the track, we had begun to appear on each other's radar. He already had a reputation as a sublime talent, and now that we were competing at the same distances, I knew it was just a matter of time before we were lining up in the same race.

His performance in winning the 1500m World Cup in Düsseldorf that summer was jaw dropping. I remember vividly crowding around our television set at home in Sheffield, with my father and friends from the Hallamshire, as the BBC broke into *Match of the Day* for live coverage of the race. We were on the edge of our seats, both with high expectation and, if I'm being honest, fearful of what we were about to witness, which was fully justified. Coming into the final curve, Steve changed pace so quickly and so violently that the reigning Olympic champion, John Walker, simply stopped, dumbfounded at what had happened, and walked off the track, holding his head in his hands in disbelief. Under the floodlights it seemed almost surreal and left David Coleman practically speechless. It was a new British record, and remains one of the most exciting 1500m races I have ever witnessed. But it was also a reality check. I might have a European indoor title, but I would have to come blinking into the daylight if I planned to take on this guy.

Steve Ovett was a phenomenon. He was winning élite-level races at 400m, 800m, 1500m, mile, 3000m and cross-country. Unbelievably, he won the Dartford half marathon, just the weekend before his Düsseldorf destruction job. It was said that the only reason he didn't compete in the world cross-country championship that year was because it would encroach on his track season. But the 800m and the 1500m and mile are not considered the Blue Riband events for nothing, and when it came to the Olympics, these would be his distances.

In the meantime, the powers in the sport – both official and unofficial – saw to it that our paths never crossed, maintaining the mystique, which was advantageous to everyone, and allowing us to keep our powder dry until Moscow. And while I knew that I wasn't yet in his class, the press were already girding up for a rivalry that would come to define not only our individual careers, but British track and field for a generation.

Whether it's football, snooker or track and field, sport has always been fired by personal rivalry, and the most hotly contested are always those closest to home, preferably with an emotional subtext. You only have to think of Rangers v. Celtic, Liverpool v. Everton, England v. Scotland. When it came to athletics, Steve and I ticked all the boxes. We were both British and yet became pigeon-holed as representing disparate strands of society. The fact that we looked so different tempted the tabloid press to polarity. Steve was the rugged one, I was the skinny one. I was north, he was south. I gave interviews, he didn't. In fact, he didn't talk at all.

There was no master plan to ingratiate myself with the press – far from it. I was just prepared to be reasonably polite. Like all good schools, Tapton had taught me respect, but the one who came down hardest on me if I was truculent or offhand was my mother. She drilled it into my brother and me that when a woman came into a room you stood up, you opened the door for a woman and let her go first, you wrote thank-you letters. I tended to answer journalists' questions in much the same spirit.

But Steve had a spectacular falling out with the press early in his career, and they would make him pay. By the mid-seventies, post-race interviews were becoming the norm. You'd be summoned up to the press box, and it could be like feeding time at the dolphinarium. A good many of the writers were both cultivated and knowledgeable – Colin Hart, John Rodda, David Miller, Norman Fox, Cliff Temple and James Coote were firmly in this camp. But there were some – usually those parachuted in from other sports or news desks – who were hardly the touchstone of grace and elegance and had scant regard and even less understanding of the nature of my sport.

So in 1975, at just such a post-race conference at Crystal Palace, Steve, having won the semi-final of the Europa Cup, was asked about his chances in the final to be held a few weeks later in the south of France. At the time, he was going out with Lesley Kiernan, a talented young 800m runner, and he replied that, as the date clashed with his girlfriend's debut in the European juniors in Athens (the meet where I took the bronze), he would not be competing in the final in Nice, but would be supporting her instead.

At this a veteran rugby correspondent from the *Daily Mail*, Terry O'Connor, who would occasionally cover athletics, lost whatever vestige of courtesy he might once have had. It's said that he was the inspiration for *Private Eye*'s 'Lunchtime O'Booze' and, true or not, he was certainly cast in the same mould. 'So let's get this straight,' he said. 'You're not going to be competing for your country because you're going to be following some bird around Europe.' Ovett got up and walked out. In fairness, I would probably have done the same. Many of the writers present were really quite shocked, not least because they realised this was a heap of rubble they were unlikely to get clear of. And they were right. To all intents and purposes, he never really spoke to the British press again.

The first time Steve and I met on the track was in the European Championships in Prague in 1978. Two weeks earlier I had won the 800m at an invitation meet in Brussels, my second visit to the Heysel Stadium, where I had broken the British record, and I was feeling pretty upbeat. I was now ranked No. 1 in Europe, my time a full second inside Ovett's, but even so, he was still the one to beat. Now here we both were in what the press was claiming was a two-horse race – the rest was just window dressing. As far as they were concerned, this marked the day the rivalry officially kicked off. What, until now, had survived on a diet of speculation and potential, was about to be turbo-charged.

We both cruised through our heat and semi no problem. Walking back from the warm-up track to the stadium just before the final, I had a few last words with Peter about what he thought I should do.

'Well, you're not going to win,' he said. Turning to look at me, he realised I needed a little more nourishment than that. 'Let's be realistic. You're relatively new to championship racing, you've got a good chance but you're not yet the real thing. You're not fully formed. But if you run as hard as you can for as long as you can, you'll get a medal.' Then, with a smile of devilment that I knew only too well, he added, 'Apart from anything else, we'll find out what the bastards are really made of.'

I was drawn in lane 5, and I ran from the front and I ran hard. I held nothing back, or very little. I went through the first 200 metres in 24.3 seconds. It was crazy. Nobody had ever run the first lap of an

800m that fast. Soon an East German in a bright blue vest was at my shoulder, fighting to take pole position. If I'd been smart, I would have let him through, and used him as a pacemaker, but I was too inexperienced and kept fighting him off, expending energy totally unnecessarily. Ovett must have thought this was Christmas come early. There he was, sitting in our slipstream, watching this carnage unfold. Then the blue vest disappeared. Now it was Steve tucked in behind me. I was still sailing along, feeling relatively fresh, but as I came off the final bend and into the straight, I suddenly knew I was running on fumes. It had ceased to be whether there was a medal in this; it was, frankly, whether I would make the finish line.

Physiologically, 800m is the toughest race there is. At that distance and at that speed you are able to absorb about 20 per cent of the oxygen you need. The rest oxidises and turns into lactic acid. By the time there were 100 metres to go, I had nothing left; it was just one foot in front of the other, running on empty. As I was mentally surveying this physiological horror show, Steve pulled alongside. I didn't need to turn to look at him, I sensed the white vest floating effortlessly by, and he at least had the good grace to smile. Another ten paces up the track, the East German came steaming past me, and I remember thinking, 'God, you're moving fast.' He had clearly not read the script that day and the next moment was across the finish line before anybody knew what had happened.

When you run 800m at that speed, it's not down to who has the fastest kick, it's actually about who slows up the least. And so it proved in Prague. But I have no regrets about that blistering first lap. At this level of running, there's an element of poker, and the truth is that I wasn't physically the finished article that night.

In the end, Ovett took second, I got the bronze, and Olaf Beyer of East Germany became the new European champion with a European record to boot.

As I clutched my sides, trying to extract enough oxygen to come back to life, I noticed Beyer about to set off on a lap of honour. Only steps into it, a couple of East German coaches rushed on to the track, wrapped him in what looked like a large horse blanket, and ushered him urgently away from the scene. Perhaps they didn't want him prey to the drug-testing systems. In 1978 these were still in their infancy and pretty *ad hoc*.

But as he was whisked off into the tunnel, the main question was 'Who was that?' If this had been the Derby and you'd gone through the list of runners and riders, Olaf Beyer would have been the 40:1 outsider. There were two other East Germans in the field, Detlef Wagenknecht and Andreas Busse. Although they rarely competed outside the eastern bloc, you couldn't discount these guys, and I'd thought, 'If anybody's going to figure in this race beyond Steve and me, it's going to be one of them.' Wagenknecht would make the final of the Moscow 800m and Busse was in both the 800m and 1500m, so they were definitely up there. But Olaf Beyer?

Beyer has since denied that he ever took drugs during his career, let alone on that occasion. But given the system he came from, I find it difficult to believe. He is known to have been on a Stasi list of athletes on a doping programme. He may well have been in a test group and given placebos but most of the athletes were never told what was in their food or 'vitamin' tablets. My reading of the situation is that he was almost certainly souped up, probably to goad Steve and me into a suicidal pace and to create the platform for Wagenknecht or Busse to pick up the pieces as we faltered in the finishing straight. What I fancy they hadn't factored in was that their pacemaker would go for broke – last the course and inflict as much damage on his compatriots as he had on us.

It could be said – and often has been – that going off like free beer as I did at the start was a grave tactical error. In fact, I know it's what got me a medal that day. If I'd sat back and allowed the race to unfold to the normal choreography, we would all have trotted around waiting for Ovett to hit us 200 metres from home, in which case we'd have been left chasing his shadow, and possibly let in other athletes who only had a fast finish in their armoury.

I learnt early on that you can race yourself to medals by being brave. Both Peter and I felt that, although we'd lost, we'd brought out a frailty in Ovett. While he had that crucial change of pace, the final sprinter's kick that was his calling card, if you took him out of his comfort zone for an extended period, he was vulnerable. My father left Prague convinced he had found the chink in Ovett's armour.

As for the attitude of the British press, the picture they ran with the next morning was Steve with his hand on my shoulder saying something. The caption: 'Even in their moment of medals they can't set aside their rivalry.' The truth would have made punchier reading. What he actually said was, 'Who the fuck was that?' To which I replied, 'I haven't a fucking clue.'

The one who really lost out that day was Ovett. Two days later he went on to win the 1500m, and so Beyer's win in the earlier race denied him the accolade of the double. Steve Cram took gold at both distances at the Commonwealth Games in Edinburgh in 1986. Kelly Holmes got both the 800m and 1500m in Athens in 2004. I never did it, but Prague 1978 should have been Steve's.

At least he had taken the British record back from me, although it wouldn't be his for long. But the lesson I learnt then was one I have never forgotten. To this day, if anyone uses that trite expression, 'This is a two-horse race', I always remember Prague 1978.

6

DODGY BUSINESS

Until the European Championships in Prague, the Ovett–Coe rivalry had existed largely in the press's imagination. No one involved in track and field took it seriously because no one believed that Steve and I were on the same trajectory. However, post-Prague everything changed. We were running the same distance and, whatever serious followers of the sport might believe of our respective talents, the public appetite had been whetted, and what they wanted was a rivalry of Homeric proportions, gladiatorial combat minus the gore.

We could have battled it out two weeks later on British soil, at the Coca-Cola meet at Crystal Palace, which traditionally marked the end of the summer season. Held under floodlights, and packed to the gunwhales with Britain's most knowledgeable crowd, there was always a phenomenal atmosphere. The race in question was two miles. Steve was scheduled to run against sensational Kenyan athlete Henry Rono, who that year had established four world records, at 3000m, 5000m, 10,000m and the 3000m steeplechase.

I had never competed at two miles, and I had last run 3000m – the metric equivalent – in 1975 when I was still a junior, but as I regularly covered much greater distances in training, I didn't see it as a problem. Brendan – who had donned the mantle of career mentor – considered it a good move, but Crystal Palace was then the fiefdom of Andy Norman, and he had other ideas. I should do the 800m instead, he said, promising an international line-up, including the Kenyan Olympic 800m bronze medallist at Munich,

Mike Boit, who had just taken gold at the Edmonton Commonwealth Games.

The version handed down to me by Brendan was slightly different. Andy didn't want anyone queering Steve's pitch in a record attempt, he told me. As it was, Steve came in eight metres ahead of Rono – who had been hoping for a fifth world record himself – clipping Brendan's time by just a tenth of a second. So Steve had the race and his first world best.

There was an upside for me. Although Mike Boit didn't show, I ran the 800m in a very good time, reclaiming the British record that Steve had taken off me in Prague – but I was still around half a second short of Alberto Juantorena's world record. This godlike, gracious and gentle Cuban had taken gold at 800m in Montreal, only the third time he had ever run the distance in competition! He was really a 400m sprinter . . . Oh, and he also took gold in that.

Elsewhere, Ovett seemed unstoppable, unbeaten at 1500m and the mile since 1977. As a final flourish to the season, he won the first of the Dubai Golden Miles, not in Dubai, as the name would suggest, but in Tokyo. As the desert climate of the Gulf was hardly conducive to world-class athletics, Dubai had donated $400,000 to the International Amateur Athletics Federation. In return the IAAF would stage eight 'Golden' élite events over the following three years, as part of high-profile track and field meetings on the circuit. And why would promoters play ball? Because being staged under the auspices of the IAAF, national federations could strong-arm the big names to appear. Individual promoters would never have had this kind of clout. And then, of course, there was the money.

In the era I started out, athletics was still amateur, run entirely by volunteers, and nobody got paid. Well that was the cover story. The truth was rather different.

When I ran against John Walker and Dave Moorcroft up in

Gateshead, while I wasn't paid, I suspect that they received something even if it was described as expenses. I find it hard to believe that world class athletes from New Zealand would travel to England's northernmost outpost on the promise of a crate of Craster kippers and a few six-packs of Newcastle Brown.

It wasn't just the big names who benefited. Athletes at every level got a look in. Steve Mitchell tells the story of a knock on the door when he was having breakfast at his house in Loughborough. Enter two officers from Strathclyde Police needing help with their enquiries. A few months earlier he had run in an invitation meet in Edinburgh. Having worked out that money was changing hands, a disaffected local councillor decided to make trouble. Mitchell was never in particular danger himself, not least because the police were uncomfortable about being dragged in. They were actually great supporters of the sport; most forces had – and indeed still have – their own Athletics Associations. Nonetheless the situation could sometimes tip into farce.

The Gateshead promoters also had their collar felt under similar circumstances but – thanks to a tip-off from the local police – by the time the heavy brigade arrived there were no books to be had. The promoters were, naturally, equipped with a perfectly reasonable explanation: 'The floodlights went out,' they said, 'so we lit some matches to find the fuse box, but one must have dropped . . .' And everything in the way of accounts, went up in flames.

Arguably, British athletics remained truly amateur longer than elsewhere in Europe, but there was an inevitable knock-on effect. In the fifties Roger Bannister, Chris Chataway and Chris Brasher all raced on the Scandinavian circuit – Stockholm, Oslo, Malmö, Helsinki – and it's hard to believe that they didn't pocket a bob or two. Running had always enjoyed a higher profile in northern Europe than it had in Britain. In the 1920s Paavo Nurmi of Finland became the greatest middle- and long-distance runner of his generation – perhaps ever – setting world records from 1500m to 20 kilometres. He won a total of nine gold and three silver at three Olympic Games, from 1920 till 1928, which no other track and field athlete has beaten. He was due to run in the 1932 Olympics in Los Angeles, but was banned from competing by Siegfried Edstrom, the first Swedish IOC president, having been branded a professional for having accepted too much in travel expenses at a meet in Germany. As everyone was doing it, one can't help feeling there was an element of a Scandinavian *schadenfreude* at work here.

Expenses, of course, were what payments to athletes continued to be called, but you were hardly going to set off from Rochdale to compete in Rieti in Italy for the cost of the rail fare. If a promoter wanted you, there was an understanding that there'd be money involved. But it was a murky world, a world where honest men were forced to become dishonest. Including me.

The first time I was paid appearance money was in Brussels on 16 August 1977, a date I remember not only as it was the day Elvis died, but because it marked my first invitation to race abroad. Had they but known it, I'd have gone for nothing. Just to be included in that kind of international field was a coming of age for me.

The event was a new addition to the summer circuit, a memorial to the Belgian middle-distance runner Ivo Van Damme, who had been killed in a car crash the previous Christmas while warm-weather training in southern Spain. Following the meet, I went to the graveyard, where I laid a wreath and talked to the family. His mother and father were like shadows, empty of emotion, and it's one of the saddest things that I have ever done.

Only two years older than I was, he had taken silver at both the 800m and 1500m in Montreal six months previously, and had he lived, I'm not sure people would have been talking about an Ovett/ Coe head-to-head in quite the same way.

Before going to Brussels I had agreed over the phone the princely sum of £100, which to put it in perspective was more than my student grant for the entire term. The promoters had booked me into the competition hotel, and said they'd settle up after the race. So I ran and came third with a time that was a personal best, so I was feeling understandably chipper.

The counting house wasn't difficult to find. A queue the length of the corridor rather gave the game away. After a wait of about an hour, all of us shuffling forward one by one, I went in, took the proffered envelope, inspected the contents, then shook my head.

'There's been a mistake,' I said. 'This should be in pounds, not dollars.' I knew that the difference between $100 and £100 was about £20, not something I was about to throw away for the sake of not making a fuss, and it's probably the only occasion in my life that I put my knowledge of economics to practical use.

The guy handing out the cash was a young journalist, Wilfried Meert – the meet being sponsored by the Brussels evening paper – and he was having none of my lip. It was a hundred dollars, he said, take it or leave it.

'I'm sorry,' I said. 'A hundred pounds.'

'A hundred dollars.'

'No, we agreed a hundred pounds. At the moment a pound is worth 20 per cent more than a dollar.' We could have gone on all night, arguing the toss over the exchange rate, until an older man chipped in.

'Give him the money, Wilfried. The kid will be really good one day. We'll want him back.' The voice of pragmatism belonged to Roger Moens, Belgium's only other world-class middle-distance runner before Van Damme. He took the 800m silver at the Rome Olympics in 1960. He should have won, but was beaten by a young upstart from New Zealand called Peter Snell.

Only later did I hear that Moens – when not involved in dispute resolution with stroppy athletes – was also head of Interpol in

Europe. Yet here he was handing out under-the-counter dosh, which I would have to smuggle back into England, putting me in double jeopardy thanks to the currency restrictions then in operation, due to an economy that was on the brink.

I wasn't the only one collecting a share of the gate money as I queued up in the hotel corridor. From what I saw everyone was doing it, from athletes at the beginning of their career, to star names, the bulk of the envelope being the only visible difference. At the top end, substantial sums were involved. In the mid-seventies, in the infancy of my career, I might pocket £100, but for big names it could run into many thousands.

In Italy, lire was the usual currency on offer, and thanks to galloping inflation, my father and I would spend as much time figuring out how to bring back carrier-bags full of notes as thinking about the race. The pair of us would end up stuffing wads of cash inside linings, up sleeves, down underpants until we'd find ourselves going through customs giving a passable impersonation of Errol Flynn.

Perhaps it was this dodgy way of doing things that attracted some dodgy customers into the sport. I remember an Italian promoter I'll call Signor Greedio. On one occasion a couple of shot-putters waiting for their cash in the hotel corridor noticed that the queue wasn't getting any shorter and shouldered the door down to find the room empty, the window open, and their cash fast disappearing across the lake in a rowing boat, Signor Greedio at the oars.

The equivalent character in British athletics was Andy Norman. A county-level half-miler as a schoolboy, he'd come up through the AAA Southern Counties. He began by organising a few events, and ended up basically running British athletics, and it was all done on the back of a fag packet.

I first met Andy in 1976 when I was 19. He paid me £50 to run around a grass track in the middle of Lincolnshire – just some tents, a crowd, a little local sponsorship and a public-address system. Later that summer, he paid me another £50 to run in the annual Emsley Carr Mile at the Coca-Cola meet. As for appearance money, Andy's line was 'it's not illegal, just against the rules', his status as a serving police officer bestowing a sheen of legitimacy on this somewhat dubious maxim. If you really had qualms, he had another option up his sleeve. 'Bet you a hundred quid you can't jump that wall,' he'd say, and point to something the height of a few telephone directories. 'Go on. Have a go.' You'd jump it, and he'd hand you the cash. Appearance money? Nah, just a wager.

Andy was completely Runyon-esque. At 23 he'd been the youngest sergeant in the history of the Met, and started his career with the Flying Squad. But his maverick streak proved a stumbling block. On duty at the Notting Hill Carnival one year, and bored with the lack of activity, he collared a young solicitor who, unfortunately for Andy, knew his rights. 'What have you arrested me for?' this guy asks. 'Don't worry about that, my son. I'll have figured it out by the time we get you down the nick.'

Anyone else would have been ejected from the force, but Andy had a protector in the shape of Gilbert Kelland, a great track-and-field fan who went on to become Deputy Assistant Commissioner of the Met – and, incidentally, Britain's representative at Interpol. The rest of Andy Norman's career was spent as desk sergeant in Bromley police station. He was famous for having two different telephones: a blue one for police work, a grey one for athletics. He ran everything from Bromley nick, from setting up meets across the country – later across the world – to deals with athletes, sponsorship, the lot. Nor was it just his own time he volunteered. The grey phone could be picked up by any of the coppers on duty, answering promptly 'Athletics', and on Thursday and Friday nights a fleet of panda cars would be sent out to fly-post meetings, specifically Crystal Palace.

Stories about Andy abound, and with reason. I remember standing next to him once in Gateshead, idly waiting for my race. Ethiopia had recently changed regimes, and with it their national anthem, and now an Ethiopian athlete was creating hell because the right anthem wasn't being played. Andy put his head in his hands, turned to me and said, 'Brown envelopes I understand, patriotism I don't.'

He was an extraordinary operator, flying American athletes in at the beginning of the season on the condition that they stopped off in London on their way back, guaranteeing a world-class programme for the Coca-Cola meet at Crystal Palace. In 1985, TV coverage of athletics was finally ceded to ITV and while Andy might not have been the first to spot athletics' potential for entertainment, he was the first to capitalise on it. He gave the punters what they wanted – personalities, records, duels. Before my races, the other guys would tell me how he'd wait till I was out of earshot before giving them their instructions: 'You've only got two things to do,' he'd say. 'Keep out of his way, and don't 'it him. The public don't like it.'

Rather worryingly perhaps, my father and he got on quite well, but he was always nervy around me personally, due in large measure I suspect to his relationship with Steve Ovett, who by then he was managing.

If the Coca-Cola meet could be said to have transformed British athletics, the Dubai 'Golden' series was the wedge in the international door, although it would take another five years before the gates were finally flung open, and it would be Andy Norman who turned the key.

There was no one at the IAAF who didn't know perfectly well that top runners were being paid top money to appear in high-profile invitation meets. Yet if anyone was discovered to have received anything more than expenses, their career was in flames. Yet however you looked at it, Baron Pierre de Coubertin's Corinthian ideals made no sense in a world where half the sport's top performers – those from the Soviet bloc – were paid to train under the guise of wearing some spurious military uniform, while the other half were supposed to be doing it in their spare time. The way 'amateur' athletics was run could have been a dictionary definition of hypocrisy, the ethos being nominally upheld by people who never had to worry about where the next pair of training shoes were coming from. And if you read de Coubertin's words carefully, which I have done, you will see that he didn't have a problem with people being paid for what they were good at. His words have been misinterpreted and taken out of context to suit other purposes.

In the meantime, how were the rest of us supposed to survive? Many fine athletes stepped off their career ladder in order to compete for their country and, like me, were largely funded by their families. Excellence doesn't come cheap, and it certainly didn't come cheaply to my parents. Although my father was on a decent salary as production director of a successful manufacturing company, I know full well that foreign holidays were something they could never countenance until much further down the line, simply because they were supporting me, and that was their priority throughout my university career and beyond until I was in a position to fund myself.

Big names or small, in the late seventies we were all in no man's land. Although the federations knew what was going on, it was still against the rules, so you were constantly looking over your shoulder. The one consolation was that, the practice being so rife, if banning became the norm, there would be no one left.

The real problem for me in all this was the Inland Revenue. Al Capone was famously nailed not for being a Chicago mobster but for tax evasion. And to précis Benjamin Franklin: 'Nothing is certain in this life except death and taxes.' It wasn't just the fear of exposure that worried me. I genuinely saw no reason not to pay income tax like everybody else, if queasy about what it got spent on.

What was the solution? The worst that could happen, I decided, was that there might be some explaining to do to the federation, even to the International Olympic Committee, but what I certainly didn't want was being faced with the full force of HMRC.

The old man and I talked about it *ad nauseam*, but it was Brendan who suggested, from his own experience, that we set up a company. All payments whether cash for appearances or the small sponsorship contract I had with a local kit company went through PNC Enterprises, and set against these were my legitimate expenses. Like any small business, I kept a box file of invoices and receipts, and every year I'd declare my earnings and pay whatever was owing. To begin with it was pretty small beer, but at least I could sleep at night. And having a system already in place paid dividends when – off the back of my world records, and then Olympic success – we went from a few hundreds a year to many thousands a race.

After Steve Ovett's *annus mirabilis* – God knows how many races he had won – he went on record saying that he intended to lie low in 1979, in preparation for the Olympics.

Moscow 1980 had been a fixed point on the horizon ever since I started running. It was the benchmark for every stride I took, in training and in competition. One year out, I too intended to take it easy, but for a different reason – 1979 was earmarked for my degree.

It was now four years since I arrived at Loughborough. With my graduation year falling in my first championship season, I'd been given a furlough of an additional year. But now it was crunch time and although I kept up my training, I hardly competed at all beyond turning out for my university and a couple of county races up in Yorkshire.

I handed in my last paper in the middle of June and breathed a sigh of relief. Never again. I'd sweated blood to get there, working till two or three in the morning, night after night, week after week, forcing myself up at seven, and into my running kit. By the time it was over I was on my knees with mental exhaustion. As for physical exertion, that was different.

The next date on the calendar was a trip to Scandinavia – first Malmö in Sweden for the semi-finals of the Europa Cup on 30 June, then my first invitation to Oslo for the 800m.

Malmö went well. The Europa Cup was the athletics equivalent of the Davis Cup in tennis. You competed for your country as a team, and it took place every two years. These were the all-male semis, the final to be held in Turin at the beginning of August. The spirit was tremendous, with all of us cheering each other's events. This was a team on the move.

I felt suddenly liberated. The pressure of my finals had finally evaporated with the realisation that I would never have to face another exam paper again – and I won my 800m with plenty to spare. Then came trouble in the shape of our team manager. I had told him I wouldn't be going back to England with them as I was heading straight to Norway. I had a couple of days before the meet, so to go home just to turn round again made no sense in terms of expended energy, plus it was cheaper for the promoter. Now the guy was telling me that I couldn't go.

'But the promoter has sent my ticket!'

'Sorry, but you can't run without a permit. It's standard procedure.'

This would be only the second venue I'd run on the European circuit, Brussels being the other. And, yes, a permit was necessary. You had a duty to inform your federation to ensure you weren't about to run a coach and horses through your amateur status. But that couldn't be a problem here.

My relationship with the federation was strained at the best of times. Added to the usual antagonism that my father seemed to engender, the tectonic plates of our sport were shifting and, in large part, the genie was already out of the bottle. The federation could sense that they were losing their grip and, like parents of teenagers on the brink of leaving home, they were throwing their weight around in a show of after-the-horse-has-bolted aggression. In reality, their power and hold were ebbing by the day. They were basically saying, 'You may get the invitation but we'll tell you where you'll compete,' which was less than code for, 'We run the sport.'

I reversed the charges to my father back in Sheffield, and his view was the same as mine. 'Tell them to take a hike.' Oslo was the big one. Simply to be invited put me into an entirely different league. There was no way I was prepared to sit out this dance.

We agreed that I should keep my head down and just disappear. This wasn't the Soviet Union after all; they could hardly frog-march me gagged and bound on to a plane leaving for London. Pre mobile phones, it was comparatively easy to give them the slip. I just claimed not to have got messages, and did a flit, disappeared into the night and headed for the airport. I found a vacant bench and lay down with my kitbag under my head. The last thing I remember thinking before I dropped off to sleep was, 'There's no way the bastards are going to find me.' Although hardly a seasoned traveller, I became positively brazen. I flew to Oslo, got myself accredited, got access to the track, and at the appropriate time turned up at the welcoming reception – the strawberry party held on the lawn under apple trees at the promoter's house in the hills behind the city that is still a Bislett tradition.

By now I felt completely at home. Bislett is a one-off. In those days it took its relaxed, family atmosphere from the larger-than-life promoter Arne Haukvik, a local politician who was instantly recognisable in his trademark burgundy velvet jacket and pork-pie-meets-the-Tyrol straw hat.

The federation eventually caught up with me, the needle still stuck in the same groove: 'We don't know if we'll give you permission to run.' Technically, they had total control. Technically, they could have turned to Arne and said, 'He's not running.' Fortunately, common sense prevailed, and not before time. I finally got the go-ahead at two in the morning on the day of the race.

The Bislett Stadium is legendary. Until 1988 the track was iced over in winter and was a major venue for speed-skating champion-ships, while the infield did duty as a football pitch. In 1952 it hosted the Winter Olympics, and in total fifteen speed-skating world records had been set there. But this is dwarfed by the number of track world records broken – 32 by 1979, 65 at the time of writing. It was here in 1955 that my Interpol protector in Brussels, Roger Moens, took Rudolf Harbig's 800m record, which had remained unbroken for sixteen years.

How to explain Bislett's unique role in the pantheon of broken records? Unusually for a major sporting arena, it's bang in the centre of the city, barely five minutes walk from the Royal Palace. The surrounding buildings provide near total protection from the wind, especially after 7.00 p.m. when the sun goes down and all vestige of a breeze goes with it, while the air stays cool and fresh. This is when the crowd-pulling races are run, the big names take to the track and records tumble.

It's a small, even intimate, space. With its antiquated clubhouse stuck on top of the tribune, it reminded me of an English county cricket ground. Until 2004 when the stadium was rebuilt, the track was just six lanes wide and had steep banking so that the crowd felt practically on top of you, while the expectation that even more records were about to be broken turned the atmosphere electric. A tantalising aroma of beer would waft across from the brewery directly behind the finish line.

As a kid I'd studied maps of Norway, and now here I was! I had never been anywhere that felt so different. My father used to say that there were two things he would always remember: sailing into a Caribbean port and sailing into a fjord. It was the smell as much as anything else. The heady aroma of pine resin pervaded everything, and I remember being knocked out by the sheets of purple irises growing wild. I felt truly excited about being somewhere I had never been before, and that excitement at finding myself somewhere new has never waned.

The name of our hotel, the Summer Panorama, belied the reality. This was student accommodation at its most basic, effectively a hall of residence for most of the year. The canteen – and it was no more than this – was decorated with lurid photographs of the dishes on offer, which we claimed probably had more nutritional value than the food itself.

There was one huge plus, however. I was sharing an accommodation unit (apartment is too glamorous a term here) with a trio of Kiwis – Rod Dixon, 1500m bronze medallist at the 1972 Olympics; Dick Quax, 5000m world-record holder; and John Walker, the 1500m Olympic champion. Being with these guys, accepted as one of them, had me walking on air. I also got an insight into antipodean antipathy. Genuine tourists were staying in the Summer Panorama as well as us, and one morning we were in the antiquated lift going down when a woman got in, heard Rod and Dick talking and said, 'Are you Australian?' Rod Dixon peered at her over his glasses and said, 'Fuck me, no!'

I never remember what I dream, but that night I dreamt that Dickie Davies of *World of Sport* – ITV's answer to *Grandstand* – was going through the running order at the top of the programme and said, 'And of course we have Seb Coe's extraordinary world record from Oslo.' All very odd.

The morning of the 17th was cool but once the sun burnt off the mist coming off the fjord, the temperature rose. It was the perfect weather for running. At lunch I bumped into Andy Norman. In those days he was married to a Norwegian, and he was there to choreograph the race. He asked me what time I wanted to go through the first lap in. That morning I'd gone to the track and run a few 200 metres. They were really fast. I wasn't straining, it was just coming naturally, so I said, 'I'll go in fifty and bits,' bits being short-hand for tenths of a second.

He paled, then laughed. 'I'm not sure I've got too many in the 400m who will do that,' he said.

'Well, you did ask. But don't worry. If you haven't, I'll do it myself.'

'OK, I'll do what I can.'

'Doing what I can' in Andy Norman's lexicon meant spotting a Jamaican runner in the stands who was there on holiday, pulling him out, and telling him he was going to run. This guy – Lennie Smith – protested he hadn't any shoes. Andy found him some spikes and we had our pacemaker.

That evening I phoned my father. 'I'm feeling good,' I said. 'I don't quite know why.' I told him the times I'd done on the 200 metres earlier, and he was as surprised as I had been.

'Well, just go out and run. Let's get a benchmark for where you are. I'll be working late tonight, so call me at the factory as soon as you're done to let me know how you get on.'

Mike Boit, the Commonwealth title holder, who I'd been supposed to run against at Crystal Palace, was the one to beat. He and I were together off the bend behind Lennie Smith. The pace was fast, but not as fast as it had been in Prague, and then suddenly I was out on my own. I had no particular sensation of speed and I think I could have run even faster. I was running tall. It was as if I was floating. A lap from home, a roar rose up from the crowd that was deafening, and as I hit the back straight I was aware of Brendan and another couple of guys shouting from the side, urging me on. If I was tiring, I didn't feel it. I was flying. I was now thirty yards clear of the rest of the field and felt on a different plane. Then, the line crossed, I eased up.

'What was it?' I asked Rod Dixon who had been watching. There was no public display of the time at Bislett. You had to wait for the announcement.

'Well, I've got 1m 42 something . . .'

'He must be wrong,' I thought as I walked a few paces down the track, waiting for the official time. The world record was etched into my psyche: 1m 43.7.

I put my head down, bending from the waist, hands on my thighs, and took my breath, turning towards the Tannoy that was crackling into life, straining to hear what it said, but it was in Norwegian, and drowned out by yet another roar from the crowd. I caught only a bit of it: '. . . another world record at Bislett!' I must have leapt two feet in the air.

I couldn't believe it! I had broken the world record! I was the holder of a world record! I had never done a lap of honour before, but I did one then . . . even so, I still couldn't believe it.

The first thing I had to do was to call Peter. The 800m had been the last race of the evening and the stadium was emptying fast. Someone pointed me in the direction of the press box. It was empty, so I just picked up a phone. When there was no reply from his direct line, I called the main number.

'I'm not sure that he's still here,' one of the girls in the office said.

'Can you check his car, see if it's gone?' A couple of moments later, she was back on the line.

'Still here.'

'I think you'll find he's down in the engineers,' I said. 'The engineers' was the creative hub, where his teams would be designing some devilish piece of machinery that would revolutionise cutlery manufacture.

'No reply,' she said. 'But if you don't mind waiting, I'll pop down and find him.'

'The thing is,' I explained, 'I'm calling from Norway.'

'Well in that case I could give him a message.'

'Just tell him his son's broken the eight-hundred metre world record.'

'All right, love.'

'Make sure you say *world* record. Thanks.'

As I heard it later, she eventually located him in the machine room. I can picture the scene. Everyone is in overalls, my father in a white coat, standing next to whatever is causing the problem, glasses on the tip of his nose, when the girl who took the call walks in.

'Message from your son, Mr Coe. Says to tell you that he's just broken the world record.'

At which point my dad dropped a large piece of metal on his foot and swore. That machine was forever afterwards known as the Jesus-Christ machine.

Back at Bislett I tried to get a lift back to the hotel, but the guys had all disappeared. There was no one I knew. Still looking for a face I recognised, I wandered back out on to the track. The stadium was empty. The sky was a deep blue – the sun barely sets that far north in mid-June – and the floodlights were still on. I decided to walk around, a last solo lap, unable to take it in. Nothing was different yet everything was different. I knew I was in good shape, but to take a full second of Alberto Juantorena's time . . .

Then I remembered there was a reception in the City Hall. The building had been pointed out to me earlier in the day and I knew roughly where it was so I started off on foot, eventually managing to flag down a taxi. But when I began climbing the steps I had serious second thoughts. I was still in my tracksuit, kitbag containing my spikes and towel slung across my shoulder. What was I thinking of? I'd do better to head back to the Summer Panorama for a beer. Then somebody must have spotted me and suddenly I was in the middle of a flurry of people. I'd had no idea that this was less a reception than a banquet. A huge deal, which is why they'd all legged it once the last race was over. So there I was, still in my kit, and everybody just stood up, a sea of faces turned towards me, and started clapping. The organisers, of course, were mortified. Everyone had thought that somebody else was looking after me. It was a surreal moment.

7

THE ELYSIAN FIELD

I N those days Oslo hosted two athletics meetings every summer, the first – where I took the 800m world record – and 'the big one', ten days later. No sports editor mindful of his budget would sanction two trips to Norway so close to each other, so they'd always cover meet number two. The only journalist to witness my achievement was a stringer from the Press Association.

I had left England unknown outside the small world of middle-distance running, but I returned home a hero. On landing at Heathrow I was told to leave the plane first. When I emerged from the cabin it was into the glare of flashbulbs, and versions of, 'Over here, Seb!' and above all, the question that would come to haunt me over succeeding years: 'How does it feel?' Nothing in my life would ever be the same again.

Like so many of the great promoters of our sport, Arne Haukvik was not only devoted to athletics, he was a consummate showman. Immediately he knew I'd smashed Juantorena's record, he'd heard the click of turnstiles. 'Of course, Sebastian,' he'd said, an avuncular arm around my shoulder, 'now you will have to do the mile!' So I found myself back in Oslo ten days later, and this time the British press were there by the plane load. It was exactly twenty-five years and six weeks since Roger Bannister had made his myth-shattering run, and their interest was spiked.

Although the mile has never featured in the Olympics, and was scratched from the Commonwealth Games in 1966, it remains an iconic distance, both for athletes and the public. Yes, there's the romance of the past, but it was the Herculean determination of athletes to break the seemingly unbreakable four-minute barrier that captured the popular imagination. Alongside the ascent of Everest and the conquest of the South Pole it ranks as one of the peaks of man's unquenchable spirit. The mile has lost none of its cachet in the intervening years, and continues to maintain a uniquely high profile, the jewel in the diadem of athletics meetings that glitter across Europe every summer. From the spectators' point of view, the mile is long enough but not too long. It's a drama in four acts. The first lap is the overture when the orchestra is warming up, the second lap you begin to understand where you think the plot might be leading, by the third lap you're into the thick of the narrative, and the fourth is about how the hell is this going to finish, with a few twists and turns before the curtain. And all in under four minutes.

Scandinavia has a particularly vibrant history with the distance. During the war years, Sweden's neutrality enabled Gunder Hägg and Arne Andersson to keep up the pressure on the elusive sub four-minute time. Together they took it from Sydney Wooderson's 4m 06.4 in 1937, to 4m 01.4 in Malmö in 1945, the record passing back and forth between them like their personal plaything, and Hägg's record remained unbroken until Roger Bannister in 1954. There's a salutary postscript to this story. In 1946, having set over a dozen middle-distance records, Gunder Hägg was deemed to have broken the amateur rules – which he almost certainly did – and barred from further competition.

The mile is the only imperial distance recognised by the IAAF. Unlike the 1500m, which is three and three-quarter laps of a standard stadium, it's precisely four. Due to its roots, it's rarely run outside America, Europe and the Commonwealth; hence Dubai's choice of the mile for their profile-raising exercise.

The involvement of the IAAF in the Golden Mile meant that Arne Haukvik had both the cash and the clout to assemble the world's top milers that year. Among them was New Zealander John Walker, Olympic gold medallist at 1500m and mile world-record holder at 3m 49.4 – the first man to run it in under 3m 50. There were Steve Scott and Craig Masback, two of three Americans in the race, the latter a student at Trinity, Cambridge. There was Thomas Wessinghage, a doctor from West Germany and the European No. 1. Eamonn Coghlan from Ireland had run the fastest indoor mile of the year in Philadelphia and was perhaps, along with Steve Scott, the joint favourite. From Britain there was Dave Moorcroft from Coventry, who had taken the 1500m gold at the Edmonton Commonwealth Games. And then there was the dark horse, an 800m runner called Sebastian Coe, although the newcomer wasn't seen as a definite threat.

However, in an interview that preceded the broadcast of the race, John Walker said I was the question mark, 'the danger man, because no one knows how good he can be'. We were all interviewed individually, an unprecedented media focus, which demonstrated the power of the cash that Dubai had injected.

Although I'd set a new world record for the 800m, this race was twice the distance, and while I had squeezed in under the four minutes two years earlier, among the thirteen starters I was the third slowest, only the Norwegian and the Japanese – both included largely for diplomatic and/or TV reasons – being slower on paper. People had always said I would end up as a miler, largely because of my build, but this would be only my fourth mile in as many years and I privately feared I'd get chewed up in the third lap.

There was one glaring omission in the line-up – Steve Ovett. While I was really only a jobbing athlete at the distance, he was the master. Not only had he won the first Golden Mile in Tokyo the previous September – and should by tradition have been there to defend it – he had been unbeaten in the mile/1500m since 1977. Initially, he had accepted the invitation, but just ten days before the race, after winning yet another 1500m at Crystal Palace, he'd had second thoughts. 'Why should we have to go over to Norway? The best milers are British. Let the rest of the world come to us,' he'd said in an interview, and in doing so had boxed himself into a corner. His rationale was that he had 'nothing to prove', while a victory without him in the field would be 'hollow'. His absence – and dismissive attitude – certainly irked the rest of the field, although from my perspective it served mainly to deflect attention from me.

The Bislett crowd are perhaps the most knowledgeable in the world, and the expectation that night was that I would run quite well, but be gobbled up and spat out by the more seasoned in the field towards the end of the third lap. Everyone knew that I was there to pull in the crowds, not to win. One person who didn't subscribe to this scenario was my father, who this time had come with me. As I finished my warm-up he said, 'You know, you can win this today,' and I said, 'Yeah, I know I can.' I was surprised at my own equanimity, but it was the truth. However, it was also true that I hadn't run a mile in competition since Crystal Palace in 1977. It wasn't my distance and these were the world's finest. At least in terms of tactics that made it easy. I decided to sit in and do no more than was strictly necessary, even remain a passenger. The less I did and the longer they failed to break me, the more I could utilise my 800m speed.

There were thirteen of us, which on Bislett's six-lane track was tight. To avoid the inevitable scrum on the first bend, where there's always the possibility of trouble, I decided to go to the front, but I wasn't there long. At around 100 yards, an American – the third, and yet another Steve, Steve Lacy, who had been pressured into making the pace – took the lead. Steve Scott followed, and I tucked in behind, lying fourth. At the halfway mark Lacy dropped out and Steve Scott went to the front. He wasn't pacemaking. He was out there to take the American record, still held by Jim Ryun. Entering the dangerous yards of the third lap had been my greatest worry, but instead of anxiety I actually felt easy, relaxed and hardly breathing. When I glanced back, I saw that we had left the rest of the field a good way behind. Then halfway down the home straight and with one lap to go, I thought, 'Sod it, I'll go it alone.' As I drove for the line, I had no idea what the time was. I had no idea what the world record was, all I wanted to do was win.

I was already jogging around the track on a victory lap, when the news came over the Tannoy that Bislett had added another world record to its tally. I had run it in 3m 48.95, slicing nearly nine whole seconds off my previous best. At the side of the track a woman was holding a union flag on a branch, and as I took it I felt a huge surge of elation. Craig Masback said later that, with the press running behind me, it looked like Delacroix's painting *Liberty Leading the People*. Ten days before I'd thought that the high of the 800m record could never been beaten, but I now realised how much more this was. This was the mile! I had brought the world record back to Britain, its spiritual home. And as the correspondent of the *Sheffield Telegraph* would later point out, I had also brought it back to Yorkshire. The last British holder of the mile world record was Derek Ibbotson in 1957.

At the end of the race, my father who couldn't resist the jibe, remarked that I'd not actually run through the line, I'd eased up. I wasn't the only one. Steve Scott missed Jim Ryun's US record by one-hundredth of a second. And my dad was right. It meant I could have been even faster.

When I returned to England, two serious students of the sport, i.e. Steve Mitchell and Malcolm Williams, were anxious not to let the momentum slip. 'You do realise, Newbold, that nobody's ever held the 800m, the mile and the 1500m all at the same time?' Newbold is my middle name – my grandmother's maiden name – and they had taken to referring to me as such to retain my anonymity.

It's fair to say that I rise well to a challenge and my interest was aroused. Next year was Moscow and everything would be subordinate to that. If I wanted to try for the triple, it was now or never.

There are moments in an athlete's life when you feel unassailable. It doesn't last long – maybe as little as one season. But I had now entered that Elysian field. However, I also knew that records are there to be broken and my 800m and mile wouldn't stand for ever.

Every summer there were – and still are – three key invitation meets in the athletics calendar: Oslo in June or July, Zurich in August and Brussels at the beginning of September. I was already committed to the Europa Cup final in Turin in early August, where I would run in the 800m.

And then Andreas Brugger phoned my dad. Andreas was the founder of the Zurich Weltklasse, the athletics equivalent of the Ascot Gold Cup, which athletes value for its quality and consistency. Thanks to its scale and pulling power, it is even known as the 'Olympics In Three Hours'.

All promoters love world records, and that summer Andreas thought he had sniffed one. In fact, the previous March I'd already been invited to run in the 800m; coming third in the European Championships in Prague had put me on the map. But post Oslo everything changed. He'd like to offer me a world-record attempt at 1500m, he said. He said that he'd pay me X and set it all up, which meant sorting out a pacemaker and putting together a strong field. 'But first I want you to try out our national training centre in the mountains to acclimatise yourself. You can come straight from Turin.'

It was a smart move. He recognised that I probably needed some space, and he was right. Since returning from Oslo, press interest had become an avalanche. If I was safely ensconced in an Alpine stronghold, perhaps I might get some peace.

Turin being done and dusted – I won my 800m although five

seconds slower than at Bislett – I flew straight to Zurich from Milan and was met at the airport by Andreas himself and his meet colleague Fred Diete, a Clark Kent look-alike complete with American accent. My first impression of Zurich's Mr Big was that he lived up to his reputation. To say that Andreas Brugger has presence fails to convey his persona. Then in his fifties, he was exceptionally tall with cheekbones you could sharpen a pencil on, and exuded power like a boxer exudes sweat. A few waves of his hand enabled us to walk straight through the airport – no nonsense with passports – out of the VIP entrance and into his purring green Jaguar.

'Ever been to Zurich before, Sebastian?'

'Never.'

'OK. So we'll go to our most famous street and we have coffee and cake.'

Personally, I would have preferred going straight to the hotel but decided that I'd be unwise to turn down his hospitality.

Zurich's Bahnhofstrasse might have a plebeian name, but it's one of the smartest and most expensive streets in the world, and for the most part, a pedestrian precinct – not that anyone appeared to have told Andreas that. The Jag nosed its way through the mêlée and, pulling up outside a café, we got out, leaving the car where it stopped. Having identified a table, Andreas went across and Diete and I followed in his wake. It was occupied by two elderly but perfectly coiffed women. Andreas said something in German, asking – I imagined – if they minded if we sat down as there were several spare seats. Instead of a smile and a wave towards the empty places, a guttural altercation ensued, and the women left in what was clearly high dudgeon. I sat down uneasily, wondering what the hell had kicked off.

'What was all that about?' I asked Fred when Andreas went inside.

'Mr Brugger asked to share the table,' he said.

'Yes, I got that. But why the scene?'

Fred looked uncomfortable. 'These ladies were German.'

'And?'

'Mr Brugger's not keen on Germans.'

'So?'

'So, he says, "OK. You lose the war, so we permit you to conquer the coffee tables!" '

Andreas was someone who spoke his mind. His children tell the story of a family walk in the mountains near their house in the Grindelwald, and crossing a paddock belonging to a local farmer. The farmer emerged from a barn shouting, 'Get off my land or I'll set my dogs on you!'

'Feel free,' said Andreas. 'But I tell you two things. First I will kill your dog, and then I will kill you.'

But underneath the hardman carapace, Andreas's generosity is hard to match. The number of athletes he has helped is legion, way beyond their sporting careers. An anecdote: in 1949 when food in Britain was still rationed, he brought over a suitcase full of prime beef, destined for Herne Hill Harriers. By chance, the customs officer at Dover, who was about to confiscate it – importing raw meat being strictly illegal – turned out to be a member of the club, and nodded him through.

Like many promoters, track and field had been Andreas's sport. He had competed at the discus and shot put, and just decided that the club could do better. A successful businessman, he had brought blue-chip sponsors to the table, including Omega and UBS, the banking giant, and raised the profile by inviting the best athletes in the world. In this way he turned a small-time regional meet into one of the most prestigious dates in the athletics calendar, for which tickets are sold out nine months in advance. Every penny made goes back into the club, which, thanks to his astute financial planning, is now sitting on millions.

Andreas drove me to the Swiss National Training camp in Macolin above Neuchâtel. It had been a long year – first my finals, then two world records, then Turin. All I really wanted to do was to chill out, go on holiday somewhere warm – and a training camp didn't quite fit the bill. However, I accepted that he had made the offer with the best of intentions and I would make the best of it.

Introductions made over the inevitable coffee and cake, Andreas left and the centre director took over. Accommodation, he explained, would be elsewhere on the site and my heart sank. I wouldn't even be at the centre of things. After a short drive we arrived at a largish chalet. As I walked down the path, I noticed running kit hanging out of the windows drying in the sunshine – female running kit. That was the moment when things began to look up. It turned out that I'd been billeted with the American women's track team. Twelve of them! What can I say? They cooked for me, they got my kit laundered, and I learnt more about the female of the species in those five days than I'd probably learnt in my entire four years at Loughborough. Among them was Evelyn Ashford, one of the great US sprinters, who went on to take gold in the 100m in the Los Angeles Games; also Stephanie Hightower, Olympic hurdler and current president of US Track and Field, now married to Ian Stewart.

Not only was the company great but Macolin's facilities, from the physios to the food, were perfect. This was as far removed from the Hotel Summer Panorama as can be imagined. In Oslo I had been able to smell the pines. Here I could run among them for hours, needles softening the forest floor, utterly alone, nothing between me and the sky but pure mountain air plus the odd kite or buzzard. It began a love affair with mountains that continues to this day.

Meanwhile, back in Zurich, word had got out about my 1500m record attempt, and after ruling himself out of the Golden Mile in Oslo, Steve Ovett – via Andy Norman – now wanted in. I didn't care who was in the line-up. On the other hand, neither was I prepared to pacemake for somebody else, nor attempt a world record in which another runner might opt for spoiling tactics. Ultimately, Andreas himself decided to leave Steve out. He could well have taken the record that night, but the buzz that summer was around Sebastian Coe. A world record in Zurich for me would make it three in a row, and in terms of both gate and media, for Andreas that was jackpot time, and he left no stone unturned to make it happen.

Only when I got back to Zurich did the enormity of what I was attempting really hit me. Holding three world records at the same time at those distances simply hadn't been done, and thanks to the deal Andreas had put together with NBC, the world would be watching. What made it even more disquieting was that I had never set out to break a world record before. The two in Oslo had been entirely serendipitous. As far as the 800m was concerned, I'd been in good shape and got slightly swept along by the atmosphere. The Golden Mile was equally unexpected, it being only my fourth race at the distance in as many years. In addition, I was about to learn that the Zurich Weltklasse is as different from Oslo as it's possible to imagine. If Bislett is anoraks and trainers, Zurich is pure Gucci, athletics' answer to St Moritz, where haute couture rubs shoulders with bankers and politics. And everyone had paid premium prices to see history made. The pressure now was exponential; the mercury risked shattering the barometer.

Everything about that evening was high octane, high expectation. My father joined me before the race, having broken into his holiday to be there. In terms of the record, he said, everything rested on the weather, and as the evening wore on, it looked increasingly unlikely. Clouds were closing in, and occasional flashes of summer lightning flickered across the sky. Although the wind had dropped, the air was hot and humid and you felt it. Peter's last words before we lined up on the track were, 'It's shit or bust, get out there and hang on.'

Kip Koskei from Kenya, who was making the pace, shot to the front, and I knew instantly that he was going too fast. Everyone had agreed that we wanted a good time, but this was lunacy. Nevertheless, I had to keep up. At the end of the first lap the old man was yelling at me to slow down. But where was Mike Boit? He'd said he'd take me to 400m. As for the others, I couldn't even see their shadows on the floodlit track. Kip got me to about 600 metres and then he began to fade. So I had no option but to go. I'd hoped that a few people would start pushing up behind me, even coming alongside, but they were all way too far behind. Digging in from so far out was tough. All that kept me going was the crowd, chanting my name and clapping in time to their repeated 'Coe, Coe, Coe', rising to a demented roar as I hit the home straight, lifting me as nothing else could.

I passed the line, shaving just one tenth of a second off Filbert Bayi's record, set at the Commonwealth Games in 1974, but one tenth was all it needed. I am absolutely convinced, however, that if the pacing had continued longer, and if I hadn't been having to struggle on my own, I could have taken another second off. But that night nobody was complaining. I was the first British athlete ever to hold the 1500m record. More importantly, in terms of the history books, nobody had ever held world records in these three distances at the same time before, and I had taken them in just forty-one days.

I have much to be grateful to Zurich for, not least that I made a lifelong friend in Andreas Brugger. He's now in his eighties, but I still go to Grindelwald every year, and have become good friends with his offspring, and now my children ski with his grandchildren. But as far as that race was concerned, I can't say that I enjoyed it. On that final straight, I was running on fumes. A few days later I pulled a calf muscle while training in Richmond Park, which effectively put me out of any further racing that season, and it's fair to say I wasn't too disappointed.

* * *

Steve Ovett had begun 1979 saying that he'd had a great 1978 and was planning to have a gentler year in the lead-up to the Moscow Games, which was perfectly reasonable. But as my star continued to rise, I think he became edgy. For years, Steve had decried the whole business of record breaking. His attitude had been that records could only be transient but titles and medals are yours for life – and actually, of course he was right. Yet the moment I'd got the triple, he began a hurried re-think. He held the world record for the two miles, which he'd taken off Brendan Foster, but that wasn't one of the classics.

Over what remained of the 1979 season he made two record attempts, first the Emsley Carr Mile at Crystal Palace, followed by the 1500m at the Van Damme meet in Brussels, both of which he missed by fractions of a second. Still nursing my strained calf muscle, I watched them both and, although it couldn't have been closer, I was not really surprised. Had he and I been on the track, racing, it might have been different, because that's what he enjoyed, pitting himself against another human being. Running against the stopwatch just wasn't his scene.

This always remained the great difference between us. I didn't need the presence of a rival at my shoulder. While it's true that I liked the bustle of a keenly contested race – and a solo effort was always tougher – the concept of man against clock was something I enjoyed. I have always felt comfortable when I've chosen to run from the front and perhaps there is something of the performer in me that responds to the undivided attention of the crowd. There is nothing to beat hitting the front two laps from home and feeling the stadium explode. They know what you're there for and they just roar.

Zurich 1979 was probably the one exception to that. Although it got me over the finish line, the burden of the crowd's expectation was one notch tighter than I needed, and with the Olympics less than a year away, the pressure could only get worse. Attention from the press was now a given at any meet I went to, but I hadn't expected it to impinge on my ordinary life.

Having given up my student accommodation in Loughborough that July, I was now back at home. And while Sheffield is by any standards a substantial city, in character it resembles a large village, and is certainly less brash than Manchester across the Pennines. As the new local hero, I couldn't go anywhere without someone stopping me and wishing me well. As for the press, there was no letting up. While I could give the British the slip by heading for the hills, French, Italian and American journalists tended to bypass convention and knock on our front door. Meanwhile, writers and snappers on the sports desk of the *Sheffield Telegraph,* who knew every track and byway as well as I did, would ensure their readers were updated on my every move. We took to driving over the county border to Derbyshire on to the Chatsworth Estate and its thousand acres of parkland, some of the most beautiful in England, where I might disturb a few deer but little else would bother me. They hadn't found me there yet, but, although private property, it was basically accessible to anyone, and as autumn slipped into winter I realised the situation could only deteriorate.

The solution came out of the blue in a phone call from my old PE teacher John O'Keefe. He had left Tapton when I was in the third year, but we had kept in touch, and he was now head of PE at St George's International School at Olgiata, on the outskirts of Rome. My father took the call and then handed me the phone.

'I don't know what your plans are, Seb,' John began, 'but if you fancy training somewhere warm, you could do worse than come here. We've got a house with plenty of room on the edge of a golf course, and the weather's nice, and you can just be part of the school.'

Suddenly it all fell into place. A Yorkshire winter with a wind-chill factor unsuited to anything less than four layers of clothing is far from ideal for a pre-Olympic training programme, and the memory of running in the Alps, and the freedom that gave me, was still fresh in my mind. Rome might not be Switzerland, but it definitely wasn't Sheffield, where every wet road and iced-up track was an accident waiting to happen, and I had as much chance of passing unnoticed as Ziggy Stardust.

The teeth of the media ratchet were beginning to grip. As far as the non-sporting press were concerned, I'd come from nowhere to break three world records in forty-one days. It wasn't nowhere, of course. In 1978 I'd taken bronze in the European Championships in Prague, but 'overnight sensation' was more fruitful, as indeed was the even juicier prospect of some real opposition for Steve Ovett. In less than two months, I'd gone from the back page of the *Sheffield Telegraph* to making the cover of *Time* magazine, and *Sports Illustrated*. I'd been the front-page lead in the *Daily Telegraph*. I'd won the BBC Sports Personality of the Year award, and the Sportswriters' Sportsman of the Year.

I left Sheffield at the start of the New Year, and was soon happily ensconced with the O'Keefes – good company, good food, the rough and tumble of normal family life and the weather was perfect. As for John's casual mention of a nearby golf course, the 27-hole Olgiata Club turned out to be the Italian equivalent of Gleneagles. God knows how much the membership fees were, but at least nobody looked twice at the pale young man they would see running along beside the fairways or doing press-ups in the rough. And with Sophia Loren's mother living just a few doors down, I enjoyed a certain frisson every time I passed, in the vain hope that I might catch a glimpse of the fabled Roman goddess.

Rome is one of the original seven-hilled cities, the others being Prague and, yes, Sheffield, and in terms of endurance training, the emphasis here would be on stamina. In Moscow, faced with two separate distances, each involving heats and semi-finals, this could be an issue. If I made both finals, I'd be running a total of seven races in eleven days.

As part of a sponsorship deal, I'd been given use of a car and before leaving England had taken my test. Some mornings I'd drive out to the coast and run up the beach at Ostia – miles and miles of sand, deserted in the winter except for the occasional dog walker – or I'd head north to Santa Marinella, where the sand gives way to rock, but a little-used coast road hugs the shore right up to Civitavecchia.

On other days I'd go inland, up into the hills, into the forest of Manziana, following ancient Etruscan trails or running along a perfectly preserved Roman road that led through a landscape that at times could have been Arizona. I was completely on my own. No training partners, and a coach two thousand miles away. As for weight training, I could use the school gym, and the old man came out a couple of times to check up on 'my athlete'. But basically for the first time in my life I was totally self-directed.

Until now I had always been a part-time athlete. At first it was school, and then there was university. Even in the summer holidays I'd worked at the factory. For the first time ever I had no homework or studying to fit in to my training schedule, which was now the epicentre of my life.

My ex-pat existence began to develop a certain rhythm. While I made friends with some of the teachers at the school, most of the time I'd be on my own, training during the day and listening to my growing travelling collection of jazz tapes, as well as attempting to catch up on ten years of reading. Like many people I know, my education only really got going when I left full-time education.

At weekends I tried to give John and his family some space. Sunday afternoons were always given over to football. And what football! Roma and Lazio are Rome's two Serie A teams. They share the Olympic stadium, playing there alternate weeks, and their rivalry is every bit as intense as that between Rangers and Celtic.

Saturday night was very different and my one big indulgence. Just as jazz ran through my father's veins, classical music was my mother's great love, and every second Friday when I was growing up she would take us to a concert at Sheffield City Hall, which alternated with Manchester as home to the Hallé Orchestra. Yet although she had a substantial collection of recordings, which would take their turn on the record player, I seemed to have baulked at the idea of opera. And while it had often been on, I had certainly never sat down and actually listened to it. Yes, opera sounded OK, but I never really 'got' it until that first evening at the Teatro dell'Opera di Roma, when I was completely blown away. This was the cultural equivalent of my first football match at Stamford Bridge, which is not a comparison I make lightly. Seeing Mozart's *The Magic Flute* was an epiphany, and it is still my favourite opera. And while I can't say that life without opera would be as devastating as life without football, nobody who hasn't experienced it can even begin to understand the power of the entire experience, let along the singing. The atmosphere is unlike anything else, from the excitement of the orchestra tuning up and people settling into their seats, to the hissing and booing by the 'claque' in full throttle, fans who were originally paid to clap the performers, but who now make their own partisan decisions. The great divas and tenors are as big in the lives of opera lovers in Rome as Gianni Rivera and other stars were in the lives of football fans. The great difference between opera in Italy and opera practically anywhere else is that it is totally classless. The auditorium is filled with as many grannies and students as moneyed patrons in their finery.

8

BOYCOTT

THE 1980s was perhaps the most politically charged decade in the history of sport and it began on Christmas Eve 1979 with the invasion of Afghanistan by the Soviet Union. I remember us all sitting at home, watching it unfold on television and having no idea how far the ripples of this particular pebble would extend.

It was just before I set off for Italy. A wonderful man called Kenny Moore – an American athlete-turned-journalist – was spending Christmas with us in Sheffield. We'd met in Oslo at the Golden Mile and he had subsequently been commissioned to do an in-depth profile for *Sports Illustrated*. Kenny was everything you like in an American, erudite and self-assured but also self-effacing. Above all, he was cuttingly funny. When he turned up at our front door my mother and sisters just melted, not least because he had the look of a youthful Robert Redford. As for his staying at a hotel, Angela wouldn't hear of it. The men in our family had rarely seen the level of customer care that was lavished on him. Tea and coffee would appear as if by magic. Most visitors would be told, 'Well, you know where the kettle is.' Kenny was different and they couldn't get enough of him.

Jimmy Carter – arguably one of America's worst presidents – was in his last year of office and grasping for a legacy. A month after the invasion he found it. If Soviet troops weren't withdrawn by the end of February, he said, the United States would boycott the Moscow Olympics. For a while there seemed to be stalemate. Then came the Lake Placid Winter Games, in New York State, which provided an unexpected outlet for cold-war tension when the Soviet men's ice-hockey team – four-time gold winners – were trounced by the unfancied Americans. In early March, Carter confirmed the US boycott, and deemed it an article of faith that other western democracies should follow suit. Where have we heard that before . . . ?

West Germany soon fell into line, unwilling perhaps to risk the wrath of those underpinning its security. Then on 19 March the boycott was debated in the House of Commons.

The previous May, Margaret Thatcher had formed a new government with a majority of forty-three. Her response to the proposed US boycott was a reaffirmation of the special relationship, watered down under recent administrations. Government papers released under the thirty-year rule show that Michael Heseltine, then Secretary of State for the Environment, stated that the Soviet invasion of Afghanistan, 'Needs to be countered by whatever means at our disposal, political or otherwise. If this means that we have to embrace the use of sport for the first time as a political weapon, I feel that the end would justify the means.'

Unlike the situation in the States where athletes were simply forbidden to compete, the decision in the UK rested with the British Olympic Association. The BOA were under huge pressure to comply, the argument being that to compete in the Games would serve the propaganda needs of the Soviet regime, and thus condone the invasion. Mercifully, the BOA's chairman was a straight-talking Yorkshireman, Sir Denis Follows, who would have none of it. His on-record response was: 'We believe sport should be a bridge, and not a destroyer.' His off-the-record views were unprintable. It didn't help that Margaret Thatcher called him a communist when he was in fact an old-school northern Tory. As a fellow Sheffielder, I had got to know him quite well, and while I believe he would always have taken the it's-for-us-to-decide-and-not-the-government route, the prime ministerial typecasting was not only privately upsetting, but a tactical blunder of some magnitude.

The BOA is one of the rare Olympic committees that receives no state funding, and there continues to be periodic debate in the British sporting community about whether or not it should get government support. However, there can be no doubt that, had they taken the Treasury shilling, the decision to go it alone in 1980 would have been much more problematic, as demonstrated by the situation in New Zealand.

The months preceding an Olympic Games are among the most intense an athlete will ever face in his or her career. Everything you do in preparation – your training programme, competitions, even where you live – is predicated on reaching a peak during a few days in July or early August. The threat of a boycott and with it the prospect that after many years – a decade in my case – devoted to your sport you will be denied the one chance in your lifetime to compete in an Olympic Games, was unthinkable. But think about it you did, and it was like a grumbling appendix.

Among those I canvassed in Rome, the prevailing view was that both Italian and British athletes would compete. And so it proved. But there were many athletes who would not have the chance, specifically Americans and Kenyans. Their governments' action in denying them the holy grail of any world-class athlete showed utter contempt for their dedication and ability.

The position of Kenya was particularly intolerable, the boycott having been forced on them by threats to trade, overseas aid and loans. At first they were going to go, but then the government changed its mind. Given that the country had also boycotted the 1976 Games – in response to New Zealand's rugby team playing in South Africa – it meant that their athletes spent eight years in the wilderness. Henry Rono was perhaps the most spectacular casualty. He had taken four world records in 1978 and two gold medals at the Commonwealth Games in the same year. Would he have made the podium in Moscow? Without a doubt. And as an Olympic hero of that magnitude his future would have been assured. As it was, the country that had nurtured his career through college scholarships – America – left him to hang out and dry. He became a drifter and an alcoholic. What politicians forgot was that they were playing God with people's lives and that the human consequences of their decisions could be catastrophic.

In Britain, when it first kicked off, public opinion seemed to favour the boycott, whereas the attitude in Italy was more ambivalent. Meanwhile, Kenny Moore kept me posted on what was happening in the land of the free, including how he'd been invited to organise an alternative 'Liberty' games to be held in Philadelphia. He refused, saying that while he might be forbidden to participate as a competitor (he had come fourth in the Munich marathon) he would go to Moscow anyway, as a journalist.

I returned to England shortly after Easter. Attempts to derail the BOA having failed, individual athletes were now being targeted with anti-Soviet propaganda. Allan Wells was sent a picture of a dead Afghan girl clutching a doll. But the most shameful example was that of Linsey MacDonald, a 15 year old from Scotland, and a preciously talented sprinter. One morning she opened a letter, addressed to her personally at her home in Glasgow, to find a photograph of an Afghan child with his head chopped off. Fortunately, Linsey was resilient enough to cope with such grotesque mind games, and vindicated her decision to go by helping to take bronze in the women's 4 x 400m relay. And, of course, Allan took gold in the 100m sprint and silver in the 200m. But all in all it was a pretty disgusting campaign.

As for the Coe household, a giant swastika appeared daubed on our garage doors, discovered by my younger sister Emma as she set off to school one morning. It may, of course, have been coincidental – whoever it was had clearly researched my mother's Indian parentage – but either way, it shows just how high passions were running. The issue really did seem to have divided the country.

Sheffield took a belligerent view right from the start. The election of a Conservative government six months earlier had come as a huge culture shock, but whatever their politics, the entire sporting community had no doubt that Britain should be represented. As for me, I did my best to assess the countervailing arguments, and there were moments when I really questioned whether I was doing the right thing, but from whichever standpoint I looked at it, all reasonable roads led back to participation.

On a day-to-day level such uncertainty was unsettling. When you set off for the training track, knowing that the session you're about to do will leave you utterly exhausted, probably wasted for the rest of the day, that you've already been doing this for over a decade, and that it may all be for nothing, is destabilising no matter how much you try to compartmentalise it.

Some British athletes, those employed in the public sector – the armed forces or the police – had a particularly rough ride. Geoff Capes, the larger-than-life Lincolnshire policeman and our team captain, fell into this category. After much wrangling he was finally allowed to take his annual leave in August and was thus able to compete, but he failed to make the rostrum. Given his performances before and after Moscow, it's hard not to conclude that the pressure had told.

Another athlete who should have done better was long jumper Sue Reeve, the Commonwealth gold medallist in Edmonton. As a civil servant, she was refused leave of absence either to train or compete. Her defiant, 'I'll go to Moscow even if it costs me my job,' got wall-to-wall media coverage, and as stories like these began to get oxygen, the pro-boycott lobby slowly lost its edge.

A minority of UK federations opted to toe the government line. As well as Britain's hockey players, these included our three-day eventers, who were then world leaders. The team included three-time gold medallist Richard Meade. As for our excluded sailors, at least three – Chris Law, Rob White and David Campbell-James – had won European titles and would almost certainly have come home with medals.

As the Games approached, I went from being irritated to angry, and in the end, given my federation's overwhelming vote to defy the boycott, and the BOA's unequivocal decision to go to Moscow, I saw no reason not to air my views when asked for them directly, as I was in Oslo on 1 July, just two weeks before the Games were due to start. I did so knowing full well they would be picked up and given wide coverage. I reiterated what Sir Denis Follows had said, namely that sport is an extraordinary bridgehead into all sorts of things, and that using it as a weapon was both craven and self-defeating. 'If the government think this is serious, then they should do something about it, but don't just use sport as the fall guy.'

My outspoken views did not play well in the corridors of power, and my father was called to the Foreign Office to be ticked off by Douglas Hurd, the Minister of State for Europe, requesting that he keep his troublesome son in check. My old man was always distrustful of politicians, and I have little doubt that he gave as good as he got, arguing along the lines that he was my coach not my keeper, and that having recently graduated in economics and social history, I could probably figure out the pros and cons on my own.

This tragi-comedic incident has a sequel. Sixteen years later, I had reason to speak to Douglas Hurd myself when I was in the Whips' Office, and I asked him if he remembered upbraiding the father of the future MP for Falmouth and Camborne.

'I've never forgotten it,' he said. 'The truth is I felt very uncomfortable about the whole business. And your father, I remember, gave me the toughest run for my money of anybody that I was asked to speak to. He didn't budge an inch.'

I'd be surprised if Douglas Hurd made much headway against Ron Pickering, either. The great former coach and BBC commentator was also subjected to the Hurd housemasterly chat. Ron told me later that he was convinced that Margaret Thatcher had left the room only seconds before. 'I could smell her perfume,' he said. Perhaps it was a last-ditch attempt to stiffen the resolve of an unconvinced junior minister.

More telling was that Britain was providing much of the sporting equipment that would be used in Moscow, a fact that seemed to be totally ignored. No one was suggesting economic sanctions, as that would affect our balance of payments, and thus jobs. Boycotting the Games themselves must have seemed a cheap option. After all, sport was only amateur, something people did in their spare time . . .

As a former Conservative MP and government whip, I never envisaged the day when I would be quoting a Labour MP, but I find it hard to disagree with Austin Mitchell's assessment at the time, that the government's stance 'was mean and petty and stupid, and a demonstration of impotence rather than anything else.'

In the United States the situation was far worse than it was in Britain. Neither federations nor individual athletes were given the option. Any hint of dissent and tax audits were ordered and passports pulled. It didn't matter who you were. World-record holder Renaldo 'Skeets' Nehemiah, who dominated the 110m hurdles from 1978 to 1981, was forbidden to compete. He never ran in an Olympic Games, and in 1982 was lost to athletics when he joined the NFL. You'd have needed an elephant gun to stop hurdler Edwin Moses from winning in 1980. He'd won the Olympic 400m hurdles in 1976 and he took gold again in 1984, but for many others 1984 was simply too late. America lost a generation of athletes thanks to Jimmy Carter. Within the sport there was a real sense that the US Olympic Committee could and should have shown a fang. But in the United States, whether the president is a Democrat or a Republican, there is a deference to the office that is not accorded to a British prime minister, even someone as powerful as Margaret Thatcher.

As for the British royal family, the Duke of Edinburgh, a keen sportsman himself, was for many years president of the British Amateur Athletics board, while Princess Anne had competed at Montreal in the equestrian team. They were, and still are, very savvy when it comes to sporting diplomacy, but while their views in private were unambiguous, the nature of the monarchy prevented them from saying anything politically controversial, which the Moscow boycott clearly was, although I have it from insiders that they were hard at work behind the scenes trying to knock heads together.

Gradually, public opinion in Britain began to shift and by the time the Games began they were definitely on the side of the angels. Sport has been called the culture of the masses, and increasingly the masses in Britain wanted to see British athletes – particularly in track and field – competing on the greatest sporting stage there is. And in 1980 that meant Moscow.

I returned to England in better shape than I had been in during 1979. But although I'd trained in a harder, more concentrated and unhindered way during my months in Olgiata, I hadn't run in competition since Zurich in August 1979, and that was something I needed to rectify. So when I saw that a cross-country race, the *Cinque Mulini*, was being held in northern Italy, I thought I'd enter, the name implying it would be run over five or so miles, and thus just what I needed.

How wrong can you be! *Mulini* means not miles, but mills. The course threaded its way between five historic water mills, some of which were definitely still lived in. So you'd find yourself running through a building where the family would literally be clapping you on your way. Nonetheless it is a highly prestigious race, and acts as a qualifier for the IAAF world cross-country championships.

Gianni Merlo, the journalist covering it for *Gazzetta dello Sport*, wondered what on earth I was doing there. I explained my fundamental error. He thought it very funny, which of course it was. I told him that what I'd actually wanted was a fast, cross-country race – not an obstacle course.

To my astonishment he immediately volunteered to organise one himself, in his home town of Vigevano in Lombardy. And he did. In the space of three weeks he had not only sold the concept to the town, but set up an organising committee and fixed a date. It would be a four-mile road race around the town, finishing in the Piazza Ducale, one of the finest squares in Italy, and held on 6 April, Easter Sunday.

My father came over to help me pack up, and we drove up to Vigevano with a couple of days to spare. But when we went over the course – consternation. A lengthy section of the route through the centre of the town was *pavé*, the Italian equivalent of cobbles, and was, we both decided, a risk too far.

'*No problemo,*' was Gianni's response and he set about re-routing the course. But inevitably there were problems, one in particular. The only way we could achieve the length needed for the permit was to take it past a church where a wedding was due to take place. This was now beyond embarrassing. Undaunted, Gianni negotiated with the unhappy couple to postpone their nuptials. Time now was very tight, and to get its official permit the route had to be re-measured. While so engaged, Gianni contrived to lose control of his car and buried it in a supermarket window. No one was hurt as it happened at ten o'clock at night. Only in Italy.

Thankfully, the following day passed off without incident, and I won. Local hero Gelindo Bordin came second. A talented distance runner, he went on to take gold in the 1988 marathon in Seoul, and also to win the European Championship in 1986 and 1990. Unusual though these races both were, they had the desired effect of easing me back gently into the reality of competition, and my dad and I set off early on Monday morning, sharing the driving on the long road back to Sheffield.

While I now believe my father was essentially a natural, someone who saw instinctively what had to be done to achieve the desired end, the scientist in him needed that instinct to be corroborated by hard fact. For this reason, a year or so earlier he had consulted with John Humphreys, professor of physiology at Carnegie PE College, now part of Leeds Metropolitan University, who ran a physiological assessment centre where the basic idea was to get under the bonnet to check out the motor.

Put simply, oxygen fuels the muscles that work the legs. The faster the pace, the higher your heart rate, the lower the level of oxygen in the blood, the less far you can run. Oxygen debt, as it's known, not only lessens muscle efficiency, but increases the level of lactic acid – a kind of blood poisoning – that results in the sudden diminishing of power that steals up on you, robbing you of pace. It's like the nightmare where you dream you are moving but are constantly held back.

Being on John Humphreys' treadmill, and those that succeeded it, was never fun, but it was an environment my father relished. Wired up to electrodes, breathing through a plastic tube, connected to dials and monitors, I would run on the conveyor belt, while my oxygen efficiency was measured at different paces and at different distances.

This time, however, the analysis couldn't have been better. I was utilising oxygen at a range of running paces more economically than ever before.

My aim was to ease into the season gradually. I ran a couple of college races, I ran the county championships, building up as I would normally do, including some early season races back in Italy.

The line-up there included international runners, but these weren't the guys I would be racing against in the Games. In April or May you don't want to compete against top-class competitors. There's no great advantage in running against people you're likely to come up against when the season is at its height.

Following my unusual debut at the Bislett Games the previous year, Arne Haukvik was anxious to get me back for a repeat performance. 'What about a tilt at the thousand metres?' he said.

At the beginning of 1979, the idea of becoming a world-record holder had been no more than a pipe dream. Now Arne's invitation put me in a position to hold four at the same time.

Improbable as it seemed, this was only my third visit to Oslo and yet it felt like a homecoming. Arne had cranked up his publicity machine till there wasn't an empty seat in the stadium. And there was one spectator new to Bislett who I hoped felt the warmth of the welcome – my mother, Angela. She rarely came to race meetings, not least because she had three other children to look after at home – Emma was still only 16. This was the first time she had watched me race abroad and, as my father would be with me down on the track, I'd arranged with John Walker that she should sit above the finish line with his wife Kim.

As well as Walker, Willi Wülbeck was also running. This was the West German whose elbow and spikes had scuppered my chances of a medal at the Europa Cup final in Helsinki in 1977, and Peter and I had decided that he would be the danger. For once I felt sorry for him. Like Walker, Wülbeck was a casualty of his government's decision to boycott Moscow.

The first two laps were fast – to the extent that the pacemaker Arne had laid on couldn't even get to the front. But that was fine, because I knew that Wülbeck wouldn't like being stretched that early on. Sometime after the halfway mark both leader and pacemaker dropped out, and with a lap to go I found I was on my own, but I wasn't running easy. The previous week I'd scratched from a race with some kind of chest infection and there was still a residual tightness and a sluggishness that seems to go along with antibiotics. But buoyed up by the Bislett crowd, and knowing my mum was there, I somehow held on and crossed the line ten yards ahead of the gaining Wülbeck. On my victory lap I spotted Angela in the stand, applauding with the rest of the crowd and felt a surge of pride and gratitude. Watching her son break a world record might go some way, I hoped, to make up for all she'd put up with along the way.

I was now the proud possessor of four world records. However, Steve Ovett had other ideas. Just a few yards away on the warm-up track, he was preparing for his own race, with my mile world record firmly in his sights.

Two weeks out from the Olympics, I was the nailed-on favourite for the 800m, Ovett for the 1500m, but barring accidents either of us could win either of the two distances we were entered for. The world knew it, we knew it. And that's what made it so addictive. There were few floating voters. People who had no connection with athletics, who had never watched a race even on television, had made their choice. You were either for Coe or Ovett. While I continued to get the better press – largely because I actually talked to journalists – Steve was playing up to his role of bad-boy in the devil-may-care way he finished his races, waving to the crowd or running across the track, adding unnecessary seconds to his time but endearing himself to the general public, who always love a maverick and slightly despise the boy with the clean handkerchief. Given that physiologically there probably wasn't the thickness of a vest between us, psychological advantage, if we could get it, became hugely important. Steve would come under starter's orders unbeaten in his last forty-two races, but with only one world record – two miles – taken at Crystal Palace two years earlier.

Olympic regulations permit just three entrants in any one event from any one country. Steve and I were taking the first two places in both the 800m and the 1500m, and the choice for third GB man in the 1500m lay between a 19-year-old Geordie, Steve Cram, and a young Scot, Graham Williamson. The mile in Oslo, scheduled to start an hour after my 1000m victory, would be the decider. Third place in the 800m had already gone to Dave Warren, who lived on the Essex coast and who was also in the line-up.

It wasn't a particularly sparkling field, but that wasn't the point here. Dave Warren had been persuaded by Andy Norman to supply the early pace and Ovett tucked in behind him. I was watching with my father, and we exchanged a quick glance. The time, we knew now, would be fast; Dave was basically running an 800m race and dropped out at the halfway mark, at which point Ovett took it up, followed by the gangly teenager Steve Cram. Although Ovett was never comfortable running from the front, he had no choice, and he crossed the line 12 metres clear of Cram.

As usual at Bislett the official time was a long time coming, but when it did – 3m 48.8 – Steve Ovett was confirmed as the new world-record holder, having beaten my time by a fifth of a second. I had never doubted that he was capable of it, so I didn't feel overly depressed. For forty minutes I'd held four; now I was back to three. But as far as the mile was concerned, I always knew it was only borrowed.

Two weeks later my nemesis was back in Oslo for a crack at the 1500m. This time he was up against a top-class international field, specifically athletes who wouldn't be going to Moscow, notably Americans, including Steve Scott, who had come second to me in the Golden Mile the previous year.

Ovett's decision to race so close to the Games was seen by many as reckless. I certainly wouldn't have done it a week away from the opening ceremony. Not only would it disrupt your training programme, but as with all competitive racing, it was risking injury.

Steve was never interested in other people's opinions, however, and psychologically he needed to dispel the taunt that, without an American presence at the Games, a gold medal would mean nothing. Not only that, but Steve Scott, who had won the US Olympic trials with a time of 3m 35.2, had made it personal, boasting that he would 'run the sting out of Ovett', which to a street fighter like Steve was a hand-delivered invitation. In the end, Steve Scott came third, with Thomas Wessinghage – also denied the opportunity to run at Moscow – second. As for the world record, it was that rarest of things, a dead heat between my time at Zurich and his. So Steve and I went into the Olympics evenly matched, with two world records apiece and one shared.

Not until the flight actually touched down was I really convinced I would actually get to Moscow. The build-up had started with the official notification of selection, a hand-signed letter from the Duke of Edinburgh, which went some way to making it all real. Then there was the team uniform. This was the first suit I'd ever owned, and I had a fitting in Hepworths in Fargate in Sheffield. It was made from a startlingly bright blue textured nylon material, with a Union flag woven into the pocket, considerably less fashionable than what the average Muscovite was wearing, and basically pretty hideous. As I followed Brendan, laughing, down the steps of the aircraft, both of us wearing these crumpled examples of British tailoring at its worst, he said, 'You'll be glad you're not a shareholder in Hepworths when these photos get beamed around the world!'

I had run behind the iron curtain once previously, in Prague two years before where you'd had to queue for everything and the food was dire. We'd all heard the stories, and most of the athletes had packed tins of potatoes and baked beans. Even I travelled with my share of carbs. In fact, Moscow was one of the finest catering environments I have ever come across. Counters groaned under the weight of fresh food. Athletes from eastern bloc countries could be seen bearing away tray after tray. They couldn't get enough. Years later I heard how trains laden with fresh produce from Poland and East Germany had brought us this sumptuous fare. If the average Russian had had any idea that this was how we were being treated, Glasnost would have happened ten years earlier.

What stays with me now is the extraordinary range of physiques you saw every day queuing up in the dining hall. It was exactly as if I had joined the circus. There were basketball players, male and female, bordering on seven-foot tall in the same queue as weight-lifters whose arms and legs were a third the length of your own but who could lift six times their own bodyweight over their head. There were gymnasts three or four years older than my sister Emma who looked three or four years younger. And, looking back, no doubt the shot-putters from beyond the Urals saw me and other middle-distance and marathon runners as representative of malnourished capitalism.

I can remember seeing Teofilo Stevenson, the gentle giant of Cuban boxing – who took gold in Munich, Montreal and Moscow – surrounded by a queue of autograph hunters. And you could never miss the East German team, who were always in uniform – trademark blue tracksuits. At the other end of the sartorial scale, the Italians had an elegance unrivalled by any other team.

You never forgot for a moment that you were behind the iron curtain. At the border I'd had Hedrick Smith's *The Russians* confiscated. My copy of *The Spectator* had also disappeared. And then there was Boris. Boris was our shadow, just one of many hundreds stationed in the village, charged with God knows what. He clearly had good solid KGB qualifications but, after a few raised eyebrows, was soon part of the furniture. At breakfast Boris was there, and he tended to be the last person you saw at night. He spent most of the time sitting in our recreation area reading, the book being covered in a brown-paper wrapper. Although he kept it close to his chest, I happened to see it was written in English.

'What's that you're reading, Boris?' I asked. Without looking up, he carefully slipped down the brown paper to reveal the title: *The Human Factor* by Graham Greene, a classic cold-war spy story set in London involving a Soviet agent . . . He had a certain wry humour, did Boris.

'So Boris,' Brendan had said early on in the proceedings. 'Where's the nearest nightclub then?'

'Helsinki,' Boris replied, with the merest hint of a beat.

The BBC crew were based in Moscow itself, at the Hotel Ukraina. The techies among them were determined to find any bugs that might have been planted in their room and, being in the trade, had every plug and every switch off the wall. They checked every chandelier, every curtain pelmet and shower head but drew a blank. Then the penny dropped. Of course! The TV. Off came the screen, out came the valves. At this point the room phone goes.

'Yes?'

'Please to leave your television set alone.'

The whole of this dismantling procedure had been done in total silence, so although they'd found nothing, there had to have been a camera in there.

Before I left England, Brendan had told me that, no matter how much I prepared, the whole experience would come as a shock.

'Don't imagine you're just going to another meet and staying for a few days,' he warned. 'This is massive. Get it into your mind that this is massive.'

The truth is that nothing anyone can say can prepare you for the reality. It really is unlike anything else. And in terms of international championships, I was a novice. My only experience was the Europeans in Prague two years earlier. Steve Ovett had not only been to Prague with me, he had also competed at the previous

Europeans in 1974, and of course had gone to Montreal in 1976. He knew what it was like to live in an Olympic village. He knew what it was like to be hermetically sealed for two weeks. He knew what it was like to be into something that was almost the office grind. He knew what it was like to queue for food, to organise your training, to utilise your time properly over an extended period. All these things have to be learnt, which is why it's so important to get athletes into that environment as soon as you can. The experience of championship racing can never be replicated.

And I, of course, had had none of that. I had missed out on a place in 1976 by a couple of tenths of a second. If I'd been in the other heat, or run the times I was running at the end of the season, I'd have probably made it to Montreal, and no matter how well or badly I'd done, the experience would have been invaluable. As it was, although I was learning my trade pretty well, getting to grips with the nature of running internationally, there is a world of difference between popping over to Brussels or Zurich or Oslo and the kind of intensity that Olympic athletes are faced with. It's two different planets.

For once, my father couldn't help. We had always had a bond that was probably closer to friendship than a conventional father-and-son relationship, and it became even closer during those two weeks in Moscow through our shared vulnerability. He had been my coach for eight years, working at the highest possible level, but this was his first Games, as it was mine. We were both feeling our way and found a degree of comfort in our mutual inexperience, even if we didn't articulate it like that.

The first heat went OK but it was nothing special. I had an irritating hamstring condition that was threatening to flare up. The British team physios worked long hours to keep it at bay. I remember particularly the caring hands of Helen Bristol. And I'd had a back problem all season, related to a slight pelvic tilt, which was restricting full range of movement in my right leg.

In the semi-final, I kept wide after the break. I'd witnessed a good deal of rough-housing in the other heats, and was concerned to stay out of trouble. While I got through, it's fair to say I didn't feel unassailable.

Saturday, 26 July 1980 was the day I had been building up to for the best part of twelve years, ever since sitting cross-legged on the floor of Tapton's gym, watching as David Hemery and John Sherwood hurdled into Olympic history, ever since my father said casually on a dark rain-soaked winter evening on the way to a training session, when I must have been all of 14, 'You'll be going to the Olympics in 1980.'

Sleep has never been a problem for me. The world can be crashing down around my ears – and, believe me, on occasions it has certainly seemed that way – but when my head hits the pillow, I'm out for the count. 'The cloak that covers all men's thoughts,' as Cervantes put it in *Don Quixote*, has always been a failsafe for me. But that night the failsafe failed. Presumably, I did get a few minutes here and there, but it didn't feel like it. And at breakfast the next morning it showed. I dropped a jug of milk. I was pouring the milk over my cornflakes and wasn't concentrating. At lunch I did the same with a carton of orange juice. No big deal, but I am usually quite precise about things, and I remember my father looking at me quizzically. But he stayed schtum, a silence that till the day he died he tortured himself for. In the whole of my career, it was his only regret. 'I will never forgive myself for not articulating or raising with you what I sensed over the hours that led up to the final. I should have.' There was nothing he could point a finger at and he knew nothing about my sleepless night. 'It was just,' he said, 'that you didn't have your normal, don't-worry-it'll-be-all-right attitude.'

And I didn't. The race wasn't scheduled till 7.30 p.m. and it was a long wait. The confidence that throughout my entire career had seemed as natural and as freely available as air, was evaporating by the minute. Looking back from the distance of thirty-plus years, the truth is that, for one of the very few occasions in my life, I was afraid. The pressure was cumulative, built up over a number of days, probably months if I'd been more alive to it. This was the Olympic Games, the biggest show on earth. The athlete's date with destiny. Clichés but true. So I had come this far. So what? To win an Olympic title, the odds are stacked against you. It was just the enormity of the moment. And the truth is I froze.

As for the race, it was a shambles, a catalogue of unforced errors. I compounded more middle-distance sins in the space of one and a half minutes than I had done in the whole of my career.

In considering tactics I'd given serious thought to going it alone, but in the end had decided on a more cautious approach. Anyway, I didn't need to be that precise, I'd decided. It wasn't as though I was the one-dimensional, evolving athlete I had been two years earlier. I had been working with sprinters on the track at Loughborough and could hold my own against any of them over 200m and 400m. I'd spent hours in training perfecting the art of kicking off the final bend, my father trackside giving me random whistles when, with no notice at all, I would be forced to change pace. All this would be money in the bank.

Racing in a heightened environment can occasionally give rise to performances that defy form and reputation. In Prague I'd learnt the hard way about acting as an unpaid pacemaker and I wasn't about to make the same error here. My plan was simple. Sit in, and take my time in the knowledge that there was no one in the field who had that raw speed.

I was drawn in lane 8, which should have made it easy, leaving all options open. But as the gun went off I did what no one in an Olympic final can risk doing: I started too slowly. When we came to break lanes, I was already seven metres adrift, but didn't realise it.

Looking at the playback, I appear to be sleepwalking, oblivious to anything and everyone around me. And God, there were chances. Steve got boxed in and had to fight his way out of trouble using his elbows. This wouldn't be allowed now but that day it was messy, practically hand-to-hand combat and if I'd been thinking straight, I should have gone then. By keeping wide I had avoided the thumping and pushing on the inside lanes, but at key moments I'd lost touch with the race. But the big brutal mistake, the one that buried me, was not following when the pace picked up halfway down the back straight. To this day my insouciance at that point remains a mystery. That basic survival instinct was deep in my DNA by my middle teens, but by the time I'd emerged from my somnolence and pulled the rip cord, it was too late. I was just too far adrift. Even when I started to close on the field like a train, I was still well out of the medals. At the crown of the bend I clawed back three or four places and got into medal contention – 80 metres out, I hit silver medal position, 30 metres out . . . but I had nothing else to give. Ovett closed the door and the race. Looking back, I'm not even sure that performance deserved a medal, let alone silver.

Would it have made a difference if my father had been braver and said something earlier? I don't know. It might have done. It might have shaken me out of my torpor. But every athlete has his or her own way of coping with pressure, and mine was always to switch off, to the extent that I wouldn't recognise my own family before races. On this occasion, the problem was that I never switched back on again.

Also, I've never been great with little homilies and words of advice, and I might not have reacted well. I remember an example of that towards the end of my career when psychologists were the new fad and were being introduced into the British team. A really nice, softly spoken guy came up to me shortly before a race, introduced himself as the newly appointed team psychologist, and said,

'I'm here to help, just let me know if there's anything I can do.' I explained my position.

'Look,' I said, 'we're here for a week and a half. And I'd be really grateful if you didn't speak to me until we get back on the plane. That way you'll be doing me the best favour that you can.'

One of our team coaches overheard my rather ungracious comment, and said, 'I think you're being a bit harsh, Seb. They only want to help.'

'I don't need any help.'

'Well, we're just trying to create a normal environment.'

I looked at him.

'Do you think I'm normal? Do you think what I do is normal? Do you think running a hundred miles a week, three times a day, is normal? I don't. Don't tell me I'm normal. I'm not normal. There's not a single person in this team who's normal. We're all fucking mad.'

9

GOING THE DISTANCE

THE Moscow 800m final had been mine to lose, and I lost it. There was nobody else to blame, no extenuating circumstances. And for an athlete, to walk off a track knowing in your heart of hearts that you just ran badly is the worst possible way to face defeat. My body language on that rostrum said it all. I was numb. Numb from shock and misery. As my dad so succinctly put it, 'First is first and second is nowhere.' As for the post-race conference, it was an autopsy.

It was generally assumed that my old man beat up on me. Actually, he didn't. It was enough to tell the truth, with an Anglo-Saxon twist of the knife. 'You ran like an absolute cunt,' he said, under his breath. Meanwhile the press were rubbing their hands. Our relationship had always puzzled them, and here they were being given ringside seats at the meltdown.

It didn't happen. If my father was beating up on anyone, it was himself. 'I'm your coach,' he said. 'You're the fastest man on the earth at eight hundred metres, and at the biggest moment of your career you run three seconds slower than if you were running in Sheffield. I can't suddenly say, "We win, you lose." I have a responsibility here. There is only one thing to do now,' he added. 'You'll have to win the bloody fifteen hundred. Now get out there, have a good run, purge yourself and come back refreshed.'

Next morning I set off for an hour's run beyond the perimeter fence, a distance I guessed of around ten to twelve miles. And from the moment my feet hit the road, I felt the tension in my body begin to ease, my mind go into neutral and finally switch off.

The sheer pleasure of running has never left me. There's still that same delight that I felt as a boy, running along country roads, opening gates, waiting for my dad's car to rattle across cattle grids, letting the five-bar gate clang shut behind me, then setting off again, tearing past the Cortina to reach the next gate, and then the next.

I hadn't given up ten or twelve years of my life to come second in an Olympic final, and yet that's precisely what I had done. To rub salt into my self-inflicted wound, I was sharing a room with Allan Wells, who had just taken 100m gold.

The Moscow suburbs were noticeably free of traffic, and I was halfway round before I heard the car. I assumed it was some kind of security tail, monitoring my run, checking I wasn't fraternising with the locals, but when it came alongside there was no mistaking the syncopated click and snap of the professional photographer. There were about six of them I guess, hanging out of windows like commuters on a Mumbai train, faces a study in grim determination behind the thicket of lenses. I ran on, the posse of paparazzi shadowing every stride. It was like a metaphor. There was nowhere to hide. I had to go on, mile after mile until I had gone the distance.

As far as the press were concerned, Coe v. Ovett was the story of the Games, the reason editors from across the globe had shelled out Monopoly money to get them to Moscow, and in the absence of hard news, rumour and speculation would have to do. Press conferences hosted by the BOA that would normally have been lucky to attract a dozen or so specialist correspondents were now standing-room only, packed out with writers who didn't know a split from a stagger, but who were desperate to learn exactly what I'd had for breakfast.

Without newsstands or corner shops, at least you didn't have to read the stuff they churned out. But two days later, sitting in the leisure area, I spotted the front page of an abandoned tabloid, with a headline so big it was impossible not to read, even from a distance of several yards: COE'S TRAIL OF SHAME, and of course that picture of me.

Over the last twelve months I'd got used to my name being hi-jacked by the press – after all, it was usefully short. I didn't particularly relish the exposure, but neither had it made me feel physically sick. This did. In retrospect, I ought to thank them because it was that picture and that headline that finally gave me the kick up the arse that I needed. Brendan had tried, Peter had tried, but it was 'the *Sun* wot dun it' – although it might equally have been the *People*. Did I really want to sink into Olympic oblivion? To become a pub quiz answer? I had another chance, and it was up to me to take it.

Quietly, behind the scenes, the team managers, Lynn Davies and Mary Peters, did what they could. Two better qualified people never pulled on an official tracksuit. Both of them had star quality. They were shrewd enough never to offer technical advice but just their presence was invaluable – almost like your parents – not least because they had seen it all before. Both had won Olympic titles, Lynn the long jump in 1964, and Mary the pentathlon in 1972. These two would accompany you to and from the first call-up room to the warm-up track, then down to the final call-up room. At that moment what you're looking for is a sense of calm, and when the moment came, they'd walk you down into the stadium. Only a handful of people on the planet know what it's like to have to leave your coach behind and they did, because they'd done it themselves. Both had had legendary coaches. Lynn had Ron Pickering and Mary had Buster McShane, who would have handed them over to their team manager to accompany them for the final walk into the tunnel.

Lynn is now president of UK Athletics and Dame Mary is Lord Lieutenant of Belfast and whenever I find myself sitting with either of them, which I have done regularly in various official roles in recent years, I still look at them as, in a way, my team managers. It was a role they both repeated in Los Angeles and I have the most extraordinary respect for them both, more perhaps than almost anyone else I can think of.

Over the next forty-eight hours I began to haul myself up from the pit, keeping moving and getting my mind in gear. And I slept. I remember lying in bed when the door crashed open and in marched Daley.

'You planning to get up by any chance?'

'What's the weather looking like out there?'

He opened the curtains. 'Looks a bit silver to me.' Welcome to the Daley Thompson school of psychology.

At some point I was handed an envelope containing a letter from Chris Brasher, athletics correspondent for the *Observer*, and of course Olympic gold medallist who helped take Roger Bannister to the first sub four-minute mile. Over ten pages he had painstakingly set out what I needed to do to win. It was a mountain of a letter, citing the great Scandinavian athletes of the past, and recommending I listen to inspirational composers, such as Sibelius and Elgar, advising me to 'run with Finlandia in your mind'. At least it wasn't Vangelis's *Chariots of Fire*. That wouldn't open for another twelve months. Visual images he thought might help included both Norwegian fjords and the English lakes. But for all his endearing romanticism, here at least was someone who knew his stuff and who thought I could do it. 'No pace can drop you off, and you are the fastest in the field. The only person who can beat you is yourself . . . All it needs is iron determination in your heart. And in the race, relax, move up and strike.'

The finals for the 1500m were exactly a week after the nadir of the 800m. This meant that the first round of heats was on Wednesday. I was drawn on the inside lane and at the gun, I sprinted out of trouble as I didn't want to get boxed in – a lesson I should have taken with me

to the semis. Although my performance was hardly scintillating –
much to Peter's annoyance I didn't even win – mentally I knew I had
started to come back. My back was easing, my hamstring was feeling
loose, and as I was warming down everything felt good. I was thinking, 'Hey, I'm feeling like I could spring again!'

In my semi-final the next day all started well. I wanted to do
better than just get through this time, but 200m out I lost concentration. The Russian cut across and I had to hand him off to keep
my position. Then there was a rush from behind coming off the
bend, and I was boxed in again. Now lying fifth, I went wide and
kicked, powering past the rest, crossing the line just ahead of
Jurgen Straub, from East Germany. I came off the track feeling
elated. I had done it! That change of pace was electric, as good as
it had ever been.

I had just got to the warm-up track and was warming down,
when my old man appeared, looking like thunder.

'Are you fucking suicidal?'

I was so excited about my change of pace that I was barely listening. 'I guess you're right . . .'

'You *guess* I'm right? You do that tomorrow and you're dead. You
cannot do that tomorrow. You *have* to maintain contact with the
athletes at the front. And I don't care if Steve Ovett runs off to the
shitter, you are in there with him before you've even realised you've
left the track. You sit so tight into that action you can smell his
armpits. Have you any idea how close you came to fucking that up?'

It was the only time in the whole two weeks that he lost it. He just
unloaded, going on and on at me as the light faded and dusk began
to fall across the stadium. The hacks, all of whom were safely downing vodkas in the nearest bar, had missed a trick, because if they
were shocked at what my old man had said after the 800m, if they'd
heard this diatribe, they'd be covering their children's ears and
phoning the NSPCC.

And all the time I was standing there thinking, 'Hang about here! What happened to the pat on the back? I've changed pace, I've come back, showing all the confidence that I've been lacking . . .'

But of course he was absolutely right. I should never have got myself boxed in. As for this verbal onslaught I think he sensed that I could take it. Firstly, having watched the race he knew that the change of pace was as good as anything I had ever done either in training or in competition, and that the only way I could lose the final was to do something really stupid . . . such as losing concentration.

It might have been just a moment, but a moment is all it takes. When someone comes up alongside you 150 metres from home and you allow him to come past, where do you think he's going to go? He is hardly going to stay running wide all the way up the finishing straight. He's going to come in front of you. And if he comes in front of you, where are you going to go? If you cede that territory, and somebody else comes past, you have created one unholy mess.

At 150 metres from home you do not yield. You do not give ground. You fight them off, keep them running wide, so they're running wider and further than you are, even if it means expending slightly more energy. Make them run even harder to get past you, and even if they succeed, you'll still have the space to respond and go past if you need to.

Given the naked change of pace I'd shown that evening, only my tactical limitations could deny me the following day. That was what made him see red. From where I stood, what made his anger so powerful was that this was cold analytical factory-floor language. He wasn't shouting or screaming and I just had to take it.'

He wasn't alone in his analysis. London bookmakers were giving 11:4 on Ovett getting the double. Most people that night had written me off along the lines of, 'If he makes a mistake like that in the semis, what's he going to do under real pressure?' It seemed as if the whole of British athletics was sitting holding its head in its hands, saying that, while I might have the speed, I didn't have the tactical intelligence to win a race of this pressure and intensity. And yet, in that semi, I had run the second-fastest 1500m of my life, a full four seconds faster than Ovett in his.

I continued my warm down and did six or seven laps in the dark, while my father was out there talking to Mary Peters, the sound of their voices rising and falling but making no sense. I was somewhere else, and as night fell, I could feel the excitement building.

When the moment came next day, I was raring to go. In the call-up area where you were corralled before you went on, we wished each other luck, and Steve suggested the three of us had a drink when it was over – Crammy had also made it into the final. And then I remember Steve turning to me and saying, 'Do you realise, we've got a hundred thousand people out there. Imagine what promoters would pay for the race that's just coming up.' I can't remember what I said in reply, if anything. But I wasn't at my conversational best.

Compared to the final of the 800m, the stadium was virtually silent as we took our places. You could hear the odd shout, the odd call, but given there were a hundred thousand people present, you could have heard the proverbial pin drop.

My mother, who was watching on television back in Sheffield, and who knew a thing or two about drama, said it felt like the whole of Britain stopped for those few minutes. As for the race itself, 'It was pure theatre,' she said. The curtain was about to rise on the final act of what the press were calling the Clash of the Titans. Would Coe bottle it, fatally holed by his failure in the 800m? Or, now that Ovett had an Olympic gold medal, had he lost his hunger?

It began slowly –a funereal pace – with Jürgen Straub leading on the inside. Having being drawn in lane 6, I moved across early and ran at his shoulder. Just after the halfway mark, Straub began winding it up and the field strung out. I was now running free and loose. Although I was running in an Olympic final, to all intents and purposes I was out there on the Rivelin Valley Road, with the old man in the car breathing down my neck. At the bell, Jürgen stretched out again and I half kicked and levelled. I knew that Steve had to be somewhere close behind me, but I couldn't see him. With 100 metres to go I kicked again, and went. If Steve had made it back to my shoulder, he would have gone on to win. But although I had run out of gears, I still had one more than he did, and all I had to do was cross the line.

Although it happened over thirty years ago, I can still remember that race as if it were last week, and not only because we now live in the age of YouTube. But as for that perennial journalists' question, 'How did you feel?' I no longer know. I'm not sure that even a few hours later I'd have given a coherent, let alone cogent, answer. When Ron Pickering, wielding the BBC mike asked how I felt minutes after I left the track, I answered, 'Christ,' an unfortunate choice of phrase given the embarrassing crucifixion stance, complete with agonised expression, I'd adopted when I knew that I'd won. The Bishop of Durham duly complained to the BBC. For once in my life I was completely lost for words. In fact, my dearth of emotional vocabulary made little difference, since it allowed the representatives of the fourth estate to supply their own – ecstasy, elation, euphoria, revenge, vindication. And it would be churlish not to admit that I probably experienced a heady cocktail of each of these during those first few unbelievable minutes. But the overriding emotion, the one that survived more than a day, was relief. Overwhelming relief. In a strange way, it was just like I'd felt after getting my degree. I had done it, and I would never have to do it again.

In terms of the press's Clash of the Titans, it was the most extraordinary outcome. The result was as perfect as if it had been scripted. There were no losers. We had both come away with gold medals. Just as no one would have tipped Steve for the 800m, no one would have tipped me for the 1500m. I was the world-record holder at 800m, and regularly ran several seconds faster than Steve did, whereas he was unbeaten in forty-five outings at 1500m. But at least one thing had been proved. He wasn't the only one of us who could race. When it came to the big moments, they had said I hadn't got it. The bookies must have been rubbing their hands.

In the end, sixty-two nations were unrepresented in Moscow. Far too many small countries couldn't afford the price of independence as we in Britain could. But while British athletes certainly didn't go with the approval of the *Daily Mail* or the *Daily Telegraph*, we came home with a total of twenty-one medals, including five golds – Allan Wells, Steve Ovett, Daley Thompson, Duncan Goodhew and myself – and nobody complained about that. The MBE, which is the standard 'well done' to Olympians offered by HM's government in the name of the Queen, was not immediately forthcoming, but in less than a year envelopes 'requesting the pleasure' were dropping on the relevant doormats.

As for the argument that competing in the 1980 Games was somehow condoning the invasion of Afghanistan, this was simply political posturing. It seems to be in the nature of politics that people neither read nor understand history before making political judgements. Afghanistan has always been a country of huge geo-strategic importance, which is why it has been occupied for so much of its unhappy past.

A question we used to ask ourselves at the time was, if we boycotted the Games, would it make a jot of difference to the internal politics of the Soviet Union? The answer then, as now, was no.

Sadly, the only thing a boycott ever really does is damage the athletes. It is brutal on careers, affecting them long after governments have forgotten that they ever thought about it. But for a period Moscow v. Afghanistan really did divide the world. People were burnt, but a lesson was learnt. After 1980, no British government has remotely tiptoed down the boycott path. Two years after the Falklands war we were playing Argentina at football, and nobody ever suggested that we should be pulling out of World Cups.

Looking back, I believe that at some stage we would have had to go through a 1980. Moscow wasn't a disaster, and who now remembers the alternative Liberty Bell Games set up in competition in the States? In all, I think the Olympic movement came out of the process a darned sight stronger and very much more independent.

The question is always asked, did the absence of the United States devalue the Moscow Games? We have to accept that some people won medals in 1980 who might not have had there been a full American presence. But as far as my own sport is concerned, British track and field was enjoying a true renaissance, and although Americans are always strong in the 100m, Allan Wells was as fast as anyone around at the time. Four or five weeks later he competed against a full field at the Golden Sprint in Berlin, beating America's finest over both 100m and 200m. So he was perfectly capable of winning the title, and I think on balance he probably would have done.

In your own event you know only too well who your main rivals are, and in the 800m and 1500m at that time no Americans were in serious contention, as Steve Ovett had demonstrated in Oslo the previous week. Of the excluded, only Thomas Wessinghage from West Germany or Mike Boit from Kenya might possibly have made the rostrum. But great talent though Mike was, by 1980 he was marginally past his best, and Thomas nearly always lost out to either Steve or me. Any doubt I might have had was put beyond doubt when I ran at Zurich two weeks later and beat both Steve Scott and John Walker.

Winning the 1500m final at Moscow changed everything. No longer could anyone query my ability to race. An Olympic gold gave me freedom to do what I enjoyed, which meant running at speed. To put it in perspective, if I had run the 1500m final as fast as I had done in Zurich the previous year, I'd have been 50 yards further ahead when I crossed the finish line. What I most wanted to do now was to improve, to run faster. I had become convinced that none of the records was so tight that, in the right circumstances, they couldn't be bettered. But that would have to wait. Within two weeks of Moscow, immediately after Zurich, I was diagnosed with what is commonly known as a slipped disc, related to my pelvic imbalance. I had been in and out of pain for nearly a year and it was a huge relief to know that it wasn't my imagination and that something could be done about it. Also, it gave me a much-needed rest.

By the autumn I was back to being a part-time athlete, having returned to Loughborough to do post-graduate research, sharing a house with Steve Mitchell. Much as I had enjoyed being in Rome, it was good to return to the knockabout camaraderie of Steve and my other training partner Sean Butler. Some might say that I had finally left home.

When I stood on the rostrum in Moscow – sadly, not with the national anthem echoing round the stadium, a consequence of Britain's official boycott – an era had come to an end. To some degree I was now moving away from my father, making my own decisions, although I never went far from the basic precepts that he had evolved, and which had got me to where I was. There was no falling out. It was simply a question of growing up.

The first world record to fall under the new regime was the indoor 800m at RAF Cosford in January. The second was in

This photograph of my mother was taken shortly after she graduated from RADA as an aspiring actress.

Miranda, Dad and me all dressed up in our Sunday best when we were living in Alcester, Warwickshire. I was about four, Miranda 18 months younger.

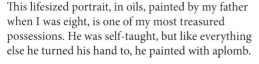

This lifesized portrait, in oils, painted by my father when I was eight, is one of my most treasured possessions. He was self-taught, but like everything else he turned his hand to, he painted with aplomb.

January 1971, aged 14, winning the Sheffield City Championships for Tapton Secondary Modern, where I was known by the teachers as Coe the Runner. My father can be seen in the background in a Russian hat, his eye on the stopwatch even at this early stage of my career.

AAA Championships at Crystal Palace, 1977. Although I came second to Milovan Savic, I pushed world champion John Walker (*right*) into third place, resulting in my first invitation to run internationally, in Brussels a few weeks later.

'Who the…?' 'What the…?' Steve Ovett and I, bemused by the identity of the winner of the European Championships 800m in Prague 1978 – Olaf Beyer. This was the first time the two of us had competed against each other on the track. Steve took silver, I took bronze.

July1978. Brendan Foster (*left*) was responsible for turning Gateshead into an international athletics venue, where he generously invited me to compete against some of the gods of middle-distance running.

Appreciating the cheers of the knowledgeable Bislett crowd after taking my first world record, at 800m, on 3 July 1979.

On my way to winning the Dubai Golden Mile at Bislett Stadium in Oslo, my second world record in two weeks. This was totally unexpected as the line-up included some of the greatest milers of the era, including joint favourite, American Steve Scott (*left*).

Andreas Brugger, Mr Big of Zurich's world-renowned Weltklasse meet, talks me through his plans for my record attempt at 1500m a week later.

In the months preceding the Olympic Games in Moscow I escaped both the media circus and northern winter by going to Italy. Running on the beach west of Rome was in distinct contrast to my usual training runs on the moors above Sheffield.

Peter checks his stopwatch during an interval-training session on the road. I don't know when this was taken, not least because it was our default way of working over twenty years and never really changed.

Chamonix, Switzerland. I fell in love with the Alps the first time I competed at the Zurich Weltklasse, in August 1979, when I set a new record for 1500m, my third world record in 41 days.

Andy Norman (*left*) and Steve Ovett in the Moscow Olympic Village. Andy was arguably the most important figure in British athletics during the most successful era the sport has ever known.

A press conference before the 800m metres final in Moscow, where the Coe/Ovett head-to-head was the story of the Games. Unfortunately, Steve had fallen out with the press years earlier so I was on my own.

I am famous for being able to sleep anywhere, even on an uncomfortable Soviet metal chair in the Moscow Olympic Village. The problem was I never really woke up in time for the 800m.

Moscow, 1980 – finally waking up after sleepwalking through the 800m final. Jurgen Straub (*right*), who came third, later helped me win the 1500m.

The 800m final was mine to lose and I lost it. I barely deserved a medal, let alone silver.

Moscow, 1500m – Coe gold, Straub silver, Ovett bronze. London bookmakers had expected Steve to do the double, giving odds of 11:4 on.

My overriding emotion on winning Olympic gold for the 1500m was relief.

Angela watched the Moscow Games from the comfort of an armchair in Sheffield. A former actress, she described the 1500m as 'pure theatre'.

Showing my gold medal to neighbours outside our house. The hills of Sheffield were the making of me.

Florence in June. I hadn't expected to do it. I had gone on my own and intended to run a 'safe' time in a warm climate. The pacemaker, a young Kenyan with limited experience, set off fast, too fast, so there was a huge risk that I'd fade. In an 800m, unlike the 1500m or the mile, you don't have the luxury of saving anything for a final kick, and it's basically a sprint all the way. From the halfway mark I was on my own, having to shout at myself mentally as I hit the home straight. It's a lonely place, not running with people all around you, and that's when the crowd can lift you up, their palpable excitement as they follow your progress on the clock is a massive, massive help. Although I never felt as easy as I had in Oslo two years earlier, this new world record gave me enormous satisfaction. I had broken the 800m equivalent of the four-minute mile. I had come in at under 1m 42.

That record stood for sixteen years, unbroken until 1997 when Wilson Kipketer took less than a second off. Only five athletes have ever run 800m in under 1m 42. It's not like the 1500m or the mile, which is regularly being broken by small increments. I have always suspected that the quantum leaps have been made by people covering the distance early on. Alberto Juantorena made the big breakthrough off his usual distance of 400m. I did the same in Oslo, and Wilson did the same when he broke mine. I certainly did it that night in Florence. There's a pattern to 800m records, which is to commit physically and mentally early on in the race. But it's tough. As Juantorena says, 'When you get to seven hundred metres, all you think is, "Who has stolen the finish line?" '

Everyone knows that Roger Bannister was helped in the first sub-four-minute mile. What was unusual was that he had two athletes upping the pace, namely Chris Brasher and Chris Chataway. I don't imagine for one minute that either of them were paid for their efforts. But by the end of the seventies a pacemaker was always paid, even though this was still the era of the amateur. For a world-class athlete it was a way of making a living, and if a record got broken, there'd be a bonus on top for having been part of it. The really good pacemakers could judge the pace of a lap to tenths of a second. Their job was to do your thinking for you during the race, so you could clear your mind of anything except running. They needed to take you to a specific distance in a specific time – they couldn't run too fast or too slowly – and then they'd just drop out. These were world-class athletes in their own right. They had to be. The best was a guy called Tom Byers. In a 1500m or mile, if you said, 'Tommy, I need to go through the first lap in 56.8,' Tommy would run you 56.8 seconds; or if you said, 'I need to be at 800 metres at 1.51,' Tommy would do that.

But it was far from being an exact science. In July 1981, following the Europa Cup final in Helsinki – where for the first time the British team saw off the Soviets in open competition – I had been invited to Stockholm for an attempt on the 1500m record, the one I had shared with Steve Ovett but which he then went on to take a few weeks after Moscow.

Stockholm is another intimate stadium, originally built for the 1912 Olympics. Like Bislett, it has an enviable history of world records and, true to form, the weather that evening was well-nigh perfect. Sadly, if Moscow was drama, this was farce.

The pacemaker was an 800m champion and I told him exactly the pace that I wanted which was 800 metres in 1m 52. My own pacemaking judgement was as fine tuned as anyone's, and I could tell instantly that he was going too quickly. It was as if he had forgotten what race he was in and was running an 800m. As we went haring off down the track, I was yelling at his back, 'You're going far too fast!' Eventually, he glanced back and slowed down. But the result was that he ran me through the first 800 metres in 1m 47, barely two seconds slower than my time in the Moscow final, at which point, of course, he stepped off the track. I couldn't believe it. I still had 700 metres of this race to go! As for help from the rest of the field, when I looked round I saw that Mike Boit and Steve Scott were about 45/50 metres back. And all I could think was, 'Aaargh! This is just going to be one tortuous evening . . .'

No one had thought to lay on someone to yell out the split times, so I had no idea where I was, only that somehow I had to hold it together, but with 300 metres to go I felt my legs begin to sag and the last stretch was like running in sand.

Meanwhile, the crowd were screaming and yelling, clearly thinking that a record was in the bag. As it was I only just crossed the line before collapsing. But when I heard the time I was apoplectic, because that night I was really smoking, and if I'd run the first 800 metres in 1m 52 as intended, and gone through economy of effort, I'd have blasted the second half and have been the first person under 3m 30 for the 1500m, and I'd probably even have taken a couple of seconds off that. As it was, I'd have done better running on my own.

I always had my suspicions about this race. Why would an experienced pacemaker and 800m champion have got it so badly wrong? I will never know the truth but I have a niggling suspicion that Andy Norman put him up to it. There was no ambiguity about where Andy sat in all this. As the back pages of the British press continued to milk every twist and turn in the Ovett–Coe saga, two distinct camps had evolved. In the Coe corner was the old man and my back-up team. In Ovett's corner was his coach Harry Wilson and Andy Norman. Andy Norman picked the races, picked the field and did the TV deals in the background, in which Steve was the drawing card.

Andreas Brugger, who knows a thing or two about pacemakers – he'd employed them for years over all sorts of races – told me later that he'd never seen such a bizarre piece of running. It's hard not to conclude that there was real malevolence at work here.

It was then that Heinz Lueger, who was organising the meet, arrived looking distinctly nervous, because he knew that this was a monumental balls-up. He looked at me, and I looked at him.

'Congratulations, Sebastian,' he said haltingly. 'You've broken the stadium record.'

I'm known as Mr Nice Guy, Mr Always Polite. Not that night.

'Fuck off,' I said.

For the rest of my career he gave me a very wide berth. He was actually quite a gentle soul, and I've always felt slightly guilty. I doubt very much that he had a hand in the debacle.

What made it even more difficult to swallow was that I knew I was in great form, not least because three nights later back in Oslo I ruptured my own 1000m world record. I was originally down to do the 800m but, ever the pragmatist, Arne decided that, given what I'd just done in Florence, he'd have more chance of a record from me at another distance.

The 400m American hurdler James King set the pace and at the start all went according to plan. Then suddenly he faded. Thankfully, he was careful not to drop out – the result of a new ruling from the IAAF. While allowing pacemakers, the new rule stipulated that they had to cross the finish line themselves, even if they took an hour to do so. Drop out and the record would not stand.

For the first time in my career I became aware of the clock. How I got through I have no idea because by the time I reached the home straight I felt my feet were barely leaving the ground. My dad called the 1000m the cruellest race on the track – all the pain of an 800m but with an extra half lap. That night I was tempted to agree with him. I did it nonetheless, breaking my own record set the previous year by more than a second. But it was tough.

My next appointment with the clock was in Zurich. This time the mile. The morning of 19 August, just back from my early morning run, I was handed a note from John Phillips, the BBC's outside broadcast editor. As the race was scheduled for 10.05 p.m. European time, he explained, they were planning to break into the *Nine O'Clock News* and go live. 'PS: This is the first time this has been done. So you'd better not screw up because my job's on the line.'

In terms of records, my aim was to take a tilt at both the 1500m and the mile in the same race. At the 1500 point my time would be clocked. With Tom Byers as pacemaker it was do-able. Two weeks earlier Tommy had ensured his place in athletics' history by starting as pacemaker in the Bislett 1500m, and then going on to win! Whoever was supposed to call out the lap times hadn't understood and had called out Tommy's split times instead of those of the genuine racers, chief among them Steve Ovett. By the time they realised what was happening, they'd left it too late.

Unfortunately, in Zurich, Tommy was coming down with a cold and faded at the halfway mark. I dithered for a second I couldn't afford to lose, but then went to the front. That dither lost me the 1500m record but as I covered the last hundred yards I was assailed by the image of Kenneth Kendall, putting down his script, saying, 'And now over to David Coleman live in Zurich as Sebastian Coe attempts to break the world record . . .' The crowd were on their feet and saw me home, just. The *Nine O'Clock News* might have had their scoop, and John Phillips kept his job, but I wasn't happy. I didn't want to beat records by fractions. I wanted to hack them off in slices. I had wanted a record that would last, which wasn't vulnerable to being chipped away, not least because I knew that a week later Ovett was running in Koblenz, another of those intimate, wind-protected tracks where, the previous year, he'd broken the 1500m world record.

My fear was justified. Steve asked the Koblenz promoters to add the mile to the programme. I was back in England preparing for the Golden Mile – this year to be held in Brussels a few days later – when I heard the news. A new world record from Steve Ovett. He had sneaked it from me, but not by much. If I had hoped for an extra kick, this was it.

Although I had taken my second world record in Oslo in the Golden Mile, this year's repeat wasn't about beating the clock, it was about beating a field of the world's top milers. Again Tommy Byers went to the front, thankfully running more quickly than he'd done in Zurich, but around the halfway point I nearly wrecked everything by stumbling against the concrete kerb, which cost me a second. At the 1000-metre mark I heard Peter yell out, 'Yes!' I had no idea what time I was doing, but his shout was enough to inspire me to stretch out and go to the front. By now the rest of the field was way behind, but I was aware of Mike Boit, the African record holder, pressing me hard. Forget the world record, this man was trying to beat me! It was a race to the finish, and Mike pushed me to the line, enough for me to hack over a second from my own world record of nine days earlier, and for Mike to set a new African record. But pleased as I was, I believe I could have run even faster had I not been holding something back to ensure that I actually won.

The final of the Athletics World Cup was held in Rome and both Steve and I were summoned to compete by the IAAF, me at 800m and Steve at 1500m. This time I had no intention of not coming first. I needn't have worried. I was absolutely unbeatable that year. I had run in twenty-two races – the most I had ever run, or ever would run, in one season – and among them I had taken four world records.

The Olympic stadium, where I had watched Lazio and Roma play – and where I had trained during the run-up to Moscow – was filled to capacity. This wasn't an intimate bowl like Bislett or Stockholm. This held 65,000 people, and I have to say that we hit the track like conquering heroes. Everyone was there, and on the last night Brendan and I, and some of the other guys who were nearing the end of their careers, hit the town. As someone with specialised local knowledge, I knew just where to go, and we had a wonderful meal, course after course and buckets of white wine. It was two in the morning by the time we were beginning to wind down.

'You know they're doing a half marathon tomorrow,' someone said. Three months before, Brendan had inaugurated the Northumberland equivalent, the Great North Run.

'And?'

'Well, what about it?'

'Well, my season's over,' I said, 'so I'm up for it.'

Then Brendan chipped in, 'You're on.'

What complete idiots.

Nine o'clock the next morning found us both bleary-eyed in front of the Vatican in our training gear. And then, dead on the peel of bells from St Peter's, bang, we were off. We just joined in. Nothing official, certainly no numbers, although I noticed a couple of dogs who were sporting them. I was always able to run comfortably over a distance, and the streets of Rome were only marginally different from the Yorkshire peaks.

It was a mass start, and I just elbowed my way through, following the crowd. It wasn't until about two miles in that the local press got wind of what was happening. And then all hell broke loose. So there I was, in the middle of the field, running side by side with my old mentor and friend, both of us laughing our heads off. And I actually beat him. Over 20,000 odd metres, I came ninth. It ended back in St Peter's Square where it had begun. Tired but happy, I cleared off and disappeared back to my apartment and bed.

10

LEVELLING THE PLAYING FIELD

Even before the blinds were being wound down in Moscow, the future of the Olympic Games was far from certain. They might have survived the US boycott, but a Soviet-led retaliation was already on the cards for Los Angeles, and alternative host cities were noticeable by their absence. Not only had the cost become prohibitive, but the Games themselves were seen as on an ebb tide.

Systematic drug use by athletes from the eastern bloc (although not uniquely) was making a mockery of the Corinthian ideal. As for state sponsorship, whether through sports academies or nominal military service, it was clear that, under communism, the amateur athlete existed in name only, as demonstrated by medal tables as skewed as pit props. Such blatant inequality not only demoralised individual athletes from the west, it damaged the reputation of sport itself. Although Olympic glory can only ever honour the very few, strong and fair competition is essential for sport's integrity and who but an idiot would dedicate years of hard grind with no possibility of a place on the rostrum.

The Modern Olympic movement was founded by gentlemen for gentlemen – fine in the context of the late 19th century, but it was still being run like a Pall Mall club a decade after Messrs Armstrong and Aldrin took a stroll on the moon. Absurdities abounded, not least the total absence of current competitors from any aspect of decision making.

In 1973 there had been some softening of the rules governing eligibility. Low-level sponsorship, if permitted by individual federations, was now allowed. Frankly, this was like using sticking plaster to stop a haemorrhage. The IOC made little attempt to shape events and at best was pretending to be only a little bit pregnant. What was needed was someone with the will to achieve radical change. And that someone was Juan Antonio Samaranch.

Samaranch was what today we would call an operator. Born in 1920 to a wealthy Catalan family, he'd been educated at a German school where sport was given more prominence than usual, particularly athletics. And sport, quite simply, became his passion. After a spell as a journalist, he began managing the national roller-hockey team, who then became world champions. A small fish in a small pond perhaps, but Samaranch's ponds had a way of getting bigger, and in 1955 he oversaw the second-ever Mediterranean Games, held in his home city of Barcelona. It was this success that brought him to the notice of the IOC. In parallel to the day job, he was now involved in politics, first as a regional councillor, and then at the Cortes in Madrid, in Franco's government, with responsibility for sport. In 1966, a failed bid by Madrid for the 1972 Olympics contributed nonetheless to his being made a member of the IOC. The signposts were all now pointing one way and by 1970 he was a member of its executive board. Meanwhile, back in Spain, so nifty was his political footwork that in 1977, two years after the Generalissimo's death, he was appointed Spanish ambassador to the Soviet Union by the new democratic government. This influential posting during the run-up to the Moscow Games provided an unrivalled networking opportunity – and ultimately a powerbase – in his bid for the presidency. While not perceived as the front runner, he nonetheless won at the first ballot, and was duly installed as the seventh president in Moscow, taking over from the Irish peer, Lord Killanin, at a time when the IOC was on the brink of bankruptcy.

Modernisation was now imperative, and Samaranch was smart enough to see that, not only did athletes need to be part of the debate, their involvement lay at the heart of it, and it had to be visceral. This was not about sentiment. This was about hard-nosed pragmatism. Without athletes there is no Olympic Games, and he couldn't risk bringing global sponsors to the table without their total and unequivocal support.

He worked quickly, calling an IOC Congress in September 1981 in Baden-Baden – the first since 1973, post-Munich – and I was one of thirty-eight athletes invited to attend. Unbelievable though it now appears, until that invitation, current competitors had never been given a platform, nor had their voice – singular or collective, – been heard at any level, the general view being that they were brawn, not brains, and not intellectually equal to the task.

From a distance of thirty-plus years, it's fair to say we were a pretty extraordinary bunch. Each one of us took our role extremely seriously, recognising the uniqueness of our position and the potential to make our mark. The first crunch moment was ditching the coaches. Their presence, we decided, was an inhibitor to athletes from the eastern bloc speaking freely. It was a mark of Samaranch's commitment that there was no quibbling. They were despatched.

Our deliberations continued for the best part of a week. Few of us knew each other beforehand and, apart from goodwill visits to local schools, we were basically put in a room, given a secretary, a list of issues to discuss, and told to get on with it.

It was utterly compelling. These were people who you would never get to meet in the normal of course of events, let alone speak to. I have the list of them in front of me now, and a more disparate group is hard to imagine. They include a Polish pole-vaulter, an Italian high-jumper, a Bulgarian rower, an East German bobsleigher, a Cuban boxer, a Spanish canoeist, an Austrian three-day eventer, a French cyclist, a Hungarian fencer, a Czech footballer, a Swiss judoka, a

Norwegian skier, a Soviet ice-hockey goalkeeper, an Australian swimmer, and of course, a British middle-distance runner.

Our first hurdle was to bridge the chasm of the west/east divide. The communist contingent had no concept of professional sport, for example. No word for professional even existed in Russian. Even though Vladislav Tretyak was nominally in the army, he wouldn't have known a parade ground from a pint of Bass. In the other corner (though not in Baden-Baden) US athletes who'd have been hard pushed to write a postcard home were sitting on scholarships. Somewhere in there we had to find common ground.

The topics we'd been given included drugs, eligibility and the inclusion of athletes in the decision-making process. But there were other issues we deemed equally as important, and one that stands out in my memory is preventing athletes from being used for political advantage. As we saw it, the games risked becoming a shuttlecock in the cold war, batted between Tweedledum and Tweedledee, or in this case Carter and Brezhnev, in their battle for ideological supremacy.

Although not party to the main debate, we'd been allocated time to address Congress on the final day – four short speeches on specific subjects, each one given by a member of the core group, who had largely identified themselves by contributing the most, and then a summing up, which I was called upon to give as a native English speaker.

Our co-opted chairman was the only IOC member among us, the talented Finnish sailor Peter Tallberg, by then in his forties, who'd carved out a successful business career. Among the scripting group were the West German fencer Thomas Bach, Bulgarian rower Svetlana Otzetova, German skier Irene Epple, Kenyan middle-distance runner Kip Keino, and American swimmer Donna de Varona, again drafted in as a senior presence, and already a high-profile TV commentator for ABC.

The more we worked on the speeches the more it became clear that the basic Olympian philosophy, however old-fashioned it might seem, had to matter and to mean something. Olympic success has to be a judgement of natural ability, talent, hard work and great coaching, not that one guy has a better set of chemists sitting in the background.

On the penultimate day, Samaranch himself came to see how we were progressing.

'Remember,' he said, 'you can tell me anything. I want you to challenge me! Challenge the movement! Challenge sport!'

In fact, our findings in general were remarkably conservative. While there were issues we felt strongly about, we had no wish to throw the baby out with the bathwater. No playing around with the medal ceremonies, for example. Athletes want them. They want the national anthems. They want to enter the stadium following their national flag. That is their moment.

By 1981 I had become used to running in front of vast crowds, but when it came to public speaking, my experience was minimal. My first public engagement had been to offer a few words of thanks to the Barnsley Miners' Welfare for raising a substantial sum for local athletics. My efforts were met with thunderous silence, but as the chairman said, putting a hand on my shoulder, 'Don't worry lad. In Barnsley we don't clap, we just let you live.'

Now, here I was, the day before my 25th birthday, about to address the most influential people in the most important sporting body in the world. In round numbers we're talking an audience of over a thousand including 500 accredited journalists, and all this at a pivotal moment in the history of the movement, when the old order was dying and the new had yet to be born.

I had four minutes. As the others made their submissions, I waited. Then came the hush. I knew my overview would be picked up by the press, not least because I was the sole English speaker, and

I wasn't planning on being particularly nice. Drug abuse was destroying everything the movement stood for, and the IOC could not sit there any longer and pretend that it wasn't going on. They had to be aware of exactly what we, the athletes – half of whom came from the eastern bloc – considered the most shameful distortion of the Olympic ideal. It was no exaggeration to say that the credibility of the movement was at stake. They had to get a grip on drugs in sport, I said. 'We call for the life ban of offending athletes. We call for the life ban of coaches and the so-called doctors who administer this evil.'

I am proud to say that, when these words went ringing around the hall, I could sense a collective squirm, first guilt, and then shock that someone had the temerity to say it. I am even prouder that, after a second's stunned silence, they rose to their feet and gave me a standing ovation.

As the result of those first tentative efforts in Baden-Baden, an athlete from the Athletes Commission now sits on every IOC commission, including the executive board, and thus has an input on every decision, and I deem it a particular honour that Samaranch approached me before the conference broke up and asked me, informally, to become a founder member. If Moscow was my defining hour in terms of track and field, the seeds of who I am today were sown in Baden-Baden in late September 1981 by Juan Antonio Samaranch. And it's fair to say that while my father moulded my career on the track, this guy moulded it off the track, and it's thanks to the opportunity he gave me that I've been able to do what I've done.

I ended my speech by saying, 'I feel that our inclusion here in Baden-Baden and the tenacity with which we have grasped our tasks buries the common misconception that athletes are unthinking robots.'

And I think it did. We have come a long way since then. Many of that core group went on to play a vital role in the Olympic movement and beyond. Svetlana Otzetova is president of the Bulgarian Rowing Federation, Kip Keino is president of the Kenyan Olympic Committee and father of African distance running, while Pal Schmitt, after a spell as vice president of the European Parliament, is president of Hungary. Robots we were not. As for Thomas Bach, he is currently vice-president of the IOC and could well be the next president. He was then a young lawyer, and over those last couple of days he and I pored over the final drafts, working well into the night, knocking the speeches into shape, giving them clarity of thought and clarity of language.

As a result we became great friends, and to this day, whenever we see each other, whether in a departure lounge in Vietnam or a hotel lobby in Guatemala City, it's always, 'Ah Shakespeare!' to which I reply, 'Ah, Professor!' while those around us look totally bemused. We never elucidate. It's like a running gag where even the protagonists no longer remember the punch line.

But the last tribute must go to Teofilo Stevenson, who died just a few weeks before the London Games aged only 60. He took heavyweight gold at Munich, Montreal and Moscow and would undoubtedly have won a fourth and even a fifth medal at Los Angeles and Seoul – he was still competing in 1988 – if not for Cuba's boycott of both Games. During his long career he rejected every inducement to turn professional and to pit himself against Muhammad Ali, then world champion. Instead, he became coach to the national team and eventually vice president of the Cuban Boxing Federation, and the most famous Cuban after Fidel Castro.

A few months later, in my new-found role as member of the Athletes Commission, I was invited to a memorial service at the Guards Chapel in Birdcage Walk, to celebrate the life of David Cecil, 6th Marquess of Exeter, who had died in October. Better known as Lord

Burghley (on whom the character of Lord Andrew Lindsay is based in *Chariots of Fire*) he took gold at the 1928 Olympics in the 400m hurdles, and was famous for having sprinted round the Great Court of Trinity College, Cambridge in the time it took the clock to strike twelve. Not only was he a great figure in our sport, but as chairman of the British Olympic Council he was largely responsible for bringing the 1948 Games to London, taking on the same role as I would sixty-odd years later.

Milling around outside following the service, I was told that Samaranch would like a word. Perhaps I would care to join him at the Ritz? I have no recollection now what I expected. What I didn't expect was to be party to one of the most bizarre meetings I will ever attend. His suite was high up above Piccadilly with a view across Green Park to Buckingham Palace. Present were Samaranch, his executive director Monique Berlioux, Primo Nebiolo president of the IAAF, Robert Parienté, the extremely well-respected editor-in-chief of the French sports newspaper *L'Equipe*, Robert's wife, Henriette, and a couple of others in Nebiolo's wake.

Monique Berlioux was a hangover from the *ancien régime*, having been Lord Killanin's executive director. A former Olympic swimmer, she is by any measure pretty formidable. During the occupation of Paris she would regularly swim across the Seine bearing messages for the Resistance. It was immediately apparent to me that she and Samaranch had the rapport of a bickering married couple, and being told what to do by a bossy Frenchwoman was not how the new president saw things continuing. In fact, she survived four years, during which time their mutual animosity provided a certain grim pleasure as a spectator sport.

'So what are we going to do about this?' Samaranch began. The 'this' in question was money. The IAAF had already taken the first steps towards making track and field professional by sanctioning sponsorship, and Primo Nebiolo was first into the fray; not for nothing was he known as the Godfather of world athletics. Football was the great enemy, he ranted, and his life's ambition was to topple it from its perch. Once athletes were properly paid, track and field would be world dominating!

The expression on Samaranch's face was that of a psychiatrist in the presence of a patient who it would be best not to antagonise, while beside him Monique interposed, 'And so modest with it, doctor!' every time the Italian paused for breath. Meanwhile, I felt increasingly uneasy. It was one of those and-when-did-you-last-beat-your-wife moments. Either I talked about payments in the abstract, in which case my views would have no real weight, or I admitted breaking the rules. Luckily, the next person up was Robert Parienté. Slowly and with great skill, this consummate journalist set out the reality of our situation. As I watched Samaranch's reactions and heard his occasional questions, I realised that we were way beyond the realm of arcane bylaws. This was about how best to 'normalise' the existing situation, to enshrine what was now common practice within the official code with as little loss of face as possible.

The more I got to know Samaranch, the more I became convinced he had never been theologically opposed to professionals being involved in the Games. What he needed at this stage was to improve his negotiating position in relation to TV rights. TV wanted the best. And if the best got paid, so be it. He just needed to know how to sell it to the public. By the time my view was sought, I knew what I had to do. The days of obfuscation were over.

'Speaking from the perspective of the athletes, none of us relishes the world we are forced to live in. Yes, we're earning money, and so we should be. I personally see no ethical dilemma about being very good at something and being paid very well for it. I don't feel that I come to my sport with any less moral underpinning because I'm able to do that. Do we treat artists like this? Is a portrait rendered worthless because the painter is being paid? Of course not. So why should we not be recompensed for what we do, and honestly, because I can assure you there's not one of us enjoys living in this murky, twilight world. What is the problem about being open and above board, and paying tax?'

At this point Nebiolo made a noise like Vesuvius about to erupt, and stared at me as if I was a lunatic.

'You want to pay tax?!'

After that things moved swiftly. All it had needed was a nod from the top and the whole house of cards collapsed.

The fly in this otherwise sweet-smelling ointment was the eastern bloc. They were amateurs, they insisted, and to compete against 'professionals' from Scandinavia, the Low Countries, Spain, Portugal, Italy and the UK was simply impossible. In reality, every last one of their athletes was a state employee who did nothing else but train. While nominally in the army or at a sports academy, everything they wanted – and, sadly, even more – was handed to them on a plate.

For all his bluster, Nebiolo and the rest of the IAAF were struggling to find the route map on this. Re-enter Andy Norman. It needed someone with his street savvy to recognise what was needed and why. With the clarity of the man who risks losing his shirt, he understood that if we didn't keep the eastern bloc, the athletics world would be split in half, spelling both sporting and financial disaster. The answer he came up with was trust funds.

It was, of course a fig leaf, but an effective one. It said, 'We're not really professional. The federation looks after the money and we draw down what we need in subvention payments.' And indeed we did. All those things that had been provided for years in the Soviet system – medical support, health care, coaching – were now ours also, so they could hardly complain. Meanwhile, the federation took 10 per cent off the top to put towards coaching and development, and you drew down what you needed for allowable expenses, the residue becoming yours on retirement from the sport. The man charged with drafting and implementing all this was none other than the avuncular and respected Robert Stinson, the man who had memorably said 'bye-bye' to me on my way to collect my first gold medal at San Sebastián back in 1977. Inevitably perhaps, the expenses expanded rapidly until you could even claim rent on an apartment or mortgage interest. And once it was seen that our sport didn't transmute into a casino culture, it quickly became entirely open. The trust-fund period was a necessary bridge, as much about keeping the eastern bloc alongside as fellow competitors as giving us flexibility and financial security.

Andy Norman never had an official role in track and field, either in Britain or elsewhere, yet for many years he held all the cards. The trust-fund solution, which would change all our lives, was not the least of his achievements. He moved mountains, but it was a life that ended mired in scandal. He had been used to roaming at will, and even when boundaries became fixed, he retained a frontier mentality and was a fearless trespasser. In the end, the absence of corporate governance in the sport was his undoing.

Since 1981 my life had been split between Loughborough and London. As commercial interest in the sport began to take off, sponsors, such as they were, tended to be London based, so one way and another, I needed to be there more often. At first I stayed with my grandmother Violet in Fulham – my grandfather Percy had died in 1974. Then, having finally got some legitimate earnings under my belt – and yes, much to the mystification of Nebiolo, paying tax – I bought an apartment a few streets away in Queen's Club Gardens in Baron's Court.

Back in Loughborough I lived at Steve Mitchell's. The house had originally belonged to Malcolm Williams, who had bought it off plan when he'd enrolled as a mature student in the early seventies. He'd gone to the site office, told them he would be starting at the university the following term and wanted the smallest property they had. Assuming he was a lecturer, they'd given him a mortgage. Then, of course, came the problem of funding it.

By the time I turned up, it had already had its share of sporting talent under the roof, particularly rugby internationals, headed by Steve Smith, England captain 1982–3. Dave Moorcroft was also a former tenant, one of a cluster of the Loughborough athletic fraternity who had passed through, including Sean Butler the third of my triumvirate of core mates, and Omar Khalifa, a Sudanese 1500m runner, who would inadvertently help me out in Los Angeles in 1984.

When Malcolm had left Loughborough for London, he'd sold the house on to Mitchell, who by the time I arrived had himself taken on the role of Rigsby, although sadly there was no Miss Jones.

In 1983, when I was at my lowest, a tabloid claimed that the 'mystery' illness keeping me off the track was not physical but mental, that in short I was having a breakdown, was estranged from my family and living as a lodger in a dingy bedsit in Loughborough. I remember laughing over this example of investigative journalism with Mitchell, his only complaint being the use of the word 'dingy', to which he took great exception. I, on the other hand, disputed the term 'lodger', reminding him that I'd never paid any rent. That evening I came home to find a large book marked RENT in the middle of the dining room table.

This schizophrenic existence actually worked very well. In London I did most of my running in Battersea Park. Battersea had been part of my landscape ever since I was a kid, when we would be taken to the funfair. While the grander parks, such as Regent's Park and Hyde Park, have their place, for me there's nothing quite like the populist Victorian examples of civic pride, the green lungs of

19th-century London carved out of marshland or former market gardens for working people – Battersea, Victoria Park, Brockwell Park – where right from the start, sport was integral to the plan to give Londoners somewhere away from the smoke. They're one of the great legacies Britain has bequeathed to the world.

I also joined Haringey Athletics Club. Not only was it a phenomenal club, but perhaps more importantly, Ron Pickering was its president. He was one of the great consciences of our sport, somebody who really understood it and was never afraid to enter the moral maze. Haringey also suited Malcolm, who lived in Chingford, a fifteen-minute drive east of Haringey's track in White Hart Lane. As well as being a PE teacher, Malcolm was actually a great conditioning coach, and every Friday – and sometimes on Mondays if I was around – I would train in a weightlifting club he ran in the basement of a primary school in Hackney. This was not a carrot-and-protein-juice gym, but a broken-mirrors-and-mesh-across-the-windows establishment. While I wouldn't want to traduce any of the guys I trained with – heaven forfend – even they would admit that their daily lives were lived around the margins. The Burberry factory was just over the playground wall, and every now and then jackets and hats sporting the famous tartan would appear. To my knowledge, not one of them was employed there. But they were great, and very, very funny, and when things got tough, they kept me sane.

Hackney and Haringey became, in effect, my home patch. Even when I moved to Twickenham a few years down the line, that part of north-east London remained a constant in my life. It was where I began to understand the incredible importance of sport in areas of grinding poverty and it was Malcolm who opened my eyes to it, who became – literally in some cases – my historian and guide.

His was an extraordinary story. Born in Walthamstow just before the war, his first job was as a machine minder at Gestetners, the duplicating machine company. Their engineering works were in

Tottenham Hale, where, coincidentally, my father was employed as a young engineer there at much the same time. Malcolm moved to British Oxygen at Edmonton, simply because his dad worked there, and this east London CV, straight from central casting, might well have continued along its well-worn ruts if not for his call-up for National Service in 1956, the year I was born. After basic training in Catterick ('mind-numbing' as he put it), Malcolm was posted to the Far East. It was during the Malayan emergency, which had been rumbling on since 1948, Britain's role being largely to protect our interests in rubber plantations and tin mining against the communist insurgents. This brought its own complications since the insurgents were the rump of the guerrilla army that had fought the Japanese, and had been trained and armed by the British, a scenario that would become all too familiar over the next fifty years, most immediately of course in Vietnam. But unlike Vietnam, Malaya was considered a British victory. It was never officially called a war because that would have negated the planters' insurance.

On the voyage out the younger conscripts were given basic lessons, and for Malcolm his Damascene moment came when his tutor asked why he had left school so young, 'because you're really quite bright, and you're completely wasted here.' He made Malcolm promise that, once back in Britain, he'd do something with his life. 'Until then,' Malcolm told me, 'I'd just assumed I was a bit dim, like everyone else who lived in our street.'

Once back in England, he passed sufficient O-levels at evening classes to go to teacher-training college. Then, wanting to go further, he took A-levels, came to Loughborough (bought the house) and completed a degree in physical education. Finally, he did his D. Phil. at Nottingham University.

Malcolm died in May 2006 of a chest infection. His GP diagnosed first asthma, and then emphysema and, as it continued to get worse, I would tell him that this was all nonsense. One day I said,

'OK, if you won't book yourself into a hospital, I'm taking you.' So I got him in there, but it was too late. He was 68. No age at all. And there isn't a day that goes by that I don't think about him, and the time he should still have had. I miss his humour and his wisdom, and I could go on. But as he would say, 'Don't get me started, Newbold.' He, more than anyone else I know, should have been at the opening ceremony of the Games.

11

ALARUMS AND EXCURSIONS

THE summer of 1982 was difficult. Although we were still two years out from Los Angeles, everything had to be seen through the prism of the '84 Games. Following the clatter of broken records by Messrs Ovett and Coe the previous year, there was a huge demand for us to meet on the track. Neither of us were averse, so three dates were arranged, the first at Crystal Palace (3000m), the second in Nice (800m), the third in Eugene, Oregon (the mile). In the end, none of them happened. I had to pull out of the first two as a result of shin fractures, and we both scratched from Oregon, again because of injury and illness.

That August, thanks in part to my enforced absence from the track, I was able to spend a week training and generally relaxing in Switzerland in the run-up to Zurich. It also meant I could spend some time with a skier I had begun dating at Baden-Baden, where she had been one of the core editorial group. As well as having a whole raft of Alpine world cups to her name, Irene Epple had taken silver for West Germany at the Lake Placid Olympic Games early in 1980. On this particular day we had come down from Grindelwald, where my parents and I were staying, because I wanted to run on the flat and there was a convenient sandy track around the perimeter of the lake. Irene, meanwhile, planned to go out on the lake for some windsurfing, which is useful training for skiers during the summer months. My parents were simply taking it easy, reading and enjoying the afternoon sunshine. Irene had just gone to the car to change, leaving her board by the shore, when suddenly all hell broke loose. A guy who I had never seen in my life before started screaming at me in Swiss German, not an easy language at the best of times, and I didn't understand a word. So I did what generations of Englishmen would do in the circumstances, and said, 'I'm really sorry, but I have no idea what you're on about.'

This only served to fuel his agitation, and so I called over to Irene but with wind coming off the lake, she couldn't hear. He then picked up her handbag – which she'd left in my charge – and, after a quick whirl above his head, launched it into the lake. Horrified, I took off in the hope of retrieving it, but after a splash and a couple of weak bounces, it sank, credit cards, make-up – everything except the car keys – forever consigned to the depths.

By now my father's sense of humour had completely deserted him, and he began remonstrating with the guy, in his proficient, if engineer-orientated German – with some gesticulation to boot. Then it got physical, at one point my father fighting hard not to fall backwards into the water. Although into his sixties, he was still fit and deceptively strong, but my mother, considerably younger, was having none of it. Hearing her shout, 'For Christ's sake!' I watched as she snatched at the guy's sleeve, at which he threw a wild punch, which fortunately failed to connect. I'd had enough. From a stack of newly sawn wood beside a wall, drying for the winter, I grabbed a log by a convenient prong, and set off towards them, shouting, 'Get off!' When I reached him, I thwacked him around the head. This wasn't the time for considered judgement. I hit him hard, and down he went.

I'd had fights before. You don't survive five years in a Sheffield secondary modern with a name like Sebastian without learning how to look after yourself. And, although I'd backed off, no one had called time. The guy improbably heaved himself up, looked at me, then began lurching forward. It was the first opportunity I'd had to look at him properly. He was built like the proverbial . . . but I still had the log. I thought, this time it really has to count. I was lining him up like Geoff Boycott, with all the focus that the great Yorkshire cricketer brought to the crease. Next thing I felt a shock of searing pain across my lower back. Moments later I was on the ground and he was on top of me, punching, fist after pummelling fist.

Angela had seen the whole thing. Two of his windsurfer mates had come up behind and jabbed me in the back with a board, leaving him to pile in on top and hammer away, and he was effective. A later tally revealed a broken nose and a ripped tear duct.

This undignified scene was set against the backdrop of a peaceful Swiss Sunday afternoon in mid-August, with grandparents wheeling pushchairs beside the lake, toddlers dripping ice-cream down their shorts, and couples strolling hand-in-hand admiring the distant peaks.

As I struggled to my feet, a grey-haired woman hurried over. She'd rung the police, she said, 'They're on their way.' My heart sank. This was Switzerland. You couldn't start bashing people around the head with lumps of wood and expect to get away with it. Moments later we were all arrested. Mum, Dad, Irene and me.

It wasn't long before an older policeman, clearly of a more senior rank, pulled out his notebook and pencil.

'Your name?'

'Sebastian Coe.'

He began to write, then looked up. 'You're running in Zurich on Wednesday?'

'Well, I'm hoping to . . .' I said, wiping blood from my eyes.

'And your name, Fraulein?'

'Irene Epple.'

At this he stepped back and stared at the 1980 German Sportswoman of the Year. You could practically hear the cogs moving as his eye shifted between first Irene and then me as it sank in: 'I've got two of the world's most famous athletes and a late middle-aged couple, and some nutter screaming on the ground.' Our assailant was now doing just that. Cue the grey-haired woman who had watched this unusual holiday footage unspool.

'I saw everything,' she said in perfect, if heavily accented, English. And I thought, that's it. She saw me hit him. I'm dead meat. 'This man,' she went on pointing to the nutter on the ground, 'his behaviour was completely unacceptable.' It wasn't enough. By this time a police car had arrived and we were all carted off to the station. Irene was released (no surprise there) while my parents were held as witnesses because, in spite of the old lady's claim that the other guy started it, I had hit him with an offensive weapon, to wit: a log. Just as in all the movies you've ever seen, I was given one telephone call. No prizes for guessing who I called.

'Andreas . . .'

'Sebastian! How is your day going? Enjoy your run? Where are you?'

'Well, actually, I'm in Interlaken Police Station, and I think I need a lawyer.'

Thanks to Andreas Brugger's intervention, I was released on bail, bound over to appear in the local court the following morning. I only understood fully what had happened when the prosecuting magistrate spelled it out the next day. It transpired that the man nursing a severe headache ran the local windsurfing school and objected to Irene using 'his' stretch of the shore to launch her board without paying. She said that there was no sign up to the effect that it was private. I certainly hadn't seen one. It turned out that there was, but hidden in some bushes. Meanwhile, there wasn't a British newshound, despatched by quote-hungry editors, who wasn't trying to get into Switzerland. The story was manna from tabloid heaven. My brother Nick was lying on a beach in Spain when he saw the headline in somebody's *Daily Mirror*: SEB IN PUNCH-UP. He said he hadn't laughed so much in years. The upshot was I got fined 170

Swiss Francs. I can't now remember what my crime was, but it was sufficient to earn me a criminal record. To this day, my name triggers narrowed eyes when passing through Swiss passport control.

As for the windsurfer, fast forward to the summer of 1992 when I was a newly elected Member of Parliament. A message came via the House of Commons switchboard that a Herr Ralph Bauman from Switzerland was trying to contact me. He was coming to London, I was told, and planning to get in touch. Ralph Bauman? The name didn't ring any bells. And then I remembered. Interlaken, August 1982. I immediately put in a call to Andreas in Zurich. 'Leave it to me,' he said. 'I will make sure that he realises such a journey would be futile.' I never heard anything of him again.

Three days after the lakeside-fisticuffs incident, and in spite of being severely bruised, I competed in Zurich as planned, winning my 800m by a good five metres, although I didn't push myself as it would be a busy week. Two days later, on the Friday, I was running at Crystal Palace – another 800m – and two days after that – the Sunday – another 800m in Cologne in Germany. The European Championships in Athens were less than a fortnight away and I could have done with a rest, but the British Athletics Board had strong-armed me, and others in the team competing in Athens, into a 4 x 800m relay world-record attempt at Crystal Palace the following weekend. This was not about demonstrating our fitness, as they claimed. It was about demonstrating their power. Quote: 'Those who do not compete will not travel to Athens.'

There were three teams. Mine consisted of Garry Cook, Peter Elliott and Steve Cram, with me taking the last leg. The south London crowd was magnificent, and when I grabbed the baton from Crammy, I gave it everything I had. And we did it, coming in four seconds inside the existing record held by the Soviet Union – an amazing result given that not one of us wanted to be there. But as an exercise in bloody-mindedness – disrupting the training schedules of the strongest team Britain had fielded in years – it was ridiculous.

The one absentee at Crystal Palace that afternoon was Steve Ovett due to injury. He would definitely not be going to Athens. In fact, he turned up as the voice-of-the-expert on the BBC TV coverage back in Britain. Coe was a shoe-in, he said, or words to that effect, over pictures of us lining up for the 800m final. 'The rest of them are running for the minor places. Seb has a hypnotic effect on the other runners in the race. They just wait for the moment when he goes.'

Minus Ovett, this was a near re-run of Prague with my old East German foes, Olaf Beyer – the defending champion – and Detlef Wagenknecht, having also made the cut. It would be my first championship 800m since the fiasco of Moscow. I planned to get my own back, taking the 800m, then with luck the 1500m, and so achieve the fugitive double.

It didn't happen. Unlike the 800m final in Moscow I did nothing wrong. I was perfectly placed in lane 5, and started well. Off the bend I was at the shoulder of the leader, West German no. 2 Hans-Peter Ferner, then at 400m I went to the front. I had only 100 metres to go, the finish was in sight, but halfway down the home straight, Ferner was at my shoulder and I had nothing there. It was Prague all over again. I just couldn't hold him off. My legs were empty.

I managed to climb up on the rostrum to collect my silver medal, and watched numbly as Ferner, who I'd beaten easily just two weeks earlier in Cologne, was handed the gold. The applause for all of us was muted. Everyone was in shock. To say I was the odds-on favourite does nothing to convey how obvious it had been to everyone that I would win. I'd been perfectly positioned. I'd run a tactically perfect race. What had happened? All I knew was that I'd been feeling a bit under par for a few days and had a couple of swollen glands. Later that night, the British team doctor suggested I might have glandular fever and I withdrew from the 1500m, which was subsequently won in great style by Steve Cram.

The hope that I might get the double, either the Europeans in Athens, or in Brisbane at the Commonwealth Games at the beginning of October, had been dealt a death blow.

The truth was that, while I was capable of pulling out the stops for a one-off race even when not at my best, the stamina needed for a championship, where you have to run several times in quick succession, requires something very different, both physically and above all mentally. There are no soft championships. I'd run seven races in three weeks after a period of very limited training following the stress fracture. I'd gone to the well once too often.

Although I was now being paid substantial fees for invitation races, money was never my driving force. In reality, I ran far fewer races than many of my contemporaries, adhering to my father's principle of quality not quantity, which applied to racing as much as it did to training. 'Never waste your assets for short-term gain,' was a maxim he'd brought with him from the factory, and I'd always adhered to it. The races I did choose to run were those that we judged, over a range of criteria, were integral to my running development, a trajectory that ended in Los Angeles.

In fact, like many athletes, my income derived less from appearance money than from sponsorship. I had sensed something of its potential in 1979 during my first visit to Bislett. Apart from championship racing where you run in your country's colours, you can basically wear what you like and I tended to wear things I felt comfortable in, at that stage the Loughborough African violet. As for shoes, Adidas had given me some in 1976. I had a small sponsorship contract with Viga, a Yorkshire-based company that had been set up by Mike Tagg, a former 5,000m athlete who'd run in the 1968 Olympics in Mexico City. Although they sourced their own textiles, as a secondary line they had the agency and distribution rights to a little-known US-based shoe company out of Eugene, Oregon – called Nike. So I would wear Mike Tagg's kit and he'd throw in the shoes as well.

On the day of that first record-breaking run in Oslo, I noticed that the experienced hands were all gravitating to the kit company reps who were hanging around the lobby of the Summer Panorama, badgering them for stuff. I was wearing an old training top at the time, which had clearly seen better days, and I thought I could do worse than to pull out the begging bowl myself. As I was wearing Nike shoes, I went up to the guy who seemed to be their rep.

'Have you anything for me?' I asked, while he looked me up and down, clearly none too impressed.

'Who are you and what've you done?'

I told him my name, and said that I'd taken bronze in the Europeans in Prague the previous year. 'Oh, and I wear your shoes,' I told him, pointing down at my feet, adding I had been wearing them in Prague, giving Nike their first shoe medal outside the United States.

'Sorry,' the rep said, 'but I've nothing left.'

I was just turning away when he said, 'Here, you can take this' and began peeling off the tracksuit top he was wearing. It had a brown nylon body and cream sleeves, but was threadbare at the elbow. Not wanting to appear ungrateful I took it, and in fact warmed up in it as it had significantly more style than my old one.

I have a distinct memory of what happened two or so hours later, on that first-ever victory lap when I'd just broken the world record. Out of the corner of my eye I noticed what appeared to be a scuffle in the main stand. It was Geoff Hollister, one of the founding fathers of Nike, desperately trying to get out of the tribune and on to the track before the other apparel reps got their claws into me. After the briefest of congratulations, he cut straight to the chase, seeing just how soon he could get me over to Oregon.

For the remaining twenty-four hours I was in Oslo, Geoff was never less than a metre and a half away from me. By the time I arrived back in Sheffield, two first-class airline tickets for Eugene had arrived.

No one goes into athletics to get rich, even now. Compared to other sports, you have to work harder and reach a much higher standard before you start earning anything at all, let alone serious money. Someone ranked twentieth in the world in tennis, or cricket – let alone football – can make a very good living. And while Borg and McEnroe can still play for an hour and a half in Miami in front of 10,000 spectators misty-eyed for an era past, nobody is going to turn up at Crystal Palace to watch me run a mile in over six and a half minutes against Steve Ovett or Steve Cram. While they may not hit the ball quite as hard as they used to, Borg and McEnroe still look like serious tennis players, whereas the two Steves and I would look like we were going for a jog in the park. In athletics, the stop-watch is king.

February 1983, on schedule again. In a GB v. France indoor meet at Cosford, I won the 1500m. A month later I came first again at Cosford in an 800m against the USA, taking a second off my own world record set there two years earlier. A week later I was in Oslo – not Bislett but an indoor track – competing against Norway, this time over 1000m, and breaking another world record. That made it a round dozen, and the fifth world record I'd taken in Oslo in as many races, but it was hardly news any more. People had come to expect it.

I was back in Oslo, at Bislett, towards the end of June. Four days earlier I had come second in a 1500m race in Paris at the *Parc des Princes*, largely as the result of some rough-housing when I tripped in the initial scrum after the gun and found myself 25 metres adrift. I did well to pull up the pace to get back into medal contention. It hadn't exactly helped that, *en route* to the stadium, the driver ferrying me there had ploughed into the back of a stationary queue of cars. Nonetheless it was the first time I'd been beaten at the distance in thirty-seven races, apart from one of the Moscow qualifying heats, and it was worrying. But Bislett yet again worked its magic – not another world record this time, but my sixth-fastest performance ever at 800m.

That was the last race where I would feel comfortable for a long time to come. I was more tired than I should have been this early in the season. Feeling tired when you are in peak training is not unusual, but that summer Steve Mitchell remembers how he would come back to find me asleep at the kitchen table, dead to the world. I'd have to slap myself awake when driving down to London, pulling into a service station on the M1, intending to snatch a quick ten-minutes and waking up an hour and a half later. I could still pull out the stops when I had to – but there was a price to pay.

For much of the season I was running on painkillers because of chronic low back ache. I raced at Crystal Palace twice in eight days. In the first, a 1500m, I came second to the Russian who'd come last in the Moscow final. A week later, in the mile, I came second again, this time to Steve Scott. The proof that something was really wrong was when I came fourth in Gateshead the following week, a 1500m won by Steve Cram, a victory for the local hero that was naturally greeted with near-hysteria by the partisan crowd. I've always savoured the ebullience and good humour of the Geordie spirit, but this time it fell on deaf ears. Beyond the confines of the North East however, the headlines the next day were not CRAM WINS as it should have been, but COE LOSES.

With the benefit of hindsight, I had been in denial about the state of my health for too long – probably as far back as Athens – trusting to physiotherapy and modified training to get me through. Gateshead was the wake-up call. There was clearly something very wrong here. Peter had been with me at the track and I could tell he was rattled, and self-critically blaming himself for not realising that there was something wrong sooner.

The next day he suggested we went over to the university playing field, the other side of our garden wall. 'Just for some gentle strides, to get yesterday's race out of your legs,' he said. In fact, he had an ulterior motive. A great family friend, Robert Haig, whose brother Ian had been a teacher at Abbeydale, was a consultant physician. His speciality was endocrinology, and he was one of the leading authorities on diabetes in the country. A great track and field fan, whenever possible he would come to watch me race, and had done since the early days. So I wasn't that surprised when he turned up to watch the proceedings.

'You don't look that great,' he said when I went over to say hello.

'Actually, I haven't felt really well for the last year,' I admitted.

'Tell you what. When you're done here, I'll give you a quick examination.' So when we got back to the house, he began feeling my chin and round my head and then started to prod under one arm. I knew just by looking at his face that something wasn't right.

'I'd like a second opinion,' he said. 'It's just a bit lumpy under there. There's a friend I qualified with. I'll see if he can take a look. He's in Leicester.'

So the next morning, we all three drove down to Groby Road Hospital where Robert's friend was in charge of infectious diseases.

'What do you think I'm going to say?' the consultant asked when he had finished giving me the once over.

I rolled my eyes. 'You're going to tell me that I'm not going to the World Championships.'

'That obviously. But also I want to do a biopsy.'

Within hours I was nil-by-mouth in a hospital bed waiting for a general anaesthetic.

'I won't pull my punches,' the consultant said when he came to see me afterwards. 'We've cut out a large node, which was horribly infected. It could be a lymphoma. But we will only know where we are after the biopsy.' All I knew was that it was painful in the extreme and I went back to Steve Mitchell's feeling dreadful.

Thankfully, the diagnosis wasn't long coming. It wasn't cancer. It was toxoplasmosis, a protozoa (from the Greek, meaning first animal) – a single-cell organism that feeds on animal or human hosts and is endemic in cats. It's acquired either by direct contact or by ingesting contaminated water or food. I probably caught it in Rome, where the feral population of cats is a part of the scenery. Around the same time – the eighties – a large part of the Royal Ballet came down with it after touring in China.

In humans, symptoms are usually minimal, similar to glandular fever and largely limited to feeling 'under the weather'. For a minority, however, it's a different story. It's back to machines again. If a hairdryer is totally furred up with dust and other crap, it will still keep going and do its job. But get a grain of sand in the shutter of a camera and it's screwed. An élite athlete, or dancer, is the human equivalent of that high-performance camera, vulnerable to things that a less-challenged immune system would shrug off. In this case, the protozoa had entered my lymphatic system and created havoc. Although the consultant said he saw no reason why I shouldn't run again, he was not prepared to give me a time scale. And that included Los Angeles.

The following weeks and months were unmitigated hell. My medication made me want to vomit all the time. I lost weight. I couldn't run. I avoided watching the World Championships in Helsinki by driving to Italy with Mitchell, meeting up with Nick and Emma, my brother and younger sister, who were on holiday there and just lying in the sun. I learnt later that the 800m, for which I'd had such hopes, was won by Willi Wülbeck, the guy who virtually up-ended me in the same stadium years earlier. As for the 1500m, Steve Cram took the gold, capitalising on a mêlée involving a lot of the field, while Steve Scott took the silver, and the Moroccan Said Aouita the bronze. Steve Ovett got himself boxed in and did well to come fourth. He might have been down but he wasn't out; less than a month later he reclaimed his 1500m world record in Rieti in Italy.

As for the press, the Coe–Ovett show was now the Cram–Ovett show. Yesterday's man barely warranted a mention, except negatively. And yes, it got to me, not least the fear that I would never run again. But at this point I would have traded all this just to feel well.

How do you come back from that? With the help of other people. Malcolm resorted to, 'Get a grip, Newbold. You're not some idiot sixth-form drop-out. You're the current world-record holder.'

Sometimes I'd have to sit in my car for half an hour before driving home as my hands and arms were so tired from the weights that I couldn't grip the steering wheel. And while sympathy wasn't in my fellow-weightlifters' vocabulary, humour was. One of the guys, a pub singer known as Mouthy Mickey, had this thing about Frank Sinatra, and one night another of the guys was winding him up.

'Who d'you think's better, then, Mickey? Sinatra or Pavarotti?'

'Sinatra,' he said as he heaved another weight.

'Pavarotti,' said another voice in mid-lift. And so it went on until Mickey conceded.

'All right, I'll grant you that Pavarotti probably is the better singer. 'E might be a fat old wop but 'e can't arf bang out a number.'

The other guy in this esoteric discussion was Bloodbath Dave, so named because someone once picked a fight with him, not realising he spent half his life weightlifting.

Athletics now had a profile that it had possibly never had before.

The IAAF had recognised this with the inauguration of the World Championships in Helsinki in 1983. Oslo had added a third meet to its already crowded summer schedule. As for Britain, our top three middle-distance runners were also the top three middle-distance runners in the world. At a time when English football was mired in violence and hooliganism – and for most of the seventies it had been almost entirely absent from the international game – British track and field athletes were suddenly doing what the public craved – breaking records and bringing home medals. We were young and clean-living (well, in public). We were the role models parents wanted for their kids before the term had been invented, and families began voting with their feet. They were not just watching it on television. When Newcastle United were setting their fixtures, they would check with Brendan to make sure a home match did not clash with his track meeting. If it did, it was football that moved. Daley, Steve Ovett, I and now Steve Cram had become household names, instantly recognisable, with all that this brought in its wake, not least the regular run-ins with the press.

When word got out that I had joined Haringey, the tabloids decided there was a story in it. As the amateur era disappeared and sponsorship stopped being the reserve of golfers and tennis players, suddenly it became financially interesting. As there was nothing out there of genuine concern, the tabloids took to invention. Given I could have joined any club that I'd wanted to, my choice of Haringey, they decided, must have involved money. Hence the splash that I had been paid £100,000 to join the club. Ron Pickering saw red and called a press conference. When the gentlemen of the fourth estate were all assembled, he let rip.

'I would just like to knock on the head the notion that this club has paid one single penny to Seb Coe. I would remind you that Haringey is a challenged community and the idea that we would countenance paying any money to any athlete is grotesque. And just in case any of you are still harbouring any doubts, perhaps I can show you this.'

At this point he whipped out a cheque, not one made out to me, but one made out *by* me to Haringey Athletics Club for the princely sum of £15, which I'd posted off with my membership form when I'd signed up, and which he then passed around the hacks.

Ron was a big man in the sport, and not just physically. Above all, he was a great visionary. An east London boy, he had married his childhood sweetheart – they were head girl and head boy at Wanstead High, the first co-educational grammar school in the country. Jean Desforges went on to became the European long-jump champion, and also took bronze in the sprint relay in the 1952 Helsinki Olympics. Ron meanwhile became national coach for Wales, and in that capacity coached Lynn Davies to the Olympic long-jump gold in 1964 in Tokyo. And then, of course, he became a broadcaster, and it wasn't only athletics fans who knew him. There wasn't a sports-mad kid in the country who didn't recognise that familiar voice saying, 'Away y'go!' at the end of *We are the Champions*. He set up quite a good business around his broadcasting career, but the rest of his time he devoted to Haringey.

Most club presidents are purely figureheads. Not so Ron. He was determined to give back what he could, both to the sport and to the community. He was determined to meet the aspirations of young athletes in the area and provide them with proper facilities. In the early seventies he spent hours every week searching for somewhere suitable and eventually came across this pile of rubble and debris on a derelict site on White Hart Lane, just up from Tottenham Hotspur football ground. Working in harness with Sandy Grey, a local councillor, and John Hovell, a photographer who would play his part in my backroom team, it took Ron more than ten years to achieve his dream. He did it in the time-honoured way of knocking on doors, calling in favours and getting local people to support it, and eventually it happened. In doing so, he turned Haringey into a club that has contributed as much to track and field as any in the country. The depth and level of excellence he achieved in a deprived area of north-east London was quite extraordinary. Sadly, he died far too young, aged just 61 in 1991, but his legacy lives on. The New River Centre is a monument to what can be achieved if you put your mind to it, as Ron did. On his death, his wife Jean and son Shaun set up the Ron Pickering Memorial fund, which today probably funds about twenty athletes a year, providing grants to help towards warm-weather training, medical needs and other key expenses.

Ron was a great believer in indoor facilities and I remember, around 1987, he said, 'Do you want to know what Germany has and we haven't? Twenty-eight indoor running arenas, while we have one.'

Although we are still a shade light in terms of Europe, we have closed the gap with our high-performance centres. No British athlete has the excuse of paucity of facilities to fall back on.

My success had propelled my father on to the list of coaches worth listening to, and in the autumn of 1983 he was invited to give a series of seminars across the United States. He told me, 'Look, it's only a fortnight, you're not training, so why not come with me?' One of the cities on his itinerary was Chicago. Chicago played such a seminal role in the development of jazz that to turn up a chance like this would be mad. And I also knew that a break would do me far more good than sitting around moping.

John Hovell in Haringey had sorted out some 14 year olds who were happy to go jogging with me, but I could do that anywhere. All I needed was shoes, an urban park or even city streets. I still believe there is no better way of exploring a city than by running in it, at least for me. I'm more observant and absorb things better than I do with any other mode of transport. Even now, when I arrive some-where I've never been before, I'll put on my running shoes and go out for an hour, just padding the streets around a hotel, picking up the geography.

That trip with my dad was the best thing I could have done, not least because I got to know Joe Newton, a Chicago High School coach who would prove quite inspirational to me in the lead-up to the Los Angeles Games. What he didn't know about the Chicago jazz scene wasn't worth knowing. In fact, my dad's tour of the States ended up being largely a tour of jazz clubs.

While distances in America are enormous, it seems no big deal when you're there. So when Peter flew home, I caught a flight to Los Angeles, took a taxi to the Memorial Coliseum, persuaded someone to let me in and then sat in the stand on my own, soaking it up, letting the atmosphere wash over me. I wanted to have a vision of the stadium in my mind, and a feel of where it was, and also to take a few steps on the new-laid track, even if I still harboured severe doubts about making it back in July.

Los Angeles is the only Olympic stadium to be used twice – the first time in 1932, the Games where Paavo Nurmi was famously barred from competing. That year the men's 800m was won by Tommy Hampson, a Londoner born in Clapham, who in breaking the tape also broke the world record, at 1m 49.7. He was the first of just three Britons who have broken the 800m world record, followed by Sydney Wooderson in 1938, and then me in 1979.

While in LA, I thought I'd take a look at the Olympic village. I knew there would be two, both university campuses. The first was at USC, University of Southern California. Close to the stadium, south of downtown Los Angeles, this was not somewhere, I decided, where you would just go out and run in the streets.

The other was several miles to the north at UCLA, University of Los Angeles, in Westwood, Beverly Hills. The moment I began wandering around I thought, if it's here, then I'm in clover, not that we had the choice.

The 1984 Games were the first to be run on an overtly commercial footing, and athletes had their commercial freedom as well. Sponsors, such as shoe companies, were falling over themselves to persuade athletes to stay in sponsored houses or hotels. Their line was, 'Why would you want to queue for food when you could be comfortable in a five-star Hollywood palace with a swimming pool?' Before 1980, you'd never have dreamt of staying outside the village, but presented with an attractive alternative, a good many athletes chose that instead. Had the British team been billeted at USC, then I too might have gone elsewhere, but luckily we drew Westwood.

Staying there had huge advantages. You had food twenty-four-hours a day, medical and physiotherapy help, plus all the facilities of a top-ranking US university, including a training track and gym. And being inside the transport system, you were spared the worry of wondering whether your taxi would get you to the stadium on time. For me, it made total sense, not least because the Hollywood hills were just on Westwood's doorstep. However, if the village had been a hell hole, I'd have walked out the first morning.

12

THE ROCKY ROAD

TRAINING began almost immediately I was back in England. Thanks to the persuasive powers of Ron Pickering and John Hovell, an amazing group of athletes allowed their sessions to be built around me and my fitness gradually improved. The weather was particularly grim that winter of 1983, and there was nothing in it for these guys beyond being part of what for much of the time must have seemed a lost cause. But they kept me buoyant, through gale, sleet and mud.

By March I felt confident enough to join other members of the club in a road relay race. It may not have been the High Peaks, but I was back running with people I trusted, and it felt comfortable.

The debate had now shifted to selection for the Los Angeles Games, little more than four months away. I have thrown a veil over the innumerable fiascos that dogged British middle-distance running in the run-up to Athens (European Championships) in 1982, and Helsinki (World Championships) in 1983, because to relate them is simply too tedious. There wasn't one athlete or coach who didn't experience some degree of exasperation with the selectors, related less to their quixotic choices than to the heavy-handed manner in which they acted.

Clearly, athletes need to be fit, but to force them to prove their fitness in race conditions can be totally counterproductive. Timescales differ between different events and different athletes, and if the more seasoned athletes were the more vociferous in their complaints, it wasn't because they expected privileged treatment.

They were simply less willing to put up with high-handed behaviour and were no longer frightened of having their card marked 'difficult' – as mine most certainly had been as a youngster because my father refused to play the game.

What the selectors singularly failed to understand was that an élite athlete has no interest in competing in a championship if he or she is not in good enough condition or serious contention. What would they have to gain? A poor performance on a public stage is more likely to harm rather than enhance the athlete's commercial pull.

I had been pre-selected for the 800m, along with Peter Elliott, a gritty 21-year-old steelworker from Rotherham, who had run the second leg of our world-record-breaking 800m relay at the end of 1982. This left one vacant spot, which in the end went to Steve Ovett. When it came to the 1500m, the two Steves, Ovett and Cram, had been pre-selected, and I was determined to get the third place, not least to defend my Olympic title. But – and this time with some reason, given my health problems – the selectors would be questioning not only whether I was the best athlete available, but also my stamina, my ability to take on both distances – a total of seven races if I got through to both finals. I would be up against runners who were four or even six years younger than me, most of them choosing to run only one of the distances.

Among those I was up against was Graham Williamson, who had been pipped at the post by Steve Cram for the place in the Moscow 1500m. And then there was Peter Elliott. Like me, Elliott ran both distances. So why should the selectors give it to me rather than him? Not only did I have to prove my worth to them, I had to prove it to myself.

The view had always been that coming back after the 800m debacle in Moscow had been the toughest hurdle I would ever have to face. But this was of a different magnitude. Moscow had been about character in dealing with defeat. Physically, there had been no question that I could go out there and win. I had all the qualities it needed and my health was not an issue. This was about having had a seriously debilitating illness, of not having trained for six months. I would have to dig deeper than ever before.

I put in the hours with Malcolm in the gym. I put in the mileage. I slogged up and down the hills in Richmond Park, did endless repetitions on the track and worked with Haringey sprinters to get the power and cadence back into my stride. But I was still two months behind where I needed to be. I had to cling on to John Hovell's mantra: 'Forget about the past. It's only the future that counts.' But there were times when I didn't think I'd make it back.

Gradually, things started to come together – first a gentle outing, running one of the legs in a 4 x 400m for Haringey; then, on 19 May, my first solo track race, an 800m, the Middlesex championships in Enfield. Supported by just about everyone I knew at the club, with the familiar sight of the old man shouting out splits from inside the track, I crossed the line at just under three seconds short of my own world record. This was the turning point. I'd stopped feeling tired all the time. Soon afterwards, although still with personal doubts, I told the British Athletics Board that I wanted to be considered for both the 800m and 1500m in Los Angeles.

Never before had I felt so determined. I'd shed everything that was secondary to this one goal: Los Angeles. Perhaps it came from spending time with the weightlifters and sprinters, but I felt harder. Stripped down. Meaner. Everything else I'd done to date seemed irrelevant – an unconnected part of my career. Maybe I had needed this time. I had called a halt to the dinners and the rest of the celebrity hoopla that was frankly redundant. It was as if I was starting out fresh again and in doing so had become more at ease with myself.

Next up was Crystal Palace – 1500m in early June. So far so good. No defeats. Then two weeks later, Crystal Palace again.

The run-off for the third place in the 1500m was between Peter Elliott and me. Six years younger than I was, he had emerged as a precocious talent, having won English Schools titles at both 800m and cross-country as a junior. The way he went into races fearlessly reminded me a lot of myself. He would always give you a race and so was the last person I needed to run against at this stage in my recovery.

The race was not spectacular. It wasn't even particularly fast, just a rather cagey affair with nobody wanting to make any tactical errors. I hit the front coming off the bottom bend, but never really with enough daylight, and Elliott proved stronger in the finishing straight. I came second, not by much, but by enough. I'd been shoved about in the early stages and should have elbowed my way out of trouble, but didn't yet have the confidence. To put it in perspective, I had run 60 metres slower than my personal best.

Peter and I shook hands and, while he went off on his lap of honour, I walked down the back straight where I was joined by Andy Norman. 'Oh well,' he said. 'Just concentrate on the 800m.' Even Andy made the assumption that the selectors would go for Elliott. That was my assumption, too. It seemed like a foregone conclusion and I felt pretty low. Over the following days and in the absence of any hard news, there was massive conjecture and speculation that Elliott would get the nod. A few people thought differently, though, including David Miller of *The Times,* the doyen of athletics correspondents, while in the *Guardian* John Rodda wrote: 'Coe will get better, Elliott will not.'

The arguments rumbled on but, in the end, the selectors gave it to me. A campaign was launched by the *Daily Mirror*: ELLIOTT MUST GO. He was certainly not happy, saying he saw it as proof of southern bias among the selectors, although whether he was faithfully reported is another matter. However, the accusation of a north/south divide was a little questionable given that he and I were actually brought up six miles apart from each other. The divide, if it existed, was subtly different. I was the economics graduate; he was a carpenter/fitter in a Rotherham steelworks.

I heard the news on the car radio while driving to Battersea Park for a training session. I remember thinking, 'That's it. I'm in the team. This is what I wanted.' And I knew that they had made the right decision. I knew that, given enough time and the rub of the green, I could still pull it around. I stayed for some time at the track, then wandered over to the little Italian restaurant across from the pedalo lido. I needed to invest some thinking time on how to proceed. That afternoon, over pasta and coffee, I decided on two things. Firstly, this was no longer about coaching or day-to-day contact with my father or John Hovell or my training group. I instinctively knew the only way I was going to do this was on my own. I didn't want to spend any more time discussing it or thinking about it. Secondly, I had to get out of England. And that was a tough call. I knew that, at the end of the afternoon, I had to talk to the guy who had steered my career for fourteen years and tell him that I didn't actually want him around. It wasn't a personal thing. I didn't want anyone around. I got in the car and drove to Fulham – he and my mother were in the process of moving down from Sheffield. And this was when you knew that Peter Coe was always a class act. He looked at me and said, 'Yeah. I get it. You know what you have to do, so you go and do it. All I ask is, every now and then, to know what you're doing, how you think it's progressing.' Then he paused and added, 'Well, where do you want to go?'

'Chicago,' I said. 'I've figured out that I can spend three weeks there, get used to the six-hour time difference, then arrive in Los Angeles two weeks before the Games start. That way I'll only have two hours to make up.' It strikes me now that if I had shown any hesitation, if I hadn't shown that I'd thought it through, he'd have punctured that lack of intellectual rigour in seconds. As it was, he said, 'Fine.'

I rang Joe Newton later the same afternoon. Before leaving, I had one major commitment – Bislett, where I ran the third-best 800m that year – but I went on my own. Then it was back to Haringey for a mile, which I won with the fastest time that year and my dad was in his familiar place, beside the track, shouting out split times. After that I didn't see him again until he joined me on the training track at UCLA's Drake Stadium a few days before my first heat.

Leaving my father behind was the single toughest decision I made in my whole career. And it is the mark of the man that he didn't feel slighted or consider this was a gross act of treason or ingratitude on my part. He was smart enough and wise enough and intuitive enough to accept my decision.

Joe Newton is straight out of the Vince Lombardi school of classic old-style American coaches, complete with beanie hat, green York High School top and megaphone, which he used when coaching from the middle of the track. He was messianic about running, and his language could be so profane that he actually once stopped a church service. While the pastor was inside instilling moral rectitude into his congregation, Joe was son-of-a-bitching it at 100 decibels on the track outside, even though he was about as committed a Catholic as I have ever met.

A high-school coach has near mythical status in small-town America, up there with the doctor and the lawyer. Joe was revered, and rightly so. He was a big figure in the community and did much more than just coaching. There was no one in that city he didn't know – including the immigration officials when I flew in – because he'd coached either them or somebody in their extended family. He also happens to be the most successful high-school coach of all time in the States. He was US team manager at the Seoul Olympic

Games, the only high-school coach ever to take on that role, traditionally the preserve of college coaches, such as Sam Bell from Indiana, or Brooks Johnson from Stanford.

Joe was completely committed to what he was doing. He believed in getting every ounce, mentally and physically, out of an athlete, and his great trick was that they did it willingly. He used sport as a stepping stone, allowing generations of young guys to understand more about themselves and pursue successful careers having established self-confidence and self-esteem through the track and cross-country programmes he set up. He had a profound effect on their lives, and Joe Newton was, is and always will be a great inspiration to me.

He picked me up from O'Hare airport and I stayed with his family in a very comfortable house in Oakbrook, a smart suburb to the west of the city. With his gravelly south-Chicago voice and high-school coach salary, nobody understood how he came to be living next door to doctors and lawyers. But for all his success, Joe remained a hustler. He somehow managed to get the car-park concession at the local racecourse, making enough money over five or six years from punters who wanted to get close to the rail to buy himself the house.

During those three weeks in Chicago I trained and slept while Joe held the watch for me. This wasn't about him giving me technical advice; this was having someone beside the track who gave me confidence. Good coaches are inevitably good psychologists, and Joe was about as good as it gets.

Daley had taken my word on the village and he and I and Britain's great hope for the javelin, Tessa Sanderson, had agreed we'd get there in good time. That first afternoon we were just chatting, catching up, marvelling at the expanse of manicured lawns with sprinklers hissing, when somebody came up and said there was a call down in the lobby. It was Frank Dick, director of national coaching, who, in fairness, brought a professionalism to the management of the team that we had never had before or have had since.

'Guys, what are you doing up there?' he said. 'You're meant to be down here with the rest of the squad!' He had set up a holding camp in San Diego in southern California where he wanted the team to train as a group. Although I knew that Frank would not have put together a dog and pony show, I didn't need to be with a gang of people. And Daley was different. Daley was completely self-contained. He and I would spend hours together without exchanging a word, just comfortable in each other's company.

'Believe me, Frank, I'm really happy here. I've got everything I need,' I said.

'You don't understand. The reason I've done this is to get you out of the pollution.'

'I can see clear across the city, Frank. The air's cleaner here than it is in London.'

'Seb, you're not listening. We need you down here.'

'I'm not moving.'

Daley's response was both shorter and blunter. When Frank asked to be put on to him, he turned to me and said, 'You're the diplomat. Tell him to fuck off.'

We really did think the world of Frank, who was as good as they get – by a distance the best technical director I've ever worked with. In fact, at that point he was steering Daley's career. But, like me, Daley was happy where he was.

On arriving at the village, I'd cast my eye down the accommodation list to find out where we were billeted, and saw that we were in with the Irish and Kiwis. Then I looked again and couldn't believe what was staring me in the face. We'd been put in 'H' Block. Clearly, whoever was in charge of the allocations had neither any sense of contemporary British history nor heard of the Maze prison.

In spite of Samaranch's best endeavours – which were considerable – the Soviet Union had opted to play tit-for-tat in retaliation for Carter's boycott of Moscow, not that they called it that. They insisted the decision of the eastern bloc not to participate in the Los Angeles Games was simply a matter of security. They didn't believe the Americans were capable of protecting their athletes they said. This was obviously the smart thing to do. Having complained about the impact politics had had on them, they could hardly be heard singing the same song.

As a result, Steve Ovett and I were the only two of the Moscow finalists to make the final of the 800m. The United States was represented by Earl Jones and Johnny Gray, Kenya by Billy Konchellah and Edwin Koech; then there was Donato Sabia from Italy and Joaquim Cruz from Brazil, the junior world-record holder, who had taken bronze at the World Championships in Helsinki the previous year behind Peter Elliott and Willi Wülbeck. Elliott had taken the third British place but ended up scratching before his semi because of a serious stress fracture.

Ovett, too, was distinctly unwell with residual bronchitis, not helped by training in San Diego rather than coming directly to Los Angeles as Daley, Tessa and I had done (the only three of the athletics team, incidentally, to win gold medals). In fact, Steve barely made the final, collapsing over the line in his semi to take the last place. But he's a fighter, and he was defending his Olympic title. I knew he would run even if it killed him.

My father and I had Cruz flagged as the danger. His time in his semi was nearly two seconds faster than mine and he was cast from the same mould as Juantorena – a giant of a man with a stride like Colossus. But I didn't need reminding that it's seldom a two-horse race, and Jones, too, would need to be watched. Nonetheless, Cruz was the one to track – in a phrase my father had so memorably used in Moscow – 'into the shitter'.

I was drawn in lane 3. At the break, Koech took to the front, Cruz tucked in behind him, Jones third, Ovett fourth. At the bell I went past Ovett, running easily shoulder to shoulder with Jones on my inside. With 200 metres to go, Cruz made his move and I went with him, down the finishing straight, fighting off Jones, who was matching me stride for stride. But Cruz was off and away and I knew I was running for silver.

The last time I stood on an Olympic rostrum having come second, I had felt nothing but humiliation. This time it was different. It would have been nice to mirror Tommy Hampson's gold of 1932, won on this same track over fifty years earlier, but it wasn't to be. Joaquim Cruz had set a new Olympic record, beating Juantorena's time set in 1976 in Montreal. Although I was disappointed, this time a silver medal didn't feel like a failure.

Cruz was also entered for the 1500m but, having got through his heat, he was scratched by his coach shortly before his semi. The official reason was a cold. The clever money (the coaches) had it that after four races in succession, he was knackered, and a defeat in the 1500m final would diminish what he'd achieved. I can't say I was heartbroken.

As for Steve Ovett, he was like the boxer who struggles to his feet, wiping the blood from his half-shut eyes, thinking 'just one more punch . . .' He had promised his wife Rachel that he'd run off the track if things got really bad. And as it turned out, that's exactly what he did.

Back in the tunnel after the 800m, putting my shoes on, getting my kit together and thinking about the medal ceremony and the ritual dope test, I looked down and saw Ovett hunched on the ground, looking really grim.

'Are you all right?' I asked. He looked the colour of dirty parchment and was struggling to unclench his fingers from cramping up on him. For a moment I thought he was having a heart attack. Then

Harry Wilson his coach came down, followed by Rachel. It struck me that they needed more serious help than the US equivalent of the St John's Ambulance Brigade and I jogged to the end of the tunnel and called out to some paramedics, 'I think you should look at this guy . . .' Next thing I heard he'd been admitted to hospital. A week later, however, he was back in harness.

There were more familiar faces in the 1500m final than there had been in the 800m. In addition to Steve Ovett, there was Steve Scott on his home patch; Omar Khalifa, sometime inmate of the Loughborough house, who had been coached by George Gandy; and of course Steve Cram, of whom I'd seen little outside the stadium as he wasn't staying in the village. Three Brits in the final line-up of twelve. People were talking about a clean sweep.

As I waited for the gun, I felt better than I had for a long time. Sure. Focused. Improbably calm.

Positioned one out from the kerb, I went straight to the front to avoid any possible mêlée, then Omar took up the pace and began to stretch it out. At the halfway mark I was lying second behind Steve Scott, who'd taken the lead and had pushed up the pace. I was feeling so comfortable within myself that I fleetingly toyed with making a long run for home. Just as quickly I decided this was not the day to bet with the till. I didn't need to. I wasn't look-ing for times, so why take that risk? At the bend I glanced quickly behind me to find Steve Cram hard on my shoulder. Abascal of Spain was now out in front and I tucked in behind him, still running easily, Cram lying third, Ovett fourth. Then, with 200 metres to go, Cram moved up alongside me, ready to pounce. When Crammy hit the front, he could be hard to dislodge. He liked a long run for home, and he liked it unencumbered. I had gone into the race with one objective other than winning, and that was to make sure that at no point from gun to tape would Steve Cram ever be in front of me, least of all on the last lap. I had seen enough of his races to know this was non-negotiable. As he came up to my shoulder, I felt his shadow, and I kicked. By sprinting earlier than I'd intended, to keep him behind me, the risk was it would empty the tank quicker. Mercifully, it didn't. Easing my way through the gears, I went past Abascal. Crammy came with me. Then it was just the two of us. But this wasn't like the Moscow final where over the last 100 metres there was an air of desperation. This time I was flying, and completely in control. As I raced down the home straight, I even knew I was smiling, grinning, jubilant, knowing that I had closed the door behind me.

But as I crossed the line, I caught sight of the press box on my right. Suddenly I was engulfed with another emotion. Even as I sit thinking about this at my kitchen table, it is still difficult to explain properly. It was anger. Raw and undisguised. Anger at how I'd been treated, dismissed, my very integrity called into question. And this anger, bordering on hatred, bubbled like molten larva from a volcano the existence of which only a few people close to me could have even guessed at. I'm not sure I knew of it myself. 'Who says I'm finished now?!' I shouted, shaking my fist, not once, but several times. 'Who says I'm finished now?!'

The anger vanished as abruptly as it had arrived, and I picked up a union flag from someone in the crowd and ran my victory lap, hardly aware of my feet touching the ground. I had done it, and done it in style. Not only had I claimed two successive Olympic victories at 1500m – which had never been done before – I had set a new Olympic record of 3m 32.53 seconds.

As for my outburst, Colin Hart, athletics writer for the *Sun* and a good friend, told me that up in the press box, the British sports writers were stunned into silence, broken when one of them volunteered, 'That's aimed at us boys.' And Harty said, 'Not all of us, you ****' Another friend was standing at the back and heard one UK hack say to another, 'Oh Christ. This means we've got him for another four years.' So much for pride in British athletics. The truth is that everyone was so fixated on the Coe–Ovett rivalry, no one outside that tight circle knew just how dysfunctional my relationship with the press had become. It was actually worse than the lowest point they ever reached with Steve, who never talked to them anyway. In fairness, while a significant few had written some pretty hideous stuff, the majority were paying the price for the behaviour of their news editors. As Adlai Stevenson famously put it, 'An editor is someone who separates the wheat from the chaff, and then prints the chaff.'

They paid a high price. News journalists, who didn't have to form a long or abiding relationship with me, could dip in and out according to the news agenda or the whims of their features editors. In doing so, they damaged the relationship between specialist writer and athlete.

A quarter of a century later I would witness the same pathology. Specialist writers on the Olympic beat, who devoted time and energy to getting to grips with the complexity of the delivery of the Games, were regularly undermined at big moments simply because a news editor had decided that there was a 'fiasco' to be reported. Some novice would be drafted in who, without the necessary background, was unable to contextualise anything but who nonetheless would write twelve paragraphs of rubbish about the ticketing process, or the torch relay, or the budget, or whatever happened to be the gripe *du jour*. I know because I had to listen, and sometimes respond, to their naive questions. All this to the chagrin of specialist writers.

The Los Angeles 1500m was run more like a Grand Prix than an Olympic final. The unexpected speed had given me more space to run in, and one by one other runners had made the pace – first Omar Khalifa, then Steve Scott and finally José Abascal – taking the strain until the home straight. The exhilaration of those last 200 metres, accelerating for the line, is something I shall never forget.

As for my old nemesis Steve Ovett, he was stretchered off for a second time. He had walked off the track halfway around the final bend when he was lying fourth, as he promised Rachel he would. As David Coleman said on the commentary to the race, he'd been 'perhaps too brave, too proud for his own good'.

I will always respect his determination not to leave an Olympic stadium cheaply.

13

CLEAN SWEEP

My long-term plan had always been to move up to 5000 metres – 3.1 miles. It's a distance that requires endurance, speed and tactics and is thus a natural progression for someone who in the early stages of his career had focused on the lower end of the middle-distance spectrum but who had a background in cross-country running. John Walker, who is just under five years older than me, had achieved the transition pretty well, making the 5000m final at Los Angeles. So that winter I started doing longer runs with this in mind, but it didn't really work out, and by the end of May the idea was ditched. In addition, my 1985 season was badly blighted by a series of niggling injuries, which were probably the residue of seven races in nine days the year before.

Los Angeles had put Steve Cram firmly in the spotlight, and in the summer of 1985 he blazed a trail across Europe. We ran against each other twice. The first time was in an early season meeting in Birmingham, an 800m, when we were racing against an American team and I beat him. In the Dream Mile the result was the other way around.

The Birmingham race is only ever remembered for one thing. During the course of the previous year, the BBC had lost one of the jewels in their crown – the right to broadcast athletics – to ITV, who clearly recognised the advertising potential around what had become our most successful national sport. Although the new team had covered the London marathon earlier in the season, the Birmingham meet was their debut appearance on the track. Andy Norman knew he had to deliver that night for his new masters – hence the Cram–Coe head to head. It would have added to the spectacle, however, had ITV not been prompted to run a baked-beans advert as the race was about to begin. I still remember fondly the way the commentator Alan Parry – seamlessly and with some ease – opened his commentary with, 'We join the athletes at 200 metres,' as though this was common practice. I subsequently made some fairly searing remarks to John Rodda in the *Guardian*, and the following day, John Bromley, the legendary head of ITV sport, called everyone in – Rodda's article, complete with my acerbic comments, providing the agenda. I'm told that when a producer commented on my parentage in unflattering terms, he was brought up short by Bromley. 'He may be a bastard, but on this occasion he's right.'

My second encounter with Steve Cram, when he beat me in the Dream Mile in Bislett the following week, left a more indelible mark. This was the race many would deem the finest of his career and I watched him control the finishing straight from about twenty yards behind the action. However, his main rival that season was the Moroccan 5000m Olympic champion, Said Aouita. Cram broke Steve Ovett's 1500m record in July, and Aouita removed it from him five weeks later. It would stay Aouita's for the next seven years.

Abandoning plans to move to 5000m left the way clear for another attack on the elusive 800m championship gold. Stuttgart 1986 was my next chance and, because by then I would be just weeks shy of my thirtieth birthday, possibly my last. I loved this race and it seemed absurd that my favourite distance should be the one that got away. I'd lost count of the number of times I'd come first, and I still held the world record, which remained unbeaten until 1997. I'd taken three silver medals, in Moscow, Los Angeles and Athens, and of course the bronze in Prague back in 1978. And although I'd won two Europa Cups and a World Cup over the distance, to me – and the purists – they didn't really count.

The 800m calls upon a greater range of physiological demands than any other distance. With this in mind, I flew to Atlanta to see the professor of cardiopulmonary science at Georgia State University.

It was probably inevitable that at some point I would end up on Dave Martin's treadmill. We had first met in Prague at the European Championships seven years earlier. I'd noticed this rather acerbic-looking American, a bit academic but built like a runner, rangy, wiry and always running everywhere. Then, while I was talking with some German journalists about my training, and struggling somewhat because of the language barrier, he stepped in to help and introduced himself. He told me he ran marathons and was working on an endurance running programme in the States. He was interested in what the human body could do.

By then I had done a couple of sessions with John Humphreys in Leeds, so we talked a bit about physiology, and a couple of days later I introduced him to Peter. Over the next year or two I would see him around the circuit; he was there when I broke one of my world records in 1979. But the next time we really spoke was in Moscow the following year.

Although Dave had done a bit of coaching, his USP was that he understood better than any practitioner of his generation the physiological DNA of the élite runner. In 1975 he had established a human performance evaluation laboratory at Atlanta, appraising élite-level distance runners who would each be tested three or four times a year, enabling them to fine-tune their training programmes. He was at the coalface. There was nobody at that time who knew more.

He'd collaborated with the American Olympic Committee and US track and field association, plus he'd worked with some individual cross-country runners in the southern states, including Craig Virgin, who won the world cross-country championship in

1980 and 1981, and Pat Porter, who won eight successive US cross-country championships through the eighties. He'd also worked with Tom Byers, my sometime pacemaker, the guy who, in that guise, famously ran away to win the 1500m in Oslo from Ovett in 1981.

As well as being a fanatical marathon runner, Dave was a fanatical photographer. In most parts of the world this was great, but not in Moscow in 1980 – spectacularly not so on one occasion.

It happened just before one of my press conferences when a couple of Russian soldiers eased gingerly into the ante room, carrying a tray the size of a card table, piled high with hundreds of small boxes stacked in the form of a giant ziggurat. Suddenly, a side of this tray flipped down, and the boxes began cascading on to the floor where they opened like mechanical oysters, revealing what turned out to be commemorative medals for the press. It was then that I noticed Dave in the corner, happily snapping away, capturing pictures of this bizarre scene for posterity. Enter the heavy brigade. A scuffle ensued, and I heard his gruff mid-western voice saying, 'I guess you don't photograph the cock-ups in Moscow,' at which point he was bundled out, camera and film successfully confiscated.

Until Dave Martin, physiology was seen as a branch of science, rooted in academia, and a lot of useful work had been done by people such as Astrand and Rodahl. What Dave was concerned with, perhaps for the first time, was the practical application of this research. It didn't just sit there as a subject for undergraduate study. What he, and my father, did (they went on to write a book together) was to bring it out of the lab and on to the running track. And, as far as I am concerned, David Martin is one of the cleverest people I know.

As a slight digression, it never ceases to amaze me how extraordinary the United States is, specifically the polarity of intellect there. I don't know another country in the world that is such a powerhouse of creativity and innovation in literature, music, art, science and technology. On one level they number among the cleverest people on the planet. Yet all too often these smart, cultivated individuals are bracketed with the rest of the population, who seem barely aware of what is going on beyond their TV set, let alone in the wider world.

I had my first session on Dave's treadmill in November 1985 and from then on, my visits to Atlanta became a three-monthly fixture. Typically, I would fly into Atlanta on a Wednesday, have my blood chemistry analysis done on the Thursday, and then on the Friday it was into the torture chamber, running on the treadmill as the speed and the gradient are ratcheted up until you reach the state of exhaustion. It's not only singularly unpleasant – you have to breathe through a plastic tube – it's also dangerous, because there comes a moment when you just can't keep going. There was always a panic button, and if you were alert enough, you'd hit it just before you needed to, but sometimes you'd be too far gone to be thinking straight. And if you lose balance when you're on the brink of passing out, and catch the side of the treadmill, then you're in real trouble. So there'd be six or seven students standing around ready to catch you. In Leeds I actually once broke the machine. Smoke started coming out and all I can remember through a sea of lactic acid was Peter shouting, 'Fuck, it's on fire!'

I'd made it clear to Dave that my primary objective in all this was Stuttgart and winning the 800m. On the basis of his analysis, I agreed with my father we should continue my weight training and conditioning further into the season and shift the focus on to speed work. I had to be strong enough and fast enough in equal measure to see off any competition. I also needed to protect against any diminution in strength, which can happen towards the tail end of the season and all too often coincides with a major championship.

Both the Commonwealth Games and the European Championships are scheduled midway between the Olympics, often within a
few weeks of each other. At least in 1986 there wasn't the time
difference issue, which prevented many British athletes from taking
part in both. Athletics has always been a Euro-centric sport, so when
it was either one or the other, the Europeans usually won. In 1986 the
Commonwealth Games were held in Edinburgh, which made
competing in both feasible. Unfortunately, the weather in Scotland
that July was dire.

In fact, the problems besetting the Edinburgh Games were more
deep seated than the vagaries of a British summer. The organising
committee had lurched from one crisis to another, problems stem-
ming from lack of secure finance and little commercial support.
The level of desperation can be measured by the appearance of one
Robert Maxwell, self-proclaimed white knight and saviour of the
championships. In the light of what we now know about his nefari-
ous activities, it is perhaps not surprising that none of the promised
money ever materialised. But with the might of the *Daily Mirror*
behind him, he was ensured front-page status, which was presumably his overall intention from the start.

Back in August 1986, my immediate concern was the weather.
My training sessions were done in torrential rain and most days I'd
return, drenched and shivering, to the university campus at Pollock
Halls that doubled as the village. Unsurprisingly, colds and flu were
not far behind. The team doctors did their best to isolate the
infected, but in the end they ran out of rooms, and many of our
team succumbed. It wasn't long before it was my turn. While I
managed to struggle through my semi, after a day and a half in the
san I was advised to go home. I would be mad to continue, the team
doctor said and diagnosed flu. Although relieved to see the back of
the rain, I was disappointed not to test the water against Elliott and
new Scottish talent Tom McKean, who had a finishing kick that I

sensed might, in some types of race, prove troublesome. I returned to Loughborough to recover. Then Steve Mitchell and I loaded up the car, drove to Chigwell, collected Malcolm and headed for Dover and Switzerland.

Macolin's wonderful mountain air worked its magic as usual, the residual effects of the Edinburgh lurgy disappeared and we spent the best part of three weeks training, interrupted by a couple of local outings to Zurich and Berne, one at 1500m, the other at 800m.

I wasn't the only athlete at Macolin focused on the Europeans in Stuttgart. With that year's venue just a couple of hours away up the autobahn, several athletes had based themselves there, including Donato Sabia, who had come fifth in the 800m in Los Angeles and would go on to make the final in 1988 in Seoul. Malcolm had spotted that the Italian coaches had taken to watching me, particularly in the weights room, after which they would quietly disappear and presumably report back. One day, when I was just coming to the end of my session, Malcolm slipped in.

'Don't ask any questions,' he whispered. 'Just do what I tell you.' I then watched as he added an extra two hundred pounds of weights to the bar. 'Now get back underneath.'

'You're mad!'

'Just do what I say. But don't for Chrissake try to lift it. When I give the word, pretend you're at the end of one of your movements and walk away.' It can't have been more than thirty seconds before Malcolm hissed, 'Now!' He had timed it perfectly. The two Italians came in, I feigned massive effort, wobbled a bit as I got up and then he and I walked out of the training room. In a flash these coaches were totting up the weights they imagined I'd been lifting – eyeballing each other in disbelief, as well they might. But they completely fell for it.

A day before the first heat, my training partners set off for England – in Malcolm's case, for one reason and one reason alone:

the start of the football season. Steve Perryman and the boys at White Hart Lane had a far greater allure than a stint trackside in Germany, so I took the train to Stuttgart in time to meet Peter and Angela who were flying in from London.

We all have our idiosyncrasies, our favoured ways of running, and you're always conscious of the strengths and weaknesses of your opponents. But sometimes it pays to think like a poker player, to come out of left field and do the unexpected, and I was lucky that I had enough weapons in my arsenal to do it.

Up to this point I'd had an indifferent season. In the Commonwealth Games, I'd travelled to Edinburgh, confident enough to attempt the double, but thanks to the Scottish summer had been forced to bail out before the final. In Zurich two weeks before Stuttgart, I'd come second in the 1500m behind Steve Scott. So I arrived in Stuttgart trailing little expectation. For Steve Cram and Tommy McKean it was a very different story. They were both on cracking form and I knew they were both a threat.

The year before, in 1985, Crammy had destroyed me in the Dream Mile in Oslo. I'd allowed him to get in front after the bell – in truth, there was not much I could have done to stop him – and he did exactly what I knew he'd do, what I'd prevented him doing in Los Angeles. With the track wide open in front of him, he'd surged ahead and taken my world record as well as the race. I wasn't about to let that happen again.

With only two laps to play with, a second's hesitation, indecision or uncertainty is enough to lose you the race. So I did what I had never done before. It wasn't planned. It was instinct plus a streak of devilment. I am known for many things – running from the front and kicking hard and late – but I could never have been accused of being a head waiter. This time I deliberately lingered at the back of the field – actually, I was in last place as I passed the bell. My mother told me later that she thought her husband was about to have a heart attack. Crammy, too, had stayed back, keeping clear of the bunching at the front, and he kept looking to his left and right, trying to see me. Now Steve Cram is tall, and I was so close behind that he couldn't see me. I could sense him thinking, 'Where the hell is he?' not realising I was in his blind spot. As Crammy began to move up, I went with him, always out of his eye line, until we reached McKean, who'd been up with the leaders from the start. I made my move down the back straight, and with 100 metres to go came up to the shoulder of both, went past Cram, but Tom McKean was more resilient and was not folding. I didn't hit the front until thirty paces from the line, but crucially got a stride on McKean and it proved to be enough.

The gold medal that had eluded me for so long was finally mine. That night I won because I'd done the last thing they expected from me. I was the threat, the one they had to keep tabs on, and I think they were thrown off balance, having no idea how to respond. They thought I was below par, that something must be wrong. Nothing was wrong. Those weeks in Macolin, and testing the water in Berne, when I didn't even break sweat – I knew that I had everything it took to control the finishing straight. And this time it was a British clean sweep, just not perhaps in the order that anyone expected.

During my athletics career I was often accused of arrogance, but more often than not, what people took for arrogance was the preference for my own company the day or so before a race, and above all, self-belief. That night in Stuttgart I had self-belief in spades. If I hadn't, I would never have risked racing the way I did. I had pushed two much younger guys – Tom McKean was seven years my junior, and Steve Cram four – into second and third place.

I didn't get the double. Perhaps I was simply not hungry enough. I had taken what I wanted from Stuttgart. I was the 800m European champion. Steve Cram won the 1500m because, at one lap to go, he was four strides in front of me, and as I've always known, that was fatal. If confirmation were needed that, in my thirtieth year, I was still at the top of my game, a week later I ran a 1500m in Rieti. It wasn't quite enough to take Said Aouita's world record. I should have clinched it, but I collided with the guy making the pace and staggered for a few strides. That made the difference of a few tenths of a second. But it was the fastest 1500m I had ever run, over two seconds quicker than my Olympic record set in Los Angeles two years previously.

The Coca-Cola meet at Crystal Palace was my first outing after Moscow and this time I won the 800m, here congratulated by Roger Bannister, the first man to break the four-minute mile in 1954.

Zurich, August 1981. Another world record, the mile again, cheered on by my father yelling out split times. The BBC planned to break into the *Nine O'Clock News* with live coverage. So no pressure then …

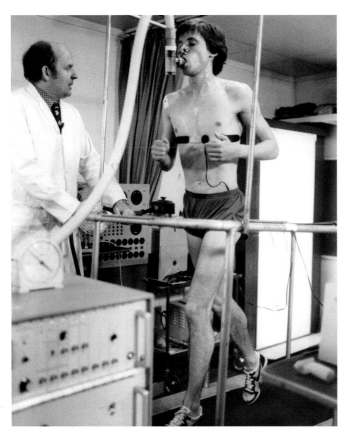

Left: John Humphreys, professor of physiology at Carnegie PE College in Leeds, puts me through my paces on his treadmill – a means of looking under the bonnet, which was torture.

Below: Not the best picture of Stamford Bridge, although to be out on the hallowed turf is always a thrill. Here I am jogging with Yorkshire-born Phil Driver, who turned out 44 times for Chelsea in the early eighties.

Slight compared to other middle-distance runners, weight training was an important part of my strength-training programme. Eventually, I could lift several times my own weight.

Richmond Park offered 2000 acres of parkland just a stone's throw from where I was living across the river Thames in Twickenham, west London. Richmond Hill, where this photo was taken, provided all the hill training I needed.

Above: Cuban giant Joaquim Cruz beats me to gold in the 800m at Los Angeles. Although disappointed not to have won, this time a silver medal didn't feel like failure.

Left: Daley Thompson and I have been friends since we first met as youngsters and we would regularly room together when representing GB internationally. Here he competes in the long jump in the Los Angeles Olympics, where he took decathlon gold.

Below left: People were talking about a clean sweep for Britain in the 1500m in Los Angeles. It wasn't to be. Steve Ovett was stretchered off but I succeeded in keeping Steve Cram at bay to take gold.

Below right: 'Who says I'm finished now?' Los Angeles, 1984.

My lap of honour at Los Angeles. Not only had I retained my Moscow title, I had set a new Olympic record.

Left: Crystal Palace, 1985, 800m. Promoter Andy Norman's instruction to athletes I ran against was 'Keep out of his ****ing way and don't hit him, the public don't like it.'

Below: Malcolm Williams was the greatest influence on my life after my dad – a great teacher, a great conditioning coach and a great friend.

Commonwealth Games, Edinburgh, 1986, after the 800m semi. I came third. Yet again, a cold prevented me from performing at my best.

Acknowledging the great Crystal Palace crowd after the last race I ran on English soil, 15 September 1989.

European Championships, Stuttgart, 1986. A clean sweep for Britain, but not in the order expected. I came from behind to take the elusive 800m championship gold ahead of Tom McKean and Steve Cram.

Left: My parents, with Wendy Sly in Basel, Switzerland. Coached by Peter after she took silver in the 3000m in Los Angeles, 1984, Wendy remains one of the best distance runners Britain has ever produced.

Below: A Downing Street reception for athletes in 1986 when I was deputy chair of the Sports Council. Few of my friends understood my admiration of Margaret Thatcher.

14

SUDDEN DEATH

As far back as I can remember the names of Olympic cities have been the fixed planets in my universe, as linked to their years as Saturn is to its moons: Mexico City '68, Munich '72, Montreal '76, Moscow '80, Los Angeles '84, and then Seoul, which had been chosen as host city for 1988 at the IOC Congress in Baden-Baden, where I had made my speech on behalf of all athletes in 1981.

One of our key demands had been for a clear separation between sport and predatory politics, our wish that the Olympic Games should cease to be used for overtly political ends. And while the Los Angeles boycott happened on Samaranch's watch, it wasn't for want of trying. Given the cold-war tensions, it was perhaps unrealistic to expect Moscow's humiliation to go unpunished, particularly when Samaranch had his tour as ambassador in the Soviet Union to thank for his presidency. With Seoul, however, Samaranch had started with a clean slate. One of his greatest diplomatic achievements – only surpassed by his persuading North and South Korea to march into the Olympic stadium in Sydney together twelve years later – was in convincing the eastern bloc that the pluses of competing in South Korea outweighed their ideological objections. In the event, just a handful of countries failed to attend, and never again would the Games be the subject of mass boycott.

As in every other Games, there were three places at Seoul for British athletes in my two distances, and my failure to be selected for either the 800m or the 1500m marks the lowest point of my career on the track, and ranks among the lowest of my life.

In the spring of 1987 a fragment of calcified bone in my right foot had embedded itself into my heel and made running impossible. It was eventually located and dissolved by a podiatrist based in Chicago, but by then an entire season had been lost. Although I had been pre-selected for the 800m in the 1987 World Championships in Rome at the beginning of September, given my lack of training I declined. I ended up watching from beside the track as one of NBC's commentary team, and it has to be said that, only a year out from Seoul, the sun was beginning to set on Britain's middle-distance empire. For the first time since 1978, we no longer held a recognised 1500m title. Steve Cram had suffered a debilitating calf injury for much of the season, finishing eighth in the 1500m, the gold taken by Abdi Bile of Somalia. As for the 800m, with characteristic grit Peter Elliott made it into the final as the fastest loser and commendably nicked a silver, while Tom McKean came in last.

That autumn I stepped up my training, and then spent January and early February 1988 in Florida with two athletes my father was coaching: Peter Wirz, who had made the final of the 1500m in Los Angeles – taciturn and very Swiss – and Wendy Sly, who took silver for Britain in the women's 3000m in Los Angeles. That race is remembered more for the Budd–Decker dust-up than for Wendy's success. Slight, smart, effervescent and with a great sense of humour, she was nevertheless hewn from granite and is one of the best female distance runners we have ever produced. My father didn't come with us, but Dave Martin was close at hand and his various tests showed no diminution of physiology of power from when I had won the 800m in Stuttgart.

A 3000m indoor race in New Jersey, which I ran simply as a break from training, would prove to be a disastrous debut on the US indoor circuit. Just getting there was the stuff of nightmares; I could almost have been playing a cameo role in the Steve Martin classic, *Trains, Planes and Automobiles*. The *coup de grâce* occurred on the

Jersey turnpike when our cab broke down in the fast lane. We ended up pushing it for nearly half a mile. It seemed safer to stay connected to the taxi than attempt to navigate six lanes of screaming traffic. The result was yet another cold. Three laps from the finish I could barely breathe, not helped by the stifling atmosphere of an over-heated indoor track. I pulled out, the only time in my entire career I failed to finish a race. But it was just a blip. A month later I came second in another indoor 3000m in Cosford in a GB v. USA match.

In terms of Seoul, I saw no reason to push things, quite the contrary. The danger lay in doing too much, too soon, particularly as the '88 Games were being held in the autumn, two months later than usual. Los Angeles remained my benchmark, and it was worth remembering that I had reached a good state of fitness just days before my first heat. But my progress was steady. I ran a series of 800m races, including a comfortable win at Crystal Palace in early July. Then in Dublin, in my first 1500m for two years, I was spiked, and had to pull out. Although we were still over two months away from Seoul, my detractors smelled blood.

Having not raced in the World Championships in Rome the previous summer, I was told that I would need to compete in the trials – the AAA championships in Birmingham on 8 August. The system used would be the most basic 'sudden death'. The first two across the line would be selected. Steve Ovett was facing the same inflexibility as I was. Yet we both understood only too well how being judged on one race alone means little when it comes to the Olympics.

In preparation I went to Switzerland for ten days' altitude training, not Macolin this time but St Moritz – to a hotel owned by friends of Peter Wirz. We'd no sooner arrived than I was informed by the federation that I hadn't yet achieved the Olympic qualifying time for the 1500m. I made the point that the deadline was still a month away, but they dug in their heels. If I didn't qualify in an appropriate race – now – I would be excluded from selection. Enter Andreas Brugger. There was a small local meet, he said, at Rapperswil, not far from Zurich. He would set up a 1500m, assembling both a local field and time-keepers, which would meet the criteria.

The next problem was how to get there. From our hotel down to Rapperswil was well over two hours by twisting mountain road. Hearing of our dilemma, the mayor of St Moritz said he would lay on a light aeroplane. The chance of a scenic alpine flight was too good to miss, so in the end, there were five of us – Wendy, Peter Wirz, another runner who had joined our small training team and my dad. It took just twenty minutes. We landed at a tiny airstrip, got into a waiting boat and ripped across the lake. I ran the race, made the qualifying time, got back into the boat and was soon back in the plane on the runway. However, it's one thing landing with five passengers on a short airstrip, quite another thing taking off when such a huge differential in altitude is involved. Time was another problem. St Moritz is a classy resort and imposed a curfew on planes after a certain hour, and we were fast approaching cut-off time. The question to be resolved was, do we go, or do we leave someone and/ or our bags behind?

'I don't think we can do this,' the pilot announced. The next moment my father had whipped out a propelling pencil and was busy scribbling numbers on a grubby scrap of paper on which he'd written my split times. Occasionally, he would look up, peer through his classes, judge the length of the runway, or some other triangula-tion, then jot something down again. I knew that this was a calculation way beyond O-level maths . . .

'Look, we have to make a decision,' I said.

'We'll go.'

Wendy was her usual chirpy self, talking about getting back in time for dinner. However, Peter Wirz – in normal life an aeronauti-cal engineer who had done his national service flying helicopters – was looking distinctly pale.

'You'd better get this right, Dad,' I said.

Just as on the way down, I was shoehorned into the front seat. The pilot set off down the runway, then taxied round to prepare for take-off.

'Stop!' my dad said. 'Back her up!' From the little I could see, we were eight metres from where airstrip became alpine meadow. So the pilot moved off, turned around and backed up. 'No, further back,' Dad said. 'As far as you can go.' God alone knows what the margin of this decision must have been. I remember sitting there, hurtling towards a mountain covered with fir trees and thinking, 'If he doesn't lift this plane up . . .' But he did, though I have to admit that my heart was in my mouth as we powered down the tarmac towards this cliff.

'Ja, Ja! We done it!' our pilot shouted triumphantly as, finally airborne, the plane swerved violently over the lake, then swooped upwards hugging the mountains all the way to St Moritz. As for the view, I wasn't really in sight-seeing mode.

'You would all do me a great honour to dine with me tonight,' the pilot said once we'd landed. I explained that I needed to sleep and that a big training day lay ahead.

'So tomorrow then. The restaurant is very close with beautiful view. It will be an honour to cook for you.'

Cook for us?

'Flying planes is only my hobby,' he said. 'I am really a chef!'

Although I had won the Rapperswil 1500m convincingly, I was soon fighting off another cold, which, according to Andreas – a man of the mountains – was the result of not having worn a jumper to warm down. Whatever the reason, I was now in a no-win situation. If I pulled out of the trials in Birmingham on 8 August, I would be accused of being a prima donna or ducking the selectors, and if I ran, I knew what lay ahead.

On the morning of the meet I drove across to Birmingham from

Loughborough. I lasted one race. I was in trouble the moment I started. I could barely breathe and trailed home fifth. Eliminated.

Based on these trials, Steve Cram and Tom McKean took the first two places for Seoul in the 800m. For the 1500m it was Peter Elliott and Steve Crabb, a local boy from Enfield. That left the two discretionary places. For the 800m, it was me or Peter Elliott. For the 1500m, me or Steve Cram.

People are inclined to remember most clearly what they have just seen, and the selectors – and more importantly the council – had just seen me lose. Yet over my last four races at 800m I had lost once, in Lausanne where Bile had beaten me by half a stride and Paul Ereng came seventh. Ereng was the Kenyan who would go on to take gold in Seoul.

Back in Loughborough, I had a call arranged with Mike Turner, one of the selectors, a former cross-country runner and Cambridge blue. The selectors wanted clarification on my health, he said. I told him that I knew I had run like a sewer but that I had a bad cold.

'I guess I'll feel better in the next few days,' I concluded.

'Well, don't push it,' he said. 'I see no reason why we should leave you out of the team. But it would probably do no harm to show everyone when you're back to fitness.'

The next morning I went to see Malcolm Read, the team doctor who was based in a hospital in Guildford. Dave Martin said he would come with me. By the time we set off I knew that I'd been unanimously selected for the 800m and that two of the six thought I could do both distances and should be given time to prove my fitness for the 1500m.

There were six selectors – Frank Dick, the chief national coach, Andy Norman and four former team managers, Mike Turner being one of them. Their recommendation would now go through to the general council who were meeting a couple of days later.

The general council consisted of about twenty-five people made up of area reps – Scotland, Northern Ireland, southern counties and so on – athletes reps and women's reps. It was chaired by Euan Murray, then chairman of the British Amateur Athletics Board, who had also chaired the selection committee.

The council's job was to ratify the decision of the selectors. Everything duly went through on the nod – except mine. I heard what happened from Frank Dick, who was sitting in. 'I suddenly sensed things weren't going our way,' he told me. Apparently, the debate wasn't limited to my fitness, or ability to perform, but included such comments as, 'Have you seen the size of the house he lives in?' this referring to a near ruin that I had brought back from the brink of demolition. Basically, this was payback time. A pathology was at work that you would probably never get to the bottom of. A few people went through the entrails of the decision a week later, and in their view the chairman's fatal error was in not closing down the debate when it veered into personal territory. Instead of using the power of the chair – and Euan Murray was a powerful chairman – to drive it through, he put it to the vote. You might as well be in the casino. By one vote I stayed at home.

Meanwhile, down in Guildford, Malcolm Read decided that I had a common-or-garden cold, which warranted no medication. He said I could start gentle running a few days later. Dave Martin, who had come with me, was in complete agreement, but as we left he admitted he was completely stunned by the decrepitude of the hospital. He and I were nattering on when I turned on the car radio for the sports news. I was in the outside lane of the A3 somewhere around Cobham. 'Sebastian Coe's international career is over. It has just been announced that the four-time Olympic medallist and world-record holder will not be going to Seoul . . .'

During the days that followed there was a generalised public outcry, which eventually became focused in a COE MUST GO CAMPAIGN led by the *Daily Mirror*, the same newspaper that was campaigning against me four years previously. It was a nice thought but basically futile since their opprobrium was wrongly aimed at the selectors. In fact, their vote was six to zero to let me go. What did for me was the collection of local councillors. At one point, Samaranch himself became involved, attempting to make me a special case, a wildcard entry in order that I could defend my title, but that too failed. It would have set a precedent that nobody wanted. Coe would not go.

The 1500m final in Seoul that September was won by Kenyan Peter Rono. Peter Elliott took silver and Steve Cram finished fourth. As for the 800m, there were no British finalists. Steve Crabb was eliminated in his semi. Cram was knocked out in his heat, as was Tom McKean. The gold was won by Paul Ereng, the Kenyan I'd beaten in Lausanne six weeks earlier.

The main argument in the press focused on my 'right' to defend my Olympic title. There is no such right, nor was that my gripe. As a patriot and somebody passionate about his sport, I simply believed that I had the best chance of any British athlete of coming home with a gold medal at either of my two distances. I had not spent the last two years in solitary confinement. I'd been in Rome and seen the best that Britain had to offer. I knew all these runners personally. I knew their strengths and their weaknesses. Nor was it simply my view or my father's view. It was also the view of a large number of the very people who could have fought for my inclusion.

So why did it happen?

First: the first-two-past-the-post system of selection. On the day, nine weeks before the first heat, I happened to have a cold.

Second: my age. I was 31, about to be 32, and was thought to be over the hill. The reality was that nobody knew. We were the first generation with the financial freedom to continue to run beyond our late twenties. My training programme was designed around a sophisticated physiological profiling that few athletes, if any, in the past had access to.

Third: the view that a vote for me would be a vote for sentiment not reason.

Fourth: the view that three bites of the cherry was simply not British; somebody else should be given a chance. Also known as Buggin's Turn.

Fifth: nobody had ever done three in a row, so clearly I didn't stand a hope. Nobody had done two in row before I did it.

It seems inconceivable now that Steve Redgrave would have been passed over for selection in '92, having already won gold twice. Rowing is an extraordinarily demanding sport. In addition, in the run-up to Barcelona he was beset by ill health, yet he went on to take a third gold medal, and then another two after that, the last being Sydney in 2000. In 1992, had the selectors decided that he was either too run down or too old at 32, the world – forget the British – would have been denied one of the most inspirational careers the Olympic movement has ever seen.

What cannot be denied is that, when the board made their decision, I was off form because I had a cold. But I knew from my times in training that I was close to my Los Angeles level of fitness and all these could have been verified, if the council had chosen to do so, as indeed the six selectors had suggested. More to the point, if I hadn't believed that I had as good a chance of bringing home a medal as any other British runner, if not better, I would not have put myself up. I would not simply have gone for the ride.

Of course, there's the issue of allowing younger talent to come through; old war horses cannot be kept on simply for reasons of sentimentality or nostalgia. The Olympics is no respecter of past reputations. But while a young athlete would be happy just to compete, get the letter from the Duke of Edinburgh and the uniform, this is not the case for an Olympic champion for whom anything less than a place on the podium would be seen as a failure. While there's a streak of madness in all élite athletes, no one but the seriously deranged would put themselves through the mill simply to run in an Olympic heat on the other side of the planet.

The reality is that experience counts. However focused, and however well trained, selection for your country doesn't equate to a place in the final, let alone on the rostrum. In the 800m, about 32 athletes run in the first round of heats, of which eight reach the final. In the 1500m, 52 athletes compete initially, of which 13 will reach the final. So out of 84 middle-distance runners, six will make it to the rostrum, and only a handful are in with a chance of being one of those six. And any bookie will tell you who they are.

There is one further factor in all this that cannot be ignored. My father and I had never been part of the inner circle of British track and field. Among the coaching fraternity, Peter Coe was a known maverick, and that was on a good day. He was a one-off, a man who didn't suffer fools gladly – a category that included many of those involved in the federation. I, too, was seen as an outsider. But anyone in Haringey would tell you that this was only half the picture. After training, we'd regularly head off to the local pub for a few beers and a laugh. I was able to compartmentalise. My mates were always nonplussed by the view of me as a loner.

Finally, in 1986 – recent history in 1988 – I had chaired the Sports Council's Review on Olympic Funding, which had concluded that track and field was already well provided for, with large sponsorships and a very healthy TV deal. We had concluded that athletics was not in need of that little bit of extra funding that the government had made available in preparation for Seoul, particularly when other sports were living a hand-to-mouth existence. While I had never openly expressed my own views on this subject, my chairmanship was sufficient to engender resentment and accusations of implicit disloyalty to my sport.

I was determined to make them acknowledge their error. So although 1989 would be my last year on the track and should have been a year of winding down – and I had made that decision long before Seoul – I would not go out with a whimper.

What the board had failed to recognise was that it wasn't for them to call time on my international career. They could call time on my ever wearing a British vest again, but for people such as Wilfried Meert in Brussels, Andreas Brugger in Zurich and Arne Haukvik in Oslo, I was still a proposition, a saleable commodity. It was they who would fix my sell-by date on the Grand Prix circuit. The federation had made it clear that it was time for me to make way for the 'young lions' in the sport, athletes who needed their moment.

In some ways their decision was cathartic, a loosening of a strait-jacket. I was freed of all the baggage and could get back to the pure enjoyment of what I was doing. It gave me the freedom to return to cities I liked and spend time there, exploring, going to galleries and jazz clubs, and just hanging out rather than chasing back for some low-level national duty and badly run press conference.

I started the 1989 season in good fettle. In early June I went to Belgrade with Haringey – a never-to-be forgotten north-east-London-meets-Yugoslavia hooley. Rejection is a powerful motivator and I was running pretty well, finishing on top of the ranking lists at every distance, 800m, 1000m and 1500m.

Towards the end of June, I was sitting with Peter and Colin Hart over a mountain of ice cream at a pavement café in Rovereto near Lake Garda when we started talking about the remainder of the season. Given the races I had already done, it dawned on us that I had qualified for the 800m Commonwealth Games to be held in New Zealand the following January. It hadn't really been on my radar screen as I hadn't intended to pursue my career beyond the end of the season. But given it was there, it was suddenly worth thinking about. In terms of the 1500m, it would be the same scenario as the previous year, a de-facto trial at the AAA championships in Birmingham. The federation had foolishly announced that whoever won the trials would make the team. So if I did win, and given my rankings it wasn't beyond the bounds of possibility, I would force one of the Steves – Ovett or Cram – or Peter Elliott out of the field.

Even my old man baulked at this. 'You can't do that,' he said. To which I said, 'Why not? Let them sweat for a change.' I knew it would give the selectors a real headache and the idea of the council being made to pick up the phone, to force them to bring me back in, would be something to relish. Also I happened never to have won a AAA championship, and I knew I had every chance. The young lions were hardly cutting a swathe through the jungle, while the old lions were falling by the wayside. Steve Ovett had largely disappeared from the international scene, Steve Cram was struggling with his calf and Peter Elliott was paying the price for being pumped full of painkillers to get through Seoul. I entered both distances and kept it absolutely quiet until the last minute which one I would be doing. In fact, there was no need for me to run the 800m because I had already qualified, but there was huge pressure to keep me out of the 1500m, which naturally was like a red rag to a bull.

And then I got a phone call. It must have killed them to do it. 'Are you available for selection for the Europa Cup?' I entered the moral maze for about three tenths of a second and politely declined. It really didn't suit my plans, I told them. Instead, I ran on a lovely track in Viareggio on the Italian Riviera, buried in the pine forest, surrounded by great restaurants. Two weeks later I was in Birmingham.

The occasion – the 100th anniversary of the AAA championships – was given an added twist in that Steve Ovett had put his hat in the ring. It would be the first time that he and I had ever run against each other on an English track. We had both come a long way since those days when we had divided the country's loyalties. I had grown to like Steve enormously. He had been totally supportive during the Seoul selection fiasco and was definitely one of the good guys.

On the afternoon of the heats I drove across from Loughborough and was just warming up with Sean Butler. Steve was standing at the edge of the track with Rachel talking to Harry his coach. I jogged past and waved cheerily.

'How times have changed!' I called out. Rather urgently, he waved me over. 'Catch you later,' I said.

'I need to speak to you now. It's really important,' he said, coming alongside. 'There's some dodgy business going on.'

'You know me, Steve. If there's any dodgy business, count me in!'

'I'm serious.'

'All right. But later.'

I didn't think any more about it until after my heat, then there he was again. This time on the edge of tears.

'I can't live with myself,' he said.

'What?'

'I've been paid to run against you.'

I was surprised. This was the AAAs and, like any national or international championship – the Europeans or the Olympics – money didn't come into it. But I wasn't about to let it concern me, not least because I didn't care.

'Just forget it, Steve. It doesn't matter.'

'But it's the principle. I've a good mind to drive home right now.'

'Now hold on. I don't think that would be a good idea. The press will murder you.'

'But you don't understand, they're paying me a lot of money.'

'I'm sure they are.'

'But they're just using us.'

'Forget it, Steve. I'm here for my own reasons. Really. I'll see you in the race tomorrow. Stop worrying about it.'

I walked away and hoped that would be that. But he was

determined to unburden himself, and the next morning I had a call from Colin Hart. Steve was now threatening to withdraw entirely, he told me, and ITV were going spare. What was my view?

'Look, Harty,' I said. 'As you know perfectly well, I race against people who are being paid all the time. I don't care if they've bought him a Lamborghini. I'm really relaxed, I don't have a problem. But if you see him, tell him I really think he should run. He can't pull out.' If he did, I thought, there was a fair chance we'd all be in for a lynching.

The worm at the centre of this particular canker was Andy Norman. Ever the showman, he knew that an Ovett–Coe head to head, the first on a home track, would be worth money, so he'd made a little investment. I would run anyway, he knew that. But Steve was a much less likely proposition, not least because he had by now moved up to 5000m. He had won the Commonwealth Games title in Edinburgh at this distance in '86, but at the World Championships in Rome the following year he finished way down the field.

By giving Steve the money in advance – and we're apparently talking somewhere in the region of £20,000 – Andy had guaranteed he would turn up. He had also implied – if not sworn blind – that I, too, was being paid. It was only when Steve had got to the track that he'd discovered that all was not as he'd been led to believe.

The race was scheduled for early evening, and the furore continued most of that day, with Steve still threatening not to run, and every last official and media schmoozer doing their best to persuade him otherwise. Steve is an emotional character at the best of times, and I have no doubt they were all battening down the hatches for the inevitable fallout. And with reason – the stadium was packed, not a seat to be had. Our 1500m had been billed all week on television as the final showdown between Steve and me and was the last race on the card. Not only had people paid good money at the turnstiles but ITV had no doubt sold broadcast rights on to the rest of the world. As for my participation, which rumour had it was now also in doubt, I told the organisers exactly what I had told Colin. That this race wasn't about money for me. All I wanted was to qualify for the Commonwealth Games. What had started over a convivial ice cream in northern Italy was rapidly turning into a Bombe Alaska in middle England.

Adding fuel to the already blazing fire, John Hovell was putting it about that, not only had I not been paid, but that I had actually paid to enter, flaunting the receipt for my £2.50 cheque to anyone who was interested. As I pointed out, 'John, this is not helpful.'

Somehow or other Steve was persuaded to run. In terms of a final showdown, with him and me battling it out to the finish line, the crowd would be disappointed. But drama they certainly got.

I was determined to leave nothing to chance and had quietly lined up Richie MacDonald, a training partner from Haringey who'd made the final and was also coached by John Hovell, to make the pace. So, as arranged, Richie headed straight to the front and I tucked in behind. Then just after the bell and with 450 metres to go, Steve Crabb, the guy who took my place in the 800m in Seoul, pulled out from somewhere behind me, but he cut in too soon. The heel of his shoe caught the guy behind him and Crabb went sprawling directly in front of me, spread-eagled across the track. I stumbled and was in danger of falling myself, while at the same time trying to avoid landing my spike plate full in his face. Somehow I hurdled over him, but by the time I regained control, I'd gone from lying second to eighth and was 15 metres adrift. Until the crash the pace had been slow, but then there was a rush for the front. I had no option but to go wide, kick and then blaze, passing first one, then a second, then a third, then a fourth. As I powered up the home straight, the crowd went wild. They might not have the duel they were expecting, but they had classic Coe being Coe, and I hit the front with 40 metres to spare.

My selection might have been secure, but the drama wasn't over. One guy was disqualified and while I was being interviewed on air about exactly what had happened, Steve was trackside in emotional turmoil, saying, 'They got me here on false pretences and lied to a lot of other people.' Upstaged to the end.

In the official AAA inquiry that followed this fiasco, Andy Norman denied offering financial inducements, although no one seriously believed that Steve had made it up. Inevitably, I was called as a witness, and at one point was asked to confirm our conversation before the heats.

'Would you say, Mr Coe, that the following is a faithful account of what passed between you and Mr Ovett on the afternoon of 12 August 1989. I quote: "If there is any dodgy business count me in?" ' I stifled a laugh.

'Well, yeah, but it was obviously a joke,' I said, and cast my eyes around the room for a show of support – a handful of lawyers, a stenographer, various big wheels, but not a twinkle in sight.

I have no doubt Steve felt he was doing the honourable thing in telling first me, and then the world about Andy's less-than-transparent offer, but racing is all about being strong mentally, and the whole sorry business clearly affected him, and affected him badly. I can't now remember where he came in the race, but it wasn't in the top five. I'm told it was ninth.

This was simply a naked attempt at putting bums on seats. Would Steve have taken me on without the incentive of the money? Andy Norman clearly didn't think so. He was the last person to throw cash around if he didn't have to, and he knew Steve as well as anyone did, although their relationship was already crumbling. But for Andy to ringmaster a Coe–Ovett clash was a prize he had always wanted, so this was his last-chance saloon. He knew it and he'd pay, no matter what the cost. And the cost was high. Steve Ovett never spoke to Andy Norman again.

I was one of the few who never fell out with Andy. The reason was simple – I was never commercially involved with him. While I accept that he was a rogue, if he was on your side, you'd never have wanted anyone else in your corner. Above all, he loved the sport and, for better or for worse, he was the architect of the most extraordinary era British athletics has ever seen.

In terms of my selection, this time there would be no debate. I would represent Britain in the Athletics World Cup in Barcelona and also at the Commonwealth Games, even though they were five months away.

I should have finished my career with a win at Barcelona, running 1500m. At the bell, after lying third for most of the race, I went to the front but was crowded by Bile to the point of obstruction. It cost me my rhythm, half a stride and gold. My father was as angry as I have ever seen him. Bile had form. He had been disqualified at Los Angeles for something similar in the semis. Against my wishes Team GB appealed, but it was never going to happen. It wasn't just Bile's reputation at stake. He was running for Africa and to remove nine points from the board would have been risking a diplomatic incident. And overall, what did it matter to Team GB who still came third, with Africa twelve points behind? More importantly, I didn't want my last race to be won in these circumstances and risk being accused of being prima-donna-ish. I'd rather come away with silver than a reinstatement.

As for the Commonwealth Games, after five glorious weeks spent acclimatising with Daley in the heat of Australia, and getting a couple of good local wins under my belt, New Zealand was dank and grey. And, yes, you've guessed it, the result was another cold. Saying nothing to my father and determined to run, I came fourth in my semi of the 800m. He claimed that it was all part of the game plan, that I was saving myself for a blistering final. It wasn't true. I came fifth. The team doctor advised me to pull out of the 1,500, but

I was still in two minds. I knew that whatever happened this would be my last race. The matter was finally settled when I was scratched by the team manager, which was undoubtedly the right decision.

A salutary story: ten years earlier, in August 1979 and flush with two world records, I was offered a lift to the finals of the Europa Cup in Turin. I was the hottest thing in town in terms of track and field, and press attention had arrived from out of nowhere like an avalanche and was threatening to engulf me. James Coote – bespectacled, knowledgeable and quirky – who covered athletics for the *Daily Telegraph*, told me, 'If you think this is bad, wait till you get to Turin!' There would be paparazzi everywhere, he told me. It was the first time I'd heard the word and I remember asking him what it meant.

In those days, you couldn't fly direct. You had to go via Milan and a coach had been lined up to take us the rest of the way, a couple of hours up the autostrada. 'Look here,' James said. 'I'm flying down. Why don't you come with me? It'll be fun!'

It was common knowledge that he had his own plane, and would regularly ferry people to and from Gateshead – a difficult place to get to in those days – where comments such as, 'Can anyone see the A1?' didn't exactly inspire confidence. But to a 22-year-old student from Loughborough, the idea of being piloted across the Alps in a little two-seater was about as exciting as it gets. This would rank among the great experiences of my life. But I was part of the British team, and the team manager put his foot down. 'This is not the time in your career to start doing this,' I was told. 'You travel with the rest of us.' So that was that. Dream over.

The reception in Milan was, if anything, worse than James had predicted and in Turin I had photographers crawling all over me. Then, on arrival at the hotel, Robert Stinson, who I had last seen in San Sebastian, told us to assemble in the courtyard for a team meeting as soon as we'd checked in.

'I'm afraid I have some bad news,' he said. 'Most of you will know James Coote, of the *Daily Telegraph* . . .' After refuelling in Geneva, he told us, James had filed his flight plan and taken off, with an unknown passenger, at 3.22 p.m. The weather forecast had been good – it was early August – and, although no one will ever know for certain what happened, it was thought that the plane had been caught in a localised storm and the pilot had become disorientated. The wreckage was found on the north side of Mont Jovet, exactly halfway between Geneva and Turin.

Athletics journalists travel as a pack. They live together, eat together, party together and they were then a pretty hardened bunch, but those who were there that day in Turin were more shaken than I ever saw them again. It's fair to say that my omission from the British team in 1988 pales into insignificance when compared to the loss of James Coote, and I can only be thankful that, in 1979, the team manager took the decision he did. As for the Alpine scenic route, as you now know I had a second chance, flying from St Moritz to Rapperswil and back again. But for the entire duration – both ways – all I could think of was James Coote and the waste of a good life.

15

SPRINGBOARDS

W<small>HATEVER</small> your particular sport, time at the top is always limited, although arguably my career lasted longer than most. In large part this was due to being coached by my old man with such care in the early years. Career longevity is predicated on not asking kids to do things too early, and thus building in the platform for injuries.

Thanks to the end of 'shamateurism', I had been able to earn a good living, even if in accounting terms I went into profit only around 1984. If viewed as a balance sheet, the greatest investors in an athlete's career are, of course, friends and family, both in cash terms and in time. On that assessment, most families rarely break even.

What to do when your competing days are over is a dilemma for any high-profile athlete. Setting off on a new trajectory in your thirties can be daunting, and success in one area of endeavour is no guarantee of success elsewhere. Sportsmen and women at the highest level have an inordinate ability to compartmentalise. At those times when things in the rest of your life are crashing down around your ankles, you learn to close the door. It's a great skill to have as a competitor, but once your career's over it's probably a hindrance. Being so focused in one area of activity often means you have bypassed some of the social skills, some of the relationship skills. And taking that attitude when you're out of competition – turning away or switching off when things aren't great – has undone more former athletes than I'd care to remember. The problem is nothing can ever replicate the rarefied air of the ten or twelve years spent on a rugby pitch, ice-rink or tennis court.

Over the course of my track career I would occasionally find myself in the commentary box, sharing thoughts and banter with the pros. Being reasonably articulate and not afraid of saying the unpalatable, a career in television might have seemed the obvious solution. There is always a demand for reasoned analysis by people who know what they're talking about – although most sports fans would argue that this doesn't appear to be an entry requirement. However, apart from the occasional foray, which was fun, over the long haul I knew it wasn't really for me. While I had never lost the sheer exhilaration of running, the weekends of cattle grids and five-bar gates were long gone. This was now how I earned my bread and butter and, once the season was over, I would take off a full calendar month when I wouldn't run at all. Taking a break from what was effectively my job was absolutely essential. While I would miss the physical pleasure, I was never gagging to get back to competition.

I was less likely to be found reading athletics magazines, for example, than biographies of American politicians, although my interests were rather more catholic than this would suggest. On the day I broke my second world record – the Golden Mile in Oslo – I passed the time before the race immersed in Chairman Mao's *Little Red Book* and found it vastly entertaining.

I'd known I'd be involved in politics one way or another for as long as I could remember. Growing up in Yorkshire in the seventies had both sharpened my focus and thickened my skin – being a Conservative in Sheffield was like being a Liberal in Shanghai. As for my admiration for Margaret Thatcher, friends were simply baffled.

Once I started breaking records, Conservative central office had been quick to seek my support, my political affiliation being known from my time as treasurer in Loughborough. But although Margaret was in many ways my lodestar, I knew that sport and politics were two very difficult bicycles to ride at the same time and I didn't propose to try. Any suggestion that I was using sport to further my political aspirations, or vice versa, had to be avoided. Just before the election in1983, Downing Street approached me again and again I said no. Not that Margaret Thatcher had any need of my endorsement by then. After a tricky first few years, her government was basking in the afterglow of the Falklands War and was returned for a second term with a vastly increased majority. She had a clear mandate for the radical reforms of her tenure, namely union reform and the move from public to private ownership, neither of which had really featured in the 1979 manifesto.

Around that time I did, however, accept an invitation to join the UK Sports Council, although I believe this was largely on the back of my appointment to the IOC Athletics Commission – and specifically the Baden-Baden speech, which had garnered wide coverage – rather than any party-political nod. The Sports Council was established by Harold Wilson in 1966 and was the first attempt by government to become formally involved with sport, and the result had been a frenzy of local-authority investment in the new concept of leisure centres in pursuit of 'sport for all'. Sadly, by the time of my appointment, the council had probably seen its best days, and it had become a rather bureaucratic, flat-footed organisation.

It was what was known as a quango – a quasi-autonomous non-governmental organisation – a body that carried out executive functions on behalf of the state, but at arm's length. It operated like the Arts Council, in that individual sports would apply for government funding, but selection and disbursement was handled by the council. We'd moved a long way from a junior minister in the department of education doling out a few quid here and there, *ad hoc* and not particularly well targeted. The council's remit was countrywide, and covered all levels of sport from the management of local-authority playing fields to the training of national coaches. Initially, my involvement was limited, but in 1986 I was appointed deputy chairman – and this was a political appointment – having demonstrated that I was both willing and genuinely interested in addressing the problems faced by sport in Britain. I had earned my spurs by chairing the Olympic review that had earned me the opprobrium of my federation. The then sports minister, Neil Macfarlane, had approached me in the village in Los Angeles. Although we'd had a reasonable showing, many sports were performing below par and the penny had finally dropped that this was as much to do with funding as anything else. Before embarking on something so time-consuming – he was talking about a six-month/year review – I had to know he was serious. Although I always believed he was on the side of the good guys, I wanted an assurance that this would go further than a feel-good press release, and that he would guarantee new money for Olympic sports, specifically targeted to the federations. He did better than that. When I told him I didn't want to be lumbered with the great and the good who would fight their own corner only, he suggested I appoint my own committee.

I knew this had to live beyond Whitehall. The economic case had to be watertight and cogently argued. I needed to include people from outside sport. To this end, I asked John Rodda of the *Guardian*, and got Vic Feather, General Chairman of the TUC, and Sir Terence Beckett, Director General of the CBI, to endorse the report. It wasn't enough to say, 'We want this money because it's sport.' All government departments were having to make difficult spending decisions and only the best arguments would cut through. Politics was then an arena of scarce resources. Above that, we needed strong stories to capture the imagination of tabloid editors. We found plenty. We interviewed competitors from all the Olympic sports. There were unemployed boxers from Liverpool who had had their benefits removed when they competed for their country in Los Angeles, because they were deemed to be on holiday. The wrestling team had to buy their own kit. John Rodda's presence on the committee ensured that these human-interest stories were given the focus they deserved. In the end, Neil Macfarlane was as good as his word – as was his successor Richard Tracey – and funding was secured. On the back of that, my chairman, Sir John Smith, chairman of Liverpool FC, persuaded a big insurance company in the city to match the government's contribution.

By today's standards, specifically the National Lottery, this was relatively small beer, but the £5 million that we were able to inject between 1986 and 1988 did make an appreciable difference in some key areas. An obvious example is hockey, which was organised into a GB team rather than the national groupings competing separately. But this was not just a carrot approach. There was stick and we were tough about it. The result was that, under the visionary leadership of Roger Self, who I got to know well in the village at LA, and the goal-scoring phenomenon Sean Kerly, bronze in Los Angeles became gold in Seoul. In many respects this was a very early precursor of the UK world-class programme now. You fund specific sports, you demand changes in corporate governance and changes in coaching structure, which Sue Campbell and Peter Keen have so admirably overseen. It all came to such obvious and delightful fruition for Team GB in Beijing.

One sport that did not get additional funding, of course, was track and field, and I have no doubt that it was this decision that led to my undoing, leading ultimately to my exclusion from Seoul.

In 1987 Margaret Thatcher appointed the first true sportsman to the office of minister for sport. Colin Moynihan was a double blue, in rowing and boxing, having coxed the Oxford crew to victory in the boat race in 1977, and competed against Cambridge in the bantamweight division. Famously, Colin had been one of those who, like me, had flouted government wishes in 1980 and competed in Moscow. He was the cox of the British crew who took silver in the eights.

We were both keenly aware of the damaging role of drugs in sport and in 1987 the Sports Council published 'The Misuse of Drugs in Sport', a report that he and I co-authored. In this, I reiterated the view, first articulated in Baden-Baden, that drug abusers should be banned for life and should on no account be allowed to represent our country. The report also highlighted the need for consistency in the lists of banned drugs and sanctions.

Following on from this report, I was appointed as a member of the IOC's medical commission, dealing with much the same issues but on a global scale. Crucially, our report introduced the concept of independent, random, out-of-competition drug testing, which would became the blueprint for today's system worldwide.

In 1989, on the retirement of Sir John Smith, Colin asked me to take over chairmanship of the Sports Council, but I declined. I was still only 33 and the energy I had formerly expended on the track needed an outlet that challenged me beyond the sporting arena. I felt I had probably done as much there as I could. More than thirty years after it was set up, there was still no coherent national policy for sport in Britain, and neither the office nor the organisation had the clout needed to change the presiding culture. It had simply run out of steam. But I had learnt a lot. I had become familiar with the machinery of government and, when I was making the case for greater funding in sport, I had recognised that there were buttons to press and buttons to leave well alone. In the end, supporter though I was of Margaret Thatcher, I tend to agree with Chris Brasher's view that she never really understood sport until it migrated – and sometimes mutated – beyond the back page, or impacted on other areas of policy.

I wasn't the first athlete with ambitions to enter mainstream politics. The obvious template was Chris Chataway, who sat as a Conservative MP, first for Lewisham and then Chichester, and went on to become paymaster general under Ted Heath. Although most famous for having helped Roger Bannister to the first sub-four-minute mile, he was a formidable athlete in his own right and took gold in the three-mile race in the 1954 Commonwealth Games in Vancouver. In athletic circles he is best remembered for his titanic battle under the floodlights of White City against the Soviet Union's Vladimir Kuts in 1954. This was London v. Moscow where, true to form, the Russians took the vast majority of the medals. An exception was Ron Pickering's wife Jean Desforges, who won the long jump.

When it came to the 5000m, from the field of four, Kuts led from the start. But while the other two were soon nowhere to be seen, Chataway never let the Russian have daylight and in the last few strides inched passed him to take both the tape and a new world record. The race was broadcast live, and was a taster of the power that TV would exert on the public perception; six months later Chris Chataway became the first winner of the BBC Sports Personality of the Year, even though the previous June it was Roger Bannister who had run a mile in under four minutes. That hadn't been televised.

Television was also Chris Chataway's springboard into politics. Having read philosophy, politics and economics (PPE) at Oxford, he turned down any number of sports-related programmes before signing with ITN, Independent Television's news channel, later working on BBC's flagship current affairs programme *Panorama*.

Over the years I had got to know all three of the country's most famous middle-distance runners. By the time I met him, Roger Bannister was an eminent neuroscientist and Master of Pembroke College, Oxford, a gentle, subtle, enquiring man. After my mile world record in Oslo, he had posted me a tie, the last of a series he'd had made to commemorate his 1954 run, and which to my enduring shame I forgot to wear when he presented me with the BBC's Sportsview Personality of the Year award in December 1979. Chris Brasher, who won gold at the Melbourne Olympics in the 3000m steeplechase, became the *éminence grise* of athletics journalism, writing pithy and perceptive prose for the *Observer* – and of course he was the author of the famous ten-page epistle that had helped stiffen the sinews after my defeat in Moscow. Of the three, Chris Chataway was the one you'd have built a party around – a languid, laid back and very funny man.

He was far from being a conventional Tory. His maiden speech, which by tradition is supposed to be non-confrontational, was on South Africa, and his hope that the English cricket team would refuse to play under apartheid. That was in 1959. Thirty years on little had changed; South Africa and cricket was still an issue.

The first time I came across racism was at the side of a track somewhere in Yorkshire when I was about 15. Suddenly, I was aware of a rumpus behind me, and a voice shouted out, 'Either you shut up or you leave.' Some Neanderthal had made a disparaging remark about a black athlete, and a group that included my parents had heard him and taken exception. The next thing he was being physically bundled out, with, 'You're watching the wrong sport, pal. We don't do that here.'

The great thing about track and field is that it's totally inclusive. Thanks to the diversity of the sport, the colour of your skin has never been an issue. There has never been the need for a campaign such as 'Kick Racism out of Football'. By the time I was competing internationally, half the British team were black and you didn't even think about it. At Haringey it was the same. Certainly, in track and field we never had any of those bizarre conversations that took place in football in the 1970s, along the lines that black players either hadn't got the right physiology or were congenitally incapable of learning the skills. Thankfully, the 'you need white working-class grit to play football' mentality has long gone, and with a vengeance. Look where black players are now.

That experience in Yorkshire when I was still a kid taught me that silence is far from golden. Many years later I was watching a rugby match in Redruth in Cornwall. Hertfordshire were the visitors and they had a black player on the wing, and then it started – monkey noises that were picked up by a section of the crowd. I remember thinking, 'Jesus, I cannot believe this.' The group I was standing with was as shocked as I was, but far too many people were treating it as something to be shrugged off. The moment the match was finished I made straight for the changing room to look for the player and apologise, but found one of the coaches instead. There was little I could say beyond, 'Please don't believe that this is the majority view in this ground.' But unless people are prepared to counter this kind of boorish behaviour, it will go on.

Pierre de Coubertin, founder of the modern Olympic movement, held as a basic tenet that racial distinctions should not play a role in sport, and in 1964 the IOC banned South Africa from competing in the Olympic Games. In 1977, the Gleneagles Agreement imposed an international boycott that included cricket and rugby, both with enormous cultural significance in South Africa. New Zealand, however, defied the ban, which resulted in African nations boycotting the Montreal Olympics in 1976. The Commonwealth Games in Edinburgh in 1986 were similarly affected, although this time the boycott was in response to Margaret Thatcher's refusal to impose economic sanctions against the overwhelming wishes of the Commonwealth, of which Britain is only one member, albeit then the most economically important.

This issue was still very much alive when I led a delegation of the Sports Council on a fact-finding tour to South Africa in early 1989. During the visit, we spoke to both sides of the divide, from Helen

Suzman and other representatives of the liberal opposition in Cape Town, to government ministers in Pretoria, including F.W. de Klerk, head of the National Party and leader of the so-called 'enlightened' group, who would eventually oversee the end to racial segregation. You could sense they all knew that the current situation was untenable and that things had to change. In fact, of course, change was closer than any of us imagined.

It was in this uncertain climate that a rebel 'England' cricket tour was announced, to be led by Mike Gatting, who'd been England captain between 1986 and 1988, and who was thus very high profile. A number of such tours had taken place in the eighties, starting with an England team captained by Graham Gooch in 1982, which resulted in three-year bans for all concerned and ended the careers of several international players, including Geoffrey Boycott. Next came a tour by Sri Lanka. This, too, was denounced. In '83 and '84 came two West Indian tours, made up of players who couldn't find a place in the then world-beating West Indian side, all of whom were ostracised. Two rogue Australian tours followed in the mid-eighties, the teams described by the Australian prime minister as 'traitors'.

This latest boycott-breaking tour was announced during the Fourth Test of the 1989 Ashes series at Old Trafford in August. Six weeks later, on 15 September, I ran my last race on English soil, an 800m at Crystal Palace. That morning there had been a press conference at which it was announced that I would be competing in the Commonwealth Games in Auckland, at both distances. As ever at these events, you do not choose the questions and given I had recently visited South Africa, a question on my views on the proposed cricket tour was perhaps not unexpected. I should have been prepared.

I found myself in a very uncomfortable position, not least because one of the names behind the tour was Ian Botham, who I liked to think of as a friend. Yet having seen for myself how things were moving in South Africa, I knew that this was the last thing the reformists needed because, with not a black player in sight, it would appear to condone the status quo. Having by then already stepped down from the Sports Council, I felt under no constraint to stay silent, so I said my piece.

Although Botham was not in the side, he took great exception to what he saw as unwarranted meddling in something that didn't concern me. Sadly, I was never able to discuss it with him face to face. At the time when it might have done some good, Ian and I weren't talking, and it was several years before the rift in our friendship was repaired.

My argument was never with Botham himself, who I admire enormously. At his best, he was one of the most exciting players I have ever watched, and as outspoken as anyone in his support of black players, not least Viv Richards. For him, this was not about money, either. He and the other cricketers involved genuinely believed that these tours would help open things up, whereas it was my firm belief that they wouldn't. Looking back, I think that the boycott lasted marginally longer than it should have done, and that had British sport responded earlier to the iniquities of the South African system and taken a more proactive role, it might have advanced the process.

As it was, the tour went ahead but proved financially disastrous when it was overtaken by history, coinciding with the release of Nelson Mandela and the 'un-banning' of the ANC.

At that stage I had no idea how the selection process for a prospective Conservative candidate might work. Biographies of political luminaries tended to skate over such mundanities, and I obviously had to be careful in whom to confide. In those circumstances, there is something to be said for going to the top. If the response was incredulous laughter, I had reason to hope it wouldn't go any further.

I first met Cecil Parkinson when he was chairman of the Sports Aid foundation. As a more-than-useful runner, he was probably the first of his political generation inside the Conservative Party really to understand the role that sport played in people's lives. As for my aspiration to enter parliament, he couldn't have been more encouraging. I was exactly the kind of young person the party hoped to attract, and he would be very happy to sign my nomination papers.

My political career began in a Holiday Inn in Slough. There were about thirty of us, all would-be candidates to be vetted by a group of Tory grandees headed by Sir George Young. In addition to general chat, where the idea was to be interesting without hogging the conversation, there was a written test and a quasi debate. For the first, we were presented with the political dilemma faced by a constituency MP, surrounding a planning application. For the second, we were given a controversial subject to defend. Luckily, mine was that old chestnut, boxing. It could have come gift-wrapped. I've been hooked on boxing ever since I was a kid. I had started watching initially just because my dad did, in the days when heavyweight boxing's top fighters included Jo Frazier and Muhammad Ali, or Cassius Clay as he was then, and of course Henry Cooper. I don't think there was a fight of his that I missed, narrated, inevitably, by Harry Carpenter. I'd loved the drama of it all, the sheer grandiosity. As the proud possessor of an Ever Ready Sky Baby transistor radio, when I wasn't searching the airwaves for jazz programmes from Holland, I'd be listening to championship boxing wherever I could find it. It might seem paradoxical, but it made great radio! Later boxing would be the glue that cemented my friendship with Colin Hart, whose passion for the sport is contagious, his knowledge inexhaustible.

Once I'd been approved as a candidate, I presented myself at Conservative central office to discuss 'vacancies'. It proved an odd meeting. A vice-chairman of the party with responsibility for these things reached down, pulled a Rolodex from beneath his desk and extracted a card.

'Take this one, for example,' he said. 'David Mudd, the current MP, is standing down at the next election. He's fallen out of love with the prime minister. Of course,' he added, 'you won't get selected.'

I looked at the card he had just passed me. Falmouth and Camborne.

'That's Cornwall.' I said.

'My point exactly. You're not a Cornishman, so you won't have a cat in hell's chance of getting it. Probably won't even make the long list. But it'll be good experience. You could consider it a trial run.'

'How many people do you think will be going for it?'

'Oh quite a few, there always are. But it won't be everyone's cup of tea.'

The more I thought about it, the more appealing it sounded. Firstly, as deputy chair of the Sports Council, I'd also chaired the council's regional meetings and had particularly enjoyed my visits to the south west. And there was a streak of bloody-mindedness in Cornwall, which felt distinctly familiar. Secondly, I felt it might suit my unusual background. Many MPs embarked on the road to Westminster after a stint in local government or as one of the many special advisors to a minister or department. Either way, they knew the system backwards and would avoid somewhere like Falmouth and Camborne, which offered little security of tenure. Being an MP in a marginal, you spend your entire time looking over your shoulder, wondering whether your career will be extended or if you'll get booted out at the next election.

That suited me fine. The last thing I wanted was to be accused of preferential treatment, and the idea of being winched into somewhere with a rock-solid majority, such as Kensington and Chelsea, filled me with horror. I had not forgotten the dire days of the early eighties during the miners' strike when I'd had to listen to well-heeled Sloanes sounding off about how it was about them and us. When news came through of pitched battles between the police and pickets at the coking plants, I would feel distinctly queasy. I had no sympathy with the miners' union leadership – Arthur Scargill had led the most short-sighted, ham-fisted strike imaginable, allowing the government to stockpile coal and thus keep the power stations going. But also I knew this landscape. Friends of mine, members of the Hallamshire who I used to run with, came from mining communities. What was happening was no fault of theirs, and yet they were bearing the brunt. Many of my early races were on running tracks owned by the Miners' Welfare, in places such as Hickleton Main Colliery, Worksop, Doncaster, Barnsley, tracks and clubhouses were all maintained by union funding. When the pits closed, local authorities couldn't afford to keep the facilities going and that was that. It had a profound impact.

I remember being at a party once, full of just the kind of braying Sloanes I loathed. The conversation turned to how great it was watching the miners getting hammered every night on the news. 'You have no idea what life in these communities is like, have you? No idea.' And I left.

My first visit to the constituency was incognito, or as incognito as I could manage. I wanted to get a feel of the place, to know where I was going. I spent two days going from café to pub, pub to café, reading a local newspaper or jazz magazine, nursing a coffee or a pint, just listening to the conversations going around me. Of course, this method had its complications. Inevitably, someone would say, 'Aren't you . . . ?' But at least it enabled me to get talking to people.

Falmouth and Camborne, one of six Cornish constituencies, was the closest you got to an industrial seat in the county, and it resembled south Yorkshire in that it was a region in decline. The areas around Redruth and Camborne still bore the scars of the once lucrative tin-mining industry, while in Falmouth, which has one of the finest deep-water harbours in the world, the ship repair industry was under threat after being the town's main employer for many years. I would ask people what their biggest challenges were, what they felt about their children's schools. Then there was the issue of Spanish and Portuguese trawlers plundering local fish stocks. Ted Heath's name was often mentioned, but never politely. They never forgave him for signing the European Treaty in 1972.

Over the years I would do that journey down to Cornwall literally hundreds of times, by road, by rail, by air. It was a long journey, whatever mode of transport you took. Whether, in hindsight, I was sensible to choose somewhere that took five hours to drive to is a moot point.

The letter asking me to attend a preliminary selection interview should have given me cause for celebration. Instead, my heart sank. The date I'd been given was Friday, 8 September – the weekend of the athletics World Cup in Barcelona. I called the constituency agent and basically said, 'Would it be OK if I delayed the interview because I've got international commitments that weekend?'

'What "international commitments" might those be?' the agent asked, making sure I heard the inverted commas.

'Well, actually, I'm competing for Britain in the athletics World Cup in Barcelona.'

I was offered the Sunday morning slot at 9.00 a.m. the following weekend. (I was later told that the only reason they agreed to this postponement was that a couple on the selection committee had promised to get my autograph for their grandchildren.)

In all, there were three rounds of interviews. The content wasn't as foreign to me as it might at first seem. My degree was in economics and social history, and much of my work with the Sports Council had been about understanding how sport fitted into local communities and making the right political arguments. But I also knew that telling them how to run things wouldn't make me any friends. We were down to the final eight when I was asked a question that I'd guessed would at some point come up, although the form of it surprised me.

'The life of a constituency MP is a fairly lonely business,' this home-counties émigré began. 'It's long hours and, to be honest, pretty thankless, and it's always useful to have support.'

'I'm sure it is,' I said, smiling and nodding.

'So my question is this,' the old boy continued. 'Do you have a doxy in tow?' I had to laugh. The only person I had heard use this word was my father when he was being skittish. It is pre-Shakespearean, and can mean anything from prostitute to paramour.

'To put it another way,' he elucidated, 'is there any likelihood of a Mrs Coe at some stage?' Ah.

'The short answer is that I don't know,' I said. 'However, let me answer the question I think you're really asking. I think you're asking whether I'm gay. And, no, I'm not. But I'm really not sure it would have any bearing on my ability to do the job if I were.' As I heard the words coming out of my mouth, I thought, 'I'm done for here. And if they don't like the answer, then I am probably not what they're looking for.'

There was an awkward silence. And then a woman began to laugh and then another. The questioner himself was obviously taken aback at being shot like this between the eyes, but by then it was too late. The woman who broke the ice was Ann Peck, chair of the selection committee, but more importantly, scion of one of the two families – the Pecks and the Muirheads – who dominated Conservative politics in that part of the world. Alan Muirhead would become my chairman when we fought the election.

On each of my visits to Cornwall I'd been invited to stay by the chairman of the South West area of the Sports Council, Richard Sharp. In his time, he had played sublime rugby for England and Redruth, and was a local legend. He was such delightful company that he probably swayed me in my view of the constituency.

The role of the selection committee is not to choose the candidate but to narrow the selection down to something like a manageable number. The actual selection was made by the 150 or so who attended the final selection meeting at which we were all present, and which was open to all members of the constituency party. Each of the four shortlisted candidates was invited to spend a day with the agent. John Herd, from Plymouth, formerly with the Merchant Navy, had retired after he lost an eye in an accident at sea, and he was a seasoned and shrewd political operator. On the morning of my visit he picked me up at RAF St Mawgan outside Newquay airport. He was gruff to the point of being taciturn and I realised that the best I could hope for was a score draw. In the circumstances, he was probably right to be suspicious. But by the end of the day he had warmed up, having decided I was both more serious and less arrogant than he had been led to believe, and over the years we actually became good friends.

My fellow candidates included Bernard Jenkin, son of Lord Patrick Jenkin, who entered parliament in 1992 as the member for Colchester North and is still an MP, although in a different seat. Jacqui Lait went on to win Hastings and Rye and subsequently became the member for Beckenham, and a whip. None of us were Cornish, and from what I know now, any one of us could have got the nomination and done a first-rate job.

Harold Wilson famously said that a week is a long time in politics. As it turned out, in the two and a half years between selection and election, the pack of cards collapsed. I had always hoped that I might witness a Thatcher premiership as a constituency MP, but when Sir Geoffrey Howe resigned in November 1990, the writing was on the wall. My predecessor David Mudd – then still the sitting Member – was one of the first to signal it when he called on the prime minister to step down on *Newsnight*, backing Michael Heseltine for the leadership.

While Mrs Thatcher continued to have overwhelming support in the constituency parties, only MPs were eligible to vote in the leadership election and they, like David Mudd, had fallen out of love with her. When in April 1992, I took my seat in the House of Commons for the first time, the leader of the Conservative Party – and the prime minister – was John Major.

And I was a married man.

16

MUSICAL CHAIRS

GIRLS never held any particular mystery for me when I was growing up, not least because I had two sisters. They were simply a part of life, at home, at school, on the track. At Tapton, girls were generally considered a good influence. David Jackson always maintained that their presence had a civilising effect in the classroom, and at any hint of too much testosterone flying about, he'd move us to sit next to them. There was certainly no doubt that girls were keener on working than we were and academically considerably more advanced.

As far as romance was concerned, there were one or two in the class who you would think were attractive, but you never did anything about it. At the English Schools meets, with barely an adult in sight, it was the same. These were your mates, the people you hung out with. Nothing more than that.

I didn't have a girlfriend as such until I reached the sixth form at Abbeydale Grange. It was the early summer of 1974 and, probably not coincidentally, it was during my break from training following discovery of the stress fracture. Girls, I now knew, needed time, and under my normal training schedule, time was in short supply.

During the four years I spent at Loughborough, having a girlfriend was a key part of student life, and I behaved with as much care and consideration as most other young men of my age, which is to say I was pretty cavalier. Retribution wasn't far behind. From the moment in June 1979 when I broke my first world record, I only had to glance in the direction of a pretty face for a tabloid feeding frenzy to follow.

There was only so much hiding away you could do, and after a couple of 'kiss-and-tell' stories in the press – sample headline: COE YOU CAD, which, at the time, I considered a badge of honour – I decided it was easier not to bother. Occasionally, as happened with Irene Epple, I was able to start seeing someone beneath the media radar, but those particular circumstances were pretty unusual. Firstly, we met abroad behind the drawn curtains of the IOC, and secondly, she was German and thus of little interest to the largely parochial British press, and not around to be photographed.

Long-term, a relationship with Irene was never going to work, if only because of the logistics of our two sports. But in other respects we were extremely compatible. We both understood the pressures of competing at the highest level, and understood what it took out of you, physically and mentally. This not only helped us to relate to each other emotionally, it gave us an equality.

Marriage never featured on the agenda during my years on the track. While some of my fellow athletes did have wives – Steve Ovett and Dave Moorcroft both married quite young – another school of thought believed it simply wasn't possible to commit yourself to your sport if you had commitments at home.

I was under no pressure from either of my parents – no wistful references to grandchildren for example. As for my peer group, Malcolm Williams went through life with a series of girlfriends but no wife. Steve Mitchell, although he had a partner, was also legally single. The only close friends who had tied the knot were John and Jane Rowlinson. John, at that time, was a senior figure in BBC sport and Jane was a barrister. If I'd had any template for a successful marriage – apart from my parents – it was theirs. Their jobs were equally pressured but they operated successfully in entirely different spheres. To this day they remain among my closest friends and confidants.

I come from a family of extremely strong women, and the girls I was attracted to were cast in the same mould. Vera, my grandmother on my mother's side, had been a great beauty in her youth, and retained an aura of glamour into old age. Angela had this same quality, plus the element of mystery provided by her Indian parentage. Miranda, the elder of my two sisters, trained at the Royal Ballet School, danced for the Rambert and then – to no one's real dismay it has to be said – joined a troupe of showgirls and high-kicked her way across the world. Her public persona – Las Vegas, New York, Paris – was glamour personified, and many otherwise Alpha males of my acquaintance would be near speechless with awe when they met her.

My single long-term relationship had been with a young woman I met through John and Jane on New Year's Eve 1983. I had returned from my recce to Los Angeles convinced that I'd be fit enough to compete at both distances the following summer, and threw a party as a way of thanking everyone who'd been involved in getting me there, including numerous medics. That afternoon, Jane rang and asked if she could bring along a friend, a girl who'd recently broken up with her boyfriend and who was feeling a bit low. Naturally, I said yes. This was Jane Williams and she and I would be together off and on for the next five years.

It was the first time I had an insight into what life might be like if I shared it with someone else. Jane understood what made me tick. She knew instinctively when I needed company and when I needed to be on my own. Most importantly, she gave me confidence at a time when it had been severely dented. Like me at that juncture, she was wary. But she was there in Los Angeles, and also in Stuttgart when I won the much-coveted gold for the 800m two years later. There were complications, however. She was divorced and had a daughter, so logistically it wasn't easy. She also had her own career to consider, and while she seemed perfectly happy to go on as we were, with no commitments on either side, nonetheless a relationship needs the oxygen of change if it's not to stagnate.

In late 1988 my morale was at rock bottom. Being dropped from the British team for Seoul was the worst thing that had ever happened to me. Looked at objectively, my career had been a series of challenges. I'd had goals, and strategies to reach each one, including eliminating as far as was possible what my father called the variables, the things you had no control over. But the summer of the Seoul selection, there had simply been too many variables at work. Now, whatever happened or whatever else came my way, I would never stand on another Olympic rostrum, and this time Jane couldn't help. While the Games were on we had escaped from the hullabaloo by going to Sicily. She did her best, but my sense of futility was crippling. In the end, I was impossible to be with, moody, irritable and generally fairly unpleasant, although we remain good friends to this day.

By 1988 I was living in Twickenham in a beautiful 18th-century townhouse a few steps from the Thames. It had been a wreck when I'd rescued it, with six inches of water on the ground floor and the front wall bowed out several feet from the plane. Slowly, I'd put it back together, the work all done by guys I knew from the sport, through Haringey and weightlifting.

From a training perspective it was perfect. I would fall out of my front door and within seconds I'd be on the towpath. Then I'd run east under Richmond Bridge to Isleworth; or head across the river into the Old Deer Park, or up Richmond Hill into the park itself – over 2000 acres so quiet you could be in the heart of the country.

Sometimes the only person I'd see all day was my younger sister Emma, who was then living with me. She had come down from Sheffield and was studying at Chelsea College of Art. I'd kitted out the top floor as a studio to encourage her to stick at it, while she waitressed in a restaurant round the corner in the evenings. At the time, I thought I was helping her, but now I realise that her presence – and the responsibility I felt towards her – kept me from really going under.

During those awful months, few people could stand my introspective company for very long, but one who did and who went out of her way to 'cheer me up' was Judy Stott who I had got to know when she worked for Mark McCormack's company IMG in the early eighties.

Mark McCormack was an American lawyer who pretty much invented sports sponsorship. He had started in the fifties representing pro golfers in the States; then when tennis went open, he took on tennis players as well. By the time athletes were given the green light in 1981, Mark McCormack was the most formidable game in town. However, I didn't allow IMG to intrude on my running. That remained in the hands of Andreas Brugger who by then was acting as my race manager. He, above anybody else, knew my current market value and when he sat down with other promoters, they knew there was little point in arguing. He never got involved in tortuous negotiations. He just gave them a figure and they acquiesced. But in terms of commercial interests outside racing, IMG was an essential buffer and a channel for the interest from abroad.

Judy never represented me herself, but she did act for Virginia Leng, one of Britain's élite riders. I'd met Ginny briefly in Los Angeles, along with other members of our equestrian team. They'd come second to the Americans in the three-day team event, while Ginny had come away with the individual bronze, a double that she repeated four years later in Seoul. Not that I understood what any of this meant back then. I just knew she was a big star in the equestrian world.

Sometime in the spring of 1989, Judy telephoned proposing a trip to the Cotswolds. Ginny was competing at Badminton, she said, and was on the cusp of winning.

'And you are not allowed to say no,' she insisted. 'You're becoming boring, Seb. You need to get out of London. Oh, and bring something you can change into for the evening. Ginny's based at her mother's a few miles away and we're invited for dinner.'

'Judy, I don't think I feel like a dinner party right now.'

'Don't be so pathetic. Her mother won't eat you and she's quite a character. Trust me. It'll be fun.'

That day would prove memorable for many reasons, not least as my introduction to a most extraordinary sport. The Badminton horse trials is one of two major events held in England, the other being Burghley, which takes place in the autumn at the ancestral home of David Cecil, Marquess of Exeter, Lord Burghley of hurdling fame. Three-day eventing is basically a triathlon of three individual disciplines: dressage, show jumping and cross-country. As a child I had caught the odd show-jumping programme on television, the patrician voice of Dorian Williams building up the tension, but I can't say it was required viewing in the Coe household. This was the first time I had seen horses and riders competing only yards in front of me. It was an eye opener. Three-day eventing is one of the rare sports in which men and women compete against each other as equals, and the sheer size of the jumps when you're standing near them is staggering. I'd had no idea just how gutsy these riders needed to be. I found it terrifying.

When I had trained in Chatsworth all those years ago, I could never understand why, in parkland otherwise immaculate, so many tree trunks had been left lying around. Logs like up-ended oaks seemed to have been simply dumped in the middle of nowhere. Only when I went to Badminton did I realise that what I'd seen was a cross-country eventing course.

That weekend, Ginny Leng added yet another trophy to her already impressive collection and the atmosphere was infectious. As for the dinner, Judy was right. Ginny's mother was a character, filling the room like a galleon under full sail, firing off her cannons one by one. Also there that evening was another eventer, Nicky McIrvine, vivacious, successful, glamorous. And, of course, that's who I was put next to.

Exactly a year after we'd first met, I was back to watch Nicky win the 1990 Badminton horse trials. At that moment of hesitation when rider and horse prepare to leap those impossible fences, your heart is always in your mouth, and not without reason. The previous year I'd been overwhelmed by the skill and physicality involved. This time I was aware of everything that had gone into getting there, not to mention the sheer danger, and I could hardly bear to look.

Nicky was tall and leggy with dark hair and a face that would break into spontaneous laughter – often at my jokes – and by the spring of 1990 I knew that in this quirky young woman I had found my future wife. All those old constraints about training and focus and commitment had disappeared.

Eventers are totally dependent on their horses and Nicky's were stabled on her parents' farm in Surrey, about thirty miles south of London on the North Downs. Horses are arguably more time-consuming than children; not only do they have to be fed, watered and mucked out, they have to be ridden. Living in Twickenham was clearly out of the question – Nicky had to ride out at 6.30 a.m. every morning – so the simplest thing was for me to move in with her.

At first we lived in a small bungalow on her parents' farm close to the stables. Then after we'd started thinking about setting up home permanently, the horses being the complicating factor, the farm manager decided to retire and move back to the west country. His role was taken by a contract farm manager. That left the old farmhouse empty. The solution was now obvious. We bought the farm from her parents and slowly began turning it into a family home.

Ranmore Farm ran alongside Ranmore Common, part of the Surrey Hills Area of Outstanding Natural Beauty, a landscape that has survived largely unscathed since it was used for pasturing sheep in the middle ages. I could run for miles along ancient droveways, across downland unchanged for centuries, looking out over the Weald with its scattered villages and isolated farms, without seeing another soul. Over the ten or more years I lived there I became very attached to this small corner of England, which explains why, when I was awarded a life peerage in 2000 and was told I needed a geographical title, I chose Baron Coe of Ranmore.

The moment I was selected as Conservative candidate for Falmouth and Camborne, I started looking for somewhere to live in the constituency. While there was no guarantee that I would win the seat, I would still need a foothold in the community, at least until the election, which was over two years away.

Stithians is a largely agricultural Cornish village built of rough-hewn granite and as typical as somewhere so individual can be. It had a pub (run, incidentally, by the former England rugby international Roger Hosen), a church, a chapel and a village shop. Most importantly, it was equidistant between the two coasts so that nobody could say I was favouring the south or the north. Sunny Corner Cottage gave us three bedrooms and a patch of garden that lived up to its name. It has to be said there are worse places to have a second home. Seven miles to the south lay Falmouth estuary with dozens of secluded inlets and beaches, while a dozen miles to the north was the surf-hammered expanse of Hayle sands.

John Major called a general election for 9 April 1992, a month earlier than expected. Conservatives had been in power since 1979 and the view from Fleet Street was that it was time for a change. Labour, led by Neil Kinnock, certainly seemed to think so. They were slowly jettisoning unwanted baggage and were no longer the dinosaur party of Michael Foot and CND. Margaret Thatcher might have gone, they crowed, but she had been neither forgotten nor forgiven by the electorate. Opinion polls seemed to agree, giving Labour the lead, but not by much.

In the west country the threat came not from Labour but from the Liberal Democrats, a merger of the former Liberal Party with what had been Labour's moderate wing, the SDLP, who had broken away from the Labour Party in 1981. There were no Labour-held seats in the south west until you got to the large conurbations of Plymouth and Exeter in Devon. A Labour victory across the country wouldn't necessarily mean that the Conservative vote wouldn't hold in Falmouth and Camborne, although an increase in the Labour vote would more likely eat into the Tory support than the Liberal Democrats, who already dominated at local-government level.

The constituency lay across the instep of Cornwall, the narrowest part of the British mainland. Only St Ives – another Tory marginal – was further south. Immediately to the north was Truro, a Lib Dem stronghold. The charismatic Liberal MP David Penhaligon had held the seat for twelve years and would probably still be there today had he not died in a tragic accident on 22 December 1986. He had been on his way to St Austell sorting office, keeping up the morale of staff busy with the last of the Christmas post – a tradition he started early on in his career and which Cornish MPs retain to this day. Halfway there his car was hit by a baker's van, which had skidded on ice, and he was killed instantly. He was 42. I met him a couple of times when I was in Cornwall on Sports Council business, and he was an exceptional man. Through appearances on TV he became one of the first celebrity politicians, known and admired far beyond his geographical and political constituency. His personal following was such that, in the by-election that followed his death, his 24-year-old assistant Matthew Taylor was elected with barely the loss of a vote. Matthew famously resigned when he became a father, saying that parliamentary life was incompatible with parenthood.

It's fair to say that on the campaign trail, one garden path is much like another, one village hall a mirror of the last. Some exchanges stick in your memory, however, and I remember clearly after one particular meeting a woman came up and said, 'It's not that I've got anything against you personally, Mr Coe, but I'm not going to vote for you because you're not a Cornishman and we don't like outsiders.' A good chunk of the room went quiet as I quickly decided that appeasement wasn't the answer.

'Well,' I said, 'I come from Yorkshire, a county where we don't much like each other, so I think I can cope down here.'

On the night of the general election, 9 April 1992, not only was there no certainty that I would win, it wasn't even clear there would still be a Conservative government in the morning. But there was, and while I retained the seat for the Conservatives with a majority of 3,267 over the Lib Dem candidate, the writing was on the wall. The majority bequeathed me by David Mudd was down by 1,500, the votes having transferred to the Labour Party. As a consequence, the constituency had become the tightest three-way split in the country. You did not need to be Bob Worcester, the doyen of pollsters, to forecast that the chances of retaining the seat at the next election were negligible.

Being a new MP is a bit like joining a huge corporation. No matter who you might have been in a former existence, you come in at the very lowest level.

On that first day, I ventured into the famous chamber with another fresh-faced newly elected Conservative MP, both of us turned out in smart suits and haircuts like new boys on the first day of school. We were marvelling at how much smaller the chamber is in real life than it appeared on television when a voice barked out from the Labour benches, 'Right, are you proper Tories or lily-livered Tories? Are you going to stand up to me?' With his red tie and tweed jacket, there was no mistaking Dennis Skinner, former miner and Labour MP since 1970. Tory-baiting was his hobby and over the next few weeks I got used to the constant – and at times, it has to be said, amusing – running commentary. One day, in the tea room after prime minister's questions, I said, 'You may not remember this, Dennis, but when I started out in athletics, you used to run the social club at one of the miners athletics associations. And you encouraged me to run in your meetings by suggesting there might be cash involved.'

'Did I do that?'

'Yes. So unless you want it generally known that you actively encouraged a youngster to stray from the amateur rules, I suggest you direct your energies away from me.' We both laughed.

My guide around both the building and the arcane rules and procedures of the Palace of Westminster was David Harris, who had been MP for St Ives, my next-door neighbour constituency, since 1983. He had already proved very helpful during my election campaign locally. We hadn't actually met before, but that first day he came up and introduced himself, as did Bob Hicks, who held South-East Cornwall, the last Cornish constituency before crossing into Devon. Both helped make my first few months in the House of Commons comprehensible, and to this day I remain grateful for the paternal role they played.

The issue that defined my term as an MP and beyond was Europe. In some constituencies the European question was little more than a philosophical argument. In Cornwall the situation was very different; a way of life that had existed for generations was in jeopardy. With trawlers tied up at the quayside – a direct result of allowing EU boats into UK territorial waters – it faced them every day of the week.

This was not an area I was familiar with, but luckily David Harris knew more about the nature and vicissitudes of the global fishing industry than any politician alive. Without the benefit of his patience and knowledge I would have been – and I fear the pun is inevitable here – completely at sea.

Traditionally, Labour had always been cast in the anti-European

Left: By 1990 I was already Conservative candidate for the Cornish constituency of Falmouth and Camborne. This iconic image with the Commons behind was taken for the launch of the Manchester bid to host the Olympic Games in 2000.

Above left: My 1992 election leaflet, published by John Herd the constituency agent.

Above right: Eating pasties is part of the political landscape, at least in Cornwall. There is no threshold of embarrassment for a constituency MP.

Below: Opening a new lager factory in Redruth, Cornwall. Would you vote for this man? In 1997, many people didn't.

As a government Whip I would regularly sit on the front bench in the chamber of the House of Commons, on this occasion at Parliamentary Questions with John Major with Michael Heseltine (*left*) Brian Mawhinney, then party chairman, with whom I would have further dealings during England's failed bid for the 2018 FIFA World Cup.

October 2000, with William Hague at the Conservative Party Conference in Bournemouth.

One of my jobs in the election campaign of 2001 was to prevent William being put into un-statesmanlike situations.

Meeting Nelson Mandela was an unforgettable moment.

Shaking hands with George Bush at the White House.

April 2004 at the launch of our bid for London 2012. With me, ranged right, are Tony Blair, Barbara Cassani and Tessa Jowell, all of whom played key roles.

This was taken immediately after I became chairman of the London 2012 Olympic bid, in our office in Canary Wharf.

27 June 2005. Setting off for Singapore with Keith Mills, the bid's CEO, a man of unmatched creative flair.

Resplendent in our London 2012 uniforms, Amber Charles and I are captured for posterity shortly after the vote in Singapore. The expression on our faces says it all.

Minutes after IOC president Jacques Rogge (*right*) announced the result to the waiting world, I shook his hand with more emotion than such a formal gesture usually evinces.

Above: Paul Deighton, LOCOG's CEO. Paul brought intellect, emotional intelligence and quiet humour.

Left: HM the Queen arrives at Holden Point, a sheltered housing tower block in West Ham, on top of which a viewing platform was built that offered a bird's eye view of the Olympic Park.

Below: The support of Ken Livingstone (*centre*), then mayor of London, was central to winning the bid. Here we are given a tour of the Olympic Park two and a half years before the start of the Beijing Games.

Left: Juan Antonio Samaranch was hugely influential in my career off the track, beginning in 1981 in Baden-Baden. Twenty-five years later we met in his home town of Barcelona, a city rejuvenated by the 1992 Olympic Games.

Below: 'Shakespeare!' 'Professor!' Thomas Bach – now vice president of the IOC. We co-wrote the athletes' manifesto at the IOC Congress in Baden-Baden, September 1981.

Below: The Duke of Edinburgh visited the Olympic stadium in 2010, two years before the opening ceremony. With us, to explain the technicalities, was chairman of the Olympic delivery authority, John Armitt.

Proud dad and proud children – with Pete, Harry and Maddy at Buckingham Palace after receiving my knighthood in May 2006.

A father and daughter moment with Alice at the World Junior Rowing Championships at Eton Dorney, Windsor, in August 2011.

role. It was a Conservative prime minister, Edward Heath, who had had signed the Treaty of Accession in 1972, taking Britain into the Common Market, as it was then called. Twenty years down the line, Brussels had become a dirty word; the promise of a united Europe was, at best, only a mirage it was claimed. Margaret Thatcher wrote in her memoirs that the atmosphere in Europe in which Britain had to operate had become 'increasingly alien and frequently poison-ous', and a small but vociferous group agreed with her, and indeed had her tacit support. In the House of Lords, she said, 'I could never have signed that treaty', describing it as 'a recipe for national suicide'.

These anti-European MPs were known as the Eurosceptics. The constant in-fighting they provoked was inevitably debilitating and provided a large part of the backdrop to the Tories losing the elec-tion in 1997. The focus of the Eurosceptics' fury was the Maastricht Treaty, which John Major had signed shortly before the election. This was the legislation that, above all, paved the way for the Euro – although he had negotiated an opt-out for Britain – and needed to be ratified by each member state.

John Major's problem was that the Maastricht rebels, as they became known, outnumbered his slim majority – twenty-one following the 1992 election. This gave them a power quite dispro-portionate to either their number or status. As an MP new to the House, I might have been forgiven for thinking that these few – Bill Cash, Teresa Gorman and Teddy Taylor among them – were the elder statesmen and grandees of the party, such was their influence. They were not. Until Maastricht they were all pretty anonymous, if a little quirky, but for a short period this handful of renegades would, from night to night, decide on the party's survival.

It was an exhausting time to be a backbench MP. Mostly, you were simply lobby fodder. The first thing I did when I arrived in the House each morning was to find the most comfortable chair in the library, preferably with a view over the Thames, and base myself there – that is assuming I had actually gone home the night before. The idea that I might be heading out of London by 10.30 p.m. was a pipe dream; you could be still going through the voting lobbies at four in the morning.

By the time of my first Queen's speech in October 1992, I had a wife and a baby – Maddy was born three months after I took my seat, and my maiden speech had to be delayed until October as a result. That drive from the House of Commons to Ranmore, down the A3 to the M25 and then across country for the last six miles, took fifty minutes – one side of a jazz tape – and on the last stretch I was more likely to see a fox than another car. I would do the journey three or four nights a week, depending on whether the Friday was a 'sitting' Friday, when meetings and debates take place as usual. If not, then I'd be heading west.

I held surgeries every Friday and Saturday, rotating between the four urban centres of the constituency: Falmouth, Penryn, Redruth and Camborne. Some weeks I'd go down on the sleeper, some days I'd take a flight out of Heathrow to Newquay on the old Brymon airways. Sometimes I would take the car, leaving at around 4.00 a.m. in time to be in my constituency by 10.00 a.m.

The idea that MPs of opposing parties are always at each other's throats is, of course, entirely fallacious. A case in point was the Penzance sleeper. The issue still comes up for debate every few years, and the most vociferous campaigners for its retention are west country MPs, of whom at least fifteen or twenty use it on a regular basis.

The Night Riviera, as it's called, would pull out of Paddington just before midnight, but we'd be let on at 11.00 p.m. The bar area would be open and, whatever our political hue, a dozen or more of us would sit down in front of family-sized whiskies and unwind before disappearing to our berths. We'd talk about cricket, about football, and sometimes about the quirkier aspects of our constituents. Raw politics were never discussed. Interestingly, some of my closest friendships were made across the party divide, not least because you're never in competition. You're not sitting there thinking, 'Same intake, bit older, might make it into the cabinet before me.' There's also a high degree of trust that allows people to become quite incautious; I've had things said to me that I wouldn't in a million years have repeated, but they could have been used to quite damaging effect had I decided to be hard-nosed about it.

I was usually the second-to-last of the Westminster cohort to leave the train, which would arrive in Redruth at about seven in the morning. David Harris would continue to Penzance, although sometimes, depending on where he'd left his car, he'd get off with me since he lived in my constituency. But however you did it, it was a strain. Most MPs have a much higher approval rating individually in their constituencies than they do collectively in the body politic, because most MPs – certainly the ones I know – possess a highly attuned sense of public duty. You certainly don't do it for the pay. Or the glamour.

In a parliament where the government majority was both small and unreliable, thanks to the Maastricht rebels, pairing was particularly important. The moment David Harris took on board the fragile nature of our majority, he said, 'These numbers are really tight. Find yourself a pair quickly, and make sure you get someone you can rely on.'

Pairing is the system where, in the interests of sanity and your marriage, your vote and that of your pair – an MP from the main opposition party – cancel each other out. It means that neither of you have to turn up for non-important votes. However, you can't just make a private arrangement with another MP. The pairing has to be agreed by the whips' office both at the outset and then on every occasion you hope to use it. Sometimes they say yes, sometimes they say no.

Barbara Roche was the Labour MP for Hornsey and Woodgreen, the constituency that included Haringey Athletics Club. We were both new and both looking for a pair. She was a barrister with three young children, so we were pretty much in the same boat.

The parliamentary gavotte began on Thursday evenings when the timetable for the following week – known as the party whip – would be read out by the senior whip on duty to a gathering of backbenchers called the 1922 committee. Debates where your presence/vote was not required would be underlined once. Those where your vote was required, but which – with permission – could be paired, would be underlined twice. Those where you had to turn up even if you were at death's door (and I'm not exaggerating) had three lines beneath them, hence the expression. A three-line whip is immutable. No pairing. That's it.

There may be some MPs who – at least at the start of their Westminster career – harbour no ambitions to move beyond the backbenches, but I have never met one. Maybe at a push Dennis Skinner. The first step on the ladder of preferment is the position of PPS, Parliamentary Private Secretary. A PPS is often characterised in the press as a 'bag carrier' but the job – deemed to be such but unpaid – is less about carrying ministerial boxes than providing intelligence on anything that you think your minister should know about. You talk informally to those MPs whose constituents are in some way affected by legislation or by any other action that your ministry might be considering, or which might impact on the health and safety of your minister – even his 'clubability'.

My first job was PPS to John MacGregor, then Secretary of State for Transport, a role I also carried out for Roger Freeman. Next I went to the Ministry of Defence as PPS to Nicholas Soames, then Minister of State for the Armed Forces. He was a true maverick – gourmet, gourmand, wit and raconteur. As they say these days, what's not to like? Then, following first the resignation and subsequent re-election of John Major as leader, I became PPS to Michael Heseltine.

For years, Michael Heseltine had been the party leader in waiting. In November 1990 he had challenged Margaret Thatcher but fell at the first hurdle. In 1995 when John Major in turn resigned – calling the bluff of the Maastricht rebels – Heseltine chose not to stand. In the ensuing election, Major won a convincing majority against the only other candidate, Eurosceptic-in-chief John Redwood, and immediately appointed Heseltine as his deputy. It was generally believed that this was his reward for not standing himself.

Being PPS to the deputy prime minister was subtly different from anything I had done before because he wasn't at the head of a particular ministry. Heseltine had no specific portfolio. He was seen as a hard hitter and, even more than the party chairman, tended to be thrown into the lion's den whenever a Jeremy Paxman or a John Humphrys was on the rampage. His role, alongside Brian Mawhinney, tough Ulsterman and party chairman, was to prepare the party for the general election. As deputy PM he would also stand in for John Major at prime minister's questions. My job involved assisting those preparations, which was fascinating. To this day, Michael Heseltine remains one of the most impressive people I have ever met.

Notwithstanding, I owe much my most interesting year in the House of Commons to the phenomenon known as 'sleaze', which blighted the Conservative Party as much as Maastricht did over the same period.

'Back to Basics' had been launched at the Tory Party conference in October 1993 and was an initiative designed to promote traditional values. However, thanks to mishandling by the press office, it was sold to the media as a moral crusade. I have always felt distinctly queasy when politicians make forays into the moral maze. A maxim current in Westminster said that 'if you want to preach, go to church.' Straying from this path made us hostages to fortune, allowing Fleet Street to shine a light on to some of the inconsistencies of members' lives. In fairness, most of the so-called scandals they uncovered were pretty small beer and should certainly never have been resigning issues.

But behind the scenes John Major exploded. He thought he had created a campaign that reinforced Conservative values and evoked a gentler age – cricket on the village green, Stanley Baldwin, warm beer and bicycles – not a reactionary roasting of single mothers and errant fathers.

From then on, Major pursued a policy of zero tolerance. Soon even lowly PPSs were obliged to fall on their swords. In June 1996 the *News of the World* published photographs of junior minister Rod Richards, suggesting an involvement with a young woman not his wife. He was immediately sacked, in parliamentary parlance he 'resigned', as per the now standard procedure.

A group of about six us, all the same intake, decided to take him out for a commiseratory lunch. Halfway through I was called to the phone, and returned to the table ashen-faced.

'That was the whips' office,' I said. 'The chief wants to see me. Now.'

Up went a combined roar: 'You've got the job!'

'I can't have,' I said. 'With my voting record?'

But although I would hardly have considered myself whip material, it seems that others did and I had benefited from the musical chairs that always accompanies a resignation. Once Rod Richards departed the Welsh office, someone from the solicitor general's office took his place. Then a west country MP, a solicitor, was moved to the now empty chair in the solicitor general's office, which left a vacancy where the solicitor had been: the whips' office.

17

A CERTAIN FREEDOM

Winston Churchill used to say that a party without a whips' office is like a city without a sewer. I would prefer the analogy of a ship without a boiler room, but it is certainly true that the whips know more about what's happening – including the effluent – than anyone in the party, up to and including the prime minister. The job of the whips is enshrined in the phrase 'to make a house and to keep a house'. Keeping a house means ensuring that enough government members are at hand to be summoned into the chamber in the event of a division, if necessary at short notice. The whips' job is primarily to get the business of the House through successfully and, crucially, within the timetable – notwithstanding the activities of the opposition – and, yes, on occasions to bring back into line the wayward in the party, which is euphemistically known as conducting 'conversations about career development'.

You are also the prime minister's Praetorian Guard. Your responsibility is really only to the prime minister. You are beholden to no one else.

A junior whip is considered a ministerial position and, unlike a PPS, you are paid in addition to drawing your basic salary as an MP. Like all such appointments, mine took immediate effect. After a brief interview in Downing Street with the chief whip Alastair Goodlad, I was packed off along the corridor with the deputy chief whip Andrew MacKay to see Sir Robin Butler, the cabinet secretary. Before being accepted, I had to be taken through the ministerial code and provide details of my assets and my sources of income.

I explained that I was technically a sheep farmer and that I had a string of health clubs and was on the advisory board of Nike. I also did odd bits of sports journalism, and in that capacity would be going to the Olympics in Atlanta as part of the BBC's team.

'Well,' Sir Robin said, 'the good news is that you can keep your sheep and your health clubs as long as you're not involved on a day-to-day basis. However, I'm afraid you won't be able to write any more newspaper articles, and I'm going to have to stop you going to Atlanta.'

What? I couldn't believe what I was hearing. 'But why?'

'Because, as a minister, you cannot be employed by an outside organisation. It truly pains me to have to tell you this, not least because I'm a sports nut and I'll be glued to the television myself, but I can't let you go. You can't be paid.'

'Well that's easy then. I won't be paid. I'll go for nothing.'

'And how do you propose getting there?'

If I was prepared to cover the costs of my own flight and accommodation and other such expenses, then I could go, he said. But it didn't take long to see that this made no economic sense. Clearly, I couldn't rack up over £10,000 just for the pleasure of sitting in the Atlanta stadium and soaking up the atmosphere.

But it did strike me, then as now, as mad. The integrity clause stated that 'no obligations should be accepted if they could undermine the minister's position', but I was hard-pressed to see how discussing the finer points of anaerobic thresholds over a period I'd chosen as my summer holiday could fall into that category, but this wasn't an argument I was going to win. It was with an extremely heavy heart that I informed the BBC of the situation.

In the end, thanks to a personal invitation from Samaranch, I was able to fly to Atlanta courtesy of the IOC and sit by the president's side for the final of the men's 1500 metres. Sadly, while it had all the ingredients of a great race, shortly into the third lap the joint favourite, Moroccan Hicham El Guerrouj, caught the heel of world-record holder Noureddine Morceli and went sprawling. The rhythm of everybody bar the leader was upset and Morceli – from Algeria – raced for the line unchallenged, in a time that was some three seconds slower than mine in Los Angeles twelve years earlier.

The whips' office is Westminster's *sanctum sanctorum* and as 'safe' a house as anywhere in Europe. Nobody has access except the whips themselves. I can still remember the moment, that same afternoon, when I stood on the threshold to be introduced to my future colleagues. It was by then half-past two, the time of the meeting that marks the start of every whip's day apart from Wednesdays when you meet in the chief whip's office in Downing Street at 9.30 a.m. and work through till lunch.

Behind the dozen or so guarded faces turned in my direction was a confusion of leather sofas with desks ranged around the edge, papers stashed on the floor, overflowing from boxes, empty wine glasses. In short, a complete tip. I felt I was peering into the inner workings of a secret society, which wasn't far off the mark. I was directed to a leather armchair – and that was it. I had no idea what I was supposed to be doing. After about a quarter of an hour of what was known as 'house-keeping', conducted by the deputy chief whip, which effectively outlined the day's duties, the chief whip appeared as if on cue. Then, one by one, the whips – in what appeared to be hierarchical order – gave what sounded like intelligence reports, including information on the guy who'd just been sacked.

'Rod Richards,' said a laconic voice, 'left the House at 12.20, in the company of John Sykes and Sebastian Coe. They took lunch at the Golden Dragon in Gerrard Street . . .' I was stunned. There I was, meandering through London's Chinatown, completely oblivious that our every move was being noted. And this was just one of an index of MPs' lunch arrangements that were recorded that day. They knew everything. And that, I soon discovered, was my new job. To know everything.

As a junior whip I had both geographical and departmental responsibility. My flock of MPs, who I was charged with both shepherding and prodding, were those from Bristol and southwards further down into the west country. I was also the whip, at different times, for social security and defence. Members had a duty to come to you if they were wobbling over a particular vote or piece of legislation, but all too frequently they kept their doubts to themselves. Your job was to winkle out such crises of conscience before they became a problem, and to use your best endeavours to comfort, occasionally cajole, and then steer into the right lobby.

Sometimes the conversations would become quite intense. This was honest talking and, while maintaining personal confidences, you would pick up hints that all was not well elsewhere in the party. The job of the whips' office is to ensure that the business of the house gets through and if that means an occasional touch of metaphorical strong-arming, so be it. Sometimes it went beyond the metaphorical. I have seen a government whip grab a member of the cabinet, pin him against the wall and read him the riot act because he turned up late for a vote. The office is no respecter of status so you could have earthy conversations with Members who were of greater seniority to you in the party.

The job had one huge plus, at least for me. While I was soon the proud owner of a ministerial 'box' – a black leather attaché case, embossed with my initials, recognisable by having its lock on the underside – not being under a government department meant no boxes packed with correspondence, no reading reports till the early hours. I took nothing home. The other great advantage was that you only worked when the House was sitting. During nearly ten weeks of the long recess – from 27 July until the last party conference was over sometime in October – I could be with my family and be working in the constituency. My task then as a junior whip was mainly to keep in touch with the flock, and this could be done from Surrey or Cornwall. Keeping in touch with those two dozen or so colleagues meant that some weekends I would be more on the phone than off. Rather than ringing solely when things were going badly, I would try to keep channels open all the time when I'd be having quasi-theological discussions about the direction of the party. It was a period of exposure to human nature that was both instructive and absorbing.

The major issue facing the whips' office during the full five years of the 1992–7 parliament was the party's ever-diminishing majority. We started with a majority of twenty-one and ended with a minority of three. By the time I arrived, there had already been two defections: Alan Howarth went over to Labour in the autumn of 1995, then Emma Nicholson, MP for a neighbouring constituency in Devon, departed to the arms of the Liberal Democrats at the end of the same year. Meanwhile, the Maastricht rebels continued to play games, sometimes voting with the government, sometimes not, apparently on whim, meaning that we could take no chances.

In any community of people, there will always be a percentage who are ill, and MPs in that situation are usually allowed to pair. But if the vote is really tight, every Member has to come in, whatever their state of health. They are not required to pass through the division lobbies, but they do have to be present within the precinct. For a period of a few months we were reduced to bringing in people on hospital beds. One, I remember, was in mid-blood transfusion, while being hooked up to a drip was quite commonplace. When the ambulance arrived in New Palace Yard just before a division, two whips, one from each side, would go down, open the door, peer in and verify that the Member concerned was actually inside, albeit not in great shape.

I remember speaking to one MP's wife, telling her that we needed her husband in that night, and asking how he was. Her reply was fairly terse: 'How do you think, four hours after a hip replacement?'

This barrel-scraping was not an edifying spectacle. One old guy, I remember, clearly had some form of dementia. He hadn't a clue where he was or what he was doing, let alone which party he belonged to. A Labour whip – a Geordie – peered down at a stretcher case I had obliged to come in and said, 'I'm not convinced this one's alive.'

'Of course he is,' I said. 'Things may be bad, but we're not reduced to bringing in dead bodies.' But I wouldn't have put it past some to say nothing if a heart monitor started flat-lining.

The usual advice given to a new MP is never get involved in a local dispute because you will wave goodbye to the votes of whichever side loses. But by 1996 I knew that the chances of retaining my seat were negligible, and a situation arose where I felt I could be useful, and maybe even avert closure of the biggest employer in the area.

Membership of the Conservative Party and membership of a trade union are not mutually exclusive and one of my constituency officials had voiced his concern about a stand-off between the workforce and the management of A. & P. Appleyard, a large ship-repair yard in Falmouth where he worked – a dry dock the size of two football pitches. The dispute had all the makings of taking a damaging turn. Unless their demands were met, he said, the workforce – then around 600 men – would down tools. If the worst happened and the owners went into liquidation, which they claimed would be the consequence of a walk-out, the knock-on effect on the whole community would be devastating. I knew I couldn't sit out this particular dance.

Thanks to my father, I had always had a greater feel for trade unions than most Conservatives. When appointed to the employ-ment select committee, I was frustrated at the tribal attitudes of a few of the committee, who in turn were similarly wary of my famili-arity with unions. The last thing that any trade union, or the average worker, wants is a strike. There are hundreds of middle-of-the-road trade unionists who know that striking hits little more than their members' disposable income and public support.

At first, both sides were wary, as indeed was my own constitu-ency association. Here was I, a Conservative MP, who appeared to be involved at the behest of the union. The issues were clear. The new owners of the shipyard were an international conglomerate who wanted to trim costs while the unions were intent on protect-ing conditions and livelihoods. A familiar story.

The first meeting could well have been the last. The antagonism between both sides corroded every word that was spoken. I sensed that the new owners – although clearly competent – had little loyalty or understanding of the local people or landscape. And they were right, of course, to point out that ship repair was becoming an increasingly competitive market place, challenged by Germany and Poland. And yet I knew grants were available for regional assist-ance, if they chose to look for them. Fortunately, common sense prevailed, and to this day A. & P. Appleyard remains a major employer in the south west, their dry dock the biggest on the south coast. It could so easily have gone the other way if either side had decided to take it to a shoot-out.

The situation with the tin mines, however, was at that point beyond my or anyone else's help. In the 1980s the price of tin plummeted on world markets and in 1991 the Department of Trade and Industry withdrew funding. By the time I arrived on the scene, South Crofty was the last operational tin mine in Cornwall, but even the unions knew that it wasn't economic, the cost of getting it out of the ground exceeding the price on the exchanges. But you can't close a mine for a few months to wait for the price of tin to improve or while you attempt to summon up interest from elsewhere. Early in my parliamentary career I persuaded Tim Sainsbury, then Minister of Trade, to agree to some short-term financing while a solution was sought. This provided a breathing space, which, combined with local fund-raising efforts, gave local people the opportunity to buy shares. Although it was still a going concern when I left Cornwall in 1997, sadly the mine ceased operations entirely the following year. However, since then the price of tin has gone up 500 per cent and metal prices generally are set to stay at sustainably high levels. The presence of copper, tin, indium and tungsten in the ore may yet bring South Crofty back to economic life. Times change. Every flat screen in the world has a thin layer of indium tin oxide in it.

Following my defeat in the 1997 election, people would ask, 'At what point did you realise you might lose your seat?' to which I replied, 'Within thirty seconds of winning it.'

In the early hours of 10 April 1992, John Herd had brought me the numbers as soon he got them from the receiving officer. I had won 36.8 per cent of the vote and the Labour and the Lib Dems were only a few percentage points behind. While the Conservatives had scraped back in for a fourth term, we were at the fag end of thirteen years of government and the natural shift over the next five years would erode my small majority. In a way, it gave me a certain freedom. It allowed me to be myself and not worry about treading on sensitive toes, if in my view they needed treading on.

At a general election, unlike a by-election, people vote for the party and not the person. If your party is flying high, you can be the most ineffective constituency MP in history and yet still be within about 3 per cent of the share of the vote in the country overall, and the 3 per cent rule applies equally the other way round.

In April 1997, shortly after John Major called the election, the whips' office ran a sweepstake. Nobody thought we would lose by less than sixty seats, not that any one of us would have made such an admission beyond the solid oak double doors, and we felt uncomfortable even suggesting such a possibility among ourselves.

Of course, politicians never admit to anything other than total confidence, even when staring disaster in the face. But in my corner of Cornwall we had some small cause for optimism. Having instigated all-women short lists in some constituencies, New Labour had parachuted in a former mayor of Islington, Candy Atherton, as their candidate. Old Labour supporters were distinctly unimpressed and had put up a local guy, John Geach, to stand against her. As a consequence, the Labour vote stood a good chance of being split. Unfortunately, the Conservative vote was similarly threatened. Euroscepticism continued to dog party unity and in late 1996 Sir James Goldsmith – multi-millionaire and previously a Conservative benefactor – formed and funded the Referendum Party, whose sole objective was for a referendum to be held on Britain's continued membership of the EU. Their candidate in Falmouth and Camborne was Sir Peter de Savary, another self-made millionaire. He could at least claim some local connection; at one time he had owned Land's End and had made money in the shipyards of Falmouth. Thanks to the continuing disputes on territorial fishing, Cornwall had become even more determinedly anti-European and so was obvious and fertile ground for the anti-European vote.

We were already well into the campaign when de Savary called. He was staying in the Falmouth Hotel and wanted to talk, he said. We had met a couple of times during my early months as an MP, and although our meetings were convivial, our 'conversation' was mainly a monologue – the world according to Peter de Savary – and I knew that we wouldn't be spending much downtime together in the Duchy.

From the moment he got up to shake my hand I could see he

looked harassed and ill at ease. Giving speeches in village halls, kissing babies and the rest of the campaign merry-go-round had clearly palled after the first few days.

'I've been reading some of your speeches on Europe,' he said, 'and you're more of a Eurosceptic than I am. So why in hell am I standing against you?' I resisted the retort, 'No shit, Sherlock,' but did venture the opinion that this could have been thought through earlier. But what he said was true. As a representative of a fishing community that was being hard hit, particularly by EU registered trawlers, I had spoken and voted against the government line whenever it was necessary, or abstained. Now, by standing against me, de Savary risked opening the door to an overtly pro-Federalist Europe MP – New Labour – to represent this constituency. 'So what I suggest,' he said, 'is that I step down.' It was an eminently sensible solution that suited us both.

I conveyed the gist of this conversation as soon as I could to Conservative central office. We had just over a week to go before polling day and I recognised that this might be the brick we needed to shore up the dam.

It was an important moment, not just for my constituency but country wide. The Referendum Party were fielding 547 candidates, many of whom risked pushing Eurosceptic Tories into second place. A press conference was called for the following Saturday. We arranged for the party chairman, Brian Mawhinney, to come down from London, plus whatever other big guns could be rustled up at short notice. But late on Friday afternoon I had another call from de Savary. He was sorry but he couldn't withdraw. 'Unfortunately,' he said, 'I'm going to have to go through with this nonsense.'

The speculation was that, while Goldsmith, the Referendum Party's prime mover, would have taken a political view, he also had a financial relationship with de Savary, and as a result de Savary wasn't entirely his own man.

It wasn't a pleasant few weeks. I knew we were in serious trouble when a woman on the doorstep told me very politely, 'Actually, I quite like you. I think you've done a reasonable job down here, even though you're an incomer. I've seen you at lots of dos, and I know neighbours of mine you've helped, but I can't bring myself to vote Conservative again. Not this time.' And this was a woman who'd voted Conservative all her life. This was not personal antagonism. They just felt rather sorry for me.

On the evening of 1 May 1997 I sat in Sunny Corner Cottage with a bottle of red wine, watching the minute-by-minute speculation that is standard TV fare before the results start to come in. Exit polls were cheerfully predicting Armageddon. The mood seemed positively festive. This kinetic energy, I decided, derived from the sheer scale of what was about to happen. It was worse than any of us had feared. It wasn't a defeat. It was a rout.

At the equivalent moment five years earlier, I had been at the count from midnight onwards, a smiling Mrs Coe by my side, radiantly pregnant with our first baby. And while it was not yet a done deal, I had done enough to dispel my own inner fears that I wouldn't be accepted or that I didn't have what it took to get to Westminster. How things had changed. For a start, I was in Cornwall on my own, Nicky understandably having stayed at home with the children – Maddy four, Harry two, and Peter just eleven months old. This time I was drowning my sorrows with my close friend Hugh Hastings, a friendship forged through our passion for Chelsea, having met at Stamford Bridge in 1978. Hugh later moved to Cornwall and, when I was selected for Falmouth and Camborne, we began to see much more of each other. He was an enormous help in campaigning, a real support and a good friend.

My secretary called. 'What are you doing at the cottage?' she said. 'You ought to be there at the count.'

'I don't particularly want to sit for hour after hour watching boxes full of votes for other people come in,' I said. 'I'm not a masochist.' The result wouldn't be in till five in the morning and I thought, 'Sod it.'

I'd finish the bottle of wine and grab three or four hours sleep. Defeat brings its own form of tiredness and mine had come early. I'd spent the day going around the constituency, not canvassing, that had all been done, but saying thank you to the party members who had made such Herculean efforts to get the vote out, those party faithful without whose graft no MP of whatever party can survive.

During the five weeks of the campaign I could be honest with nobody, not even with John Herd. When asked what my plans were if I lost, I refused to be drawn. 'I'm fighting to win,' I'd say. 'I don't contemplate losing.' But I knew I was about to get my P45 in a very public way. I opened another bottle and rang a few mates in the House to commiserate.

I got to the count around 1.30 a.m., by which time I'd personally downed the best part of a bottle and a half of claret. By now, I was pretty demob happy, sitting in a corner of the hall laughing with John Geach, the Old Labour candidate, who told me how his troops had been quietly campaigning for me on the doorstep, saying, 'If you can't vote for us, vote for Seb. At least he's not New Labour.'

Peter de Savary came up looking like Coleridge's Ancient Mariner after he had shot the albatross. 'I can't believe what I've done,' he said.

The ballot boxes would come in, be emptied and divided in piles according to the candidate. The tellers were all girls from Barclays. John Herd was pacing up and down, chain smoking his usual Hamlet cigars, and would come back and give me occasional updates. The Lib Dems, he said, thought they were in with a shout and seemed to have a bit of a party going on, but Candy Atherton (New Labour) was looking distinctly nervous. Meanwhile, Old

Labour and I had now moved on to the beer, as unconcerned at the outcome as Freddy Zapp from the Monster Raving Loony Party.

A TV screen had been rigged up in a back room, where talking heads on *Newsnight* were filling the dead space between results. Among the high-profile mug shots that formed a shooting gallery of likely victims was my own, at that stage one of the minority still intact.

'You'd better sober up, boy,' John Herd said suddenly. 'I think you're ahead. There are only a couple more wards to come in, and they're ours!'

My only thought was, 'Oh God . . .' Not only had I not prepared a speech, I was a couple of bottles of claret the worse for wear, topped off with a few pale ales courtesy of Old Labour. At the very least I would need to be coherent.

But he was wrong. He'd got excited because it was nip and tuck, and the three wards that were yet to come in were traditionally strong Conservative wards. But this time they had either sat on their hands or gone over to the Referendum Party, while the Labour vote stayed solid, and this was pretty much the story of the night. However, those five minutes when I thought I might have to make a victory speech, clearly the worse for wear, were the most stressful of the entire campaign.

It must have been after three when the result finally came in. New Labour had won with a majority of 2,500, I was second and the Lib Dems third. As for Peter de Savary, he came fourth, polling just over 3,500 votes. If he had withdrawn as promised, and if those who voted for the Referendum Party had voted for me, then I would have been 1,000 votes ahead of New Labour and we would have retained the seat. As it was, I can take some pride in that the swing against me was 5 per cent against an average across the country of 11 per cent – the smallest that night against any incumbent Conservative MP.

Dawn had already broken by the time I got back to the cottage, the birds already announcing another fine Cornish spring day. In London, New Labour were whooping it up in the Festival Hall. I went to bed, had four or five hours kip, got into my car and drove home. My career as an MP was over. I never went back.

One person who was not unhappy at the result was Nicky. Although my last year in the whips' office had made day-to-day living easier, it was still no life for her. The logistics alone were a real struggle. I mean, what do you do when you have three children under four? Drive them down to Cornwall every weekend? That's six hours in a car – twelve hours in total there and back. Or do you stick them on an aeroplane, all throwing up with turbulence? If I went alone, I might finish late on a Saturday night in the constituency and drive back early on Sunday morning. Or if I'd gone by train, I could get the early morning flight up from Newquay at 7.00 a.m. Either way I'd be knackered and of little help to a harassed mother of three children under five, who was also trying to pursue her career as a horsewoman.

The pattern of life imposed by parliament is simply not one that works in a modern marriage – in the days of MPs with private incomes and stay-at-home wives, maybe. Things have improved a little, but during my term the earliest you could expect to be out was 10.15 p.m., home at 11.00 p.m. That was a result. Your wife might actually be awake. You wonder how any MP's marriage survives at all.

The vast majority of Britain's MPs live outside London. Some of them rent flats or make other arrangements during the week within the area of the division bell, which means they can be back in the chamber in time to vote, while their families live in Scarborough or North Wales or the Scottish borders or wherever their constituencies happen to be. This might appear to be the most practical solution – and in some cases it is the only solution – but it goes without saying that it brings its own problems. I wasn't prepared to be a part-time husband and father, seeing my children at weekends only, and waiting for the division bell in the bar with a well-thumbed, eight-hour-old copy of the *Evening Standard* for company. I made it clear from the outset that my home would be in Surrey, where my wife and my children lived, and I went back there every night, even if the reality meant that I barely saw them.

I might have been disillusioned by the life of an MP but I was far from disillusioned with politics. Even so, my main emotion as I drove back on the morning of 2 May, listening to the mellifluous sounds of the great jazz pianist Bill Evans, was relief that an era was over, a door closed.

A month or so later I was standing in Guildford livestock market discussing the price of sheep with Alan, our farm manager, when my mobile rang. Most of our flock went to Waitrose, but we had a few still to be auctioned off and I could barely hear who was calling over the lambs' chorus.

'It's Alan Duncan,' the voice said. Alan was the same intake as I had been. He had been PPS to Brian Mawhinney and I'd spoken to him only a few weeks previously over getting his boss down for the de Savary press conference that never happened.

'Who should be the next leader,' he asked, 'off the top of your head?'

'William Hague.'

I didn't need to think about it. Although I didn't really know William personally, I knew he was the shot in the arm the party needed. Although by far the youngest of those whose names had been touted in the press – he was 36, five years younger than me – he was a brilliant orator and more than capable of giving Blair a pasting across the despatch box.

'Though if you're asking me if this is the right time,' I continued, 'that's another matter. But there's no question that he has the intel-lectual muscle and resilience.'

'So if it came down to him or Michael Howard?'

'Oh, no competition.'

It was early June. The Conservative Party were in freefall. John Major had resigned on 2 May, the morning after the election. Michael Heseltine, who although nearly 70, had been widely expected to succeed him, had been admitted to hospital the same night with a suspected heart attack. If Heseltine had been seen as the leader for the Europhile left of the party, the Eurosceptics' choice, Michael Portillo, poster child for the right, was also now unavailable, having lost his seat in the most rejoiced over defeat of the entire election, and not only by Labour supporters. Half the cabinet had been culled. Of those remaining, only Michael Howard and Ken Clarke had ever been in opposition. In the party outside Westminster, Ken Clarke was much liked. But while the press saw him as a white rhino – an endangered species and the sole political heavyweight capable of inflicting serious damage on Labour's mastodon majority – his colleagues saw him as a rogue elephant, who had left too much wreckage and debris in his wake to get their support. This left the field wide open.

William himself never intended to run. His first choice for party leader to replace John Major was thought to have been Michael Portillo, now *hors de combat*. His second choice was Michael Howard, who, in return for William's endorsement, had offered him the deputy leadership. When word got round that the deal was all but sealed, Alan Duncan, Charles Hendry and others – all young and on the right of the party – had seen that this was an unsustainable and unnecessary alliance. They were convinced that William could win on his own. A few days later, Alan Duncan called me again.

'Bearing in mind what you said before, would you be prepared to get involved?'

'Alan, it may have escaped your notice but I'm no longer a member of the parliamentary party. I don't have a vote.'

'No, I know that, but we're thinking of organising a regional campaign meeting or two. And we were wondering, would you be prepared to introduce him? Nothing too onerous.'

'Well . . .'

'In fact, we've got one up in Coventry this Saturday. I know it's short notice but it would really help us out.'

In 1997, only MPs could vote in a new leader, but by including the regions in his campaign, William hoped to get grass-roots' support, which could help sway the vote in Westminster. There was no doubt that some MPs were intending to consult their constituencies before either endorsing or voting for any of the candidates.

The traffic going north proved horrendous and I ended up driving the last two miles on the hard shoulder with my hazard lights on. Luckily, the police were too busy getting things moving to notice. I got to the venue with minutes to spare, ran on, said my piece, ran off.

'Thanks very much,' William said when it was over.

'My pleasure.' We shook hands, and I set off back to London and Stamford Bridge in time to watch Chelsea.

The next week, I got another phone call from Alan. 'That was great,' he said. 'Really terrific. Everyone was so grateful. Now we've a bit of a problem and wondered if you could help out. We're somewhat short staffed and really need an old hand who's been in the whips' office, you know, those sorts of skills.'

The campaign HQ was in Stafford Street and I was greeted warmly by James Arbuthnot, MP for Hampshire North East, William's campaign manager who subsequently became his chief whip.

'I can't tell you how pleased I am that you're here,' he said. 'Everyone's saying that they're going to vote for him and I know that they're not.' The usual story.

That's how I became a number cruncher, sitting in the bowels of a building that a benefactor had lent the campaign, cross-indexing names with James Arbuthnot, while the rest of the team wandered the corridors of Westminster, building up caffeine levels in the Members' tea room and alcohol levels in the bars, listening, quizzing and reporting back, making their way through the 165 Conservative MPs who made up the electoral college – only half the number who had been in place little over a month before.

By 12 June there were five definite candidates – from left to right, Ken Clarke, William Hague, Michael Howard, Peter Lilley and John Redwood.

Once William had thrown his hat into the ring, Michael Howard's campaign imploded, given the *coup de grâce* by Ann Widdecombe saying there was 'something of the night' about him. In the first round he ended up with fewer votes than he had had proposers; having seen the way the wind was blowing, they had jumped ship. Ken Clarke had come top with 49 votes, William second with 41 votes and John Redwood third on 27 votes. Lilley came fourth and so he and Howard withdrew.

From here on the number crunching became essential. Forty-seven votes were now up for grabs and while both Lilley and Howard had given their support to William, that meant nothing. At the next ballot, Clarke took 15 of these while William took 21, and John Redwood, the most Eurosceptic of the candidates, increased his total by just 11. The writing was on the wall. With Redwood out of the running, it was down to a stark choice: Clarke, experienced but damaged, versus Hague, less-experienced but with youth on his side.

John Redwood had gone out with 38 votes. He told his supporters that these should now go to Clarke – apparently, a deal they had cut previously but which made no sense at all given that Ken was as Europhile as Redwood was Europhobe. All now depended on how these votes would be distributed, and when Margaret Thatcher broke her silence and endorsed William, it was all but over. William Hague was elected leader with 92 votes, a majority of 22, far greater than any of us had dared hope.

With the benefit of hindsight it's easy to say that William should have trusted his instincts and waited. That unparalleled parliamentary majority meant Labour were in for at least two terms, and any leader of the Conservatives – even if Mother Teresa had suddenly turned up to endorse him – was on a hiding to nothing. William's line on this was clear: 'Politics is competitive. If this goes to somebody else, there is no guarantee that I'll be seen as the leader-in-waiting five or ten years down the line.' Although no longer an MP, Michael Portillo was still a presence in the wings, and in fact he returned to parliament on the death of Alan Clark, in the rock-solid seat of Kensington and Chelsea, in November 1999.

It's always nice at the end of a campaign to have a win, and I had enjoyed being right in the thick of things. But now it was back to the sheep.

18

THE NIGHT SHIFT

'SEB? Charles here. Some good news. William's made me his chief of staff.'

Charles Hendry was the same intake as me and, like me, had just lost his seat. He'd worked for the Hague leadership campaign, much as I had done, because he believed that William was right for the future of the party. He had been William's PPS for a year in 1994 when William had been Minister of State at Social Security, so this was an eminently sensible appointment.

The role of chief of staff was a comparatively new departure in British politics. Jonathan Powell, a former Foreign Office diplomat, had taken on the job for Tony Blair both in opposition and in government, and I could quite see how William had warmed to the idea of having one person co-ordinating his team. So, of course, I offered my congratulations.

'And on that note, Seb,' Charles continued, 'I was wondering if you could give us a couple of days. We've simply not got enough people on the ground. I've got to get William up to Scotland this weekend and I've no one to do it.'

'OK. I'll give you two days just to help out. But I'm not coming back, do you understand?'

'Yes, yes. All right.'

Charles Hendry was one of my oldest parliamentary friends. On our first day in the House of Commons we'd ended up sitting next to each other while the chief whip gave us a pep talk about how we had to toe the line and generally behave ourselves.

'My God,' whispered Charles. 'We might as well be back at bloody school!' He had gone to Rugby, and I soon realised that being at a famous public school like that was not so different from going to Tapton Secondary Modern. If the chief had thrown a bunch of keys at me and threatened me with a car aerial, I wouldn't have been in the least surprised.

Two days became another two days, and soon I was doing two days a week. However good a politician you might be, you still need to be prepared, and I sensed in William an unease when we were criss-crossing the country, largely, I realised, because he wasn't always adequately briefed. And when the leader of Her Majesty's opposition gets off a train, while you don't expect the pomp and sheen of a colliery brass band waiting on the platform (although that would be nice) nonetheless the visit demands a certain level of dignity and preparedness. As it was, everything would feel sloppy. It became abundantly clear – if not always to others in the team – that, above all, William craved routine, order, punctuality and no surprises. One thing I have always been able to do is organise. And in the post-election vacuum, when all those with careers at stake were chasing their tails and trusting that within a year New Labour would quietly implode, I found myself doing more and more.

The leader of the opposition, necessarily, has a lower profile than the prime minister. However, at least once a year at the annual party conference the presence of journalists is guaranteed. Our 1997 conference in Blackpool provided a double magnet since it marked not only William's first conference as party leader but also the twentieth anniversary of his first speech to conference as a precocious 16 year old, also in Blackpool. At that juncture I was little more than a stage manager, so when the press team suggested a visit to Fleetwood – a once-prosperous fishing port just north of Blackpool – I was deputed to sort it out. A week beforehand I went up for a recce, spoke to the skippers of several trawlers and discussed the problems facing the community – catch quotas v. declining fish stocks. I felt comfortable about it making a good story, a serious issue but with plenty of human interest and non-frivolous photo opportunities.

It was a car crash. I forgot the one question any former MP from a fishing constituency should have known to ask. We arrived at the quayside to find that the tide was out. A storm the previous night had kept most of the fleet at sea and those boats that remained in harbour were sitting there, unable to move, on mud banks. For the press who turned up it was Christmas come early. The metaphors were all there for the taking, along with the snaps – washed up, tide out, beached, William a lone figure looking vacantly seawards at the gathering storm clouds.

It was a good lesson. Don't get clever. If you can't choreograph something down to the last detail, steer well clear. It was my old man's mantra again about limiting the variables. While I could do nothing about the weather, I could have done something abut the tide. All it would have taken was one simple question.

William, although no doubt quietly seething at this incompetence, heard my lame apologies with the inscrutable face of a poker player, and was his customary charitable self. From that moment on I planned meticulously. I became positively anal. I would never again put the leader of the Tory Party into a position where tabloid subs or snappers could exercise their creativity.

The first major issue we faced was money. Conservative coffers were empty, run into the ground. As late as four days before polling day, when even the most loyal party member could see we were heading for the recycling bin, in a last throw of the dice £600,000 was sanctioned for a poster campaign. The lead-up to the election had been notably long – six weeks, nearly double the usual time. One reason had been the expectation that Labour would run out of money, but thanks to the phenomenal fund-raising efforts of Lord

Levy and the huge growth in membership of the Labour Party under Tony Blair, plus pragmatic donations from those groups wanting to emerge on the right side after the election, the opposite had been the case: *our* coffers had run dry, not theirs.

We had emerged from our election spending spree four million in the red. As we approached the end of the financial year, there was real doubt that the auditors would pass the accounts as being those of a 'going concern'.

The Conservative Party has always relied heavily on private donations, and in November 1997 I accompanied William to keep up the morale – and yes, the donations – of the million expatriate Brits, many of whom we knew to be Conservative supporters and the majority of whom were eligible to vote in a general election.

No politician really enjoys pressing the flesh in this way, but it is necessary. The state provides limited financing for the party in opposition, called 'Short money' after the politician Edward Short. Unfortunately, it was also proving short in the literal sense, since it's distributed on the basis of number of seats held and votes garnered, which in our case was catastrophically low. Not only did we have the deficit to replace, but without serious investment in research, data collection and analysis, we couldn't hope to compete with the machinery of government that the Labour Party now had at its fingertips. To provide effective opposition is difficult enough at the best of times, but given our limited resources, it was all but impossible.

Anyway, back to Spain. By this time I had been working for William off and on for about four months, and while I was committed to making a go of it for his sake, because I had come to admire and like him in equal measure, I had begun to wonder what I thought I was doing, where my life was going. I had to think about earning some money, and did I really want to spend endless nights on the Wheel Tappers and Shunters circuit in southern Spain or anywhere else? Alicante in November is a pretty bleak and barren place – not a season that features in the holiday brochures. One night we got back to our hotel and were sitting in the bar (the name, I recall, was the Peanut Bar, risibly appropriate) and William said, 'Do you think you could give me a bit more time?' And I sat there, incongruously drinking a pint of British lager, and thinking this is not really the moment to ask. Perhaps if we were speaking to well-heeled farmers in leafy Hampshire or to perfumed ladies in a smart supper club in Kensington, or even up in Yorkshire. Particularly up in Yorkshire. But here? This was hard work.

'Look, I'm happy to do two or three days a week.'

'I don't think two or three days will do it, Seb.'

So I compromised. I did seven, becoming William Hague's chief of staff. Charles Hendry had decided to concentrate on finding a new seat, which he did, becoming MP for Wealden in Sussex, a few miles from where he was born.

Although it would have been hard to distil into a formal job description, my role was to head up William's support team, juggling people and politics, publicity and fundraising, ensuring nobody was – or felt – left out; and later on, watching his back.

I also instigated a training schedule. The morale of the local constituencies was as bad as it had ever been and a visit from the leader would go a long way to keeping them buoyant. Yet William's Westminster duties alone – management of the parliamentary party, management of the shadow cabinet, management of central office – were incredibly taxing. Add to that a diary weighted by both domestic and international travel, and the physical wear and tear was not marginal.

William was smart enough to recognise this, and one day asked, 'What do you think I should do to keep in shape?' The answer was simple: 'Do what you like doing.' However, William's favourite outdoor pursuit – fell and mountain walking – was in short supply within the radius of the M25. Then he volunteered that he'd always been interested in martial arts. Now while I didn't know the first thing about any of those disciplines, I knew someone who did. Ray Stevens had got a silver medal in judo at the Barcelona Games and was now managing a martial-arts club in Fulham, Budokwai, so I rang him up.

'Ray, how do you fancy a private pupil?'

'Well, I'm a bit pushed at the moment. Who is it?'

'William Hague.'

There was a theatrical silence at the end of the phone. He didn't quite say, 'Yeah, very funny,' but it was close. A week later I introduced them. Judo is about using the least amount of physical strength to throw your opponent and it's not something you can practise on your own, which is why I decided to learn with him. I didn't last long. My years of competitive racing had made me nervous of injury and I was never entirely comfortable with being flung around. However, from then on William set aside regular blocks of time in his diary for exercise. He was under enormous pressure and I knew from my own experience that regular exercise maximises your physical and mental energy.

At first we used the gym in the basement of the apartment block where Jeffrey Archer had a penthouse. This had the advantage of being close – just across the river from Westminster – and free from mocking eyes.

I had known Jeffrey for over twenty years. A former sprinter and hurdler, he was famously obsessive about track and field and was actually the first face I recognised on my lap of honour in Los Angeles after winning the 1500 metres. I was obviously aware of the public perception of him, but in person he was always charming and good company, and when he offered us the use of the gym I had no hesitation in accepting. Jeffrey had a talent for resurrection as well as reinvention, and having won the Conservative nomination for London Mayor in October 1999, he looked finally to be on his way to senior representative office. However, the arrangement came to a sudden and grinding halt that November when Jeffrey was first accused – and eventually tried and sentenced – for perjury.

The offices of the shadow cabinet and leader of the opposition were not impressive. I had paid my first visit during my number-crunching days. The place was totally unlived in and there was a definite smell of mice. It must have been months, if not years, since New Labour closed the door on it, having moved their entire operation over to a super-high-tech communications centre in Millbank Tower. There was a broken fax machine, a couple of telephone lines that went nowhere, a beaten-up desk or two and that was about it. It looked as if Tony Blair had only ever dropped his coat off in this place.

The Conservatives had been in power for eighteen years. Now that they found themselves ranged on the wrong side of the Speaker's chair, with no ministerial boxes to busy themselves with, they looked lost. Of the shadow cabinet, only a handful had ever been in opposition. There was no hinterland. No researchers to speak of. No think tanks or policy units. In government there had been battalions of back-office staff – civil servants, special advisors, a hundred people behind every big name providing all the support you wanted. Not so in opposition. It is, by a distance, the most thankless job in politics. Malcolm Rifkind once memorably described it as, 'getting into the back of your car and going nowhere'.

At the party conference in Blackpool in October 1997, John Major – in his outgoing speech – had delivered a prescient warning: 'It's a simple choice. Reform the party, back William Hague, rediscover the art of working together, fight every seat for every vote – or fight one another and lose elections.'

Sadly, that is pretty much what happened. Yet while the

arguments over Europe didn't entirely disappear, William ensured that the range war stopped. There were inevitable skirmishes, but the internecine bloodshed in the Tory Party over Europe was no longer the lead story every morning. William was more sure-footed than his predecessor had been. John Major's inherent affability meant that everyone thought he was talking their language. William planted his flagpole and moved neither towards John Redwood's Eurosceptic right nor closer to Ken Clarke's position. Everyone knew where he stood and eventually ceased to lobby him on the subject.

The squabbling over Europe had been immensely damaging to the party in the run-up to the '97 election. In the eyes of the electorate, we were a querulous, mutinous lot who didn't deserve to be in government.

There was also no question that the political landscape had changed, but then so had the language. After '97 we'd got the Middle Way, or the Third Way. In the States, Bill Clinton had emerged. Princess Diana had died. This was a very difficult topography to gauge. Had the electorate really rejected Conservative policies? Or had they rejected the way Conservative policies had been presented? Or portrayed? As it turned out, New Labour jettisoned very little of what we had bequeathed them. They didn't fight the election on re-nationalisation. The 1997 battle was not danced to a theological tune. It was simply that, unpalatable or not, we had had our time. And you have to say that the electorate were right. For all the erudite scribblings, opinion polls, press conferences, initiatives, counterblasts and clever posters that are the scenery of every election, the electorate knows when time's up and instinctively makes a judgement.

As for reform, the party remained traumatised, still reeling from defeat. Everyone knew that there had to be changes. The electorate had told us loud and clear that it no longer wanted what we had on our stall. On Europe, we appeared introspective and absorbed in an issue that in reality rarely featured the top four or five electoral issues. The party's grey beards who could have come to the rescue and knocked a few heads together, were either sniping from the sidelines or no longer in play.

One who was still around, albeit in the House of Lords, was Lord Parkinson. Although he had largely retired from politics, as a former party chairman Cecil knew how Conservative central office worked, and he certainly knew about the dog days of opposition when he and Nigel Lawson and Norman Fowler were the young Turks fighting it out with Labour hand-to-hand on the backbenches in the late seventies. One of William's first actions was to re-appoint him as party chairman. Cecil had the advantage of having seen it all before, and with his wonderful sense of humour it was a delight just to be in his company. He was that rare combination – a serious politician who never took himself too seriously. Also he did calm the horses and would become a crucial cog in William's wheel, particularly when it came to putting our financial house in order.

William Hague and Ffion Jenkins met in 1995 when he was Minister of State at the Welsh Office, where she had worked for him and famously taught him the Welsh national anthem. They married on 19 December 1997 in the crypt below Westminster Hall, the bridegroom having spent his last night as a bachelor at Ranmore Farm. Above us, in the House of Commons, parliament was still sitting. Also in session, although the bridegroom didn't know it, were our auditors in the final stages of authorising the party's accounts. A collective decision had been taken not to tell him this was happening. It was a wedding present he didn't need and it wasn't as if there was anything he could have done. As the reception got under way, Cecil Parkinson kept popping in and out giving us the latest position. There was a real risk that the party could go under before Christmas, and the fact remains that William could have returned from honeymoon as leader of a party that had ceased to exist.

Meanwhile, that other Westminster honeymoon – the ceasefire traditionally accorded to a new administration – showed no signs of losing its bloom, and Tony Blair's personal star continued to rise. One reason was the signing of the Good Friday Agreement in Belfast, ending decades of civil war by another name. In spite of an appalling massacre in Omagh two months later, the hard-won deal would lead to a ceasefire by the Real IRA and meetings between David Trimble of the Ulster Unionists and Gerry Adams of Sinn Fein. Tony Blair claimed to have felt 'the hand of destiny' on his shoulder, but little mention was ever made of the role played by John Major in earlier negotiations, which made it all possible. Party-political point scoring would have been entirely inappropriate, but in terms of William's or the party's visibility, it did not help.

The 1998 party conference was held in Bournemouth. The first evening was always given over to the party's agents – the only non-volunteers in local associations – when they would be addressed by senior members of the cabinet, now the shadow cabinet, and the leader. We were roughly halfway through the speeches when I was called by the press office. The *Sun* was putting William on the front page in the guise of an upside-down parrot, hanging from a perch, echoing the famous Monty Python sketch, the text taking up the entire front page: 'This party is no more . . . it has ceased to be . . . this is an EX-party.'

'Everything all right?' asked John Major when I'd finished the call, having seen me looking a little wan. So I explained.

'But that's completely outrageous,' he said. 'Are you sure? Who did you hear it from? Well, one thing's clear. You have to tell him.'

'I don't have a problem about telling him. But what difference is it going to make?'

By this time I was beginning to get the measure of William. If I did decide to say something, it certainly wouldn't de-rail him. But of course for John Major this was a case of déjà vu. His relationship with the *Sun* had ended brutally on the night of Black Wednesday, and arguably ended our relationship with the electorate as well. Kelvin MacKenzie tells how – probably on the advice of the communications team – Major rang around all the national newspaper editors. When it came to the *Sun*'s turn, the conversation started well enough: 'Hello Kelvin, how are you?' etc. to which he replied, 'I'm fine, Prime Minister, but I've got a bucket of shit lying on my desk and tomorrow it's going to be all over you.'

With William, I knew that mention of the *Sun* wouldn't evoke any such Pavlovian response. He would have put the information to one side and dealt with it later. In the meantime, he would have the agents – emotionally still in the recovery ward – rocking in the aisles as he always did.

In the end, I decided to wait, and for the record, his reaction when he saw the parrot next morning was to laugh. I told him I wasn't sure the party membership or our donors would find it quite so funny.

John Major always remained very fond of William – not least because William was to some extent his protégé. John had made him the youngest member of cabinet since Harold Wilson. For his part, William was always grateful for the platform Major had given him.

Relations between Margaret Thatcher and her predecessor were not as cordial. In fact, they were toxic. With party unity high on the agenda, it was decided that having both former PMs on the same platform would send out a clear message. Both were well past retirement age – Heath was 80 – and in a combined comfort-plus-money-saving exercise, we bought some chairs from Ikea. It turned into another PR disaster when we were pilloried for appearing to ape Labour's Cool Britannia. Meanwhile, during the debate on Europe – the occasion for their presence – the cameras did not lie. They showed Margaret and Ted sitting in identical blue bucket chairs, either asleep or, when awake, refusing to look at each other.

For the entire four years I worked with William, fundraising was never off the agenda and it was hard pounding. Following the Bournemouth party conference, somebody suggested auctioning the chairs. Owning the chair that Margaret Thatcher had once sat in might have an appeal to a certain kind of party activist it was thought. I have no idea how much money was raised, but they all went, notably one to Elizabeth Stevenson, scion of the powerful Stevenson family who ran most of the trawlers out of St Ives. But it was not about to become a family heirloom. Instead, she and her fellow anti-Europeans – everyone in the fishing industry in south Cornwall who wasn't at sea that day – assembled on the quayside and with great ceremony set it alight, although not before strapping in an effigy of Edward Heath. Both Ted and the Ikea chair were burned to a cinder, the whole episode being filmed and then broadcast by BBC South West television. No surprises who delivered this piece of news from the front line.

William's resilience to adversity was almost superhuman and he had the great gift of being able to laugh at himself. He has the original of a *Times* cartoon showing a series of outline drawings of his head, captioned 'Hague Happy', 'Hague Furious', 'Hague Irritated' and so on, each one of them identical. And like many good caricatures, there was some truth there. William had an inbuilt imperturbability which was fireproof. Only once in the four years I worked with him did I see a chink in that armour. It was mid-April 1999 and we were heading for Liverpool for a day's campaigning and meeting with local businesses ahead of the following week's local and devolution elections. The previous evening Peter Lilley, William's deputy and head of policy, had given a speech at the Carlton Club, the R.A. Butler memorial lecture, which the party were using as a platform for Conservative policy reform. William had, naturally, read the speech but not, it transpired, the final draft. The next morning it was head-line news: LILLEY URGES PRIVATISATION RE-THINK, LILLEY KNOCKS UP THE FIRST PLANK IN THE TORY LIFE RAFT. The tabloids were content with the simpler: END OF THATCHERISM.

The next few days would be marked by real anger, with calls for either Lilley's resignation or William's, or as the press put it, 'Tory Party in Mutiny' and 'Hague Fights to Save his Political Life'. In a speech a few days later, William repudiated the idea that he was abandoning Margaret Thatcher's free-market policies, but acknowl-edged that Conservatives couldn't live on 'the glory of the Thatcher years' for ever. And while the party wasn't prepared for a wholesale rebranding as New Labour had done, there was an argument for some degree of brand decontamination. May 1997 had been a watershed and it would be foolish not to recognise it. Peter Lilley's speech was a departure, and would prove the first step on a journey that would eventually take David Cameron to Downing Street.

I remember standing in Battersea heliport that morning, wait-ing for the fog to lift so that we could get going to Liverpool, and for the first time seeing William despondent. I told him, 'Look there's nothing you can do now. Just punch on through and deal with it tomorrow.'

At the first opportunity I rang James Arbuthnot, by now William's chief whip.

'James, I will keep this rolling today, but when he gets back tonight, he's going to need some support. I've not seen him like this before.' And I hadn't. For two years he had worked tirelessly to jolt the party into some semblance of an opposition, into a party that once again had a vision of where it was going and what it wanted to achieve, but it was like trying to inflate a hot-air balloon with a bicycle pump.

Once the helicopter took off and we were headed for Liverpool, I felt his mood lighten. Having been delayed by the fog, we were running late and immediately on landing we went straight into a press huddle. Although this was mainly for the benefit of local TV and newspapers, a northern stringer from the *Daily Express* was there. I can't remember his question, but I will never forget William's answer. 'In the twenty years I've been in politics,' he said, 'that is probably the most stupid question I have ever been asked.' And then everyone began to laugh. The journalist was stunned. And I thought, 'Good. He's through and out the other side.' And from then on, whenever things got hairy, I'd say, 'Now don't forget: the spirit of Liverpool.'

Going north in William's company was always a tonic. He grew up midway between Barnsley and Rotherham, just ten miles east of Sheffield. His constituency is in Richmond, just south of the Co. Durham border, and on the train, when we hit Peterborough, the change was palpable. From then on, every mile north you could feel him unwind. He'd open a bottle of beer, or pour himself a glass or two of wine, and by the time we got to Darlington he was a changed man.

If William had a weakness, it was his lack of interest in popular culture. 'You should try to be more normal, William,' the media people around him would say.

'Meaning?'

'It would help if you knew what was happening on *Brookside*, for example.'

'Why?'

'Because people will think it's normal.'

'But I am not normal. I want to be their prime minister. That's not normal. What value or quality do I bring to people's lives by knowing what's happening on *Brookside* or *EastEnders*? That's not what they're voting for.'

Someone even suggested a compilation tape, a weekly update of all the key soap moments on video.

'You're mad,' I said. 'He hates television.'

The thought that these products of St Paul's and Westminster could begin to tell William about what the ordinary person wanted to hear was ridiculous. This was a guy who went to a comprehensive on Wath-on-Dearne, South Yorkshire. He was born in Wentworth, three miles from Greasbrough colliery. He grew up alongside coal miners, steel workers and farm labourers. His parents might have been middle-class – they owned a local soft-drinks company – but when they sent him to a local prep school, aged eight, after less than a week he asked to go back to the local primary. They tried again when he was older, this time Ripon Grammar as a boarder. This was equally short-lived and he insisted on going to the local comprehensive. He and I get on fundamentally because we were hewn from the same South Yorkshire landscape and share such similar backgrounds.

For once the press have it right. He is a straight-talking Yorkshireman. I remember him saying to me once, 'The problem is, I'm conservative with a small c. I never get too excited by the best but I never get too depressed by the worst, because reality is usually somewhere in the middle. And I can't keep flying into these synthetic rages to order.'

Tony Blair, of course, was just the opposite. He had total conviction, or appeared to. Even the most mundane subject would be imbued with a fervour that it rarely deserved, and when it came to the death of Diana, he reached his apogee. Once Blair had encapsulated Diana as 'the people's princess' he became her champion and until Iraq, could do no wrong. William was not cut from the same cloth.

I was on holiday in Portugal with my family when the news came through. Portuguese TV covered the tragedy as assiduously as everybody else and I could see that, while Blair had judged it completely right, down to the setting outside the local parish church, William's response didn't match the mood of the country, let alone lead it as Blair's had done.

When I got back to England, his team were still berating themselves. The mistake had been to send him out too early, they said. They should have waited to see the lie of the land. But William remained adamant that he could not have reacted any differently however long he'd waited.

'You've got to do these things as you feel at the time. All right, perhaps the response was a bit early. And what did I say? That I was desperately sorry and at that moment I felt most sorry for the children? These are two young boys who have just lost their mother. I can't go into a eulogy, I don't do what he does, that's why I'm different.'

Just as the misconceived 'Back to Basics' sounded the death knell for John Major, William's speech to the party in April 2001, at a spring forum in Harrogate, was similarly misconstrued.

This was a thoughtful, hard-hitting, prepare-for-election attack on New Labour, presenting the harrowing spectre of yet four more years of a Blair-led government. 'Try to picture what our country would look like. Let me take you on a journey to a foreign land.' It was nothing to do with immigration, but that's how it was spun. And there was some suspicion that this had been oversold by Nick Wood, a former *Times* journalist, who was then William's communications director, and Amanda Platell, former editor of the *Sunday Express*, his press secretary. I can picture the pair of them now. When a lobby correspondent asked, 'Does William here mean asylum seekers?' they looked at each other. It looked to me like they were saying 'Let's go for it.' In doing so, they were promulgating their own political preferences. And this is very, very dangerous.

In the press coverage the following day there was nothing about lowering taxation or constitutional reform, or any of the other issues that William addressed. The focus – and headlines – was Britain as a 'foreign land'. And with only a few months to go before the election, this was not helpful. It was 'Back to Basics' revisited – big moments when things get spun by over-zealous press teams who trim and often interpret. This is not limited to the Conservatives. At certain key moments in recent history, the way that communications directors and/or press secretaries of whatever party speak on behalf of their masters, the tone adopted and selective reportage have been enough to change political fortunes.

A severe outbreak of foot and mouth disease postponed polling day until June. As in 1997, we began the campaign determined to give our all, and just as in 1997, there was little hope that we would actually win. The party fought the only campaign it could.

One hundred and seventy seats previously held by the Conservatives had been taken by Labour in 1997. While not all could be clawed back, a considerable number might be considered marginals, constituencies where an appearance by the leader could tip the scales. The election was called on 8 May for polling on 7 June. This gave us twenty-eight days – seven marginals a day, excluding Sundays. The only way we could physically get around this number was by using a helicopter. Yet as any general will tell you, an army moves only as fast as its slowest component, and the slowest component in a political campaign is the media entourage. There was little point in getting William somewhere, fêted by thousands after a barnstorming speech, if there was no one there to put it on television that evening. Campaigning at this level is about building up a head of steam, and for that you need constant exposure.

While you could get the press to a local airport in a jet from Northolt, you still had to get them off the plane and into mini buses to ferry them to the next staging post. Realistically, the most we could hope for was two big moments a day. In the meantime, by using the helicopter we might be able to visit six or seven marginals in one geographical area.

Timing was a huge part of my job. Stay five minutes too long at the 11 o'clock slot and by 5.00 p.m. you're running an hour or more late.

'So how long did it take you?' I asked the party worker who claimed the two hundred yards between the drop-off point and the venue was walkable.

'Half a minute,' she said.

'Great. So that's William, Ffion, me and one tubby cameraman moving at a four-minute mile pace. I'm not sure even I'm up to it any more.'

Two hundred yards may be walking distance but, unless you're a Jamaican sprinter, it takes longer than thirty seconds to cover it, and over two hundred yards of open territory anything can happen, and for one week it often did.

From 15 to 19 May we were dogged by a journalist from the *People,* dressed as Krusty the Clown, a character from the Simpsons. The plan was clearly to snatch a picture of Krusty and William together and caption it 'Which one is the clown?' And I made it my life's work to stop this happening. It's fair to say I became completely obsessive. Krusty made his first appearance in Salford on the Tuesday. I just assumed he was some kind of nutter and wrestled him out of camera shot. This then became the story. He told reporters he wanted to shake hands with the biggest clown in the world . . .

I remember the next few days as a series of pitched battles. On Wednesday we were at the other end of the country in Portsmouth, but there he was with his tufts of orange hair and red nose, glasses and shoes the size of lacrosse sticks. William's itinerary wasn't restricted information and Krusty used to drive overnight to where he knew we would be. I became obsessed by this guy whose face I had never seen. I would dream about him. I would wake up in the small hours thinking, 'How far has the bastard got?' By this time I'd recruited a couple of friends who had helped me on my Cornish campaigns, simply to stop this jerk from getting close to William, but Krusty was by now a *cause célèbre*. A clutch of teenagers would be chanting 'Free the clown'. Meanwhile, his circus jokes continued. I was 'Coe-Coe' the clown while he claimed to be William's 'new running mate'.

In Southsea he ambushed us by the helicopter, but I managed to get William in without being snapped. The next day we were in St Albans. William was about to board a campaign bus when I spotted Krusty among the well-wishers, waiting for his hand to be shaken.

That Saturday night, I knew it was time to move on when Pete, then aged four, said, 'Dad, why are you on television punching a clown?' I can't now remember whether it was Portsmouth or Southsea or some other end-of-the pier resort, but I was on the ground, in the dust, wrestling with this fucking clown, locked in mortal combat. I remember thinking, 'I've got him. I've got him now', and the guy looking up at me with what seemed like resignation in his eyes. He said, 'OK. That's it. I'm not doing this any more. I'm not paid enough.' As he pulled off the latex mask I said, 'Neither am I.' And we both started laughing.

Before the election William had quietly told me that he had set himself a target of thirty additional seats, as well as a sizeable increase in the Conservative vote, and if he didn't get them he would resign. Only three people knew – Ffion, James Arbuthnot and me. The target was non-negotiable.

I was with him and Ffion at their constituency house in Catterick waiting for the results to come in. Richmond itself is a large, rural constituency and the count wouldn't be held until the following day.

Huw Edwards, then presenter of BBC's *Six O'Clock News*, was standing in the road with an outside broadcast unit, being badgered by London for the latest information from the beleaguered Conservative leader. Although it was June, the weather was terrible, and as I peered through the drawn curtains I couldn't help feeling sorry for the guy. Every now and then my mobile would ring – Huw Edwards wanting some colour.

'So would you describe him as pensive?' Huw suggested. I turned and saw that William was deep in a book, an empty bottle of claret by his side.

'We're just having a really nice evening,' I said.

'Would you be happy to say that you're eating curry?'

'Fine. We're eating curry.'

'Washed down by beer?'

'Why not.'

'And this curry, I take it it's home-made?'

In due course the BBC cut to the shivering figure of Huw Edwards, clutching his microphone.

'I can see that the light is still on downstairs where a pensive William Hague will be anticipating a call from the party chairman relaying the first exit polls. The curry prepared earlier in the evening by his wife Ffion, washed down with local beer, has been enjoyed and cleared away. All he can do now is wait.'

Once we saw that nothing had changed, I knew what William's decision would be. I was in no position to offer him advice, only support.

'If you decide to stay on,' I told him, 'you know I will stay and do what I can. But you should also know that if you decide to go, you have friends for life, and life goes on.' Clichéd but true.

In the event, we got one additional seat. To all intents and purposes it was a repeat of 1997, as if the last four years simply hadn't happened. My belief is that when it came to the 2001 election, nothing could have altered our fortunes. In the circumstances, I think William did extraordinarily well to have kept the party intact, with no loss of seats. This was less about winning an election than about whether the Conservative Party survived.

Or as William would put it, 'Somebody had to do the night shift.'

19

MARKING TIME

IN November 1999, William let me know he was going to nomi-nate me for a peerage. I am not often lost for words, but I was then. It came as a total surprise. I neither expected it nor saw it coming. Generous as this was, I didn't believe it would actually happen. It's in the interests of the party in power to limit the numbers of peers taking the opposition whip, and I knew that few of William's nominations – given to the appointments secretary twice a year, the New Year's honours in January and the Queen's birthday honours in June – had actually materialised. But that November, following the first stage of the reform of the House of Lords, the vast majority of hereditary peers had their voting powers removed. From a total of around 700, only 91 remained. Membership of the upper house would henceforth be by appointment – life peers – a mix of political appointees and people who had made their mark in another field and could 'make an effective and significant contribution to the work of the House'. Their role remained the same, namely to review and amend bills passed by the House of Commons. This drastic cull had left a sizeable hole, which needed to be filled, and four months later, at the end of March 2000, thirty-three new working life peers were created, twenty Labour, nine Liberal Democrat and four Conservative, of which I was one.

In spite of our overwhelming defeat in the 2001 election, William Hague had retained his seat with an increased majority and his Yorkshire constituency was now the safest in Britain – they don't count William's votes, they just weigh them. As for the Conservative

Party, it would be for others to go through the painful business of trying to get the show back on the road. The future of the party was no longer in William's hands. During the following two terms, while continuing to represent his constituency as a backbencher, he wrote two magnificent biographies of two formidable parliamentarians: William Pitt the Younger, prime minister at the age of 24, and Pitt's contemporary and friend William Wilberforce, the anti-slave-trade campaigner.

Over the last four years I had come to admire William's courage, his intellect, his wit and his honesty. I had also become his friend. Loyalty at any level in politics is hard won. When your party is in government, you remain loyal to those who might one day give you a job. But the frustrations of opposition can often lead to the party and some of its bigger hitters turning the gun on themselves, occasionally inflicting more damage than the official opponents on the benches opposite.

To some extent, every marriage is a leap into the dark. That first decade, when married life should be at its most vibrant and joyful, was effectively sabotaged by Maastricht and our tiny majority. From my perspective, these were exciting years, years of high drama. Understandably, not so for Nicky.

No one sets out on the path to matrimony with anything other than optimism that it will all work out, that the family will remain together. No one goes through a marital break-up without deep wounds, and for me it will always be a monumental failure. We formally separated in 2002.

As a temporary measure I moved in with Malcolm in Chingford. I then found an apartment overlooking my beloved Battersea Park. There were moments when I thought, 'How have I got to this position? Two years ago I was married and my life had a recognisable structure.' But I had a new, unnerving flexibility and, perversely, through having sole responsibility most weekends, I became conscious of just how wonderful our four children were – Alice, the youngest addition to the family, had been born at the end of September 1998.

My father had, of course, been through the same thing himself, and while he was not about to judge me, he did offer me some advice. 'There's no halfway house,' he said. 'If you can't be there full time for your children, it's probably better not to be there at all. I feel desperately sorry for you, but it's a moral maze only you can negotiate, a decision only you can take.'

The break-up came at a particularly difficult time for him. In 2001 my mother had been diagnosed with PSP – Progressive Supranuclear Palsy – a degenerative brain disease. For the last few years we had been aware that something was not right. Gradually, her balance and eyesight had deteriorated and she had problems with speech. Angela had always been someone who fired on all cylinders – she was the beating heart that had kept the family functioning and healthy. Now all that was gone. She was only 72, the age when you ought to be able to wind down and enjoy your grandchildren. She had always been a voracious reader with never less than several books on the go, but even this pleasure was now lost to her.

During my career on the track – and perhaps more importantly when I was still at school – whenever I had become too tunnel-visioned about running, it was Angela who made me lighten up and ensured there was balance in my life, not least through music. She had a wonderful, if sometimes crushing, sense of humour, and everyone who met her fell in love with her. Now it was just a question of time. She had never wallowed in self-pity, but with her frustration at the things she could no longer do, there was also fear. For those around her, particularly Peter, who had to cope on a day-to-day basis, it was deeply distressing. On a practical level it was also worrying since his own eyesight was failing, his glaucoma getting worse.

* * *

If the Blair revolution hadn't happened – or if Peter de Savary had quit – I would probably have survived in Falmouth and Camborne and would certainly have committed the rest of my working life to a political career. My time in the whips' office was undoubtedly one of the most exacting periods of my life. Being part of that élite club, the banter and the camaraderie, the shared and competing ambitions, was a daily excitement. I knew that nothing in politics would ever be so exhilarating – at least for someone like me. Where could I ever hope to find that intensity again?

Throughout all this I was never too far away from sport. In 1997 I was appointed to the Sport for All commission of the IOC. In 1998 I took on the presidency of the AAA. In 1999 I won the British Sports Writers' Award for 'most outstanding contribution to sport in the last fifty years'. In 2000 I went to the Sydney Olympics, where I commentated on track and field events for the Australian TV channel Network Seven, and continued to cover athletics for them at all the major international meets over the next few years. Back in Britain I was a regular contributor to BBC's sports channel Radio 5 Live, and also did a fortnightly comment column for the *Daily Telegraph*.

I have always loved writing and, as my column then appeared on a Monday, I would set aside the whole of Friday to do it. Sitting down at your kitchen table with a blank sheet of paper and a pen – I still write in longhand – can be quite daunting when you haven't an idea in your head and you know that by the end of the day it has to be filed, as it has already been trailed. Like anyone with a regular column, I would focus on a topical issue, and in early February 2001 Linford Christie, Britain's most successful sprinter, was back in the news.

A two-year suspension following a failed drugs test had just come to an end and in an interview in a women's magazine, which led to banner headlines in the mainstream press, he accused officials of the International Federation of being 'corrupt', and said he wouldn't want his children to follow him into the sport. I located a copy of the original article and started from there.

A bit of history: 1999 was not the first time Linford had failed a drugs test. Eleven years earlier in Seoul, after his 100m semi-final, he tested positive for a stimulant. He claimed that instead of his usual ginseng, he had been given a different sort, which contained this stuff. Given the benefit of the doubt, he progressed through to the final and finished fourth, a race now sadly cast in Olympic history as it was won by Canadian Ben Johnson, who was subsequently disqualified for failing a drugs test – and not marginally. His body contained forty-two times the permitted level. Carl Lewis moved up to take gold, elevating Linford's fourth place to third and Olympic bronze.

Then in early 1999, now at the tail end of his career on the track, Linford was tested positive for the growth hormone Nandrolone at an indoor meeting in Germany and banned for two years. Nandrolone is used in the treatment of breast cancer to rebuild muscle. In my opinion, it's very difficult to test positive if you haven't taken something.

Linford put it down to avocados and vitamin supplements, and UK Athletics, which supplanted the British Athletics Federation in 1999, decided it was too close to call and they, too, gave him the benefit of the doubt. Coming only four years after the federation had lost a long and costly battle with the 800m Commonwealth Games gold medallist Diane Modahl, perhaps they had neither the stomach nor the coffers for a sustained fight. Modahl had claimed innocence after failing a drugs test at the 1994 Commonwealth Games in Canada and subsequently sued the federation for £450K. By the time the case ended the federation was broken, hence its reincarnation as UK Athletics.

Unlike in the Modahl case, where her name was cleared, the

International Federation were not minded to do the same for Linford, and he was banned for two years – hence his claim that they were 'corrupt'.

However, Linford remained an influential figure in the sport. His status was iconic, he was a role model, and in that sense I felt it was important to rebut his accusations. Never underestimate the impact of individuals. If Andy Murray were to win Wimbledon, it would shift British tennis; the well-stocked shop window is a more potent driver of participation than any amount of money spent by the LTA encouraging people to take up the game. Kelly Holmes inspired more girls to take up sport than any government or sports council initiative, simply by winning the double back to back in Athens.

I know that most athletes would rather jump off Beachy Head than take as much as an aspirin. Yet not long ago, at a school athletics meet, I overheard a parent saying, 'Well, I wouldn't let my kids go into track and field.' And why? Because of drugs, and I found it deeply depressing.

Although Linford is a little younger than me, he and I are of the same generation. I had known him over a number of years and we actually got on pretty well. When in the summer of 1989 he was made captain of the British track and field team, to many in the team – of which I was one – it appeared a brave decision.

In early 2001, I used my regular column to counter what I considered damaging observations from Linford about our sport. I now accept that the language I chose was unnecessarily inflammatory. I knew he wouldn't like it, but the firestorm that followed took me totally by surprise. The day after it appeared in the *Telegraph*, the gist of my broadside was splashed across every tabloid. It wasn't long before Linford took to the airwaves. Interviewed on Radio 4's *Today*, he offered the thought, 'Maybe it's because Seb feels that he is more upper class than I am?'

I was still working for William at this stage, and our daily early-morning meetings always started with a press report. So that Tuesday, when William said, 'What have we got in the papers today, Nick?' to his head of communications Nick Wood, I knew what was coming.

'Your chief of staff, William, pretty much across every front page.' At this Michael Portillo, by now shadow chancellor, turned to me and said waspishly, 'Well I hope you've got a good lawyer.' Ours was never an easy working relationship.

Four years earlier, in November 1997, I had been assigned to shepherd the former secretary of state for defence around Winchester, where he was supporting our candidate at a by-election. At one point we went into Marks & Spencer to grab a sandwich and if I hadn't got him out of the building, they'd have buried him face down in the yogurt counter. He was practically lynched. This was the moment when I realised just how unpopular both he and the party were. I genuinely felt sorry for him. Nobody deserved this kind of treatment. But it didn't stop there. As we hastily made our exit, these ordinary middle-aged, middle-class women – not obvious Labour supporters, quite the contrary – followed us out on to the pavement, hurling more abuse. It was bordering on violence and he was visibly shaken. Until that incident it was hard for us to grasp the enormity of the repair job that lay ahead. But this was a turning point.

In February 2002, a year after the furore over my *Telegraph* comments, I was a guest on Simon Mayo's Friday afternoon show on Radio 5 Live. Nicky and I were by now separated and my new weekend routine was to pick up the children from school and take them back to the house I had rented about five miles away from Ranmore. I'd made it clear to the production team that I'd need to leave promptly.

The show's format was answering questions sent in by email with a few people phoning in. It was all basic stuff, like why Britain didn't have any 1500m runners any more. Then, around 2.30 p.m., during the break for weather or traffic, Simon said, 'Look, we've got so many callers, would you mind staying another four or five minutes?' So I looked at my watch and said, 'OK. But five at most. I must be on the road by three – I can't afford to hit the Friday night snarl up.'

The moment the red 'on-air' light lit up, Mayo wasted no time. 'There are moments in the life of a broadcaster,' he said, 'when your heart skips a beat. We have a Linford from London on the line.'

My heart sank as I listened to Linford's voice through my earphones, saying how I'd misunderstood what he'd said, that he was talking about the IAAF and not about the volunteers in English track and field who basically run the sport. I hadn't misunderstood. I had written my piece with the original interview in front of me. He might have had an issue with the piece but I knew exactly what I'd read.

Having gauged the direction of travel, I ceased to listen and was figuring out what my options were. I could either remove my earphones and head for Surrey or engage. I decided to stonewall. Then came the inevitable: 'This is your moment, Seb. You apologise to me now.'

'I don't think so,' I said. 'I'm not really in the mood to rewrite history just because you are on the telephone. I'm not suddenly going to say that I was wrong because I don't think I was.' And then he came back at me and it went on and on. In truth, Mayo had lost control. He should have jumped in and stopped it, but he sat back, arms folded and just watched, yet he was sharp enough to know that this exchange could have gone anywhere. The exchange continued for twenty minutes or more, a combination of abuse and counter punching, until mercifully the three o'clock news intervened. It was clear none of them – editor, producer or presenter – had any intention of pulling apart the pugilists if they hadn't had to break. A radio studio is basically a sound-proof glass box and when I turned round to look at the production team, about half the station had their faces pressed to the glass. They had clearly enjoyed every second, which is more than I did.

I was out of there and into the sanctuary of my car within minutes. But no sooner had I switched on the radio – pre-set to Radio 5 Live – than I found they were trailing it. 'If you missed the extraordinary exchange between Seb Coe and Linford Christie, don't worry. We'll be re-running the whole broadcast after the seven o'clock news tonight. Stay tuned to Five for ear-catching radio!'

By the time I got to the children's school, even their teachers knew what had happened. When Harry appeared he said, 'Dad, were you really on the radio fighting with Linford Christie?'

My tough stance on this has in large part been echoed in sport. The British Olympic Association takes a zero tolerance stance on drugs. Linford Christie's exclusion from the Athens torch relay, and again from our own torch relay in London, had nothing whatever to do with me. Dwain Chambers and cyclist David Millar were in the same boat. I happen to agree with the decision even though it was ultimately overturned by an IOC ruling. The message has got to go out loud and clear. In my view when it comes to drugs, there should be no second chances. You blight your life and your entire career – not for two years, but for ever.

Only once did I witness drugs being used on the track. It was in the eighties, in Italy. I was just warming up when I spotted somebody injecting themselves before a race. I took the attitude at the time that it was none of my business, but looking back, I shouldn't have let it pass. As Edmund Burke said, 'All it takes for evil to triumph is for good men to do nothing.' But when you're half an hour away from a serious race, it's not the first thing on your mind, although it's fair to say that had it been somebody who was competing against me, it might have been different.

My position has been clear and unambiguous since 1981 in Baden-Baden when I was outspoken about the misuse of drugs before it became *de rigueur*. It was certainly going on when I was competing and I know that I was tested more regularly than others, because I was known to be clean. I was a safe test; it helped the stats look better. I also know that some athletes were tipped off in advance by unscrupulous federation officials and meet promoters. In the report on drugs I co-authored with sports minister Colin Moynihan, we recommended that drug testing be taken out of the hands of the governing bodies and not just during competition but also out of competition and entirely random. Funnily enough, the better the technology has become, the more 'innocent' people get caught.

In all, it's a pretty tawdry and twilight world. In the days when I was competing, drugs fell into two categories, immediate stimulants, which for a sprinter would be a serious thing, and growth hormones, which heavier guys can take. Now it's become more insidious. There's blood doping, which introduces substances into the bloodstream that have greater oxygen-carrying capacity and can improve endurance. Over 10,000 metres, the effects of this can be quite profound – the human equivalent of turbo charging. Then there are the THGs (Tetrahydrogestrinones) known as designer steroids because they were designed to evade the usual testing procedures. Not only do they build muscle but they reduce the fatigue associated with training. Dwain Chambers was banned after testing positive with THG. Not only are they illegal in sport, but they have unpleasant and dangerous side effects. Jaws start growing, hands get bigger. It is generally considered that Florence Griffith-Joyner – Flo Jo – died as a result of this manipulation. She was 38. In 1984 she set a new world record over 100m and nearly thirty years later it is still the world record. And here you have the real damage. A whole generation of female sprinters have looked at Flo Jo's time and thought, 'I'll never close that gap, so it's pointless devoting my energies to that particular target.' I wonder how many promising athletes have gone on to ply their talents in other sports as a result?

We know most about what was happening in East Germany in

the seventies and eighties because of the Stasi's obsession with documenting every facet of life in that era. Twenty years of systematic doping.

It's very easy to unload only on the athletes. The truth is that they are almost certainly a small part of a complicit and illicit network where, sadly, the coach all too often sits centre stage. I have never believed that an athlete suddenly wakes up in the small hours and thinks, 'I've had a gutful of finishing outside the medals, so I'm going to take drugs to get me up on the rostrum.'

And here I know I was lucky: I was being coached by my father, who not only plotted my athletics career, but also mapped the moral boundaries, as do the vast majority of coaches. If anyone had come up to me at the age of 15 or 16 and suggested there might be a quicker way of doing this, I know Peter would have put them in the hereafter.

I was discussing this issue not that long ago with the great American sprinter and four times Olympic gold medallist Michael Johnson, who still holds the record for the 400m he set in 1999. He agreed with my analysis, citing exactly the same experiences with his coach Clyde Hart, who in many ways reminded me of Peter. Hart had created exactly the same moral landscape for him, Michael said, and if anyone had offered him a little chemical enhancement, Clyde would have happily killed them.

Of course drugs in sport is nothing new. When big money was involved at the end of the 19th century, doping was rife. Strychnine and cocaine are two examples of the drugs that were common then. In ancient Greece, including the Olympic Games, the eating of bulls' testicles was thought to provide that extra edge. It is generally assumed that Dorando Pietri, winner of the marathon in the 1908 London Olympics, who collapsed four times during the final lap, was on a whole cocktail of things to get him across the line. He was later disqualified, not for drug abuse, but for having accepted assistance from the officials who got him moving again.

There will always be some individuals who choose to step beyond the boundaries. But where do you start when it comes to natural advantage? Kenyans have the natural advantage of having lived for thousands of generations at 7,400 feet above sea level. But the only sustainable competitive advantage we all have is the ability to learn quicker than the opposition. Ron Clarke who was breaking records in the sixties, Emil Zatopek in the forties and fifties, and before them Paavo Nurmi from Finland in the twenties, were ahead of the game because in their era they were doing what nobody else was doing.

The situation with athletes coming out of the eastern bloc was different. These were kids who had been identified at the age of nine or ten, sitting at breakfast in their state-sponsored sports school in Leipzig or wherever, and unquestioningly downing the 'vitamin' pills that they were given along with their morning milk, thinking, 'Well, this is what you have to do to become a top athlete.' Anyone who refused was ignominiously sent back to their shamed families.

I have a good deal more sympathy for them than for those athletes coming out of a liberal democracy, knowing exactly what the rules are. When they say, 'Oh, I didn't know what I was taking . . .' Please. Of course they know. It's called cheating. And we should not be coy about saying so.

20

NO TOMORROWS

THE road to hosting the Olympic and Paralympic Games is strewn with boulders. Selection of the host city by the IOC is made seven years in advance from a short list made up of candidate cities – five in the case of 2012 – selected from those who put themselves forward two years before that, known as applicant cities. This makes nine years in all. But long before the IOC get involved, people have to start wanting it and thinking about it, not to mention all the soil tilling that needs to be done in persuading governments that it might be something worth doing.

London had already hosted the Games twice, in 1908 and 1948, but on both occasions we'd been the fall-back option. The 1908 Olympics had been scheduled for Rome, but when Mt Vesuvius erupted in 1906, the Italian capital pulled out as the money was needed for the reconstruction of Naples. Then in 1948 London stepped in when no one else was prepared to shoulder the burden so soon after the war. Had London not taken up the challenge it is questionable whether the Games would have survived the twelve-year hiatus, especially as the last Games, Berlin 1936, had been an exercise in propaganda for the Third Reich.

In 1985 Birmingham was a candidate city for the 1992 Games, planning to develop a site next to the National Exhibition Centre, which had opened ten years earlier. However, with IOC president Juan Antonio Samaranch in his home-city's corner – Barcelona – Birmingham's bid was probably doomed to fail. Four years later, Manchester tried for the 1996 Games, and four years after that revamped its bid for 2000. Any number of factors contributed to its failure to cross the line, but the facilities that the city fathers had already started to put in place formed the basis of their highly acclaimed staging of the Commonwealth Games in 2002.

At some level or another I had been involved in all these bids in that I had been asked to endorse them and I had talked them up whenever I'd had reason to speak to an IOC member, one of the hundred or so who would ultimately make the decision. Although my involvement was never more than that, it gave me a valuable insight into how things worked. The Birmingham bid had been led by Denis Howell, former sports minister under both Wilson and Callaghan. Ron Pickering and I were drafted in because Ron knew everyone who mattered in international sport and I was on more than nodding acquaintance with a good number of IOC members – this was five years after Baden-Baden and I was on the athletes' committee. The presentation was at IOC headquarters in Lausanne and I remember watching the Birmingham team as they made their final preparations. Denis was sitting in a chair on the rolling lawns of the Renaissance Hotel on the shores of Lake Geneva with a cigar the size of a missile. It was a preparatory Q & A session, so he was fielding questions, pre-empting anything that might get thrown at him the following day. Responding to a googly from one of the technical team, he came up with a raft of statistics.

'Denis,' this guy said. 'That's not the right answer. You're way overstating the situation here.'

Pulling the cigar out of his mouth, Denis gave this innocent a withering look and said, 'Of course it's not the "right" answer. It's an election. Everybody lies.'

Shortly after Manchester's second failed bid in 1993 (for 2000), I happened to cross paths with Samaranch and he could not have been clearer. 'Come back with London and we'll take you seriously,' he told me.

Around 1994 a small group of people started to think about what it might take to mount a successful London bid. They included Sir Craig Reedie, a shrewd Scot and very well connected. As well as being chairman of the British Olympic Association, he was one of Britain's four IOC members. A former president of the Badminton World Federation, he was largely responsible for delivering that game's Olympic status.

By 1997 work started in earnest on a feasibility study to set down what might be needed. The job was given to consulting engineers and designers Arup. This was familiar territory for them. Ove Arup had designed the futuristic stadium that had been the centrepiece of the failed Birmingham bid.

In November 2002, Arup's report was made public. It was an impressive and powerful document. While demonstrating the scale and complexity of the project, Arup nonetheless came out in favour. I needed no persuasion. Even before my conversation with Samaranch, I thought London was realistically the only runner.

My *Telegraph* column that week spelled it out. 'The challenges are formidable,' I wrote, 'if only overcoming the urge to doubt our ability.'

That spring, I was asked by some head-hunters to come up with a few names, people who I thought had the necessary background, skills and commitment to lead the bid. But while my own name was being touted in the press, it failed to feature on the relevant 2012 radar. My position from the start had been clear. I'd be happy to turn up to support the bid, to be around every couple of months whenever an IOC member was in town, but if they wanted a more serious involvement, it would have to be properly structured. And then I heard that Barbara Cassani had been appointed.

It struck me, at best, as counterintuitive. An American high flyer, she had worked for Bob Ayling at British Airways in setting up their budget arm Go. Three years later she had led a management buyout and became Go's first chief executive. The airline was then bought by easyJet. Barbara was clearly a talented businesswoman, and a business, whether retail or wholesale, whether it's a factory making doughnuts or machine tools – or indeed an airline – is underpinned by the same management principles. Sport is different . . . therein lies its attraction. It has an ethos and language all of its own, understood by anyone who's ever been involved, but double Dutch to anyone else. It thrives not on profit but on passion.

As to why Barbara Cassani had been chosen, there was much speculation. But with Manchester's failed bid fresh in their memories, when the traditional bid-leadership background had clearly not cut it, perhaps it was felt that somebody with more of a business locus was needed. Two years after the attacks on the twin towers, international tension was high. The Iraq war was under way and while understanding that the special relationship probably necessitated a British commitment to what, in essence, was US foreign policy, to have an American heading up our bid was a problem doubled. In addition, this American was a woman and, however unpalatable, this could be an inhibitor in a large part of the world, especially Africa and the Middle East. Notwithstanding all this, in my *Telegraph* column of 18 June 2003, I wished her well, and indeed gave her some advice about where to look for help and who to steer clear of. At the top of the latter list were politicians, who, I wrote, 'have an unerring sense of preservation at the first whiff of grapeshot. And there will be times in the next few years when the air will be full of it.' She would need them for access to the Treasury, 'but don't let them anywhere near the coalface because overnight they will become instant experts in every aspect of mining. The sound of collapsing pit props will soon follow. They will then remain one step ahead of their own rubble by setting up a select committee of enquiry into the failure of British universities to produce properly trained mining engineers.' Or as the subs' headline had it: Dear Barbara . . . Keep the politicians at arm's length.

Meanwhile, the press kept up its pressure, and I guess for Barbara this began to become irksome. You could hardly open a newspaper without reading that I'd been shunned. My absence, they trumpeted, was a glaring omission. Eventually, I got the call. She'd love to get me involved, she said. I should go see her and hear what she had in mind.

First impressions, although not necessarily accurate, are important, particularly in what, in many people's eyes, is a communications exercise. Her opening salvo was generous – with all that sporting excellence behind me, she was keen to give me the opportunity to come on board. 'So what I had in mind,' she said, 'was chairing a group of celebrities.'

I hadn't been sure what to expect, but it wasn't this. I explained, gently, that it wasn't quite my style and that I didn't think this was really what I was best placed to do. But, of course, I'd be happy to offer advice or to continue in an informal role. And it was true. I am above all a patriot, and I truly believed that London was the right city for 2012.

Over the next few weeks, I continued doing what I was doing – acting as advisor for Nike, and writing my column for the *Daily Telegraph* – while the press continued to speculate on my involvement. Then in November 2003 came another call, offering me one of the three vice chairman's jobs, along with Olympic hurdler Alan Pascoe and Charles Allen, former CEO of ITV, who had successfully chaired the Commonwealth Games organising committee in Manchester. So I went along to see her.

As she explained it, the role was hardly onerous. There would be the odd board meeting but in reality I'd be doing little more than I'd been doing anyway, picking up what intelligence I could through international sport and generally talking up our bid to any IOC members I came across. Just simple stuff – how committed the British are to sport, how London had shouldered the burden of the

1948 Games when nobody else was prepared to do it so soon after the war, and listing the Olympians we had produced and continued to produce.

'So I see it as a half-a-day-a-week job,' she explained, to which I replied that sounded a little light. 'And out of interest, Barbara,' I added, 'how many days are you doing?'

Shortly after taking on the London bid, Barbara Cassani had been appointed as a non-executive director at Marks & Spencer. Although the chairman's job came with a salary attached, it wasn't overgenerous, at least compared with the kind of big-city pay cheques she could certainly command elsewhere, but to get this Leviathan going would take belief, energy and real dedication.

'Oh, I'm doing about two days a week,' she said. I stared at her.

'So let me get this right, Barbara. You're doing two days a week, I'm going to do half a day a week. Is that it?'

'Give or take, yes. So what do you think?'

I folded my arms. 'We'll lose.'

'But how can you say that?'

'I know we'll lose because I've got friends who have done this before. The guy who headed up the Melbourne bid did it seven days a week for two years and he didn't win. They went out in the second round – Atlanta got it. A friend in Athens, who did win, ended up in a sanatorium for months afterwards. Then there's Jean-Claude Killy, one of the greatest skiers of all time, who went on to carve out an extraordinary business career. He brought in Albertville in 1992 and said it was the hardest thing he'd ever done. These people gave up two years of their lives. And they did nothing other than this. There are no tomorrows here, Barbara. This is what you do.'

To have even a bat's squeak of a chance we had to canvass 116 IOC members spread liberally across the globe, from Fiji to Guatemala and every stop in between. You could not do this job without travelling. I have no idea whether she took any of it on

Carole and I were married in July 2011 in a quiet ceremony for family and close friends. Harry, my eldest son, was best man.

Left: I can't even swim, but I can recognise talent when I see it. A year after his tremendous success in Bejing, I conducted Tom Daley and his namesake Daley Thompson around the Olympic Stadium.

Below: London mayor Boris Johnson joshes with Paralympian Ade Adepitan at the two-years-to-go celebrations in Trafalgar Square, August 2010.

The torch relay touched millions in its journey around the country. The design was unveiled a year earlier at St Pancras station, where I was proud to share the stage with Olympic gold medallists Jonathan Edwards and Denise Lewis together with Austin Playfoot, torch bearer from the London Games, 1948.

As one of Britain's four IOC members, the Princess Royal has been tireless in her support of the London bid. Together with David Beckham – another stalwart supporter – we flew with the Olympic flame from Greece, here photographed with deputy prime minister Nick Clegg just after landing at RNAS Culdrose, near Helston in Cornwall.

Appropriately, I carried the torch through my adopted home city of Sheffield, where my Olympic dream first began.

A successful Games must have buy-in from the very top. Like Tony Blair before him, David Cameron has been wholly supportive, here making a last-minute visit to the Olympic Park the day before the opening ceremony.

The mad professor, aka Danny Boyle, our Prospero.

The majority of the volunteer cast in the children's literature segment were health service professionals. Spot the odd one out.

Above: Making finishing touches to my speech moments before the opening ceremony began.

Right: The opening ceremony, addressing the largest audience I have ever faced, or will ever face.

Below: Little more than 24 hours after the historic helicopter descent with 007, I was able to introduce the Queen and Prince Philip to volunteers at the Aquatics Centre.

Chatting to Ellie Simmonds in the Paralympic village, just days before she won her two gold medals and the hearts of a nation.

Zara Phillips, riding Toytown in Greenwich Park, celebrates her silver medal – presented to her by her mother, the Princess Royal, who represented Britain in the Montreal Olympics.

Watching Chris Hoy win the keirin final, with the Princess Royal (*right*) and Carole (*left*) while Prince Harry and Peter Phillips, Zara's brother, celebrate. John Major is sitting immediately below, one of the Games' biggest supporters and whose National Lottery made so many of those glorious moments possible.

Greg Rutherford is the first Briton to take Olympic long-jump gold since my old friend and former team manager Lynn Davies in Tokyo in 1964.

Presenting Jessica Ennis with her flowers at the medal ceremony, I reminded her of my prediction one year earlier in Daegu, that she would take gold at the London Games.

David Rudisha's win at 800m was for me the stand-out performance of the Games.

Kenya dominated the 800m, my favourite distance. Gold medallist David Rudisha (*left*) with Timothy Kitum (*right*) who took bronze.

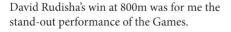

Track and field being my sport, I derived enormous pleasure from simply watching the best athletes in the world compete in the Olympic stadium.

A poignant moment shared with my sons, Harry (*left*) and Pete (*right*), right when I took them onto the track at the end of the Paralympic Games. All over.

board. I suspect not. In terms of getting the bid up and running, she did a really good job and brought in some exceptionally talented people, not least Keith Mills as CEO, a man of extraordinary ability and creative flair, who had invented Airmiles and changed the way people shop from Burnley to Beijing. But while Barbara Cassani clearly had all the business acumen, her world and that of the IOC had very different orbits.

The first hint I had that all was not well was when Keith button-holed me during a fundraising dinner at the Natural History Museum early in 2004. He wanted to sound me out, he said, while ushering me into the dinosaur galleries. Only once we were out of earshot did he speak, and then it was barely above a whisper.

'Do you think you can give some more time to this, Seb?'

Over the preceding six months I had come to value and like Keith. He was exceptionally open and straightforward, but on this occasion he was totally Delphic. I had no idea what he was talking about. I decided to take his question at face value. Could I give him more time? Yes, of course. 'But if I'm being honest, that's not the right question. The real question is can you get more out of what I'm doing already?'

At this point, he moved in closer and, lowering his voice still further, said, 'Let me get this right. Are you saying that you'd be prepared to do a little bit more?'

'Well, yes, Keith, if . . .'

'Fine . . .'

'That's it?'

That was it. The subject was never raised again.

In mid-May, London squeaked through the initial evaluation, with some big question marks around transport. Rio, Leipzig, Havana and Istanbul were now eliminated, so nine had become five. In fact, when the news broke, I was in Lausanne at the SportAccord Conference, where the world of sport meets the world of business. Just before lunch, I took a call on my mobile. It was Tessa Jowell, secretary of state for culture, media and sport, and the driving force behind the government's backing of the bid.

'This probably isn't a good time, but I need to ask you a question,' she paused, 'on behalf of the prime minister. Barbara Cassani has decided to step down . . .'

She didn't need to go on. I knew what was coming.

Although privately surprised not to have been spoken to in the early phase of the whole process, my feelings had ultimately been, 'Oh well.' But over recent months I'd felt a deep frustration. The bid, it seemed to me, was heading nowhere fast. It was obvious that most observers had already written us off, which was ridiculous given the unique nature of London, the history of our involvement in the Olympic movement and the genuinely smart people in the executive team combined with the inordinate ability of Keith and Craig on the front line. But day by day our chances were diminishing. While outwardly supportive, people I trusted in the movement were shaking their heads. I was at my best when the odds were against me. And London 2012 wasn't a chimera. I knew that it could be done and that this was the job that my whole career, perhaps my whole life, had been leading up to.

But I also knew that it could be a poisoned chalice. Gianna Angelopoulos, who drove the Athens bid and was a good friend of mine, had her health shot to pieces. At my age – then approaching fifty – and as the father of four young children, it was something I had to consider.

I told Tessa I needed time to think things through.

'I'm sorry, Seb, but I can't give you long.'

'I know.'

I snapped my phone shut, and went to look for the man I'd last spoken to on the subject under the thigh bone of a triceratops. The moment he saw me his face creased into an embarrassed grin.

'Was this your definition of a bit more time, Keith?' I said.

'Sorry Seb, but it was important you didn't know. This way you can't be accused of being involved in a palace coup,' he added, 'because there isn't one. She just doesn't want to do it any more.'

'Thanks . . .'

'I really hope you can do this. Blair's very keen, you know.'

Just how keen was a question that badly needed answering. We had a year, fourteen months to be precise, before the decision would be made in Singapore. If this was to have even a chance of working, I had to know that the support we were getting from government wasn't just Tessa's personal crusade, influential and welcome as it was. I needed to know there was buy-in from the commander in chief. We had squandered an opportunity to host the 2005 athletics World Championships because we could not deliver a stadium in which to hold them, or the political or sporting will to see it through.

The relationship with the prime minister is crucial. All successful bids have had unswerving political support from the very top. It was a key component in the success of the Sydney Games and was what helped get Athens across the line. Nor can it be partisan. Similar assurances would need to be sought from the Conservatives, in case of a change of government.

I was at Geneva airport just about to board my flight when Downing Street called.

'Lord Coe? I have the prime minister for you.'

Tony Blair and I knew each other of old, but not well. In 1992 he'd been shadow home secretary when I was a new MP. I was in the chamber the night he made his reputation over the James Bulger murder and I remember thinking at the time, 'This is a prime minister in waiting.' Now we could be working on the same side.

After the briefest of civilities, he asked me to spell out where I thought we were. Keith had brought me pretty much up to speed. I told him that we could still win, but this was an ebbing tide, and there was considerable ground to catch up, that we were not sailing along at full steam, but neither were we holed below the Plimsoll line.

'There's one question I do need to ask you, Prime Minister. And I do understand, probably better than anybody, the pressures on your diary, because it was my responsibility to sort out the diary, as you know, for William when he was opposition leader, so I can only imagine what yours looks like. But I do need to know that when I need you, you will be there. I don't know yet what I'll need you for, but you must be able to trust me when I say, "This is an important moment." I know I'm not going to have you on tap. But if you can agree to that, then I'm happy to do it.'

There was barely a pause.

'I agree,' he said. 'I understand entirely what you're saying, and I agree with you.'

My question may have been elliptical, but I couldn't have asked for a clearer answer. There was no prevarication, no, 'Well, you must understand . . .' He just said, 'You have my word on that.' So I said, 'Fine,' and boarded my flight.

There was one more person I wanted to speak to before I signed on the dotted line, and that was Malcolm. I went straight from Heathrow to a favourite Italian restaurant of ours in Soho. It was late and the place was beginning to empty. Malcolm was already there, glass of wine in front of him.

'What do I think?' he said when I told him. 'After all the things I've shown you, the history I've drummed into you, the places I've taken you to in east London, you ask me what I think? I'll tell you what I think, Newbold. I think that if you don't understand that now, you never will. So don't do it.'

'No, I know I've got to do it.'

'Good. But I'll tell you this. Screw up and you won't be carrying the torch, you'll be carrying the can.'

Although I had effectively said yes to the prime minister, Tessa Jowell still needed to hear it formally from me. It was midnight by the time I called her. 'So,' I said. 'When do I start?'

The next afternoon Keith and I walked side by side into the office. They knew I was coming – there'd been a press conference that morning at the ministry, so they'd had some hours to get used to the idea – but even so, when Keith said, 'Welcome to your new chairman,' the shock was palpable.

There was also some anger. I saw faces turned away, and I understood that. Loyalty to the person who had recruited them was natural, and there was also the speed of events. The day before Barbara Cassani had been in charge, now they had me. I knew this would take time.

And the rumours were wrong. The decision to leave was Barbara's. As she put it at the press conference, she'd got the London bid across the line from applicant city to candidate city, but it needed someone with a deeper knowledge of sport, she said, to take it to the next stage. 'The one thing I don't possess is two Olympic gold medals, and unless you have those, nobody takes you seriously.' I bit my lip and smiled for the sake of unity. Most people who win bids, of course, are not Olympians.

The bid itself wasn't in terrible shape, but everywhere I went there seemed to be the smell of fear. I sensed people were so nervous about making the wrong decision that they made no decisions at all.

Clearly their motivation wasn't in question. Judging by our previous bidding track record, this wasn't a career move, it was a cause. Many had left serious, secure jobs to join something with a less-than-certain outcome. I sensed they just needed space to get on with things, instead of which there seemed to be a culture of endless meetings, so frequent there was no chance to report on any real progress between them. So the first thing I did was to cancel all but a handful of key meetings for a couple of weeks.

'You're all smart people,' I told them. 'Just go away and do what you're good at. And for God's sake start smiling because this is a long haul.' It didn't take me long to discover that these were a really talented group and, with Keith heading up the executive team, I became more confident by the hour that we could pull it off.

The agreement Barbara had struck was that, while I would take over as chairman, she would stay on as vice chair. She had always operated more as a chief executive, and in doing so, I sensed, had stifled Keith's undoubted skills. Although with no previous experience of the IOC, he had taken to it like a duck to water, building relationships from day one. I also came to understand that Barbara hoped to continue to run the ship on a daily basis but she would slip anchor on the foreign travel. Relationship building with IOC members would be down to me, shepherded by the wily Craig Reedie, in addition to explaining what it was all about to head teachers around the country, keeping local councillors happy and government and opposition parties on board.

The situation was far from ideal but I put the best gloss on it I could. A few days later, however, I had dinner with Ian Todd, one of the founding fathers of IMG and my first agent, a guy with a pristine corporate record, much of it in sport. He could not believe what I had agreed to. His assessment was harsh.

'You do know this can't possibly work, don't you?'

'Why not?'

'Because you're the chairman and you've already got a chief executive. You have to have people on the team who are 100 per cent committed and think they can win.'

'Well, I have to try and make this work.'

'Believe me,' he said, 'it won't.'

I didn't leave our dinner feeling comforted.

Just weeks later Ian was proved right. Despite our best efforts, it became obvious to us both that it wasn't working. However, Barbara generously remained supportive, was part of our team in Singapore and focused on delivering important legacies in equestrian sport.

21

THE PERSONAL AND
THE POLITICAL

Back in September 1984, a month or so after the Los Angeles Olympics, I was at home with some mates, watching football, and during the commercial break, an ad came on, along the lines of 'Read all about sizzling Seb in your soaraway *Sun*.' I thought it was a joke. I thought one of the guys, who worked in TV advertising, had slipped a video in while I was in the kitchen getting a cup of tea. So I looked round and said, 'OK, good joke.' And everyone went, 'Er, no . . .'

The following day, sure enough, there it was. A professional tennis player I'd dated the previous year had sold her story – the whole deal, photographs, the lot. Even though it was total crap, the *Sun* managed to squeeze two days of 'revelations' out of this. Particularly galling was stuff about a dinner I'd taken her to. It was the annual Athletics Writers' Association's do, an institution in the track and field world, and she'd claimed that I was drunk and disorderly and throwing food around like some yob. I was incensed, not only because it was totally untrue, but because I had a really good relationship with the *Sun* through Colin Hart, their athletics and boxing correspondent and one of my oldest friends. So the first thing I did was to ring him up.

'Harty. What's going on?'

'Listen. I'm the last person they'd ask about this. They know what my view would be. It's down to the editor.'

The *Sun* was still in Bouverie Street then, just off Fleet Street, so I took a taxi, went to reception and demanded to see the editor.

'I'm afraid you'll have to make an appointment.'

'Fine.'

I walked straight past her towards the staircase. At the next land-ing I got into the lift and went up to the editorial floor.

'May I help you?' Another desk, another young woman. I repeated my request.

'I'm afraid Mr MacKenzie isn't here just at the moment.'

Yes, the very same.

'Fine,' I said. 'I'll wait.'

'He's probably not going to be around for the rest of the day.'

'Well, I've nothing to do, so I'll wait until he comes back.'

If I'd been anyone else, they'd have thrown me out. But this was a matter of weeks since I'd won my Olympic title in LA. Finally, when the great man appeared, I was ushered into his office and sat down.

'I'm going to ask you a really simple question,' I began. 'How bad do you think my relationship with your newspaper has got for you to be comfortable running this load of bollocks?'

I didn't know Kelvin MacKenzie from a bag of flour, but, as it happens, this was probably the right kind of language.

'To start with,' I continued, 'you get more exclusives out of me than any other newspaper. Your athletics correspondent is a friend of mine. He gets access to me nobody else gets. He gets access to races. And when any of your hacks want to organise anything, they always go through him. So why were you prepared to put that in jeopardy? Because you do realise, don't you, that I cannot speak to your newspaper ever again.' At this point I could see that he was actually quite shaken. 'Apart from anything else,' I said. 'It's crap. You surely don't believe this do you?'

And he looked at me and he laughed. 'Believe it? Of course I don't believe it. It's just a good read.'

And I walked out of the building, straight into the first phone box I saw, and dialled Ian Todd at IMG.

'I'm going to sue them,' I said.

'I'm not sure this is a good idea, Seb.'

'I'm going to sue them.'

Less than three hours later I was in a solicitor's office a stone's throw from Bouverie Street in Lincoln's Inn. It didn't matter how long it took. I knew that at some point they would have to back down, because the guy hosting the table at the Athletics Writers' dinner was none other than Colin Hart. They'd not done their homework.

Every now and then Ian would ring up and say, 'Your costs are nudging a hundred grand . . .' I was lucky in that by then I had Nike and some other sponsors, but in my private moments, I was beginning to sweat, particularly as the case dragged on for nearly a year. However, I had witnesses. In addition to Harty, Frank Bruno's manager Terry Lawless and his wife were on the same table, and prepared to swear that I had not even been drinking that night.

They settled the day before the hearing and I was awarded costs – all my lawyers' bills – plus sizeable damages, which I donated to the Sports Aid Foundation.

One person who was glad it was all over was Harty. A month or so after it started, a process server turned up at his house and thrust a subpoena into his hand. He took it thinking it was somebody wanting his autograph. When the guy had gone he called me up.

'Thanks very much,' he said.

'Well, you were there, weren't you?'

So the next day, Colin Hart slings this subpoena across his boss's desk and says, 'I think you should see this.' If anyone was a match for Kelvin MacKenzie it was his senior sports writer, an uncompromising East Ender, son of a market trader.

So MacKenzie reads it, looks at Colin and says, 'I do hope you know where your loyalty lies.' And Harty takes it back and says, 'If you think I'm going to perjure myself, the answer is no.' And walks out.

Twenty years later it was the turn of the *Daily Mail*. Around June 2003 they claimed I was involved with a young Australian middle-distance runner called Tamsyn Lewis. I had met Tamsyn two years earlier at the Edmonton World Athletics Championships when we had talked 800m tactics. She was already a serious talent, a Commonwealth gold medallist. I was with Daley at the time and we were struck by both her eagerness to learn and her sheer Aussie ballsiness. She was coming to London that summer, she said, and asked if I could give her some sessions. Why not? She duly arrived, and one afternoon we'd all been at the track in Battersea Park – Daley helping out – when it started to rain, so I said I'd give Tamsyn a lift back to her digs in south London. She directed me down some grim street in Brixton, and then said, 'OK, I'm just here.' And I looked at this house with smashed windows and thought, 'No.' She was just a kid, a fantastic athlete, and sleeping on the floor in some grubby bed-sit just wasn't right.

'Do you know what? Get your bags. You're coming home with me.' And we drove back to Ranmore and Nicky was great about it. The kids, of course, adored her, and still do. Twelve years down the line she's like a member of the family, comes over every summer, moves in and sorts everyone out with her straight Aussie talking. The *Daily Mail* duly climbed down. I won an apology and my costs. Daley thought the whole thing was hilarious. When door-stepped by the media, he said the only mystery was why she'd gone for the ugly one.

The following year, a Saturday afternoon in June 2004, a few weeks after I'd been appointed to head up the London bid, Tamsyn was over for what had become her annual summer visit. We'd been training in Battersea and I turned my phone back on to find a message from someone at the *Sunday Mirror* saying they wanted to talk. I called Mike Lee, our communications director, who had done the same job for UEFA and who later helped bring in the Rio bid.

'They said they'll only talk to you.'

I knew then this was serious and probably personal, and so it proved. A woman was claiming we'd had an affair and they wanted me to confirm that I knew her. They were running a story the next day, they said. Unfortunately, this time it was true. The relationship was long over but I had been married at the time and had small children, so it wasn't an episode that showed me in a particularly good light and I had no excuses. But she and I had remained friendly – or so I thought.

I never found out if the *Mirror* had been sitting on the story for some time, but it followed the usual format – they leave it till the very last minute before they tell you. So I said, 'Fine. Thanks for letting me know.'

At this point I should just have battened down the hatches, and followed Disraeli's maxim: 'Never complain, never explain'. But I didn't. I rang a media lawyer I knew, and asked him to find out what they had. They were being very cagey, he said. 'Given you haven't much time, I suggest you go for an injunction.' Big mistake. I should just have said I don't care, do your worst, because once the injunction was denied – which it was – it gave the green light to more serious newspapers, who would never normally have touched the story, to regurgitate it.

And while at this point Nicky and I had formally separated, Maddy was then 12 years old, the age when to hear something like that about your father is not great. It's fair to say that it did damage our relationship for quite some considerable time, which was the most painful element of the whole business.

I had been chairman of the bid for just a few weeks, and when I walked into the office the next morning, everybody had their heads bent over their laptops. Obviously, they all knew – it would have been difficult to avoid – so somehow I had to defuse the situation. When I reached the centre of the room, a former trading floor, I turned round and said, 'OK, lock up your daughters!'

I did the same thing with the press and decided to come out fighting. This was not a resigning issue. The bid was far too strong and well-founded to be rocked by a lurid tabloid kiss-and-tell.

As for my personal life, I was by then very happily involved with somebody else, who would eventually become my wife. Luckily, Carole is exceptionally calm under fire.

In 2003 I had been appointed a member of the council of the IAAF, and in March 2004 Carole came with me to Athens, a pre-Olympics meeting of the council offering an opportunity to check up on progress of my sport at the Athens Games a few months away. The day before we were due to fly back, Carole got a call on her mobile in our hotel room.

'Sorry to bother you,' said the voice. 'British Airways Customer Service. I just need the details of your flight back to London, because we want to upgrade you.' Smart, and a journalist to boot, Carole smelled a rat.

'Well, I assume that if you've got my mobile number and you're sitting at a computer at Heathrow, you've probably got my flight details as well. But as I don't have the tickets with me, give me your number and I'll ring you back.'

The number didn't exist. Meanwhile, back in Canary Wharf, the bid office gets a call from the *Daily Mirror* or the *Daily Express*, I can't remember which now.

'Would your vice chairman Lord Coe like to explain why, using tax payers' money, he has taken his girlfriend to Athens on Olympic business?'

'Tell them to print it,' I said, when Mike Lee called. 'Tell them to print it verbatim in tomorrow's paper. They'll be doing me a huge favour.'

Of course, once they did a little homework, they saw that it wasn't Olympic business. It was IAAF business. But they'd snatched a photo anyway of Carole and me walking together, taken with a lens that could have picked out the craters on the moon. We had no idea it had been taken until it appeared on page six of whichever tabloid it was. No reference to the Olympics, merely 'Seb's latest squeeze' or words to that effect.

How Carole's mobile number came to be in their possession had always remained a mystery. However, events thrown up by the Leveson inquiry have gone some way to answering that particular question.

Compared with many people, I've had a very easy run with the fourth estate, and when things have got out of hand, I have been quite bullish. I am battle-hardened and when I have had to, I can pick up a phone and call a media-savvy lawyer and get it sorted out. The people I feel for are those who're not in a position to know what to do when they get caught up in this maelstrom. For some time now, newspapers have had out-of-court settlements built into their business plans. There is, of course, a balance, and even though on occasions I've been on the wrong end of their intrusion, overall I am ferociously protective about the need for the press to hold public bodies to account. When governments win landslide majorities, the media are often the only effective opposition.

One such investigation, however, proved a baptism of fire I could have done without. It was a classic sting. The BBC's *Panorama* had used undercover reporters posing as businessmen attempting to buy IOC votes for the London bid. In the immediate run-up to the Athens Games, the timing couldn't have been worse, not least because everyone who mattered in the Olympic world was now heading for Greece where we were intending to canvass support for London. The moment our communications team got wind of what was happening, we alerted the IOC. But in the wake of the UK broadcast, a rival bid city helpfully suggested a private screening during the Games for the benefit of any IOC members who had missed it.

From our perspective, it was essential that the membership recognised that the London bid committee had no involvement whatsoever in the programme. To this end, I decided that the team and I would position ourselves outside the doors of the room where it was being shown, so that we could immediately rebut any misconceptions. I also knew that sitting parrot-like on the shoulders of any member intent on making mischief during any subsequent interviews would prove a powerful disincentive. The strategy worked.

The IOC ethics committee duly investigated and the allegations were found to have substance. The Bulgarian IOC member Ivan Slavkov was subsequently expelled.

By the time I became chairman, in May 2004, London was probably lying third, possibly fourth behind Paris, Madrid and Moscow. We had six months to prepare our candidate file, spelling out in detail exactly how the Games would be staged and funded. Everything – our ability, and suitability – would be judged on this. And then, of course, came the *Panorama* sting. Luckily, it detonated with less collateral damage than we anticipated, although it did reinforce the nervousness of some members in staging a Games in a country where the media were prepared to secrete cameras in briefcases in pursuit of a story.

In terms of our bid, Athens proved fertile lobbying ground. Finally, the IOC were beginning to take us seriously and the whole team felt we were closing the gap. Certainly, the other bid cities knew we had found our stride. From being jolly and collegiate in the early days, which told me they didn't really rate our chances, the conversations were now nowhere near as free-flowing.

Among those present at the Athens opening ceremony, raising the profile for London, were the Blairs. Cherie really knew her track and field and while the prime minister was less obviously a sports buff, he understood exactly what it would mean for Britain. One of the first things he'd done when I became chairman was to ask what we needed, and I said, 'Our embassies.'

As in any election, the important votes are those that can go either way. Keith, Craig and I were beginning to understand who were emerging as swing voters, identifying the regions where we really needed to focus our prospectus.

Jean-Claude Killy was the first person to both win a bid and deliver the Games –Albertville in 1992. He became a great friend of mine and I said to him once, 'What's the secret? Tell me how you do it.'

'Oh, it's very simple. You just fly round the world twice.'

'I can't do that now,' I said. 'It's not allowed. And, unlike you, I don't have my own jet.'

Following revelations of the Salt Lake City scandal, when ten IOC members had stepped well beyond acceptable limits, bid teams had been expressly forbidden from canvassing members directly. This had been more than just the odd bad apple – the city itself doled out around $5 million in sweeteners – so something radical had to be done. Understandable but drastic. Now you could no longer just turn up in someone's country with a brochure and a video, and go through the bid in person; nor could you say, 'We've got a fantastic bid. I'd love you to come and see what we're doing, meet our teams and see how we're planning to deliver transport.' It made it very much harder to get our message across.

In the last year or so, they have made it a little easier for bid teams to canvass legitimately. However, back in 2004, we were in a fix. We had somehow to get international traction. Luckily, there was nothing in the rules to prevent our embassies from hosting receptions for anyone in the country who mattered, including their national Olympic committee. I'd fly out and we'd talk about legacy, about involving young people, about our plans to have the village at the heart of the Games and all the other key elements of the bid. While

IOC members themselves could not be invited, we reached out to almost every cultural commentator and opinion-former from sport, business, politics or the arts – and asked them instead.

Major championships were outside the embargo on one-to-one canvassing, Athens that July being the prime example. Every candidate city and their team were accredited and IOC members were thick on the ground.

My approach to vote gathering was actually pretty similar to my approach in Falmouth and Camborne. Set out your stall and let that do the talking. In 1992, Matthew Engel – a great cricketing writer who also covered politics for the *Guardian* – had been commissioned to follow me on the election stump. Although his politics are certainly left of centre, I didn't see giving him access as a threat. It was coverage, and Matthew is a good writer and actually a nice guy. And there were *Guardian* readers in my constituency, although probably not too many of them.

It was my first day of campaigning and I was coming back down somebody's garden path, and my constituency chairwoman was standing at the gate, holding her clipboard aloft and said, 'Well?'

'Well, what?'

'Well are they going to vote for us? Or are they undecided?'

'I don't know. I didn't ask.'

At this point, Matthew collapsed with laughter. He said it was the funniest thing he'd witnessed in politics, because of course she was looking at me in complete bewilderment. In fact, I went through the entire campaign and never once asked for anyone's vote. I'm not the only one who considers it bad psychology. In Singapore I sat through thirty-four head-to-head meetings with Tony Blair, and on no single occasion did he ask an IOC member for their vote.

Being involved in a whips' office, and a very effective one, had given me a feel for this sort of thing. There were 116 IOC members, each with one vote, and just like the election for the Conservative leadership, there were several rounds of voting. Members from countries with cities in contention cannot vote until their city is eliminated. This meant that, with numbers as they stood, 99 people could vote in the first round. The winning city needs more than 50 per cent of the vote. So on this occasion, to win in the first round, a city would have to get 50 votes. With five candidates on the ballot paper, this was unlikely. The lowest-scoring city is then eliminated and the whole thing is repeated, the number of voters having increased by the eliminated country's two or three members. This continues until the magic 50 per cent is reached. As it turned out, 97 IOC members were able to vote in the first round in Singapore, which increased to 104 in the final ballot.

Deals would be done, of course, although not necessarily adhered to. This is politics at its most raw. There were traditional loyalties – the Spanish-speaking South Americans would probably vote for Madrid, for example. But if Madrid went out at the first round, say, where would their votes go? Rumour had it that there was a mutual deal between Moscow and Madrid, that the one who went out at the first ballot would then vote for the other. And it was felt that once Madrid went out, the South American votes would come to us rather than Paris. However, just like Tory MPs in the leadership election, people will happily tell you one thing to your face, and then vote entirely differently.

The IOC membership is a very mixed bag, ranging from a good chunk of European royalty, the Princess Royal included, to sports administrators and athletes spread across five continents. An argument that might work for one category, probably wouldn't work for another, and finding a common denominator to fit the aspirations of such a spectrum of history, ideologies and economies is well nigh impossible.

One of the first things I did on taking up the job was to structure in a small unit – quite separate from the rest of the team – where people just number crunched. They did nothing else and only three individuals outside this unit ever had access to that room – Keith Mills, Craig Reedie and myself. Only we had the whole picture, not least because it didn't matter to anybody else. We did not want our teams to be living and breathing the minute-by-minute rumour and counter-rumour that are the inevitable hallmarks of most elections. In the final moments, even Jackie Brock-Doyle, our deputy communications director and one of the most talented people I have ever worked with, nervously asked me, 'Just tell me we're not going out in the first round.'

'No, we're not going out in the first round.'

I knew because of the numbers. But psychologically it was important that people at the heart of the operation didn't take to barometer gazing. On some days the numbers didn't look great and that could have been destabilising. My background in politics told me that these things change from day to day, reflecting little more than your last pitch, or the last bit of gossip. Keith understood that, as a good marketeer. Craig understood because he understood the IOC. I understood it because I've been there, sailing along quite nicely with a fair breeze, and then for no apparent reason finding myself totally becalmed or in the centre of a squall. This is the nature of campaigning. For those who don't know, it can be a little unnerving, like chasing spilt mercury across a laboratory table. Now you have it, now you don't.

I've always been able to read people pretty well, but there is no doubt that my year in the whips' office honed this instinct into something of an art form. While you may not need a degree in behavioural psychology to be a whip, nonetheless you get to learn when somebody is being evasive. So often the clues lie not in what is being said, but in the questions that are not being asked.

When I arrived in Westminster, we had a majority of twenty-one. Heading for the '97 election, we were dealing on a day-to-day basis with negative numbers, finally descending to minus three. With a majority of a hundred, if someone says, 'Yes, you can count on my vote,' your observational faculty doesn't have to be quite as acute as when you're down to parity or lower. Then it's a question of, 'Actually, if you're lying to me, and this is either tied, or we lose, there's the risk of a vote of no confidence followed by a general election.'

One thing I learnt early on during my years as an MP is that you don't have to be tribal. The school of politics that says when you've done the brain work, you put the boot in, is in my view entirely self-defeating. It's enough to win the argument. During the fourteen months leading up to Singapore, I built up a clear picture of where the other bids were because they felt they could share information, knowing that I wasn't going to use it in a way that would ultimately damage them.

Intelligence gathering was crucially important, both in terms of what other cities were doing and how our bid was being received. For that we had what we called the hidden wiring, people operating at a high level – business leaders, politicians, figures in the cultural community, who could sit around a supper table somewhere, probably overseas, and ask a question that didn't look as though it was planted, and where it didn't look as though they were on the payroll. They certainly weren't on the payroll. Cherie Blair and John Major were early cheerleaders and both had access to heads of state and opinion-formers across every continent. They were particularly helpful in this regard.

Some of the most unlikely people were prepared to go the extra mile. One was John Prescott, who, I knew from my years in Westminster, was Old-Labour tribal. When the decision was made to appoint me, the then deputy prime minister was marked as a stumbling block. I was, after all, a Tory. Richard Caborn, Labour's minister for sport, and a long-standing personal friend of Prescott's, was sent to soften him up. He told me the story later.

Caborn: 'Do you want the good news or the bad news?'

Prescott: 'Give me the good news.'

Caborn: 'The American's gone.'

Prescott: 'Thank fuck for that. And the bad news?'

Caborn: 'We've asked Seb Coe to do it.'

John Prescott was politically very shrewd. In the first cabinet meeting I attended, when everyone was exclaiming, 'Fantastic, marvellous,' he was saying, 'I don't care what you say, this is going to cost a lot more than anybody thinks. Let's just get numbers out there quickly, take the pain early, and get on and build the damn thing.' Actually, of course, he was dead right. He was great at cutting to the chase. He helped us get outline planning permission for the Olympic Park in just under six months during the lead-up to Singapore.

On the other hand, Gordon Brown at the Treasury refused to engage with the project until Blair had gone. This was not ideology. It was simply totemic of the state of the relationship between these two. London 2012 was seen as Blair's success story. Had the chancellor engaged, we could have settled the budget a year earlier and prevented some collateral damage in the media. The only person who truly stood up to him was Tessa Jowell, who was simply incredible. On two or three occasions, she fearlessly lay down in the road in front of the juggernaut that was Gordon Brown and his Treasury team, and in the end won through.

My most unlikely ally in the lead-up to Singapore was Ken Livingstone, then Mayor of London. We should have been like oil and water, but in fact, we got on incredibly well. He happily told me, 'I hate sport. I'm doing this because I know I can get money out of government.' He claimed that the only sporting event he had ever been to was a Test match at The Oval, and even then he had fallen asleep. Bringing the Olympics to Stratford was simply the quickest way to regenerate East London. He also knew it was a way of gouging a deal on transport.

I used to say, 'Look, Ken. It would be nice if, occasionally, you could just acknowledge that we are hosting a sporting event. The IOC gets a bit jumpy if all you are really saying is, "We're going to use the brand as crowbar to get money out of government." We have to make some finely balanced, nuanced arguments here. It's not quite clambering into the Treasury with a claw hammer.'

Ken was the ultimate pragmatist. Although always a battling socialist, when it came to what would happen to the athletes village after the Games, he said, 'The last thing East London needs is another slice of social housing. We need to get the middle class in there.' There was a touch of Margaret Thatcher about him too. He once said, 'Don't tell me when things are going well. I want to hear from you either when you need something or if it's going to damage me politically.' And he was very open about that. 'I don't want to get turned over on this. I've got an election to win.'

Ken is a one-off, and I'm not sure we would have nudged across the line without him. During the bidding process, I had watched him be gratuitously and wonderfully rude to civil servants. While they would be sitting there, trying to figure out the sums, Ken would say, 'What, ten million a year? Is that all? That's only 0.1 per cent of my budget. I'll do it.' And you could see these Treasury officials looking at each other, thinking, 'Can he? Does he have the authority?' And he'd go, 'So what's your problem? I've just told you, I'm doing it.' He did know how to cut to the chase, but he worried people.

When I arrived in the House of Commons in 1992, Ken was an MP and clearly disinterested in the whole business. It just wasn't his scene. He didn't feel he could have much impact, nor did he. But the second he got back into London politics, everything changed. Born in Lambeth, Ken is quintessentially a Londoner. He's like a dodgy wine – he doesn't travel that well. In the streets of London, he was in his element. He walked everywhere, and when I walked with

Meetings involving Ken were structured but often very funny. In his office he had a Hugo Chávez doll – the extreme socialist leader of Venezuela – that someone had given him on a trip. You pulled a cord and it went into a robotic dance, and Ken thought this was hysterical. We'd just finished a meeting one day and I knew his staff were getting mithered about the time as he had another one scheduled.

'Look,' I said, 'we're finished here, Ken. Go and see to your visitors.'

'Why don't you stay? They're a delegation from Beijing. Could be useful.'

So in they trooped. And the interpreter was just doing the introductions when Ken cut in and beckoned them over to the doll.

'Have you seen my pride and joy?' he said, and pulled the rip cord. The Chinese minister looked on, not understanding a word and totally bemused. 'Do you know Hugo Chávez?' Ken added. A pause while this was dutifully translated. Then the interpreter turned back to us.

'The minister says yes, he does. Who do you think put him there?'

At this point I felt it was time to go but Ken insisted I stay and the meeting went on its surreal way, ending with, 'You do know, of course, that we have a very different foreign policy in London from the rest of the country.' And the minister smiled and looked benignly on.

22

THE ROAD TO SINGAPORE

Back at the end of 1979 – the year I graduated, the year I broke three world records in forty-one days – if I had asked myself then, 'What are the things I will have to do, the skills I will need to acquire, the people I will have to meet, in order to seize one seismic moment twenty-five years from now?' I could not have written a more precise brief than the set of experiences that took me to Singapore.

Thanks to our extraordinarily talented team, we now had a superb technical bid, and a compelling vision – the belief that London 2012 could inspire young people to take up sport, not only in Britain but across the world.

London's bid for 2012 didn't rely on past glories, although our country's contribution to sport is unrivalled, the British having created, codified and finally exported the most successful team games the world has ever seen. In 1908 we constructed the first purpose-built Olympic Stadium. In 1948 we pioneered the use of volunteers and initiated the Paralympic Games. Even the renaissance of the Games at the end of the 19th century was the result of de Coubertin's conviction that the English education system, with its emphasis on sport, was the blueprint for a healthy nation. We were going back to first principles: the future of Olympic sport lay with our children.

This was not some cleverly orchestrated PR ploy. When I went to Singapore, I could see no better vehicle in my lifetime to improve sustainable participation rates for kids in sport, which year on year are diminishing. And young people who learn to play sport together can learn to work together. They also learn to win with dignity and lose with magnanimity, and develop an *esprit de corps* that few other activities engender.

This focus was mirrored in our presentation, which concluded by bringing in thirty pupils from Langdon School, a sports specialist comprehensive in East Ham, less than a mile from the proposed site for the Olympic Park, that reflected London's rich cultural diversity. Each candidate city was limited to a hundred accredited supporters, and while those of our rivals were made up of business partners, trade unionists and sponsors, the vast majority of whom were men in suits, ours included these young people, a potent and demonstrable symbol of what our bid was about.

Their trip to Singapore remained a secret. When I saw them in Downing Street for a flag-signing session, I had asked, 'So tell me, when are you guys leaving for Singapore?' They said, 'Don't know what you're on about.' And I went, 'Yes you do!' Then I realised that the you-don't-say-a-word, you're-not-going-anywhere mantra had sunk in so completely, they weren't prepared to concede it even to me.

Passion is an emotion not often associated with those who inhabit our islands, but whatever their geographical, racial or social origins, nothing unites the British so much as their love of sport. However, its health depends not on those who cheer on their football team, or listen to ball-by-ball cricket commentary by Jonathan Agnew, or pack the stands at Crystal Palace. The future of élite-level sport depends on those young people who are inspired enough to get out there and train, hour after hour in whatever the weather throws at them. My own training schedule, though gruelling, was by no means unique. Apart from the odd runner at the side of the road, the time spent by athletes in training – at whatever level, at whatever sport – remains largely hidden from the public at large. The level of commitment is something only they, their coaches and their families know about. Sport is the ultimate iceberg. Nine-tenths of it goes unwitnessed. We see the precision curve of a ball towards a goal mouth, the zigzag dash to score a try, the insouciant flick from one hockey stick to another, the sweep of oars as they pull through the water, the perfect parabola of a diver in midair. We don't see the rest.

And let's not forget the parents who – like mine – make it all possible, prepared to stand in the cold and rain, or drive their sons or daughters miles to the nearest pool or ice-rink, or running track, several times a week, throughout the year. They do it not because they expect their child to play for England or stand on an Olympic rostrum but because they know the difference it will make to their child's life.

In this age of instant gratification, the challenge to get young people involved is greater than ever. Yet they thrive on competition and games. Many of the screen-based activities that keep them tethered to their iPads or phones are closely related to sport. The challenge is to get them away from the virtual world into the real world, be it tennis court, golf course, swimming pool or running track.

We had positioned our bid around young people. In stark contrast to the other four bids, our presentation was not about what the Olympics could do for London, but rather what London could do for the Olympic movement.

The road to Singapore had been clearly waymarked. In May 2004 we had made it through as a candidate city. In November 2004 we submitted our candidature file and, in line with the central thrust of our bid, it was presented to the IOC in Lausanne by 14-year-old basketball player Amber Charles.

In mid-February 2005 the IOC's evaluation commission arrived in London. This was the moment to demonstrate that we had listened to the concerns voiced the previous May, and acted upon them.

Although the rules stated clearly that one candidate city cannot undermine another, nonetheless there was a deal of gamesmanship.

Paris claimed that London's was '*un offre virtuelle*' – that we were asking the IOC to buy off plan – which of course we were. It required considerable imagination to superimpose the architects' model on to the blighted wasteland. The marker for where the stadium would be was a 50-foot pile of rotting fridges, and when I pointed out the site of the aquatics centre – beside a polluted river so thick with sludge it could have done duty as a crime scene – I felt like a time-share salesman on the Costa del Sol.

It was essential to show that the transformation could happen. One key element was Stratford International railway station, which fortunately was already finished, as was the four-mile tunnel that would eventually take ultra-fast Javelin trains to and from King's Cross/St Pancras. To demonstrate just how close we were to the centre of London, I persuaded the Metropolitan Police to drive the sixteen IOC members through it in a fleet of Range Rovers. This was high risk. Although the tunnel was safe, it was pretty basic. And although they were probably the best drivers in the country, driving in convoy down a dead-straight tunnel into the depths of the earth is far from easy. It felt like going into an unlit sewer – lighting was minimal – and if any of the evaluation committee had been subject to claustrophobia and had started screaming, it would have been a disaster. As it was, they disappeared into a hole in the ground in East London and emerged just over twenty minutes later at King's Cross to prove that there was nothing *virtuelle* about this tunnel. It would eventually transport 25,000 people an hour in and out of the Olympic Park, the journey taking seven minutes. The unspoken message was that it would be a darn sight easier to take the train to watch the London Games than it would be negotiating the Paris *périphérique* to get to the *Stade de France*.

One French voice that continued to be a distinct irritant was Pierre-Yves Gerbeau. Dubbed 'the Gerbil' by UK tabloids, he had come to prominence in 2000, brought in to turn around the

Millennium Dome after its disastrous opening and subsequent poor performance as an 'attraction'.

The experience of the dome had had a profoundly negative effect on public perception of our proposals for the Olympic Park, tainted as 'another Wembley', 'another dome'. In fact, the dome came in on time and on budget. What failed was not the building but the concept. Fatally, politicians and others among the great and the good thought they knew better than the Disney Corp what to put in there.

In late 1999 I visited it with William Hague, the various 'zones' then being in the fitting-out stage. I was doing my usual four-paces-behind thing, ensuring no negative photo opportunities cropped up, no one-way-street, no-right-turn or slug repellent signs. When we reached the end of the tour, Bob Ayling, chairman of the operating company, asked me what I thought.

'Extraordinary,' I said. 'But what does slightly surprise me is that in the year of an Olympic Games [Sydney] you're not including anything about sport. And this in a nation that is sporting mad.'

He didn't quite pat me on the head but he said, 'You don't get it, do you?' and I thought, 'Go on then. Tell me.'

'This is going to be so much bigger than the Olympic Games.'

And in that one sentence I knew that this project was doomed. In May the following year, when I heard he had got his P45, I was not surprised. Harry summed it up when he went there as a five year old on a school trip shortly after it opened.

'So, what do you think?' I asked him that evening.

'Well,' he said, 'I like it from the outside, Dad, but there's nothing in it.'

Quite. It was basically sterile and uninteresting, and represented the classic arrogance of political thinking. From the day I began working on the bid in May 2004 until September 2012 when I made my final goodbye, that vast bubble with its tent-pole spikes was visible from just about every window in the office – a permanent reminder of the hubris of those politicians, and others involved, whose egos were matched only by their lack of commercial acumen. Now, in its reincarnation as the O2, run by the Anschutz group, it's highly successful. It needed someone like them involved from the start.

Gerbeau had been appointed chief executive when Bob Ayling left, as he provided the politicians with a firebreak against accusations of folly, which were manifold. (The dome would stay empty until 2005.) In 2003, once Barbara Cassani was appointed, she brought Gerbeau in as an ambassador to the bid. I can see that having a high-profile Parisian on the London team had its attractions, but when she stepped down, he assumed, quite erroneously, that I had been instrumental in toppling her. He resigned very publicly, saying that her treatment was 'shocking'.

'I'm a man of principle and loyal to my friend. She was the main reason I was there.' He continued sniping from the sidelines, the general tone being that her replacement wasn't up to the job. I told my teams, 'I do not want to see this man in the building.'

At the four-years-to-go point, in August 2008, I was doing an interview with Nicky Campbell on Radio 2 when he asked if I'd read something that Gerbeau had written in *The Times* that morning. I said, 'No. But then I make it my life's work never to read a word that man says.' End of interview.

Back in the spring and early summer of 2005, our roving ambassadors, both official and unofficial, were quietly lobbying opinion-formers and IOC members wherever they found them. We listened and we learnt. The election of a city to host the Olympic Games is by one member one vote, and the vote of a former shot putter from Eastern Europe or a sports administrator from an African state that many would have difficulty pinpointing on a map, has the same value as that of Jean-Claude Killy or the Grand Duke of Luxembourg.

Everything was focused on the 117th session of the IOC in Singapore, specifically Wednesday, 6 July 2005, a date as fixed as the Games themselves. In early June, the evaluation reports were released. The five candidate cities were neither ranked nor scored formally, but plenty of commentators were prepared to evolve their own formula for a ranking list. By their reckoning, the report on Paris came out the strongest, with London running a close second.

When the news came through, it was met by huge relief. Little over a month before we had come perilously close to disaster when we introduced the concept of 'charters' to the campaign. This offered practical support to athletes in the form of grants towards their preparation costs, defraying the first $50,000 if a national Olympic or Paralympic committee (NOC or POC) chose to base their athletes in one of our world-class training camps, the money being paid directly to the venue – whether it was the Chinese track-and-field team staying at St Mary's College in Twickenham, or Usain Bolt and his compadres in Birmingham. Not only has the welfare of athletes always been my principal concern, but the concept would also reinforce the growing perception that we were running a proactive, innovative campaign. Admittedly, it would have made very little difference to the big battalions, such as Russia or the USA, but it would certainly help level the playing field for less well-heeled NOCs. Equality, after all, is a core Olympic value and 50 per cent of competing nations were bringing in ten or fewer competitors and would have little chance of offering acclimatisation. Knowing how sensitive the IOC was about accusations of unfair inducement, the charters were carefully crafted to remain safely within the regulations.

This late addition to our prospectus was launched at the SportAccord conference in Berlin in mid-April 2005. The response from our audience of international federations was extremely positive, which came as no surprise as our sport team had been testing the idea among the federations before the announcement. It went way beyond the warm words that other bid cities were offering. This was practical help.

It would not go unchallenged by our rivals. The main accusation was that it hadn't been specified in our original bidding document. However, I know that the real, though unspoken, irritation was that they hadn't thought of it first, and that we had stolen a march, which of course we had.

Over the succeeding days the heat rose. First came media interest on the news that we had been reported to the ethics committee. Then liberal use of the word bribe. Then the witch-hunt. Surely, they wrote, this was a calamitous lapse of judgement. In twenty-four hours the heat turned up from gas mark 3 to gas mark 8. We had a decision to make. We could either soldier on, and risk collateral damage to the bid, or jettison the commitment.

Local intelligence at Olympic HQ in Lausanne indicated presidential unease. Jacques Rogge, who had succeeded Juan Antonio Samaranch in 2001, was understandably twitchy at any inference that the IOC had not learnt its lesson following the Salt Lake City scandal. Once this was apparent, I immediately made a call to the president, explained the thinking behind the concept, apologised if the offer had in any way been misconstrued, and, crucially, told him it would be immediately removed from the table. I saw no great advantage in picking a fight with the returning officer on the eve of an election. Concede and move on under the circumstances seemed to be the prudent route. The storm abated and progressed to the next phase.

OLYMPIC BRIBES ROW FORCES LONDON INTO £15M U-TURN was typical of the headlines in the British press that weekend. The charge was that we had effectively thrown away the momentum built up over six months of effective campaigning. There were calls for heads to roll, particularly that of our communications director Mike Lee.

By Sunday I decided to go live on *The Garry Richardson Show*, on Radio 5 Live. Now Garry, although a friend, is a very punchy journalist. I expected no favours and got none, and the same accusations were being liberally thrown around the studio by Garry and guest pundits alike, but at least it gave me the opportunity to counter the wilder assertions of the Sunday newspaper coverage. As far as I am concerned, the tougher the cross-examination in these circumstances, the better. It also gave me a chance to recalibrate the direction of the press for the following week. And it worked. My radio appearance, at least in part, did seem to dampen the flames a little.

The mood in the office next morning was febrile. Although many of the team had joined the bid from high-level positions in other fields, few had been exposed to a full-blooded savaging by the British press. Some thought that the onslaught would be terminal to our campaign. Some began looking for scapegoats, the communications team – fingered in the Sundays – being the obvious target.

Recognising that the wound needed cauterising if it wasn't to go septic, I called everyone from the receptionist to the chief executive for a 'clear-the-air' session. It was vital that each member of the team be given the chance to say anything they wanted to say. First, they were given a full explanation of the thinking behind the concept – particularly important for those unfamiliar with athletes' preparation – and an account of the events that the charters had triggered.

'I know some of you are looking to apportion blame – the sport team who fine-tuned the proposal, the communications team who delivered the message, even the chief executive. Actually, the person you are looking for is me. I am the chairman and I take responsibility for this. I should have seen the sensitivities behind the offer at such a critical stage of the bid, and should have read the likely response of an organisation I have been close to for twenty-five years, and I apologise to each and every one of you.'

In closing the meeting I told them I would sit in my office for forty-five minutes with the door open. In that time they had the chance to unload on me. But after that time, the only sackable offence was if anyone continued to focus on this, or utter another word on the subject. If they did, I would escort them from the building personally.

It had the desired effect. It didn't close down all the external sniping, but it did pull the team back together and a united team is much better able to weather external storms.

What are the lessons to be drawn here? First, it is critical in any organisation to have strong leaders who will take responsibility for the actions of anyone within the organisation and let the buck stop with them. Second, people have more to fear from *not* having strong leadership in an organisation; strong leaders tend to make decisions when everyone else shies away from them. Third, it is better to take a decision that may turn out to be wrong, and you might even have to unpick, than to take no decision at all and drift in limbo; inertia is a killer. Fourth, the more profile you have as a leader in the market place, the more chance you have of getting issues over to the public when they inevitably occur. Fifth, you must always be prepared to defend your organisation in public but never be afraid to hold up your hands, on occasions, and say, 'Yup, we got it wrong.'

Oh yes, I almost forgot. Sixth: be consistent. Two weeks after we won in Singapore, we put the charters back on the table, because they were right. An impressive percentage of NOCs and POCs took them up – a small investment for LOCOG that has generated millions for local communities hosting the teams.

In terms of our presentation in Singapore, everything had been meticulously planned. There would be no equivalent of finding the tide out at Fleetwood. Also I had been to enough party conferences to see what happened if the leader's speech hadn't been sorted out beforehand. I decided to do what I would do as an athlete: get there early. Get the feel of the place, get acclimatised. We had one shot at this and everything had to be ready and pitch perfect. I did not want to be sitting there the night before trying to figure out whether the video would work or if the words were in sync. It's like an Olympic final. Preparation is everything. No surprises. There would be no second takes. Keith Mills, who is a more than accomplished sailor, understood this; and coming from the world of advertising and marketing, where presentation is everything, he was a great proponent of meticulous planning.

Around twenty of us flew over two weeks beforehand. We didn't want to be anywhere near downtown Singapore. I wanted the equivalent of Macolin, away from the hurly-burly, somewhere we could fine-tune, do everything we needed to do so that we could emerge fresh. We booked a resort hotel on the island of Sentosa, which was once a military fort. Appropriately enough, the name means 'peace and tranquillity' in Malay. It looked seaward – you could watch vast container ships passing through the Malacca Straits *en route* from Shanghai – and felt comparatively remote, not least because you were cut off from the city, both literally and psychologically.

We arrived long before any of the IOC members were in town, so there was no sense that we should have been out schmoozing. Instead, we spent twelve or fifteen hours closeted together every day, focusing on those forty-five minutes that would determine the future of London's bid. Only those directly involved with the presentation came with us: Keith Mills, Mike Lee, Craig Reedie, Jackie Brock-Doyle, David Magliano our marketing director, production people, speech writers and, last but far from least, Susie Black, as effervescent as she is dependable. Susie was one of William's team in Conservative central office and has been with me ever since.

That week on Sentosa we argued the toss over every last dot and comma. It was ball-breaking but we just kept on honing until it was perfect. This was the first time some of us had seen the filmed sections – and their quality and powerful message gave an extra lift to our determination to go the extra mile. We ate at the same time, we started work at the same time, we knocked off at the same time and then enjoyed what the resort had to offer.

Then it was over. On Friday, 1 July, the day before the session started, when IOC members had started to arrive in town, we moved into the Swissotel Stamford, part of the Raffles City complex.

By now, everybody knew what they had to do, everybody knew what they had to say. They could run through it in their own minds, but it was nailed, it was absolutely nailed. There was nothing else to do, other than, of course, get some proper rehearsal time in the conference centre next door.

As for my own speech, I had written it shortly after arriving. I had woken early, jet-lagged, and thought, I know now what I need to write.

In the meantime, there was some serious canvassing to do; not by me, or the team, but by those who the IOC saw as delivering the goods – the British government and London itself, which is to say the prime minister and the mayor.

The only complication was that the UK was chairing the G8 summit at Gleneagles on 6 July, the day of the presentation and of the vote. At one point, I sensed that Blair was wavering. I reminded him of that first conversation and that he had to trust me to say, 'This is an important moment.' That moment had now arrived. His presence, I told him, could tip the balance between success and failure.

The evening of Sunday the third I went to meet him, Cherie and his immediate team at the airport.

'How's it going? What do you think?' he said.

'Well we're in good shape, we've got the presentation, now we've just got to nail it.' I have rarely seen a politician so obviously excited and raring to go. But then politicians are by nature election junkies and he was quite good at them.

'So what do you need me to do?'

'Nothing tonight. Just get yourself sorted. We start tomorrow.' We had thirty-four meetings lined up for him, spread over two days. His list comprised those IOC members for whom a meeting with the British prime minister, our intelligence told us, would make a difference. In addition, there were a handful of those who we knew wouldn't be swayed but, in status terms, we could not risk snubbing. The British prime minister was a huge pull, one of the most famous people on the planet, and people wanted to say that they had met him. It was as simple as that.

In addition to those scheduled to see Tony, Keith Mills had put together a whole matrix of meetings for Ken and Tessa, as well as Cherie, who had worked tirelessly in seeking out IOC members over the past two years. Each meeting would last fifteen minutes, although we had scheduled on the basis of three an hour, and all had been set up well in advance. The last thing we wanted was to grab people at the last moment. These were invitations issued by personal request of the British prime minister. Even so, to get through them all, keeping nobody waiting, would be a close-run thing.

We started early on Monday morning and worked through the day. At one point, when Tony was beginning to flag, room service brought up a plate of sandwiches. 'Don't eat those,' I said. 'Have something warm.'

'Why warm?'

'Because that stuff is just energy sapping.'

He laughed and ordered up some pasta.

'Just keep drinking water,' I said, 'and you'll be all right.'

He didn't want written briefs, only a list of names, but during the few minutes between meetings I would give him a thumbnail sketch, such as, 'Right. Next one in, member of the athletes commission, cross-country skier, two Olympic gold medals, recently married, two young children. Interests: athletes' welfare. Plus he has a degree in environmental sciences.' And he would just absorb it. If anybody was put on the planet to do this, it was him. As for those conversations, it was like watching a surgeon at work. There was no, 'Hi, I've had a great holiday in Romania,' or whatever. He just cut in at precisely the smart moment.

There has always been this view that Gordon Brown was the one with the eye for detail while Tony Blair got the bigger picture. In my experience, I think it's the other way round. What Blair required from me was of a significantly more detailed order than Gordon ever wanted. He was always pin-sharp.

Inevitably, there were a couple of glitches. When a javelin thrower from Ostrava in the Czech Republic was next up, I gave Tony the basics – about the huge contribution this guy had made to East European sport and so on – but when the door opened, in came a rather cerebral speed ice-skater from Oslo. I recognised him immediately, but with no time to convey the confusion, I made my first and only intervention.

'If I might digress here for a moment, Prime Minister,' I began, before turning towards this guy. 'One of my great moments in Olympic sport was watching you compete in Lillehammer.' I was not in Lillehammer, had never been near Lillehammer. 'And you live in such a beautiful city, which is of course where I broke the world records. In OSLO.' The penny dropped. Blair opened his eyes, looked at me. He got it immediately.

23

ONLY ONE OF YOU

I have no idea now whether I had been to Singapore before. It's possible. During the previous year and a half I had spent just forty-three nights under my own roof and it's fair to say that one international hotel is much like another. My itineraries were such that I rarely had an opportunity even to put on my running shoes and pad the streets.

The Raffles City conference centre, so called because it's across the street from the legendary Raffles Hotel, takes up an entire block and includes two hotels, the Fairmont where the IOC members were staying, and the Stamford – at seventy-five storeys, the highest in Asia, and named, I liked to think, after Chelsea's home ground, rather than the founder of Singapore. My suite was large enough for meetings, and with all our key people on the same floor, the eighteenth, it effectively became the war room.

As expected, the atmosphere here was entirely different from the atmosphere on Sentosa. The lobby was seething with bid teams chasing IOC members like border collies rounding up sheep, ears pricked for any intelligence, real or imagined. The levels of adrenalin and panic were palpable – and got far worse once Blair arrived. Word had it that our rivals had been severely fazed on discovering we'd already been in Singapore for a week. It made us look organised, planned, ready for war, which we were.

The first break in the non-stop schedule of head-to-head interviews was on Monday evening when the British High Commission hosted a welcoming reception. This was a moment to take breath, meet up with our bid ambassadors and other supporters who'd just flown in, and generally build up team confidence. Everyone who had come from the office was there, as well as Bobby Charlton, Steve Redgrave and Matthew Pinsent, Ken, Tessa, Daley, HRH the Princess Royal and David Beckham. David turned out to be a complete natural. He instinctively knew what to do and needed no preparation. He just fitted in. What everyone remembers about him to this day is what a good team player he was.

The following evening was very different. This was the IOC's welcoming reception on the eve of the opening session, held at Singapore's main arts venue, the Esplanade: Theatres on the Bay. In addition to the hundred or so IOC members, a small contingent of the great and the good of each city's supporters were also invited. This was the last chance for Tony to shake hands with those he hadn't met individually. Although we were allocated a bare minimum of tickets, either six or eight, I put in a small team of 'spotters' whose job was to identify and locate the next person Tony should see.

At a nod from a spotter, I would extricate the prime minister from one IOC encounter and ease him over to the next. All was going smoothly until Jacques Chirac walked in.

Just three days earlier, the French press had reported on a meeting between the then French president and his Russian and German counterparts. Referring to the upcoming G8 at Gleneagles, Chirac was quoted on the prospect of eating haggis. 'That's where our problems with NATO come from . . . You can't trust people who cook as badly as that. After Finland, it is the country with the worst food.'

Finland had two IOC members, including Peter Tallberg, the sailor who famously chaired the 1981 Baden-Baden group of athletes. Through friendship and good judgement, they were probably coming our way anyway, but if there had been any lingering doubts, this would have quelled them.

Before the reception, Blair made it clear that there could be no photographs of him and Chirac together. This was nothing to do with the injudicious crack at British food. This was entirely political. Ten days earlier, Blair had made a hard-hitting speech in Brussels, arguing for major change in the way the EU was run. Chirac had not taken it well and words had been exchanged. EU stresses and strains had finally surfaced and now there was the real possibility of a bust-up.

The Downing Street protection officers were hovering, but I couldn't let them interfere with the choreography that the team and I had so painstakingly worked out.

'I do not want to be seen with that guy,' Tony kept muttering.

'That's fine. It won't happen,' I assured him.

Then a few minutes later, the same thing. And I gave the same response. But he was incredibly twitchy.

'Listen, I really can't have a photograph taken with Chirac.'

'Trust me, Prime Minister. It won't happen.'

'How can you be so sure?'

'Think about it. I spent four years keeping William out of photographs with you.'

'Really?'

'Really. That's what I do.'

It was like a re-run of the 2001 election, with Chirac in the Krusty role. And this time I was thinking on my feet. Chirac had arrived late but I wanted him to leave before our man and to be seen doing so. I told my team, 'Once the door to the Citroen closes and Chirac's gone, then fine. But not a second before. We keep the prime minister here until the coast's clear. He does not go out first.'

In the meantime, my job was to keep the choreography moving, ensuring the British prime minister didn't get caught up in meaningless conversations while ensuring the two groups remained safely apart. Then, out of the corner of my eye, I spotted Cherie heading like a heat-seeking missile towards the French contingent. Above the hubbub her voice rang loud and clear.

'I gather you've been saying rude things about our food,' she said, at a volume that would have done justice to a packed courtroom. Her husband, who could hear what was being said as well as I could, had assiduously turned away.

'I think we might have a problem here,' I muttered.

'Madame Blair, you must not believe every-zing you read.'

'I didn't read it. I saw it on television.'

'She's getting really stuck in,' I said to Tony's back. Then came the moment when I thought things were about to go belly up; she seemed intent on bringing the president over for a face-off.

'The thing about my wife,' Tony said, still turned away from the action, 'is that when she says something, she really means it.'

Meanwhile, Chirac was massively discomforted. As it turned out, Cherie's Exocet intervention had played straight into our hands. She was at him like a Banshee and he couldn't get out of that building fast enough. The moment we had the word that the presidential entourage had beat a retreat, we got Tony out and back to the hotel where he hosted a Commonwealth IOC members' drinks party in his suite. It was important that they knew we weren't taking them for granted either.

That left only one IOC member who hadn't had the prime ministerial *tête-à-tête*. As the Blairs' flight left shortly after midnight, and couldn't be delayed, time was tight.

'OK,' I said to our guys. 'I need a small group to come with me, and I want you all looking as if you've just got up. So go and shave and put on a clean shirt.' The prince was staying in the IOC hotel next door. We were there bang on time. Eventually, our last IOC member emerged, resplendent in flowing white, gold-trimmed robes and red-and-white chequered headdress held on by a black weighted coil. Six of us escorted him down in the lift, through the walkway into the lobby of the bid teams' hotel, where the French had already knocked off, and were lounging on banquettes, ties askew and champagne on the go. As our phalanx swept through in freshly laundered blue shirts and striped ties, escorting the regal figure of the Arab suzerain, I watched their heads turn, first in disbelief, then dismay. I will remember that look until my dying day. I knew exactly what they were thinking: Blair was still in the building and still working. As for Chirac, I later learnt that on exiting the reception he'd gone straight back to his hotel. Yes, he would be there the following day for the presentation, while we would have our country's leader only on film, but everyone knew there was a very good reason for that. More importantly, there wasn't a single member of the IOC that Blair hadn't spoken to, while Chirac had met nobody who really mattered. He had thought it sufficient simply to grace the session with his presence. But then he was 73 and at the tail end of a long political career. While winning the Olympics for Paris might have seemed a good note to go out on, he appeared tired and uninterested.

'What you've done these past two days has been Herculean,' I told the prime minister when, meeting with Saudi prince over, we hurried down to the waiting car. He was perilously close to missing his flight and commercial airlines don't wait, even for a British prime minister. 'I don't know anybody else who would have done this.'

'Well, let's just keep fingers crossed,' he said. 'I'll speak to you tomorrow.'

Then the door closed and he was off, headed for the airport, Scotland and the G8.

The kind of schedule we were running was both physically demanding and psychologically draining. A couple of months before, when the plans for Singapore were shaping up, I'd made it clear to the team what my position was.

'This is an important moment in all our lives. We're going to have early mornings and late nights and we need to be at the top of our game. So I intend going on the wagon until this is over.'

Alcohol posed another, equally pertinent, issue. While hanging out in bars is a useful means of picking up intelligence, it also loosens tongues. We were aware that several journalists following the bid process were discreetly working on behalf of rival cities, so anything said in an unguarded moment could, within minutes, be sitting at the heart of someone else's war room. It was far better to be clear-headed with a glass of coke or sparkling water than risk saying something that could be overheard, which you would regret the following day.

In the end, while it was by no means a three-line whip, everyone followed my lead. I knew I was in good shape, because I ran and worked out regularly, but I had to be conscious that while the majority of our people were considerably younger than me, they weren't actually as fit. The intensity of this schedule was a serious departure from their daily lives.

It was a lesson I had learnt from politics and being on the stump. It can be a long day. I needed everyone to know that this was going to be tough. The good thing about being in conference-style hotels is that there is always a gym. Every morning, well before the business of the day kicked off, I worked out, and encouraged everyone to do the same.

As I said goodnight to those who didn't have an on-stage role to play the next day, people assumed I'd be watching the other presentations, which started at 9.00 a.m.

'Not me,' I said.

'You're not going?'

'Why would I do that? What have I got to learn? They're bidding for the Olympic Games, the biggest prize the world of sport has to offer. They've got this far, so they must be good. And if they raise things we haven't thought of, what are we going to do? Change the film? Change the words? The only thing I want to know is what questions are going to be asked, because whatever three or four questions Paris and New York get asked, the chances are they'll ask us. That is the only information worth having.'

Apart from wondering what my children are getting up to, I have never had any trouble sleeping and that night I slept as well as I always do, and woke refreshed, ready for whatever the day might throw at me.

Until London's presentation, there was nothing I or anyone else could do. It was very like a general-election day when canvassing is over. You go round and thank a few people in your association, and then you go to your ward and you vote.

Paris started the proceedings, Chirac putting in an appearance before flying off to join the G8 in Scotland. Second up was New York, then Moscow. We were first after lunch at 1.30 p.m. Finally, Madrid. Voting was due to start around 4.30 p.m.

The one thing I was focused on that day – and this has been essential to everything I have ever done competitively – was having my own space, not least because I sensed nervousness in the team and nervousness is contagious. I took the opportunity to go and buy presents for my children, whom I'd barely seen since Christmas. Meanwhile, our competitors were taking their turn in front of the massed ranks of the IOC.

'Where is he?' the team were asking in the holding room when I still hadn't arrived. Susie was well aware of my routine.

'Don't worry,' she said. 'He knows what he's doing.'

I had no wish to dissipate my energy by counting down the hours. All energy is total; physical energy and mental energy are inextricably linked. You summon it all up for one really serious moment. You don't start eating away at it.

I've heard commentators watching lacklustre England performances and they've focused on somebody yawning before the game, seeing it as boredom, as a lack of commitment. It's a physiological response. It's actually a sign of stress. You'll see athletes yawning before major championships. It's just that they're nervous. The more relaxed you can stay, the stronger you will remain.

I learnt long ago that the best way for me to remain relaxed and stop my mind whirring is actually to go to sleep. I would often do it before races. Later that morning, after the shopping trip, I was lying on my bed dozing, listening to jazz piano, occasionally drifting off. For lunch I had a small plate of pasta and juice. You don't want to divert energy sources into digesting heavy food. This was a race day.

I took the lift with just fifteen minutes to go. I took my time. I had to be really tough on this. We all needed to deliver Oscar performances, including me.

The moment came, the door of the holding room opened and I led my team in. On the dais, ranged to the left was the president, Jacques Rogge, and the executive board of the IOC. To the right, the trestle table where the bid teams made their presentation. In the first two rows of seats were the IOC members who would make the decision. Behind them the remainder of our supporters, our contingent of a hundred. We were just twelve on the dais. And so it began.

Every city is given forty-five minutes. We knew what the template was – the mayor had to speak, and we had the prime minister on film. The Princess Royal – an IOC member and Olympian herself – read a message from the Queen. Then we had Tessa Jowell reinforcing government commitment and Denise Lewis representing the athletes. Then me.

Most of the team were comfortable with what I intended to say, but there had been a couple of voices who considered it too personal. 'The IOC won't like it,' they said.

'Well, if there is one word in those five minutes that any other bid leader can say, then I'm not nailing this properly.'

But I didn't believe it. I was the only one who had been an Olympic athlete, and I thought, 'This is the moment when I have to trust my instincts. Why throw that away?' I knew from everything I'd learnt over the previous twenty or more years that if you can make that connect, that personal connect, that was what mattered. It isn't a question of telling people you are an Olympic champion – that's just crass. But if you can tie it into your own personal journey, you are saying something much more subtle. You are saying, 'You know where I ended up, but do you know where I began?' And for me read millions of children, if they are given the right opportunity, exposed to extraordinary things at formative moments of their lives. And I *was* going to mention my family and I *was* going to mention standing beside a scrubby municipal running track in Sheffield, and I *was* going to mention John Sherwood and watching the 1968 400m hurdles final in a school hall, because this was my story.

The French team had made the fatal error of thinking that anyone cared that the Games would take their economy out of the doldrums, and that politicians and trade union leaders could deliver the message. And while the IOC did care that the London bid would transform 500-odd acres of the capital, rebuilding infrastructure and communities that had been criminally neglected by successive British governments, ultimately the Olympic Games is about one thing and one thing alone – sport and its ability to change lives. And that's what I showed them. Because it changed mine.

As Keith and I left the hall, presentation over, a few of the IOC members who were supporting us slapped us on the back, and said, 'You've won it!' And I went, 'Whoa guys. There's still Madrid to go.'

We made our way to the Carlton Hotel, a block away from the Raffles Centre, where most of the team members were staying. A function room had been booked with a big screen so that everyone could watch the presentation, and then the voting, together. A roar went up when we went in and then clapping and cheering. A voice shouted out, 'The presentation rocked!' I might not have used exactly those terms, but it felt really good. There had been no dropped catches. The films had worked, everybody had really turned it on – Ken, Tessa, Denise Lewis, little Amber Charles, who came up on the stage during the presentation, Craig Reedie and the Princess Royal. Everybody had played a blinder.

But without the energy and commitment of the backroom teams, it wouldn't have happened and I told them the truth, that, whatever the outcome, I felt really proud to have led them. Then I turned to Susie and said, 'Come on, we're going.' There was still a good thirty minutes before the Spanish presentation ended and voting began and it was time to come off the wagon. So we found a bar around the corner with a small TV and ordered a couple of beers. An English couple happened to walk in and obviously recognised me.

'Shouldn't you . . . ?' they began.

'Believe me,' I said, 'this is the best place I could possibly be at the moment.' At 4.30 p.m. Singapore time the voting began. On the little TV screen above us on the bar wall, we watched as Jacques Rogge took to the lectern.

'The city of Moscow will not participate in the next round.'

That was good, because we thought Moscow would be first to leave the table. Theirs was not a good bid and those who had voted for them had done so out of a desire not to embarrass them. They didn't want a city that had hosted the Games in 1980, and had produced some of the greatest sporting names in Olympic history, going out with only two votes. There was also the view that, as Samaranch had at one time had such close links with Moscow, having been the Spanish ambassador there between 1978 and 1980, he had pulled in a few favours. They wouldn't be embarrassed. They went out with fifteen votes.

'The city of New York will not participate in the next round.'

So far, so good. It was still playing into the pattern we had envisaged. There was a bit of Hispanic interest in New York and people voted for all sorts of business and family reasons. New York went out with sixteen votes, three less than it polled in the first round. The bulk of Moscow's votes had gone to Madrid, which again did not surprise me. The voting results were near instantaneous. Each city had been allocated a different letter of the alphabet, which the members pressed on their hand-held electronic voting devices. We were A.

The next round was the big one. There were now three cities left: Paris, London and Madrid. This was really the only time when I felt on edge. This was now serious. The Spanish are very good lobbyists. They had a good product, and they do everything with grace and elegance and couldn't be underestimated. Perhaps I was biased in that I had always had a good relationship with Samaranch, and later with his son, also an IOC member. Doña Pilar, the king's sister, was a good friend, as was her daughter. They are very smart and easier to do business with than the French.

'The city of Madrid will not participate in the next round.'

At this point I took a large intake of breath, closed my eyes and thought, 'OK.' This was now a London–Paris play-off. Although the IOC voted immediately, we wouldn't know the result for two hours. These days it's a TV show with global reach, and the organisers needed time to get both cities back in the conference centre. When the final result was announced, the teams from Paris and London would be in there, and, of course, the cameras, to witness jubilation on the one hand, heartbreak on the other.

Susie and I left the bar and on the walk back to the Stamford bumped into a few of the team. Everyone was in a state of high tension. Given where we'd been just a year earlier, to have reached the final was itself pretty improbable. Some people were excited, some looked like death warmed up, knowing we had another two long hours to wait.

The votes had all been cast but no one except the three scrutineers knew which city had won. All depended on how the votes previously given to Madrid had been redistributed. In addition, of course, Spanish IOC members themselves had been entitled to vote for the first time. It was too close to call.

Back at the hotel I showered and changed, put on some jazz, and made a few phone calls. I rang Carole. She'd heard the news and was on her way to Trafalgar Square. I knew my children were still in school, although they told me later that the teachers had brought everyone out of the classroom to watch when the show started.

Again I took my time. On my way into the conference hall my phone rang. I told the others to go ahead.

'Lord Coe? I have the prime minister for you from Gleneagles.'

'Seb, hi. How are you?'

'I'm fine.'

'So what happened?'

'I don't know.'

'No, I mean what's the result?'

'We don't know. I'm on my way in there now.' It was then I realised that he imagined it would be like a British general election. 'Prime Minister, there are no exit polls here and I genuinely have no idea what the situation is, and if I talk any longer, they won't let me in!'

'OK, OK. I know that. So you really don't know anything?'

I thought, 'I can't even continue this conversation,' because the doors were beginning to close and I wasn't prepared to sit this moment out. I snapped the phone shut, made a dash for it and was probably the last one in.

It must have been about 7.15 p.m. when the show started. The layout on the stage had been changed to allow all the IOC members to sit in rows behind the president, who stood at a central lectern. It was a show in the traditional sense of the word, complete with a local celebrity and trio of singers. I was sitting next to Keith and remember saying, 'If I see another holiday video, or a lesson on the importance of the national flower, I will scream. Just get on with it, mate, and open the envelope.'

To our left was the French team, and in front of them a battery of press – photographers, journalists, cameramen – about five deep. In front of us sat just three people, including Giselle Davies, the IOC's communications director, who happened to be British and probably thought a touch of solidarity wouldn't go amiss. John was there, too. He had started photographing me in Moscow and followed me to Los Angeles and I don't think he ever missed a race – a really nice guy. But all the press interest was down the other end. Behind them, the French supporters were standing with arms interlocked, as if waiting for a rugby international to kick off. Steve Redgrave, sitting behind me, said it didn't look good.

'On the BBC's *Review of the Year*,' he explained, 'you always know if you're in because they've told the cameras, "We want this angle." I think the word must have gone out to the photographers. Why else would they be down there?'

'Hang on,' I said. 'They're journalists and they can't be in two places at once. They have to make a choice. And they're better off being down there because either way they have a story. If Paris win, it's a story, but more importantly, if they lose, it's an even bigger story. So if you're a photographer, you're down there.' Paris had been favourites from the start. They had failed to win the 1992 Games (Barcelona got it) and 2008 (Beijing), and there was a sense that they'd paid their dues and it was their turn.

'Do you reckon?' he said. The truth was that I didn't even believe it myself.

The singing finally over, my old friend Thomas Bach appeared – he who would hail me as 'Shakespeare' after our all-night sessions working on the Baden-Baden speeches. Thomas was one of the scrutineers and I looked hard at his face, but he was giving nothing away. Another scrutineer, Francisco Elizalde of the Philippines, was as blank as a poker player.

Finally, the waiting was over. Jacques Rogge praised both cities for their bids but said, 'Only one of you can be elected as the host city.' He then spent a good thirty seconds wrestling with the Sellotape that Thomas had over-engineered, removed the card and looked up.

'The International Olympic Committee has the honour of announcing that the Games of the Thirtieth Olympiad, in the year two thousand and twelve, are awarded to the city of . . . London.' And our lot just erupted.

My first thought was, 'Have I heard this correctly?' Beside me, Keith was saying, 'Oh my God. Oh my God.' Everybody was jumping around, hugging each other. I will never forget the expression on the faces of the IOC members looking down on us from the stage. Some of them looked utterly shell-shocked. The voting had been close. Fifty votes for Paris, fifty-four for London. Madrid's votes had gone mainly to Paris. But, unknown to me – or anyone else at that point – London had led all the way, except in the second round when Madrid had pipped our total by five votes. At no point had Paris been in the lead.

There was one thing I knew I had to do, and quickly, and that was to commiserate with the leader of the Paris bid, Philippe Baudillon. I genuinely felt sorry for them. It was a good bid, they had worked hard to address past concerns about aloofness and arrogance, and then, during the critical run-up to the vote, in four sentences their president had effectively unravelled all their work. I know how I would have felt if a flat-footed, out-of-touch politician had marched in and done the same to our bid.

Having said that, the last few days had been fractious. The French had complained at the presence of David Beckham on the grounds that he was not an Olympian. Of course, this was entirely specious. Our rebuttal was that he was born and brought up within a stone's throw of the Olympic Park. Baudillon had sniped that their supporters 'were not celebrities, just people who are working inside the bid'. It had become quite personal and I didn't trust them not to spin afterwards that I couldn't be bothered to go over and offer some fellow feeling.

With all our lot going mad, I decided that this was the moment. I walked down to where the French were and waited in the shadows. It was like arriving at the scene of a motorway pile-up. Shocked faces, drained of blood, nobody knowing what to do. Some people were crying. The mayor of Paris, Bertrand Delanoë, was talking twenty to the dozen, beside him Philippe was verging on the catatonic. He didn't see me standing there. I was just out of his eyeline and everyone else was too traumatised to notice. I waited until Tele France went into the interview, then as the lights came on, I walked straight into shot, saying, 'Commiserations, Philippe. You fought a good campaign,' which of course went live on French TV, so they would never be able to say I hadn't done the decent thing.

Keith had already booked dinner for the whole team at a restaurant alongside one of the quays. Win or lose, we had to thank everybody. It was only then that the enormity of it sank in. The BBC had set up a huge screen to link to in London. In Singapore it was midnight.

It was like an out-of-body-experience, not dissimilar to being in the Games themselves. You've won your Olympic title, you've been in the village for two or three weeks, out of contact with anyone back home. You don't know what's been happening, what's been said. You've been in a cocoon. Then suddenly you're watching *The Six O'Clock News*. Huw Edwards is looking to camera and saying,

'London has won the bid to stage the Olympic Games.' And then up come the pictures of Trafalgar Square, and the London parks, and Leeds and Edinburgh, thronged with people – and you think, 'Oh my God ...'

Our flight back wasn't till the following evening. After a last press conference in the morning, people did what they wanted. Half-a-dozen of us walked down to Clarke Quay – no longer in our suits, but in shorts and T-shirts, and had a relaxed lunch at a Chinese restaurant. Susie was there and Andy Amery, the chief inspector in the Met seconded to us for the duration, Keith Mills's assistant Sam and a couple of our media team. We had just ordered coffees, enjoying the warmth, the sense of well-being that comes from sitting in the shade in the heat, when Andy got a call on his mobile and got up to take it. When, after several minutes, he hadn't returned I went to find him. He's a good copper and doesn't give very much away. But I looked at him and thought, 'Hmmm ...'

'I'm waiting for a call back from my office,' he explained. 'There's been a power surge, so the tube is down. That's what I'm telling you. But I'm also telling you that it's more serious than that.'

'OK ...'

'Much more serious.'

Five minutes later his phone went again. It wasn't a power surge, he said. 'They think a bomb's gone off on the tube.'

In the space of five minutes we had gone from elation to dumb incomprehension and horror. My first reaction, of course, was, 'Where are my kids?' I called Nicky. They were all in school.

And then I thought, 'Oh God.' Although it was three in the afternoon in Singapore, it was the morning rush-hour in London. Carole was already in her office when I called. There'd been some kind of disruption, she said. I told her not to move. And definitely not to take the tube.

As for Ken Livingstone, I only saw him once we'd arrived at the airport. I have rarely seen anyone so angry. We were shocked, but he was outraged. On the flight back he spent the entire thirteen hours writing what he was going to say when he got back to London.

A party had been planned for the children at Heathrow, but obviously that couldn't now happen. We couldn't be seen celebrating and I had to explain to them that there could be no laughing or giggling. It would take one snatched photograph for us to be accused of insensitivity. Willie Walsh, chief executive of British Airways, met us on the tarmac and we were all taken quietly out through the VIP gate. Then we said goodbye and went our separate ways.

24

TURNING BACK THE CLOCK

THE last question following Madrid's presentation – the last question of the entire session – had come from Prince Albert of Monaco when he raised the spectre of terrorism. Sixteen months previously, in March 2004, 191 people had been killed and nearly 1,800 injured when a series of timed explosions wrecked four commuter trains in the Spanish capital.

Now London had been targeted . . .

Until Munich 1972 when eleven Israeli athletes were massacred, sport had been considered immune from the threat of terrorism, but from then on security has represented a large chunk of any Olympic budget. However, a terrorist outrage on our own doorstep had transformed a figure on the bid document into a horrific reality. Fifty-two people had died, the majority on their way to work, and the date, 7/7, would be etched into the country's psyche.

For two years our focus had been 6 July 2005. Now we had a new date: 27 July 2012, the opening ceremony. We had seven years to build a project twice the size of Heathrow's Terminal 5 to be completed in half the time. It demanded a hugely accelerated life cycle. The London 2012 Bid Company had to be wound down, and the London Organising Committee of the Olympic Games and Paralympic Games – LOCOG – set up. An athletes committee would be appointed; we would not lose sight of who was at the heart of these Games. Keith, who did not want to continue in the CEO role, became my trusted deputy. He had established excellent relations with the IOC and continuity was very important to them. Our first task, however, was to find a new chief executive. We knew we needed somebody of exceptional talent, who could not only handle a budget of £2.2 billion but could master all the complexities involved in the project and pull it all together. The search began almost immediately. It would take us three months.

Most companies grow organically. Not this one. We took as our ethos the can-do attitude that had carried us through from the start. Rigidity would not work. Instead, our compass would be enthusiasm and shared values. It would be the largest workforce ever assembled in peacetime.

Paul Deighton (pronounced Di-ton) was appointed just before Christmas 2005. He responded to an advertisement in *The Economist*, prompted by his wife, and joined us from Goldman Sachs where he had been in charge of its European operations. At the end of the interviews of short-listed candidates, I asked if they had any questions. Paul's was the sharpest.

'Look,' he said, 'I don't want to be insensitive but I noticed that even in Sydney, which I guess is the template for a successful Games, they got through four CEOs – not the most reassuring thought when contemplating a serious career move.'

I laughed. 'You can be comforted by the fact that when the chief executive goes, the chairman usually goes with him.'

The truth is that it is very unusual for anybody, either chairman or chief executive, to make it through from beginning to end. Sydney was a high-water mark in terms of what you hope to get from a Games. You want full and passionate venues; a city that embraces it, with celebrations spilling from the stadium on to the street; athletes returning happy; great service from your volunteers. Nonetheless, they did indeed get through four chief executives and four chairmen. One chief executive didn't even make it to the press conference to announce his appointment.

Paul was a uniquely flexible peg for 2012's ever-morphing hole. In addition, he was a Londoner, extremely clever, clearly got sport and was an Arsenal supporter – although I don't remember spotting that on his CV.

The financing of any Games is complex. Put simply, there are two separate budgets, the infrastructural budget and the operating budget. The former – a £9.3 billion public-sector-funded package – was in essence a government investment in sporting venues and the regeneration of East London triggered by the Olympics. LOCOG, on the other hand, operated as a private company and was responsible for raising the operational budget – £2.2 billion – from the private sector.

During the first two years of LOCOG's existence, the British economy was buoyant, showing no signs of the aggressive downturn that lay ahead, but the lion's share of the sponsorship money was raised after the global financial crisis had become a reality.

Fortunately, our ambitions for the Games set out in Singapore chimed with the social-responsibility agenda of many of those companies we approached, and we spent considerable time understanding and identifying how the Games could best be used to achieve these ends. There wasn't a single category of sponsorship – from petro-chemicals to airlines – where our teams weren't totally familiar with that particular market place.

The Olympic Games is not like Formula 1, or cricket, or football, where the viewer or spectator is surrounded by hard-sell advertising. There is no branding at the venues, so these weren't classic sponsorships. They were partnerships that had to work over a period of four or five years. As a result, they tended to be with some of the most creative companies, whose ability to think outside the box, and to see this as a long-term undertaking, helped deliver the Games by helping us meet some of our legacy commitments.

One of the practical reasons why the relationship with the IOC remained crucial throughout the process was that we were now in uncharted waters. A successful bid is one thing, delivery quite another. None of us had ever done this before – not me, not Paul, not Jean Tomlin, our head of human resources, who was charged with putting together a permanent staff of 6,000 plus 70,000 volunteers. The IOC had, and in a multitude of environments.

Take the two Games I competed in. Moscow was pure command and control communism, while at Los Angeles you had the almost cartoonish extravagance of eighty-four white grand pianos, Liberace look-alikes and a Rocket Man who soared to the heavens, all in the opening ceremony.

What is certainly true is that delivering a Games in a liberal democracy, with all the tiers of public scrutiny that go with it, is a greater challenge to an organising committee than putting them on amid the opacity of a Moscow or a Beijing. In Singapore I was asked by a journalist what I'd have been doing if we'd lost the final vote. I told him I'd be spending the foreseeable future in front of a select committee in Whitehall and a plenary session at the Greater London Assembly, explaining why we'd spent £30 million to come second.

When Samaranch left the platform in Singapore, he turned to Gilbert Felli, estimable Games director of the IOC, and with a parting shot said, 'Well, good luck with the British press for the next seven years.' And he was right. Along with political scrutiny we also knew that delivering this project under the all-seeing eye of the British media would be equally stretching. With less than four years to go, Athens had been two years behind schedule. They would never have been allowed to fall so far behind had Fleet Street's finest been snapping at their heels.

A successful Games depends on successful partnerships, starting with the mayor's office. Without Ken Livingstone's wholehearted support, we wouldn't have got to the starting gate, let alone crossed the line, not least because the mayor is responsible for London's transport. Then there's government. In all, nineteen departments were involved in delivering the Games. As an example, the Home Office, together with the Foreign Office and our embassies, processed in excess of 60,000 additional visas – athletes, support teams and visitors – as well as collecting thousands of biometrics of thousands of athletes and officials around the globe. The fourth leg of the cauldron is the IOC themselves and their 'transfer of knowledge' programme – the theory here being that every Olympic Games should be better than the last because you have access to, and understanding of, the previous one. But there are different cultures at work and some Games are easier to understand than others.

A Chinese proverb says, 'If you would know the road ahead, ask someone who has travelled it.' The following March, a seventy-strong delegation arrived in Beijing, of which the LOCOG team was only a small part. Officially, we were presenting ourselves formally as the new host city. But Ken Livingstone saw China as a very important market place and was anxious to drive the London–Beijing link for all it was worth. He spent much of his time signing partnership agreements as well as opening offices in both Beijing and Shanghai.

Not surprisingly, our first photo shoot was next to the countdown clock, which turned out to be in Tiananmen Square . . . I wasn't at all sure that this was a good idea, but the ITN camera was already turning. First up was Simon Harris, political correspondent of *London Tonight*:

'Mr Livingstone, are you comfortable to be standing in a place where a hundred and seventy-one people were killed and seven thousand wounded in the fight for democracy?'

Nothing daunted, Ken went off on one of his Paul Merton style perambulations. 'Well,' he began, 'no country can escape its history.

In 1819 in Britain, we had the Peterloo riots when the cavalry charged into a crowd of protestors.' Next he drew a questionable parallel with the poll-tax demonstrations in Trafalgar Square at the end of the eighties, ending with, 'And, don't forget, the British used to chop the heads off Tasmanians.'

During this master class in diplomacy, I had been inching away from the camera. A guy from Ken's office was standing nearby.

'Listen,' I said, 'I think he needs a press officer here, and quickly.'

'I am the press officer,' he said.

Next stop was the new National Stadium, known as the Bird's Nest. On the way, I asked Ken whether we were in line for another history lesson. This time it was Sky's turn. I can't now remember the question, but instead of answering, Ken just said, 'Your outfit wouldn't be anything to do with Rupert Murdoch, would it? The man who, in order to get the ban on his operations in China lifted, stopped Chris Patten's book on the handover of Hong Kong being published?'

We had come to Beijing to learn. After all, they were five years into the delivery of their Games. We had been doing it for six months. But trying to extract information from our hosts, unfailingly polite as they were, was tough. At the end of these exchanges, our hosts would regularly thank us adding, 'We are going to learn so much from you.'

What was abundantly clear, however, was that cost was not an issue. This was a massive project to define China's global status. Beijing had created a new subway system, completely renovated its sewage system, doubled the size of its airport, and cleared vast tracts of the city – no doubt all much needed but one did not sense that there was a great deal of local consultation. One of the Beijing deputy mayors asked how we acquired the land to build the Olympic Park. Being by now pretty familiar with the process, having spent fourteen hours sitting in a planning enquiry just to get permission to develop the main site, I explained that, obviously, first we had to consult.

'Consult?' he queried. So then I went through every tier in the process, explaining about local concerns, those of archaeologists and cultural historians, the environment, health and safety and so on, and how then we would need to make a planning application.

'And what if the planning people say no?' he asked.

'Well, as a last resort we have something called a compulsory purchase order. A CPO.'

'A CPO?'

'Yes, a CPO.'

'In Beijing we don't have CPOs. We just have JCBs!'

Two years out from the Olympics their main concern was how the population of Beijing would respond to an invasion of hundreds of thousands of visitors, and most importantly, the world's media – people with lifestyles radically different from their own. They were putting out public messages, such as 'Don't spit in the street', and 'Allow visitors to get on and off public transport'.

Every organising committee tries to take the best from Games that have gone before. From Sydney, we wanted the party atmosphere; from Barcelona, the spirit and the humanity; from Vancouver, the way the city itself had embraced the Games. Beijing really did put the athletes centre stage and what we took from them was the need, above all, to plan, plan, plan and deliver. Everything was focused on detail, to the point where they were blasting pneumatic air up through flagpoles to get the flags to flutter on days when there was no wind.

The message that China was giving to the world was, 'We are too big to ignore. We are here. In five years', ten years' time, we are going to be the world's largest and most powerful economy, and this is the invitation to the grown-ups' party.'

Beijing 2008 was a triumph for British Olympic and Paralympic sport, the teams coming fourth and second in the medals table respectively, compared to tenth in Athens. A raft of new stars emerged – Chris Hoy, Rebecca Adlington, Victoria Pendleton, Ben Ainslie, Bradley Wiggins, Tim Brabants, Ellie Simmonds, Aileen McGlynn, and of course, Tom Daley, all of whom would become household names. Back in Britain that autumn, I began to notice a nuanced shift in public perception. The oft-aired accusation, 'Why are we spending all this money?' had transmuted into, 'OK, we accept it may cost, but look at all the things we're going to watch!' It became much easier to rationalise the expense once you knew you had home-grown athletes who would compete with distinction.

The level of expectation for the host city is not a straight-line graph. Typically, when you win the bid, the approval rating is high, verging on euphoria. Then public confidence flags – 'This is a huge project, we won't get it done on time.' The bottom of the curve is about halfway through, which often coincides with the Games that immediately precedes yours, when, if your teams perform badly, the view in the street is, 'And we haven't even got anybody who's any good anyway.' In our case none of this applied.

Unlike most bids, the euphoric stage ended very quickly because of the bombings. So we had to work our way back up very carefully. But by 2008, Londoners had begun to see the phoenix rise from the ashes. A centuries-old blot on both the physical and psychological landscape of the city was being transformed before their eyes. They recognised the quality of our teams in the face of the constant media glare. We'd hit every milestone up to Beijing, and now Team GB had stormed its way through the Games. I sensed on return that most people just wanted to bring it home and bring it on.

On a personal level, our success in Beijing 2008 will always be overshadowed by grief. My father had been ill for some time. I delayed my departure for the Games to be with him, and missed the opening ceremony. After one long bedside vigil during those last days my brother turned to me and said, 'What do you think Dad would be saying if he knew you were still here?' We laughed, knowing full well it would have been barely printable. In this knowledge, I left the hospital and headed for the airport. He died on 9 August, a few hours after I arrived in Beijing. Twenty minutes after hearing the news of his death from Nick, I was speaking to 400 people at a reception at the British Embassy.

Without Peter's tenacity, vision and forensic attention to detail, combined with sheer bloody-mindedness, it is highly unlikely that I would have become the athlete I did, or have done this job.

He was the first person I called when we won in Singapore. I spoke to him immediately after the prime minister had rung from Gleneagles to offer his congratulations. Peter, more than anybody, knew what this meant to me, and his response was a suitably restrained, 'So you did it then.'

If my mother had still been alive at the time of my father's death, I would probably have returned to England to support her. But she died in March 2005, six months before we won the bid, her illness having taken its inexorable course. While Peter lived to a good age – he was 88 – Angela was only 75. Far, far too young.

These had been difficult years. My guide to east London – its heroes and villains, its troubled yet powerful history – had been my old friend Malcolm, who died in the spring of 2006. At least by then he knew that the passion he had inspired in me would not go unrecognised.

Malcolm Williams was born in Walthamstow, a mile to the north of the Olympic site, where the River Lea becomes a series of lakes and reservoirs, where he roamed as a boy. These were dug at the beginning of the 20th century, the first national scheme in the country to give work to the unemployed.

The Lea is a major tributary of the Thames and has wound a significant course through England's history, forming the boundary between land ruled by Alfred the Great and the Danelaw. It rises in the Chiltern Hills north-west of London and runs east through Hertfordshire before heading south to join the tidal estuary in a false delta known as the Essex marshes, which formed a natural boundary to the capital itself. Edmund Spenser in *The Faerie Queene* described it as 'the wanton Lea that oft doth lose his way'. Until the 19th century, the further side was accessible only by boat or toll bridge on the old Roman road to Colchester. Then, as the industrial revolution took hold, its various inlets, creeks, gullies and lesser streams were shored up to make deep-water docks, the canalised branches providing navigable waterways to transport coal north in barges. The land in between, previously used for grazing cattle, was now partially drained, and heavy industry – steel, ship-building and rolling stock – began to move in. Further upstream were the 'stink industries' – tanneries and chemical works that needed to be kept upwind of the city. Where there was work, there were workers and it was soon a free for all. Housing went up on the dykes, the ditches now doubling as sewers.

The coming of the railways in 1841 didn't help. The area around Stratford became a shunting yard and more workers poured in. In 1857, a few affluent residents petitioned the government's Board of Health to do something about the squalor. One of their surveyors, Alfred Dickens, was sent to investigate. He in turn brought his brother Charles. The district, he wrote, 'is most safely explored on stilts . . . It lies just without its [London's] boundaries, and therefore is chosen as a place of refuge for offensive trade establishments turned out of the town – those of oil boilers, gut spinners, varnish makers, printers-ink makers, and the like.' The ditches that now criss-crossed the marsh, he described as cess pools, 'so charged with corruption, they are bubbling and seething with the constant rise of the foul products of decomposition.'

It was also an area prone to severe flooding, and lying two metres below high-water mark, it was impossible to drain, even with pumping stations. Not only did water come down the river from higher land north of London, bringing effluent with it from overflowing sewage works, but the flooding would happen in reverse, when sudden surges from storms in the English Channel would wreak havoc. In addition, the concrete sides of the waterways prevented the water being absorbed naturally into the surrounding land.

Then, with the advent of the Second World War, came the Blitz, when the grid of docks, railways and factories provided the Luftwaffe with easy target practice.

The Thames barrier, designed to prevent the tidal surges, was in place by 1982 and docklands' regeneration began almost immediately. But the cost of decontamination of the Lower Lea Valley, polluted by two hundred years of chemical discharge, was prohibitive and meant that it remained a post-industrial wasteland, used for warehousing and little else.

We were not the first host city to identify the Olympics as a springboard for major urban regeneration. At the end of 2006 I visited Barcelona, where the waterfront, previously a site of run-down docks, slums and brothels, had been totally revitalised by the time of the '92 Games, giving the residents access to a clean shore for the first time in centuries. They transformed a provincial industrial backwater into a cultural icon, one of the most visited and dynamic cities in Europe. We too wanted to make London 2012 a catalyst for change.

In shape, the Olympic Park resembles a misshapen sausage. An area of a little under 500 acres, it is the size of 297 football pitches, bounded on the west by the Lea navigation canal, on the east by the Lea Valley railway and in the south by the A11, where historically the river was forded, giving Stratford its name (ford over the Roman road) and now the biggest transport interchange in the country.

Before anything could be constructed, a colossal clean-up operation had to be undertaken. Some two hundred buildings, mainly small factories, were demolished. Newer, steel-framed warehouses or light-industrial plants were dismantled to be re-sited elsewhere. Only the main London sewer outlet was left in position, reincarnated as a path and cycle track running west/east. The site was then flattened, involving the excavation of a million cubic metres of earth. The soil, contaminated from centuries of pollutants, was washed in specialist machines, removing petrol, tar, oil, arsenic and lead, before it could be replaced and planted. We had a target of recycling 90 per cent of all materials. Crushed brick and concrete rubble was used to create roads and foundations, 6,500 tonnes being used in the stadium alone. While most of this recycling was done by machine, during the final stages it was hand sorted.

Vast underground tunnels were constructed to take power cables and other services. It was a central tenet of the project that the only permanent structures would be those that had a viable future after the Games. Temporary venues – the basketball arena for example – would be dismantled and re-erected elsewhere in the country where they are needed.

In addition to the main Olympic stadium, there was the aquatics centre, the velodrome, a multi-sports arena and a vast media complex to accommodate the 22,000 journalists and broadcasters from across the world who would be covering the Games. The athletes' village would be located on the north-east side of the park, just a stroll away. Post the Games, this would become housing, half of it 'affordable'. It will never become a sink estate.

In all, five miles of waterway have been restored, the concrete walls that choked and confined the river have gone for good, reducing the risk of flooding for thousands of homes to the south. The river has been dredged, its banks planted with native trees. What was once a desolate landscape is now a mixture of wet woodland, grassland, ponds for frogs, otter halts and reedbeds. As a result, the River Lea is now healthier than it has been for generations, perhaps for centuries. Birds, fish and animals are already moving back in.

The result is visible to all. Not so visible is the sustainable nature of what has been achieved. The stadium was designed around a bowl excavated into the substrata, thus minimising the steel needed for its construction. A new lock was created on the river so that 50 per cent of construction materials would arrive by barge. We built one of the world's most advanced sustainable draining systems, including the country's largest waste-water recycling scheme, used for irrigation and toilets, plus cooling in the energy centre, reducing the use of fresh water by 40 per cent. The energy centre itself produces enough low-carbon energy to power more than 10,000 homes. If I sound evangelical, it's because I am.

On the day we won the bid, Ken Livingstone said, 'Go and see the area now so that you can compare it later.' And, thanks to time-lapse photography, the transformation would be captured on the web site. However, it goes without saying that witnessing this transformation on a day-by-day basis, as I did, was an extraordinary experience. In its history, the Lower Lea Valley has gone from pastoral wetland to industrial wasteland back to an ecologically sustainable environment. We did the impossible. We turned the clock back.

And that is just one part of the legacy. Five of the London boroughs involved in the Olympics are among the eleven poorest in the country. Three of them are in the top five. Top of all is Newham. The broadcast and media complex and the Westfield Shopping Centre are now thriving commercial hubs and the source of ten thousand new jobs. The whole package will make it a prime place for companies to relocate, with access to London and the south-east and also to the north of England, with London City airport just down the road, and less than three hours by train to Paris.

* * *

In February 2005 the Queen hosted a dinner at Buckingham Palace for the IOC evaluation committee. One of the jibes made by Paris had been that we lacked support at the highest level, but with several members of the royal family among the guests – the Princess Royal, of course, had been intimately involved at every stage – as well as the Blairs, the evening went a long way to knocking this particular *canard* on the head.

Once we had won the bid, the Queen expressed an interest in what was happening, and a visit was arranged for the following October. One of the first things we had done was to organise a viewing gallery – an upmarket version of a Nissen hut – to be craned on to the roof of a residential tower block to the east of the site. From the point of view of international sponsors, it was crucial to correct the allegation that we had stuck it out in the wilds of Essex. At twenty-one-storeys high, the building was one of the tallest in the area and provided a panoramic view, not only of the site itself, but of the Thames, the NatWest Tower – all the way across London to the Wembley arch. It clearly demonstrated that we were the same distance east of Tower Bridge as Trafalgar Square was to the west.

Holden Point was actually sheltered accommodation for old people, and the lift was operated by the caretaker. Its interior was some kind of polished stainless steel and as it rumbled its way up to the top, the Queen commented favourably on its shine.

'Johnson's Baby Oil, Ma'am,' the caretaker explained. He then itemised a variety of other uses to which it could be put, and equally the uses to which it should never be put, as the lady-in-waiting and the protection office looked increasingly uncomfortable.

Looking down on the maze of railway lines and sidings, the first thing the Queen said was, 'That one over there. That's the line we take to Sandringham.' And indeed it was.

With very little to see at this point, barrage balloons of different colours had been tethered to key sites to show both the scope of the park and to enable me to point out where the different venues were going to be built. Unfortunately, I am mildly colour blind and, while I knew which balloon represented which site, differentiating the different colours was another matter. 'I must apologise, Ma'am, but I am really struggling here.'

By the time of her next visit, in November 2009, the floor of the stadium was well on its way to resembling a running track, and I walked her down what would eventually be the finishing straight.

'So where am I now?' she asked.

'Well, Ma'am, if you put in a surge over the next twenty metres, you would be the new 100m Olympic champion.'

The next member of the royal family to visit the site was the Duke of Edinburgh. He was fascinated by the detail of the interior of the aquatic centre – why this wood was chosen over that, what effect it would have on the acoustics and on how the reduction in spectator seating from 17,000 to 2,000 post-Olympics was going to work. Although an expensive way of doing things, I explained, it would save on upkeep over the next half century. Luckily, John Armitt was at hand, chairman of the Olympic Delivery Authority, the body responsible for the actual construction. After a long and distinguished career in the industry, he was well able to field the technical questions.

A photo call had naturally been arranged and, knowing the Duke's reputation for cutting to the chase, I was feeling slightly nervous. ITN were there and a little pen of photographers, already snapping away. I was mainly aware of the big directional microphone hovering above us, and thinking, 'Right, let's just get through this as quickly as we can.' By this stage, we were on a viewing platform high up in the stadium. John Armitt was explaining the architectural nuts and bolts of its construction, and Prince Philip was listening with rapt attention, as he had been throughout. With me, his focus was almost entirely on athletes and their welfare. Although nearly 90 at the time, he was very engaged. He didn't really like watching sport, he told me. Competing was what he enjoyed, which also applied to his daughter, who, I told him, I thought was doing a phenomenal job for us.

'Well, she's been around the IOC for long enough and she knows what she's doing.'

And he was right. Princess Anne has all the traits of the élite competitor. When you're in a sport that demands buckets of bravery, where the only thing that matters is the next training session, whether cross-country or show jumping, with an eye always on the welfare of your horse, you don't have much time to worry about niceties. To know that the press is there solely in the hope that you will fall into the water must be hard to accept. Within that context, her 'This-is-who-I-am-and-what-I-stand-for' attitude becomes totally understandable.

A footnote to the Tiananmen Square photo shoot. The authorities were well aware of the historical significance of Tiananmen Square, and although we had all the right accreditation, one branch of security had omitted to tell the other, so when we turned up, film crews and the rest of it, they went into red alert and it very nearly didn't happen. In the end, this jaw-dropping expanse became quite familiar to me, and I saw it at its best – completely empty – when, during the Games themselves, I would run every morning from the hotel, through the Forbidden City and around Tiananmen Square.

One person not at the closing ceremony in Beijing, and the handover to London as the next host city, was Ken Livingstone. Just three months earlier he had lost the election to Boris Johnson. In Singapore, on the night we won, he thanked everyone involved. What he said was simple but immensely moving. 'You have changed the face of sport. You have changed the face of the East End of London – and God knows they have waited long enough.'

25

STRAINS AND TENSIONS

O NE thing I learnt from my time in politics is choose your fights. Pick those you know are small enough to win but big enough to matter.

The Olympic Park aside, we had over a hundred individual planning applications to cope with. Every site you develop, every change of use, or use of fresh land – whether for a sporting venue or any other building – needs planning consent. The only one that caused any real concern was Manor Allotments, four and a half acres of vegetable gardens between the Lea navigation canal and another tributary in Hackney Wick. I knew this had salience when Alice, then aged 10, asked me why children in her class had told her that her daddy was digging up people's gardens. It was eventually agreed that they be moved to a temporary site, to be reinstated once the Games were over.

I always knew that the real test would be Greenwich, our proposed venue for the equestrian events. I entered the fray more prepared than the opponents might have expected, thanks to the years I spent with Nicky.

In organising something as complex as an Olympic and Paralympic Games, you have an impossible range of people to please. But, looked at objectively, one group's needs supersede those of everybody else put together. I was not doing all this for the benefit of the sponsors, however important they were, nor even for the spectators. The only people I never wanted to be accused of neglecting were the athletes. On too many previous occasions they had been the first thought but the last consideration. And my template, whatever the sport, was to put competitors at the centre, because if you succeed in doing that, then so much else falls into place.

Back in 1984, I had bumped into the British equestrian team arriving at Los Angeles airport, and I never saw them again. Why? Because the equestrian venue was at Santa Monica racetrack, on the outer limits of the San Fernando valley, between two and four hours' drive from the Olympic Park, depending on the traffic, which in Los Angeles is beyond parody. The same logistics held true for all subsequent Games. Over the years I had got to know them quite well – Lucinda Green, 'Tiny' Clapham, Mary King and Ian Stark – and, once I became involved with London 2012, their view was unanimous. 'Don't leave us three or four hours away. We want to be part of the Games.'

The choice of Greenwich did exactly that. It was the only venue that would put the riders slap bang in the heart of London. In Beijing, the equestrian events were actually staged in Hong Kong, over a thousand miles away – although, in fairness, in that instance it was due to quarantine. In Barcelona and Athens there was no such excuse, but they were still way out of town. Even in Sydney the equestrian park was 45 kilometres distant. The reason is primarily lack of space. But by one of the miracles of English history – the royal parks – this was not the case in London.

There was another consideration, as well as the riders wanting to be an integral part of the action. One of the propositions I took to Singapore was to connect young people to sports they may never have encountered, and eventing seemed to me a prime example of this. Stick it out in the country and that wouldn't happen. I wanted children who lived in Lewisham or Deptford or Tower Hamlets to be able to watch the world's best dressage riders, the world's best show jumpers. I wanted them to smell the horses, to experience the adrenalin of a jump-off, to have the thrill of watching horse and rider in perfect harmony competing in one the most demanding disciplines there is, and to be excited by it. Excited enough to think of taking it up themselves, or even maybe becoming a groom or a vet.

We knew that selecting Greenwich would raise hackles. It is a royal park and a UNESCO world heritage site, and there was no denying it would cause some disruption to the local community, but not for as long as a year, which is what the scaremongers were claiming. We were committed to returning it to its former state within days of the competition. The Beijing equestrian event was held on a Hong Kong golf course, and the members were back playing just three days after the teams had left.

The rumblings started early, first in the local and then the national press. The core of protestors were well-heeled – the houses that back on to Greenwich Park itself are among the most sought after in London – vociferous and media savvy. A pressure group was formed called NOGOE.

We were accused of planning to cut down 700-year-old oak trees, and of desecrating an Anglo-Saxon burial ground. There were claims that the riders would rip up the turf, and that rare grasses would be destroyed.

So, viewed pragmatically, what were the alternatives? There was Richmond, in west London, my old training patch. Here, too, there were major planning constraints. Here, too, the same genus of well-connected protestors would undoubtedly muster an anti-Games campaign, using the self-same arguments. But Richmond had one major drawback. It was nowhere near East London while Greenwich was a couple of miles across the Thames.

Then there was Windsor. Not only was it even further out – 34 miles – it had always had problems with irrigation, the ground becoming hard and unyielding in the summer months when the Games would take place, so there was the risk of serious injury to horses.

Greenwich's closeness to the Olympic Park had benefits beyond the emotional one. Most obviously, there was the financial consideration – there would be no need to procure satellite accommodation with all the additional security that would entail. A tangential beneficiary was the modern pentathlon, a trial of endurance and skill involving fencing, running, swimming, shooting and riding. With the show-jumping element in Greenwich, and shooting down the road in Woolwich, all five disciplines could be completed in a single day, adding dramatically to the atmosphere.

The majority of the eventing fraternity, including the British Equestrian Federation and the International Federation, was on our side. And while privately the Princess Royal probably didn't think Greenwich was ideal, as a member of our board, collegiately and characteristically, she accepted the decision.

There were some dissenters, however, who believed that in opting for Greenwich, which could never be a permanent site, we were depriving three-day eventing of a legacy. But what about exposing kids from the inner city to a sport they've never seen? Arguably, hearts and minds are of greater significance than bricks and mortar. For some time the three-day event has been at risk as an Olympic sport, and no building will save it from being jettisoned from the programme. I happen to know how brave those riders have to be, and what an exhilarating spectator sport it is, but not enough people do, because they have not experienced it first hand.

If we opted for Burghley, or Badminton, or Bramham, or Woburn – any of the traditional venues – the sport would largely be seen by established enthusiasts and remain marginal. Give the equestrian teams a chance to show off their wares in the heart of the city and there was a good chance they could attract a new and younger audience.

The more we thought it through, the more we were convinced that our decision was right and worth fighting for. We put in for planning permission on 8 December 2009 and on 23 March 2010 battle was enjoined.

We arrived at Woolwich Town Hall for the planning committee meeting at six o'clock, feeling distinctly wary. As required, our dossier had been made available to the public five days beforehand. This would be our last opportunity to defend it publicly. The proposal could be approved, rejected or deferred. We had put everything into it; complex issues had been investigated and resolved. But as a former MP, I knew that this was not always an exact science. There was no Plan B.

By the time we arrived, some thirty or so demonstrators were milling around the forecourt, holding placards declaring COE MUST GO. (A rather different meaning from the *Daily Mirror*'s exhortation in 1988.) They were clearly hoping for a photo opportunity, expecting us to arrive in a flotilla of limos. As usual, however, we had come on the DLR direct from the office, and had walked through the demonstrators without being noticed. Once in the hall, however, a young woman approached me.

'Would you mind coming out and having your photograph taken with us, Lord Coe?'

With those placards? Maybe not.

Not all local groups were against us. The Friends of Greenwich Park, for instance, had come out in our favour, and were working alongside us. We had invested hundreds of hours making our case at a local level. In addition to attending numerous public meetings, we'd had people answering questions in the park itself at weekends, and had opened an information centre in Greenwich High Street.

But this was no time for complacency. That morning, historian David Starkey had upped the ante in a letter to *The Times*. 'Greenwich faces its gravest threat since the 19th century,' he fulminated, 'when it was proposed to drive a railway through the park.' Interviewed later, he managed to bring in the Luftwaffe for good measure.

Clearly there were important issues here. Greenwich does have a unique place in the history of our nation. But accusations of historical desecration were not the only hurdle we had to vault. I had become an expert on the reproductive patterns of owls and of bats. Then there is a rare form of grass, unpromisingly known as acid grass, which had been designated a priority habitat for conservation.

Our plans had been drawn up in consultation with the various interested parties, including English Heritage and Natural England. Both bodies were represented on our team that night, to confirm that there would be no long-term damage, and that we had agreed to all the mitigating actions required to return the park to its full glory. We also had a couple of local councillors on our side, who understood that being an Olympic venue would be a force for good. (Apart from the area directly around the park, the Borough of Greenwich faces economic challenges.)

On the other side of the room were ranged the NOGOE group. This was a public forum and I could see at a glance that we had a fair sprinkling of the flamboyant and eccentric. Our proposal's opponents started the proceedings, and the first speaker was a woman who, on sitting down, was heard to mutter, 'But then I always preferred Steve Ovett.'

There, I thought, you have it. Our hefty submission, which had cost us both fees and time, was as nothing compared to this woman's memory of something that happened thirty years ago.

The next speaker looked like everyone's favourite history teacher, complete with tweed jacket, elbow patches and half-rimmed glasses, and he was indeed a local historian. As he introduced himself, I put my head in my hands, and thought, 'Here it comes. The David Starkey re-run.' How wrong can you be! One by one, he demolished Starkey's arguments.

'Let me remind you,' he concluded, 'that the parcel of land that David Starkey is talking about, which is so scientifically sensitive and of such historical importance, and where the organising committee are proposing to build the temporary arena, during the last war was allotments!'

I glanced at Jackie, and the expression on her face mirrored mine. Is this guy for real? Sadly, he disappeared back into anonymity before I had the opportunity to thank him.

As for Dr Starkey, while he is undoubtedly an amalgam of bile, erudition and pomposity, we need people like him. We certainly need a world where he can exist. I just didn't need him existing in my world at that particular juncture.

The intervention of the avuncular historian would be my last moment of relief. I knew I had to win this planning committee over, and the last chance I had was my final speech. Just as in Singapore, they had all the technical data in front of them, my job was to lift it from the page and make it personal. The protestors were all local residents, and I needed to show that we weren't about to ride roughshod over their precious park, because I knew exactly what it meant to them.

'Like millions of other Londoners, I have vivid memories of being taken to Greenwich as a child. It was a favourite day out, and with the Royal Observatory and the international dateline, it's not something you forget.

'And then when I started to run, making my way up through the junior ranks to the senior ranks of track and field, Crystal Palace became an important venue for me. By chance, one of my father's closest friends lived in Blackheath, just off the common. And so I would base myself there, and before the big meets, I would warm up and take time out in Greenwich Park, getting my head together. I know that this park matters to local people. I know because it matters to me.'

As for what they'd been told, I said, it was simply not true.

'We are not chopping down trees. We are not ripping up children's playgrounds. We are not bringing in JCBs to bulldoze seven hundred years of Anglo Saxon burial grounds. We are taking everything you say very seriously. But this is a temporary venue. Your park will be back, in some places better than it is now, and you will be an Olympic borough. And what will that mean? Not only the romance of having the Games at your front door – something you can tell your grandchildren about – it also means that your transport system will be upgraded by nearly £17 million.

'At the end of the day, you either trust me on this, or you don't. I have to deliver this sport to the world. I would rather deliver it by creating an equestrian theatre in the heart of London – no city has ever hosted a three-day event like this before – but we have to deliver it, and if we are turned down tonight, then we will go elsewhere.'

Then the questioning began. Most of it was civilised, and largely un-rancorous, until an elderly woman began to speak.

'I was a maths teacher for many years,' she said. 'But more than maths, I taught my children integrity. Lord Coe, I never came across you in any of my classes.'

The woman who had compared me unfavourably with Steve Ovett had nothing on this one. This was sheer malevolence. I felt Jackie digging her thumb into my lower arm in warning.

'No,' I said. 'It's highly unlikely you ever saw me in any of your classes, because I was educated in the state system.' It was an instinctive call, but a good one.

The questioning went on until well after midnight, until everyone had had their say and the planning committee felt ready to deliver their verdict. At no stage did they disappear behind closed doors to talk among themselves. All six and a half hours were conducted in public. My mouth was dry as the first councillor got up.

'I don't accept the arguments put forward tonight,' he said. 'But I do accept that this is an important decision for the borough, so I am abstaining.'

The next councillor, however, found in our favour. Then the next one, and once we got past five, I knew we were home. The end result was nine for, with one abstention.

Had the proposal been turned down, we wouldn't have gone to appeal. We had done the right thing by the competitors in coming this far. I had done the right thing for the aspirations of local children. But I was not prepared to tie the organisation up in knots for a sport that, however much I personally value it, rarely finds its way into the top two-thirds of Olympic TV audiences. At that stage, we were still three years out, so we weren't on a critical path. We'd have looked at other locations and we'd have found somewhere else. But an extraordinary opportunity would have been lost.

We emerged about 1.30 a.m. The night was cold and there was a mist coming up from the river. After a brief shaking of hands and the odd clap on the back, we made our way home. It had been a long night. But actually that's the way it should be. I'm glad I live in a country where these things happen. What began in uncertainty, ended in our favour, and on the way reinforced my faith in local democracy.

The 2010 Winter Games were held in Vancouver. However different in terms of the sports involved, the organisation boiled down to the same things – people shifting, venue management and security – and the closer you get to the field of play, the more transferable the project management becomes.

In Beijing we were limited to observing from the sidelines, but in Canada communication was simple. Although small in relation to London, it nonetheless provided a unique window on city operations. There were distinct parallels. We both had borough and city representation. They had the Mounties. We had the Met.

London has long been a terrorist target, whether by the IRA or other nationals taking exception to various strands of British foreign policy, and the Met's intelligence has a global reputation. They helped in

Sydney, and Sir David Veness, then Assistant Commissioner for Specialist Operations, unofficially chaired the security teams in Athens. Those Games were staged just three years after 9/11, and the organisers faced a very different situation from the one they had anticipated.

The real challenge for any major championship, or any global event, such as the royal wedding in 2011 and the Queen's diamond jubilee in 2012, is the seamless integration of all the facets of security, including homeland security, counter-intelligence and the local police. Delivery of this level of protection is way beyond the resources or skill sets of an organising committee. One clear difference between the security issues raised in Vancouver and London was the number of VIPs involved – in London, around seventy heads of state attended the opening ceremony; in Vancouver, the highest-ranking VIP was Joe Biden, then American vice-president, although admittedly he arrived with a fleet of thirty-six cars.

An innovation of the London Games of 1948 was the concept of volunteers, and the volunteer I was assigned in Vancouver would have met with Lord Exeter's approval. If an organising committee is smart, it tries to match people with volunteers who they think they'll get on with. And when you're away from home for that length of time, it makes a huge difference to be with someone with whom you can build up a rapport. In Beijing I'd been assigned a very bright young graduate. In Vancouver my volunteer was Tracy, in real life a management consultant, who had become involved in order, she said, 'to take myself out of my comfort zone'. She was good company and I decided she would be the perfect commentator on sports I knew little about. This wasn't in her brief, but in the circumstances I thought I could probably swing it. While she would have to retain her volunteer accreditation, she'd need to wear something less obvious than her official uniform I told her.

All went according to plan. We were watching the ice-skating when the head of protocol spotted me and came over.

'Great to see you, Seb,' he said. 'Joe Biden, vice-president of the United States is also here. Would you mind if I introduced you?'

'I'd be honoured,' I said.

So during the intermission, I took Tracy up to what is called the IOC family area, where we were offered coffee and cakes. The king of Sweden was there and Doña Pilar, sister of the king of Spain. Tracy stood beside me, understandably feeling a tad fazed. Here she was, a volunteer, in the Olympic holy of holies. Then a man came into view who I at first took to be Burt Reynolds. To Tracy's clear discomfort, he began giving her the eye. I soon realised this wasn't any aging Hollywood star, but Joe Biden. I quickly decided to introduce myself.

'Mr Chairman,' he said, grabbing my hand in both of his. 'If I had a head of hair like yours, I'd have been President of the United States years ago!'

As for Tracy, he immediately put his arm around her. 'Know what?' he said. 'If I wasn't American, I'd be Canadian!'

At this point, his security detail skilfully ushered him back into the arena.

The one sport I did become hooked on when I was in Vancouver was ice hockey. Just hours before the final, my opposite number, John Furlong, had been showing me the medals Canada had already amassed – more than they had ever won in the history of the Games, winter or summer. 'But I would swap them all to get the ice-hockey gold this afternoon,' he said. America were the favourites. They had trounced Canada at the round-robin stage with a score of 5:3. Six days later, both teams had made it through to the final and the stakes were high.

This was the third time that Canada had been Olympic hosts. They staged the Montreal summer Games in 1976 and the winter Games in Calgary in 1988. And yet they had never won a gold medal on home territory. So there was a lot of pressure to deliver.

Banners proclaiming 'Our Home, Our Game' seemed a little optimistic. But in Canada ice hockey approaches a religion. After all, they gave the game to the world.

That final was simply one of the top four or five sporting events I have ever witnessed. The Canadians looked as if they were home and dry when they scored late in the second half. But then twenty-six seconds before the whistle, America equalised, sending the game into sudden-death overtime. When Canada scored the winning goal seven minutes in, the stadium erupted and Vancouver itself came to a standstill. You couldn't have scripted it.

Canada was criticised at the time for having a policy called 'own the podium', which meant that they invested, and invested heavily, in élite performers, and there was some criticism that other teams had not being given access to the venues for training.

While the policy might have seemed rather alien to the generally unassuming Canadian character, the Vancouver organising committee knew damn well that there was a direct correlation between performance and the atmosphere in the streets. If at the end of the first week you have nothing, it colours the whole perception of the Games, which risk being written off as an expensive waste of time.

On this side of the Atlantic, you'd have been forgiven for thinking the Vancouver Games were a disaster. Press coverage was minimal, largely because Britain wasn't winning medals. When they did write, it was negative. It was as if there were two parallel worlds. I saw venues filled with people who looked like they wanted to be there, and who then flowed into the streets, where a permanent party was going on. John Furlong decided to have it out with the British press pack.

'Look, guys,' he said, 'if you were food critics, I guess you'd have tasted the food. But I don't see you in our venues. I see you sitting in here all day deciding where the next disaster story will be.'

I don't like picking fights with the sporting press, but there needs to be a balance. Instead of saying, 'Actually, we got this wrong. There's a great atmosphere here and it's buzzing,' they sat on their hands and did nothing. I felt it was important to demonstrate some support for Furlong and his team, who had shown us great courtesy, particularly during our first tentative steps as a host city. Under Jackie Brock-Doyle's direction, we began to seek media opportunities to talk up their Games, which I know helped flick the tiller back a bit.

On our return, we had a massive debrief, downloading everything we had learnt. It has to be said, we took far more practical knowledge from Canada, particularly around city operations, than we did from Beijing, perhaps not surprisingly as some of our people had been working in the observer programme for five or six months.

The worst moment of the Vancouver Games came five hours before the opening ceremony, when Georgian luge athlete Nodar Kumaritashvili lost control of his sled on a particularly challenging bend, left the slide at 90 mph, hit a steel stanchion and was killed instantly.

I was standing in Associated Press's huge operations centre, with a hundred or more journalists and agency people. It was around 11.00 a.m. and a group of us were waiting for a press conference, idly watching what had been a practice run on a large screen. There was a sudden intake of breath, followed by a horrified silence as the guy fell to the ground. Then the whole day imploded. But it was a salutary lesson.

What contingencies and resilience do you have in your own teams to deal with the unexpected only a few hours before your opening ceremony? It's not necessarily a question of terrorism or even accidents to competitors. What about a volcano erupting five days before the start and you can't get athletes and your heads of state into Britain? That was a scenario that hadn't even occurred to us before mid-April 2010. The board and I were down in Weymouth, the site of our sailing centre. This was a once-a-year thing, a working day, when we would just consider things in a calmer environment than usual, bearing in mind that this was a group of people who would never in normal circumstances find themselves together. As well as representatives of the British Olympic Association and British Paralympic Association, Justin King, the CE of Sainsburys, was there, and Sir Charles Allen. It gave them a chance to get out of their own pressured environment, and a little time to reflect on the Olympic challenge.

The night before, we would have a presentation on a particular subject, and the following day take a granular look at one or two big issues. That year it was about how we were going to get across the line with revenues and costs all roughly in kilter.

So I woke up on the Thursday morning, switched on Sky and there it was – volcano, ash cloud, and news that airports were going to be closed.

We had the IOC coming in the following week for a six-monthly 'project review'. We had the International Paralympic Committee coming in from Bonn for the remainder of the week, and the following Monday I was supposed to be going to Dubai, to present an update on our progress to all the international sports federations. In one instant, we all recognised the importance of the 'what if' scenario. And to deal with the unexpected, we needed, not experts, but people who could think outside the box.

Take the Vancouver luge tragedy as an example.

Question No. 1: you have a death, a tragedy for a young man's family. You hope that his parents were not watching, but nobody is sure of the time difference. They may have been. This, after all, was a big moment for him and everything is filmed. It's up to national TV companies what they broadcast. So what do you do? Announce his death to the press, who saw what they saw? Or do you hold off until his family have been informed, in the knowledge that the press will think you're prevaricating, not telling them the truth?

Question No. 2: next comes the issue of legality. Your legal teams are soon buried in safety certificates. Was the course properly tested? Who signed off on it?

So then, Question No. 3: what do you do about the opening ceremony, which is seven hours away? If it's a massive celebration with fireworks, what on earth do you do to mark the tragedy? Do you ask the Georgian team to walk in silence? Does the Georgian team not compete at all? Does the Georgian team go home? Do other athletes say, 'This course is too dangerous, I'm not going down it?' Does your health and safety person walk in and say, 'This is the scene of a fatal accident and I'm closing it down?' In which case you've probably got NBC saying, 'Hang on a minute, you can't do that. We've sold the advertising.' So what do you do?

And all this time somebody is trying to find the guy's parents, and you've got the press breathing down your neck, and now you've also got unscrupulous news groups trying to download from the main feed footage of him flying through the air.

And this is not the only accident. You've not only got a young athlete who has died in horrible circumstances, but a young camera-woman has crashed off a 3-metre high dais, because she was filming it, fainted and fell.

So what does Jacques Rogge say now? Does he change his speech? What does John Furlong say? How do you alter your opening ceremony? How do you suddenly take this celebration down from gas mark 10?

When asked by a journalist what the biggest challenge was for a statesman, Harold Macmillan replied, 'Events, dear boy. Events.' The same could be said about chairing an Olympics organising committee.

26

THE SMELL OF DEATH

WHILE running was always my passion, football was my obsession. Like most small boys, I enjoyed kicking a ball around and when *Match of the Day* appeared on the schedules, it was soon unmissible. My first live game was Boxing Day 1967. We were spending Christmas with my grandparents in Fulham and that afternoon, leaving the rest of the family behind, my dad and I walked down the North End Road towards the Chelsea ground at Stamford Bridge, swept along in a current of blue-and-white scarves converging from across west London. Sixty-one thousand people watched that year and for an eleven-year-old boy sitting on the old wooden benches in the west stand, my ears filled with the roar of a partisan crowd, it was an unforgettable experience. I was hooked for life. Naturally, my ambition was to become a professional footballer, preferably with Chelsea, although the nearest I ever got was playing for Stratford-on-Avon primary schools when I was 10.

Once we moved to Sheffield, trips to London became less frequent, and while Chelsea was always 'my club', Sheffield Wednesday took on adopted-team status, not least because their ground was next to the municipal track where the Hallamshire Harriers were based and my mates were all supporters. I would go there most weekends. It's still the second result that I look for, and if they're playing in London, I'll do my best to catch them, so long as the match doesn't clash with a game at Stamford Bridge.

A Chelsea season ticket was the first thing I bought when the sponsorship money started coming in. At first, I had a seat in a rather smart part of the ground, but soon returned to the terraces where I'd sat as a kid. I'm still there now – shed end, upper tier right at the front, behind the goal – along with many of the same people I've sat with since the beginning. I'm not a particularly materialistic person, so it's probably the single biggest indulgence that I have. It's certainly the first thing I buy every year and, if times got hard, would be the last thing I would give up.

If I can't make it, my kids now go on their own. A football stadium is a relatively safe place these days – football is certainly much more of a family game than it was in the seventies. I remember once when Sheffield Wednesday were playing another club and my mates and I ended up being chased by skinheads through the middle of the city. Looking back, I wonder my parents let me go at all. As for Chelsea, it had one of the worst reputations going.

The nadir of English club football, however, was the 1980s. In 1985, on the afternoon of 15 March, an FA sixth-round match between Luton Town and Millwall was stopped by a riot, leaving 81 people injured. A little over two months later came the Heysel Stadium disaster in Brussels – the same stadium where I had run my first international eight years earlier. This was the European Cup final between Liverpool and Juventus where 69 Italian fans died after being crushed by a collapsing concrete wall. In the after-math, English clubs were barred from playing abroad indefinitely. The ban was eventually lifted in 1990, the year England came fourth in the World Cup in Italy.

The FIFA World Cup is the Olympic Games of the soccer-playing world. The only time it has come to England was in 1966 and the result is engraved on the hearts of all English football fans. We were still living in the Midlands then, but at the end of July we were back in Fulham. Having decided that my grandmother's house wasn't the best place to watch a World Cup final between England and Germany, my dad took me to the flat of a friend of his, an artist, half-Scottish, half Russian, known as Jock. This bizarre character lived directly opposite the Chelsea ground and from his sitting room window painted the evocative crowd scenes that he was famous for. Over the years we would regularly drop in on him before the game. When he opened the door, you'd be assailed with an unforgettable aroma of whisky and linseed oil, the entire flat being littered with half squeezed tubes of paint and empty bottles of Johnnie Walker.

On the afternoon of 30 July 1966, Jock's split loyalties were sorely tested. As a Scot, he hated anything to do with the English. However, the Russian half hated the Germans even more. Amusingly, it was a Russian linesman, Tofik Bakhramov, who allowed Geoff Hurst's controversial third goal, later found not to have crossed the line. Some claimed he was swayed by the USSR's defeat by Germany in the semi-final. However, there is an apocryphal story that he gave his reason as 'Stalingrad'.

That year, 1966, was the end of an era. In 1970, in Mexico, we made a reasonable attempt to defend our title, making the quarter-finals but losing to our nemesis Germany. After that, it was downhill all the way. We failed to qualify in either 1974 or 1978, while Scotland did. Given this was our national game, it was an appalling admission.

Twenty years later, following our successful hosting of Euro 1996, the way seemed clear for another World Cup bid. It was led by Tony Banks, Labour MP for Newham Northwest (later West Ham), sports minister under the new Blair administration, but we went out in the second round, and the tournament went to Africa for the first time.

Plans to bid for 2018 emerged shortly after our success in Singapore, when Gordon Brown, then chancellor of the exchequer, launched a feasibility study into possible funding. An official announcement was made by the FA in 2007.

My interest in football is hardly a secret, and at the end of 2006 I was appointed by Sepp Blatter to chair FIFA's first ethics committee. But when, a little over two years later, I was asked to join England's 2018 bid, I felt I should do what I could to help. I had never seen staging the Olympics as an end in itself, but the opening of a door, which would encourage other championships to our shores, and with them greater participation in sport in general. We already had the Commonwealth Games coming to Glasgow in 2014 and it would be an extraordinary decade for sport if we could bring the World Cup in 2018. I called Sepp to explain my predicament – the two roles were obviously incompatible. He understood entirely.

'You have to do this, Sebastian. You have to help them and it's important that we have good bids.' Effectively, he granted me leave of absence from the ethics committee.

'So what do you think?' Keith Mills said as we emerged from my first board meeting in February 2009.

'You really want to know? It's got the smell of death about it.' He had got there before me.

I had never been involved with football in England other than as a spectator and in an ambassadorial role at Chelsea. Keith was a more seasoned observer of the game at this level, having recently joined the board at Tottenham. He had been involved in the bid from the start and it was Keith who had suggested that I might be a useful addition. But I had been truly shocked by the vituperative nature of the meeting I had just witnessed. There was thinly disguised contempt around the table.

For reasons of better corporate governance, the FA had decided they needed an independent chairman and had appointed David Triesman, a Labour party politician and former Foreign Office minister now Lord Triesman. His connection with football was emotional rather than practical, having been a lifetime supporter of Tottenham Hotspur and sometime referee. However, his lack of experience in the upper echelons was a serious disadvantage. He was also chairing the bid committee, which in its composition looked like an extended arm of the Labour Party. This unnerved the sport in general and FIFA in particular. There was Baroness Amos, Foreign Office spokesperson in the House of Lords, appointed because it was thought she would have some influence in Africa. There was Richard Caborn, sports minister during the Olympic bid, who Gordon Brown had moved when he became prime minister. Officially, Caborn was there as Number 10's observer and didn't have a vote. Then there was Caborn's replacement, Gerry Sutcliffe. Yet another politician was Brian Mawhinney, although in fairness he was a good chair of the Football League. On the commercial side, you had Martin Sorrell, a giant in communications and marketing. Representing the Premiership, as well as Keith, there was David Gill, chief executive of Manchester United, clearly very bright and successful, but not always finding it easy to disguise his frustrations. Finally, as deputy chair you had Sir David Richards, chairman of the Premiership, best described as a rough diamond.

Dave Richards was a Sheffielder, a former chairman of Sheffield Wednesday who still had shares in the club. At one stage, I had been part of a small group who knew the club to be a sleeping giant with huge potential and were interested in buying it. In the end, it didn't happen but one result was that I knew Dave quite well.

Keith was involved because no one else on the board had any experience of a bid, successful or otherwise. Above all, he is a great patriot and, as he reminded me when I was vacillating, football had not held back when we were globalising our bid. Banners in support of 2012 were strung across every stadium in the Premiership, the London 2012 message going out to 700 million viewers worldwide every week. He felt it was his duty to help, he said. And that pretty much summed up my own feelings. I, too, was a football fan and wanted to see the World Cup back here in my lifetime.

Keith and I were the only members of the board who came with neither a political nor a football agenda. We were also the only two who were 'non-executive' i.e. not being paid. I had made it clear that I wasn't prepared to have the press on my back doing a 'snouts in the trough' number.

The voting at FIFA is similar to that of the IOC, in that members vote for the country they want on the basis of a bid document. There are 24 members of the executive committee (ExCo). Like IOC members, they are spread liberally across the world, and one of these 24 was Geoff Thompson, former chairman of the FA, who had been moved aside when David Triesman came in. Geoff not only had a vote, he was a friend and a colleague of the other 23, who he would see on a regular basis. It seemed inconceivable that the board thought they could run this campaign without involving him. It would have been like me saying, 'Right, we're going to bid for the Olympic Games but we're not going to invite our four IOC members to be a part of it.' It was that basic.

In the immediate aftermath of the failure of the England bid, the finger was pointed at the British media. I am less willing to lay the blame at their door. Ultimately, the fault, I believe, lies with the awful dysfunctionality of the English game, its personalities and its politics.

First, you have the FA, which is the regulatory body. Then you have the Premier League, effectively the creation of Sky TV and Murdoch money, and we're talking billions here. Then you have the big clubs and the moguls, including Abramovich at Chelsea and the Glazers at Manchester United, not forgetting the big-beast managers, such as Alex Ferguson and Arsène Wenger.

This has always been a very uncomfortable set of relationships, at best strained. The fact that they didn't trust each other and didn't much like each other, was a problem. Briefings and counter-briefings were going on all the time. I knew journalists who would tell me what had been said within minutes of our leaving the room – on one occasion by text during the meeting.

I joined in February 2009 and six months later nothing had changed, but I'd seen enough to know that this was going nowhere fast. As the only board members independent of either politics or football, Keith and I decided we had to do something. As I happened to know Geoff Thompson personally – he too is a Sheffielder – Keith and I informed the board that we intended to persuade him to get involved.

'You'll find he's tricky,' someone said.

'Has anyone actually spoken to him?' No.

So we took him out to dinner, and he said yes immediately.

So on 12 November 2009, following an emergency board meeting, five of the existing members of the Board departed. First the current and former sports ministers; both equally frustrated by their inability to persuade Government to meet the shortfall in the bid campaign. We'd figured out how to meet the shortfall by other means, although it seemed particularly bizarre as the whole bid had effectively been launched and pushed by Gordon Brown.

Keith also stepped down but said he would come in and do whatever was necessary on the marketing and strategic front. Martin Sorrell made the same commitment. Last was Karren Brady, who had taken over from Baroness Amos, following her appointment as high commissioner in Australia. Karren, who the following January became vice chairman of West Ham, also agreed to stay involved. Geoff Thompson came in, as well as Paul Elliott, a highly articulate footballer, anti-racism campaigner and former Chelsea captain.

Equally importantly, we brought in Simon Greenberg, former sports editor of the *Evening Standard* and latterly communications director at Chelsea. He would have a role as chief of staff, sitting in on our meetings and generally co-ordinating the messaging. We had a little over a year.

The England bid had three things going for it. First, we already had the infrastructure, that is the stadiums. Second, we had the security. Every week millions of people go to football, they arrive safely and they leave safely – local police forces handle this very well. World Cup games would be more complicated since they would involve more people – the need to accommodate sponsors and TV coverage for example – but this was well within our national comfort zone. Third, we already had supporters of just about every footballing nation living within travelling distance of the venues. We could guarantee full stadiums of enthusiastic fans.

If Sepp Blatter had been looking at this purely in terms of commercial potential and ease of delivery, together with an unbeatable atmosphere, England would be a near-automatic choice, as he told me.

But against us was the perception that we were arrogant. Back in 2004, as chairman of London 2012, I had started my campaign in Africa, track and field being so strong there. I soon discovered that many of the relationships I'd developed over the years and had thought were in really good shape, had clearly been badly damaged by England's 2010 World Cup bid, the we-gave-football-to-the-world sense of entitlement. That could not be allowed to happen again. There could be no hint of 'football coming home'. The byword had to be humility.

The most difficult thing to contend with, however, was the internecine warfare at home. The FA distrusted the Premiership. The Premiership distrusted the FA, and Brian Mawhinney, as chairman of the Football League, wasn't comfortable with any of them. I sometimes suspected that their only common ground was a mistrust of David Triesman. Many seemed puzzled as to why Triesman was there, including myself.

Less than two weeks after the reshuffle we had the first meeting of the new, trimmed-down board. We had barely started when

Triesman said, 'I understand there's a letter on its way from Dave Richards saying he's resigned.' He'd been called by a journalist, he said. To lose the chairman of the Premiership at this stage of the process was a kick in the teeth. I'd had a gutful of this pussy-footing around and said I was going to make two calls. I left the boardroom and went into a side office, taking Andy Anson, the CEO, and Simon Greenberg with me, putting the phone on speaker mode as I wanted them to hear the exact exchange.

The first call was to Richard Scudamore, one of our most talented sports administrators and chief executive of the Premier League.

'I'm at a board meeting of the England bid and we've just been told that a letter of resignation is on its way from Dave Richards. So I have only one question. Is this just his personal view? Or is this you, as the Premier League, saying you now want nothing more to do with the bid?'

'No, no,' he said. 'We are absolutely supportive, but I can't control my chairman. He doesn't like David Triesman,' which was not the best-kept secret.

'Be that as it may,' I said, 'do I have your assurance that this has the support of the Premier League? Because if it doesn't, we might as well go to Weston-super-Mare for the day.' He assured me that it did.

Then I rang up Dave Richards.

'What the hell is going on here?' I said.

'Don't get me wrong,' he said. 'It's just me. The Premier League's right behind you, pal. Right behind you.'

'I know that, Dave, because I've just spoken to Richard Scudamore.'

'What the fuck did you ring him for? I'm the fucking chairman, not him.'

Gordon Brown's championing of an England bid had struck me as false from the start. Tony Blair would have the Games as a legacy, so Gordon wanted the World Cup. This wasn't about football. This was about New Labour's obsession with football and specifically football's ability to connect with middle England. In October 2007 Brown had invited Sepp Blatter to Downing Street and had clearly not been properly briefed. It was all 'England for the World Cup!' During the photo call that followed, Blatter made it clear that a) the campaign hadn't been announced, and b) *he* would decide where the World Cup went, not a British prime minister.

After the departure of Dave Richards, a period of stability followed. Board meetings became quite pleasant, and as chief executive, Andy Anson got into his stride now he was not being undermined every five minutes. Brian Mawhinney did a sterling job in gaining political support for our choice of the fifteen or so venues, pulling in cities and communities as far apart as Plymouth and Middlesbrough. Then on the afternoon of that year's Cup Final, 15 May 2010 – Chelsea v. Portsmouth – I was sitting in Wembley with my kids, thoroughly enjoying watching us win our second trophy of the year, blissfully unaware of the storm that had already broken over our heads in the posh seats.

I switched my phone back on around 7.00 p.m. to find a message from Simon. Apparently, the story had been bubbling up around Fleet Street for a couple of days, but Simon had only just heard. The *Mail on Sunday* had got hold of a tape involving David Triesman, which risked derailing the whole bid. It was running the following morning. As quoted by the *Mail*, Triesman was alleged to have said, 'My assumption is the Latin Americans, although they've not said so, will vote for Spain. If Spain drops out, because they are looking for help from the Russians to help bribe referees in the World Cup, their votes might switch to Russia.'

This was during a wired conversation with former employee Melissa Jacobs. There may be various interpretations and arguments about where he had got this story and if it had any validity, but that was not the point.

We now had just six months to go before the vote. Two days

previously the bid had been officially launched with David Beckham fronting it. The timing could not have been worse.

The first thing I did, of course, was to ring Keith. We both agreed there were two things to be done immediately, before the story became public the following morning. First, contact Blatter and FIFA and warn them. Then, send overnight messages to the Russian and Spanish federations, apologising and attempting an explanation. They had to wake up to an email from us putting the whole thing in perspective before being assailed by lurid headlines in *El País* or whatever the Spanish or Russian equivalent is on a Sunday.

The next morning Keith and I spoke again. By now, we had both read the coverage and it was ghastly.

Meanwhile, according to Andy Anson, Triesman was focusing more on the nature of the sting than on the substance. But this had gone well beyond the hows, whys, wherefores and who saids. The reality was simpler. Is it out there on the record? Yes it is. Is it plastered across a newspaper with a large circulation? Yes. Has it been carried in other newspapers? Yes. Was it leading every television and radio news bulletin? Yes. Will there be a follow-up on Monday? For sure. Is it the subject of radio phone-ins? Yes it is.

Then we have a problem.

Our gut instinct was that it was much better to wake up the next morning to headlines that Triesman had gone, rather than that time-honoured journalists' taunt, 'Why is he still dangling there?' Keith and I agreed to speak to him together on a conference call. We both knew that this would be one of the tougher conversations.

On a personal level, we had both got on well with David Triesman. He was polite. He chaired meetings pretty well. And while it was clear that he was slightly out of his depth in the bidding world, there was nothing you could really take exception to. I might not always have shared his interpretation of conversations and events but, having said all that, football didn't like him simply because he wasn't one of theirs.

Some things are too important to miss and that Sunday morning I was watching Harry play in a five-a-side football tournament in a local village. Pretty much every parent there knew who I was and what I was dealing with. Every time one of them walked by I'd get the benefit of their expertise. 'He should go.' 'He should stay.'

So, finally, the three of us were on the line. Keith at home in Kent, me at the far end of a perishingly cold village football pitch in Surrey and Lord Triesman in North London.

'Look David,' I said. 'I thoroughly disapprove of the way this story has been put into the public domain. We've all been at the wrong end of that kind of salacious stuff – at least I have – but I'm afraid we don't have the luxury of trying to figure out the ethics or practices of the British press. My gut instinct is that this will not go away easily while you are in post, and that this can do nothing but damage to the bid.' Keith cut to the chase. 'I'm sorry to have to tell you this, David, but I'm afraid this leaves you in an untenable position, and if you stay, it's going to be death by a thousand cuts both to you and to the bid.'

'Look, I'm prepared to step down as bid chairman, but I want to stay as chairman of the FA.'

'In the eyes of everyone out there, these are inseparable posts, David,' I said. 'I don't think that will wash.'

He was very emotional, and who wouldn't be? But he agreed to go away and think about it. Finally, he agreed to step down and it was left to Andy and Simon to sort out the details.

What was incontrovertible was that the football-loving public were angry. Later that evening I was listening to Radio 5 and the guy running the phone-in said, 'I know the BBC don't have the greatest relationship with the *Mail on Sunday*, but please, we are not censoring these calls. If you want to ring up and support the newspaper's approach on this, please do, the lines are open.'

I sat listening for an hour and a half and no one did. Gary Lineker, who had written a column for them for years, resigned.

Next on my list of calls had been Geoff Thompson. It was then mid-afternoon. 'I'm afraid you've got to do this, Geoff...' Once that was done, the next day's story could be positive: Triesman's gone, we have a replacement and he's a football man, a member of FIFA's executive committee.

That left the one conversation I did not want to have. Sepp Blatter. He had been emailed the previous evening, but I knew I had to speak to him personally. The call was booked for 4.00 p.m.

'First, let me tell you that this is a very bad day for all of us,' I began. 'I have a fixed view on the journalistic ethics of how this was done, and we are obviously very sorry it got into the public domain. But you need to know that these are not the views of the bid team, these are not the views of the FA and that David Triesman stepped down as of an hour ago. Geoff Thompson, who of course you know, is the new chairman.'

'Thank you,' he said. 'And it's the nature of the sport that you are prepared to come on the phone and speak to me personally.' Then there was a pause. 'But I am shocked. We refer to the English FA as *the* FA. You are the mother of football. How can you possibly have a chairman who could even countenance these thoughts?'

'You do have to understand that the woman was wired up to electronic equipment. This was a private conversation that was never intended for public consumption.'

Our swift action minimised the fallout and we even managed to gather some momentum. We persuaded David Dein, former vice chairman of Arsenal and a former president of the G14 group of the biggest European football clubs, to take on the role of international president, and David started a bridge-building process immediately.

However, the trial by press was not over yet. The next nail in our coffin was a *Sunday Times* investigation, covering the same sort of territory as *Panorama* had done in relation to IOC members during the Athens Olympic Games. This time, Simon and Andy had unearthed a bogus lobbying company trying to buy votes for America's World Cup bid – America was bidding for 2022. The undercover reporters had managed to get two FIFA executive committee members, one from Oceania and one from Nigeria, saying they were prepared to trade. Although we didn't have the details until the story went live, our bid team knew enough to warn FIFA that something was going on. And whether we liked it or not, the *Sunday Times* story had legs. The fact that one of the two was prepared to trade for development programmes in his country, while the other was trading for himself, is irrelevant. They were trading, and if you represent an international federation, which they were, and are members of a panel choosing where a championship should go, a championship which is worth billions to the country involved, your choice can only be predicated on the ability of the host country to stage the event, and their plans to have the competitors sit centre stage. It cannot be about whether your country might end up with more football pitches and some development money.

The *Sunday Times* investigation was an entirely different level of journalism from the David Triesman sting. It had exposed something that needed exposing. FIFA's ethics committee eventually suspended both members for three years.

However, once again for us the timing could not have been worse. We were a month away from the vote on 2 December 2010. The gap of four weeks meant that the scandal got wide coverage and the consensus was not 'bad apples have been successfully exposed', but 'the British press are at it again'. The final *coup de grâce* was yet again *Panorama*, just one day before the vote. More damaging than the programme itself, which was simply an opportunistic rehashing of something that had already been investigated, was the fact that it had been trailed for several days beforehand.

Singapore 2005 had become the template for how bid cities now presented their case. You bring in the big guns. Putin supported Sochi in Guatemala in 2007. Obama and Lula from Brazil flew to Copenhagen in 2009. It is now generally accepted that this is what you do.

On arrival in Zurich, David Cameron and his team went to see Blatter. He told them, 'Don't worry. Our decision will not be based on the *Sunday Times* or *Panorama*.' But minutes before the final vote, in his speech to the twenty-four members who would decide the matter, Blatter devoted his concluding remarks to comments concerning press intrusion. I know because, of course, Geoff Thompson was there and he emerged with his face the colour of chalk.

England needed six or seven votes in the first ballot to progress to the next round. I hadn't been involved on the front line, but I'd been told by David Dein's team that we had probably got six. Once we got through to the second round, then things looked less precarious.

We got two votes. Geoff Thompson and one other. Eliminated.

Call me an old romantic, but I do think that when somebody shakes the hand of a British prime minister or a future king of England and says, 'You have my vote,' they are both entitled to believe the deal might last for more than five hours. When Blair shook the hands of all those IOC members, not all said they would vote for London, but I have no reason to believe that those who did commit to us did not subsequently honour their pledge.

My instinct was that Blatter always wanted Russia. He sees himself as a buccaneer, cast in the same mould as Juan Antonio Samaranch, as Bernie Ecclestone – the last of the big visionaries.

He'd taken the World Cup to South Africa. He'd taken it back to South America. Now here was Russia. This was about him opening up football, although I suspect Qatar wasn't in the plan. He probably wanted Russia 2018 and the USA 2022. That way he could be sitting with Putin and Obama either side of him. That would have been the big picture.

Most people get Sepp Blatter wrong; they say he hates England. He doesn't. He's Swiss, and like a lot of Swiss, he's rather fond of England. He likes the political stability. He likes the pomp and tradition. What he has always had a problem with is the English game. And, from his perspective, it's not hard to understand. As president of an international federation, he sees the unwillingness of English clubs to release players for international duty. He sees the purchasing power of the English game – big-name clubs buying up players from all over the world. And he sees a national federation that, at the time of the bid, had no chairman or chief executive. And then he sees our press, permanently focusing on his organisation.

Blatter once said to me, 'Your game is run by idiots. It's not run by bright people.'

As someone involved with the bid I was obviously disappointed. Very disappointed. But if I had spent two years of my life on it, I would have been absolutely gutted. I can only imagine what I'd have felt like if I'd been on the wrong end of the vote in Singapore and we'd been ejected in the first round.

But for those people sitting in that room, who had lived London 2018 for two years, and who had done a supreme job in terms of both the bid and the presentation, it was a full stop. They were devastated, and I don't blame them.

When Sepp Blatter opened the two envelopes, I was standing alongside Bobby Charlton, then 73, one of the original Busby Babes, who survived the Munich air disaster, scored more goals for England than any other player, was a crucial member of the triumphant 1966 World Cup team, and who had been there for us in Singapore – a great ambassador for the game. He turned to me and said, 'This means I'll never get to see a World Cup in England in my lifetime.' Neither will I, Bobby.

27

INSPIRE A GENERATION

'To everyone in this stadium attending our opening ceremony, to every athlete waiting, ready, prepared to take part in these Games, to everyone in every city and village in the world watching as we begin, welcome to London. Welcome to the 2012 Olympic Games.'

Thus, on the night of Friday, 27 July 2012, I began my address to the largest audience I have ever faced, or will ever face. The phantasmagoria that was Danny Boyle's Isles of Wonder was in its closing stages, athletes from the competing nations formed a patchwork of colour at the centre of the stadium, individual national flags had been placed on the slopes of the hill representing Glastonbury Tor in preparation for the entry of the Olympic torch and the lighting of the cauldron. Looking over this mass of multi-hued, multi-tongued humanity, I continued, 'I have never been so proud to be British or to be part of the Olympic Movement, as I am on this day, at this moment.' And it was true.

Little over a week earlier I had packed three bags full of everything I might possibly need over the coming month – suits, casual clothes, running kit, travel jazz collection and a couple of books – and moved into the Intercontinental Hotel, just across the road from the Hilton on Park Lane where the IOC were staying. The Hilton was an island site and protected like Fort Knox and, while I could have based myself there, Carole and I decided we'd prefer a hotel where we could come and go without having to run the gauntlet of the loitering press or the ever-present security. To make ourselves as anonymous as possible, I borrowed my grandmother's maiden name for the duration and we were registered as Mr and Mrs Swan.

As for my plan to head off into Hyde Park every morning, it lasted one day, not because anyone recognised the lone figure padding around the Serpentine in the near dark, but with morning meetings under way by 7.15 a.m. and working till two in the morning most nights, I realised it was self-defeating. The thinking was sound, but even I recognised that exercising on effectively four hours sleep was not a good idea. So I ate carefully, didn't drink – beyond an occasional beer late in the evening – and tried to get what rest I could.

Athletes had been drifting into the village from the moment it opened two weeks before the Games. Almost immediately they started social media conversations, tweeting that London 2012 was the best village they had ever stayed in. Before the rise of Twitter and Facebook, this kind of information would have eventually filtered down via individual teams' *chefs de mission*, but here we had instant feedback. Nothing is more important to me than the wellbeing of athletes – if they're happy, then I'm happy. So that was the upside. The downside was shown when it was claimed an American hurdler had been stuck on a bus for four hours getting to the village from Heathrow.

Just as smart phones have turned everyone into potential paparazzi, social media has turned millions of us into pop-up stringers for journalists who are lurking in chat rooms for just this purpose. Kerron Clement's journey didn't take four hours. It took two and a half hours. And yes, the driver missed one turning, but suddenly this transport hiccup became the lead story of the day. In earlier times, when journalists actually dug out stories for themselves, the editor would ask, 'Where did this come from? Who are your sources?' Or a sub-editor or fact checker would say, 'This doesn't make sense.' Social media has none of those governors or constraints.

This was the territory we were in during the weeks preceding the Games. It was like a phoney war. Until the sport started, they had columns to fill but not much to fill them with. And while the general consensus was that we'd done a good job *so far*, the thinking – at least among some of the British press – was that maybe it was all a bit smoke and mirrors. Maybe it would all unravel.

Two weeks before the opening ceremony, the harbingers of doom had been given succour by the announcement that G4S would not be able to provide the agreed quota of security personnel.

G4S are the largest security services company in the world, operating in over 100 countries, and *en route* to fulfilling their contract with LOCOG they had interviewed, trained and vetted tens of thousands of people. The problem was that at the critical moment they couldn't find them. They couldn't get back into their system and put those who were already trained and accredited into rostered jobs. So we had to make a very quick decision. The armed services were already involved, so why not use more of them? Immediately, the press began to carp that this would change the very nature of the Games: 'It'll have military overtones.' Frankly, I didn't have one moment's unease about that. First of all, these guys get it right. Second, people skills form a key element of their training and they are socially very adept. Army training these days isn't only about a muscular military presence. Being able to talk to children at the roadside in Kabul or Helmand province is now all part of it.

Also, I had already seen for myself just how their presence had gone down, with both the public and athletes. It was the last big set of test events we held on the Olympic Park, the British University track and field championships, together with hockey and water polo. This was in late May, after which the stadium would be closed to get ready for the opening ceremony. Over the course of that weekend, we had some 140,000 people in the park, and – for the first time – a military presence. This was long before the issue with

G4S; the military had always been part of the security mix. To pick up the atmosphere I walked around the park incognito – wearing an old anorak, hood up, head down – listening to what people had to say, about the length of the queues ('better than I expected'), the coffee ('not good enough'), their excitement at being in the park and everything in between. The military were there, in full battle-dress, and I watched as, far from giving them a wide berth, grandparents rushed across with their grandchildren to have photos taken. Even more extraordinary, athletes were breaking off from their warm-up to be photographed with them, too. In my experience, you barely recognise your family twenty minutes before a race, let alone curtail those crucial last moments to be snapped with a total stranger. So I knew that the presence of the military was not going to be a problem. If anything, I think it gave the public massive reassurance.

In the end, they stepped up to become one of the defining images of the Games. By the time we were halfway through, they were as hot a photo opportunity as the mascots. Over the ensuing weeks, athletes talking to soldiers in berets and peaked caps became a familiar sight. Guys who weeks earlier had been crawling around the backstreets of Afghanistan were being photographed with toddlers. The motto for the Games had been 'inspire a generation' – to go into sport, obviously. But I think they might well have inspired that same generation to view the armed services in a completely different light, seeing for themselves that 'these are really good people' and even, 'for a few years, I'd quite like to be part of that'. London 2012 was never going to be like a church fête where security was a team of boy scouts under the semi-watchful eye of the vicar. Whatever journalists might have chosen to imagine, anyone with any experience of major sporting events in this country knows that there is always a strong police presence. I have been involved in sport for forty-odd years now, and at some cross-country races the military would even be marshalling the course. An annual equestrian event in Tidworth, run by the army, is one of the best organised sports events I have ever been to.

Security was obviously a hugely important issue for us, but there had to be a balance. You want visitors to feel they're coming to a city that's embracing and warm, and you want them to come back. You don't want them feeling they're being pushed from pillar to post by guys touting machine guns every thirty yards. Achieving this balance was important and overall I think we did it, but at the same time there could be no appetite for risk.

During the run-up to the Games I was regularly asked, 'What is your biggest fear?' My mantra was always 'I don't have sleepless nights over anything.' And I genuinely don't. But this was a tad disingenuous. Day and night I lived with the fear that, while our superb security services were working hour by hour, minute by minute to guarantee our safety, some lone wolf could do their worst.

In the small hours, back at the hotel, I would wake at the sound of a police siren punctuating the night, and think, 'It's four in the morning. Where's it going? What's happened?' I was less concerned about a twin-tower scenario because, with missiles on tower blocks and navy seals in exercise boarding boats on the Thames, the message was out there that we were deadly serious about this. But I was haunted by the fear that when people were celebrating, having street parties or watching television screens in pubs ten deep, it could all come to a grinding halt. That fear never left me. I counted off the days, counted off the hours. Even by the end, when the athletes were celebrating at the closing cere-mony, I was thinking, 'Our job is not done until each one is home and safe.'

For those first two weeks, it was a strange landscape. On the margins, while I was involved in other things, the press continued to snipe, and that's when our communications director Jackie

Brock-Doyle truly showed her mettle, dealing with everything, continually going to the well, mentally and physically. Interestingly, anybody who actually had experience of a Games – specifically members and officials of the IOC – were remarkably sanguine about it all. They would just smile and say, 'Guys, this happens all the time.' They see the landscape during those tense two weeks in every host city. And I have seen enough Games from close quarters to know that it's true. You cannot escape it.

The opening ceremony of any Olympic Games sets the bar for everything that follows. And since Beijing in 2008, the view from the Clapham omnibus was, 'How can we top that?' But even had our budget been as big as China's, we knew we didn't want a Brand Britain marketing tool. What we wanted was a celebration of what we can achieve together, of our confidence in ourselves and our history, our tolerance, our passion, our cultural diversity, but above all a sense of a people coming together. A celebration of our identity as a nation.

And we did not need to go beyond our own shores to put together a world-class spectacle. In a country renowned for great theatre, great musicals, great pageantry, great cinema, great television – at the cutting edge of creativity across the full spectrum of performing arts – why would we not go British? In Danny Boyle and Stephen Daldry we had two global talents. Danny won an Oscar for *Slumdog Millionaire*, having opened his cinematographic career with the radical *Trainspotting*. Stephen – who, along with the very talented Catherine Ugwu, would oversee all four ceremonies – is a three-times Oscar-nominated film director, including for *Billy Elliot*. Both started out in the theatre as mavericks, used to loaves-and-fishes funding constraints, both were now at the top of their game, in cinema and live performance. Stephen's ground-breaking production of *An Inspector Calls* is still pulling in theatre audiences around the globe, while Danny's *Frankenstein,* an electrifying production at the National Theatre, was subsequently filmed and screened to great acclaim world wide.

I first met Danny a few years ago when we were guests on Radio 5 Live, and we started chatting, not on air, but at the margins of the programme. And he said to me, 'I've lived in east London for twenty-five years and I can't wait to see the sport. I'll be right in there.' And I remember saying to him, 'Well, it would be great if you could be involved in some way,' and his face lit up like an eight-year-old's. 'I'll do anything!' he said. 'I'll even make the tea! Anything!'

So I fed this conversation back to our teams and when we came to look at the opening ceremony, we talked to him about what difference he thought he could make. Previous opening ceremonies, he said, had been televisually 'very one-dimensional' and that was something he felt should change. This struck a distinct chord. I had commentated for the BBC on the opening ceremony in Sydney in 2000 and it hadn't been easy. What looked like a haphazard grouping of people down in the stadium made sense only when seen on a television monitor where an aerial shot showed them forming the pattern of a dove. He wanted to make both the TV and stadium experience more multimedia, and especially, he wanted to involve the spectators.

The stadium had been locked down at the end of May to allow time to build the infrastructure and install the lifting equipment needed to raise, among other things, the chimneys. Soon there was an entire subterranean world down there. The set was built several metres above the level of the running track, providing all the space needed for storage and construction, where vignettes could be filmed to be spliced into the live TV coverage to give granularity. I remember being down in the bowels of the stadium watching Danny demonstrate to some of the volunteer cast how to lift a sack of 'coal' that in reality was as heavy as a block of polystyrene. 'You've got to put your back into it,' he told them. The success of his overall vision was built up by detail piled upon intimate detail.

Danny saw the opening ceremony as an opportunity to celebrate 'the creativity, eccentricity, daring and openness of the British genius by harnessing the genius, creativity, eccentricity, daring and openness of modern London'. All these elements were present in the Happy and Glorious sequence. In what other city's opening ceremony could you have cut to James Bond walking through Buckingham Palace before accompanying the Queen on a helicopter ride to the stadium, and then jumping out?

When Danny came to us with the original idea, and said, 'Do you think she'd do it?' we honestly didn't know. I thought it was brilliant, but whether the Queen would acquiesce . . . that was another matter. As luck would have it, when I was William's chief of staff, his head of media for a time was Edward Young. Some years later, Edward became the Queen's deputy private secretary. He and I had stayed in touch, so my first move was to take it to him. He, too, thought it very funny, 'though I think this will take some very careful choreography,' he advised. And Edward was as instrumental as anybody in getting it through, stage by careful stage.

The opening ceremony of London 2012 would attract the biggest global audience British television would ever have, and obviously the prime minister needed to be kept in the loop over the general direction it was taking; the government weren't there micro managing, but they needed to know what we were saying about the country. When the James Bond idea was put to the prime minister and his deputy, they both thought it was fantastic and David Cameron agreed to raise the possibility at his weekly audience with the Queen.

The plan was as top secret as it gets and kept to a very tight circle of people. But in March, Daniel Craig was spotted filming around the palace, and the *Sun* ran a story putting him and the Queen together and making an educated guess. Fortuitously, they ran it on 1 April and there was a lot of noise around the activities for the Jubilee Celebrations, so when the rest of Fleet Street called to check it, the story was stopped in its tracks. Run on any other day and we'd have struggled.

I'll never forget when Danny showed Paul and me the finished film. We were in the Portakabin in the stadium that was Danny's makeshift editing suite, and even though we had been involved at every stage from storyboard to final script, the wit, fun and sheer audacity left us speechless and if I'm honest a little nervous. When we saw those shoes and the peach-coloured dress disappearing into the night sky under a billowing parachute, we looked at each other, both thinking, 'Oh my God! What have we sanctioned here!' From the outset, everyone had agreed that there was a really important balance to be struck. It had to be done in a caring, affectionate, admiring way, and Daniel Craig got it exactly right, even down to looking through the gaping helicopter door to check it was safe for her to jump.

If we had judged this wrongly, we knew it would be the only thing anyone would talk about until the athletics got going in the second week, and not in a good way. And, given that Her Majesty's reputation stood at an all-time high following the extraordinary pageant of the Diamond Jubilee weekend, it was a risk.

During the opening ceremony itself I was sitting next to the Prince of Wales, with Prince Harry and Prince William directly behind us. None of them knew about the Queen's involvement, nor that the film even existed. So when the sequence began, with the corgis racing up what were obviously very familiar stairs, Prince Charles looked at me and began laughing rather nervously, wondering where on earth this was going. And when the film cut to the shot of the royal back, he had exactly the same reaction as everyone else which was to assume it was the lady who does the impersonations. But the moment she turned around, and everyone realised, 'My God! It really is the Queen!' he began roaring with laughter. As for his sons, they were beside themselves. As she started her descent two voices shouted out in unison behind me, 'Go, Granny!'

For me that was the nicest thing. It was a complete surprise, not just for the world, but for the entire royal family apart from the Princess Royal. As a member of the LOCOG board she was obviously in the know. And if at any time she had said, 'Absolutely, under no circumstances am I going to allow this,' I'd have said, 'Fine. It was a fun thought.'

Apart from this stunning *coup de théâtre*, which remained totally under wraps, we had done considerably more pre-setting than is usual with an opening ceremony, working behind the scenes with Fleet Street editors, taking them discreetly through some of the content and some of the challenges, making sure they were around for rehearsals. They needed to know they weren't going to get the Coldstream Guards and Spitfires doing barrel rolls followed by a tribute to West Ham football club. We weren't ticking the usual boxes here, and we didn't want to wake up the next morning to headlines screaming, 'What was all that about?'

Every theme, every idea, every decision about what stayed in and what went out, was Danny's. He was our Prospero, and I was determined to protect him as much as I could from others who might want to shape things their way, as inevitably they would.

On 1 July, with a little under four weeks to go, I was at Warwick School for a charity cricket match. It coincided with the torch relay going through the town. Standing at the side of the road, waiting for the runners with the rest of the crowd, people were coming up to me and saying, 'Can't you stop the newspapers giving the game away?' Already helicopters were flying over the park trying to get shots of rehearsals, trying to second guess who the headline talent would be. 'We don't want to know what's in the opening ceremony. We want it to be a surprise.'

They weren't the only ones who felt frustrated. I was particularly nervous about details of the cauldron, and how it would be lit, getting out, which I felt would have been disastrous. Danny was irritated largely on behalf of the cast, who were working their socks off, hour after hour after hour in monsoon conditions. And when they weren't soaked to the skin, they were freezing. If certain sections of the media were intent on letting the cat out of the bag, and succeeded, they would end up spoiling the party for everybody. So I started speaking discreetly to senior editors, saying, 'I need your help here. Please don't kill this.' The one who really got it was Paul Dacre on the *Mail*. 'I can see that this is wrong,' he said. 'We shouldn't be doing it,' and he made me a commitment – not only would he pull all his journalists off the story, but if anything came in from elsewhere, they wouldn't use it. The Mirror Group was also good, as was James Harding of *The Times*, but with the dress rehearsals coming up – being played to near-full capacity – there was understandable concern that it couldn't be contained. Danny could have asked for camera phones to be banned or for everyone to sign confidentiality agreements, but he just stood up and asked people to 'save the surprise'. The tag #Savethesurprise, which was then spelled out on screens across the stadium, had been Jackie's idea and soon it was trending globally on Twitter. And it worked. Tens of thousands of people saw the technical runs and the dress rehearsals, and commented on their feelings and impressions, but gave nothing away about the content of the show.

During those last few days, Danny's hair, unruly at the best of times, became wilder by the hour. He was like the mad professor. It's easy to forget now how nervous we were about the opening ceremony's reception. Paul, Jackie, Keith, Charles Allen and Bill Morris, our director of ceremonies, and I would watch rehearsals when we could, often into the early hours of the morning. There was a real buzz among the volunteers, in spite of the atrocious weather, and we became increasingly confident that we were about to see something special. But this was a vast operation and with so many moving parts, and so many disparate elements, any number of things could have gone wrong. 'Say some of the winding gear doesn't work and the chimneys don't come out. Or a key performer trips over and breaks a leg.' After all, they were, literally, dealing with a cast of thousands. I remember going into the control room after the opening ceremony to congratulate the teams and it was like being in the boiler room of a vast ocean liner. Both Danny and Stephen looked as if they were expecting the men in white coats to come through the door. They could barely speak.

While I knew we had a winner, I have to admit that I was taken aback by the level of approval it did achieve. The following morning we woke to superlatives across the spectrum, from the *Guardian* to the *Daily Mail* – proof if ever it was needed that we had got the balance right. The international response was even more of a surprise. Quirky and eccentrically British as it was, they got it.

The only dissenting voices were a right-wing commentator or two, who complained that it'd had a left-wing bent. It's fair to say that I found that slightly odd, given that the chairman of the organising committee is a Conservative peer, as is the chairman of the British Olympic Association, and both the prime minister and the mayor of London are Conservatives. Were all these people outflanked by the left? I don't think so. There was no political bent. This was British history. It was a parade of Britishness, from the industrial revolution to the digital revolution. It included the suffragettes, it included the Jarrow crusade, it included the National Health Service, which was not the creation of any particular party but of a postwar consensus. It was never going to include everything that Britain has ever achieved, if only because of time.

Eighteen months before the Games began, the government invested in the ceremonies. We hadn't gone to them with a begging bowl, far from it. The one thing we were very focused on was aligning creativity with the budget, and we would never have breached it. It was simply that the prime minister had seen our storyboard and liked what he saw. Critics implied that the government had been forced to increase their investment because they didn't consider what we were proposing was good enough. As I said at the time, 'I have rarely known an environment where somebody has put money into something they didn't like.' I know the PM's thinking had been, 'This is the first time the Games have been here for sixty-four years. There's nobody living who's going to see them back in the UK again, certainly not a British prime minister. We will never have another opportunity of showcasing Great Britain to such a global and concentrated audience. So with this in mind, let's do it.' And I am grateful. We would have had a good show whatever happened, but there were things we were able to do with the extra funding that wouldn't have been possible without it, including some of the infrastructure, particularly the extraordinary light display on individual seats we called the pixels and which we went on to use at the closing and Paralympic ceremonies – and after big moments in the stadium.

One of the most memorable moments for me was a couple of years earlier when I took Danny into the stadium for the first time. As we walked in, he stopped. 'My God,' he said. 'This isn't a sports stadium! You've given me a theatre!' And that's what he in turn gave us. Theatre.

From the end of May till the end of July, the neighbourhoods and streets of Britain had themselves become a theatre for our torch relay, eloquently dismantling any thoughts that the Diamond Jubilee pageant would be the high point of the year and that the Games would leave people disengaged – as some had suggested. Immediately the sport started, they were out again in force. Among the professionals, both the federations and the IOC, there were those who were genuinely surprised at how full our venues were, right from the start. But if you'd lived through our ticketing process as I had, you weren't surprised. It had been a bruising process, but the one thing you did know was that your tickets were selling. So for me, the bigger pleasure was the sheer numbers out on the streets. On that first morning of sport, half a million people lined the road-cycling course to see Mark Cavendish. They were forty deep on Box Hill! And once the medals started coming in, the crowds increased exponentially. The view from some quarters was that the country had been force fed into ersatz excitement by the organising committee. It simply wasn't true. Fifteen million people had been out on the streets to watch the torch relay because at each stage we had involved the local community. The torch bearers were often local heroes, sung or unsung, each with their own unique story. I ran with it in Sheffield – a lovely moment. As the headline in the local paper put it that evening, 'We are all part of Olympic history', and that was the feeling I encountered everywhere, because people got it. We had more than an inkling then that, even beyond the massive demand for tickets, people weren't going to sit this dance out.

One of the biggest moments of the Games for me was a personal one. On the first day of the athletics I flew down to Weymouth by helicopter with the president of the IOC Jacques Rogge. I am no sailing expert but it is Jacques' sport. He is a three-times Olympian, having competed in the Finn class in Mexico City, Munich and Montreal, and had come to see his hero Ben Ainslie. That morning 4,000 people were watching from the Nothe, a restored fort on a promontory jutting into Weymouth harbour, and the place was rocking. The sailors said they could hear their names being called above the roar of the sea and the wind. It was the first time, they said, that they had ever been that close to a crowd. A huge screen allowed spectators to follow the action in close-up, as well as watching the racing itself as the boats sped across the bay.

Jacques had decided to go onto the water, but I didn't plan to spend five hours finding my sea legs and took the opportunity to go round Weymouth, thanking everybody for the work they'd done leading up to this moment. I was in the Olympic hospitality area in the sailing centre, watching that master of everything, Ben Ainslie, inching his way to yet another gold, when they cut to the first day of track and field in the stadium. There wasn't an empty seat to be seen. Seconds later Jackie sent me a text saying the stadium was full. Soon messages were raining in from IAAF members who'd been to every World Championship, some of them having done five Olympic Games, saying they had never seen anything like it. 'What are all these people doing here, watching heats?' I knew that we'd sold every ticket, but even so, the night before I couldn't help wondering, 'Are they all going to come? Am I going to end up with flak about the stadium not being full?' As for Lamine Diack, the IAAF president, that night at the stadium he told me, 'I could not believe it, I just could not believe it!' He couldn't even get into his own seat because we'd done such a comprehensive job of allowing the military and games makers into any unoccupied accredited places, and selling overnight those seats allocated to the federation that they felt would be surplus to requirements. Whatever irritation he might have felt at not being able to sit in the presidential box was wiped away by the glorious sight of a packed stadium. The same thing happened to Jacques Rogge at the gymnastics; he couldn't get into the IOC box!

Why did this matter to me quite so much? I'd had years of what I call three-and-sixpenny conversations about the future of the stadium, where I'd be regularly informed that track and field was a dead sport and the only hope lay in a football club taking it over. But can anyone now imagine, had one of those football options been accepted and bulldozers moved in, razing it to the ground only to build another football-only stadium in its place?

It is not up to me to mark my own homework, and I'm not going to. For this reason we called off all interviews towards the end of the Games; if other people want to call them the best Games ever, then fine. What I can say, however, is that all the people who mattered – the athletes, spectators, national Olympic committees and federations – were happy, and that's good enough for me.

I went to as much sport as I could and saw every sporting discipline. I took particular pleasure in the success of one particular venue – that most glorious of south London parks, Greenwich. The BBC has never had viewing figures like this. For the opening ceremony we had 27 million people. At midnight, 20 million were still glued to their screens. If that wasn't enough, the London Games broke all American TV records as well. And in large part, we got right the fusion of sport and landscape. After a private dinner, only weeks after Singapore, Jacques Rogge said to me, 'If you use just ten per cent of what London has available, you'll finish ahead.' We used central London for the marathon course. We had tennis at Wimbledon, and archery at Lords, which I have to say was fantastic. I knew we were winning when my daughter Alice sent me a text saying, 'Archery's sick, Dad!' Apparently, when you're a 13-year-old girl, 'sick' means 'very cool'. She hadn't particularly wanted to go, but it was what we had got in the ballot.

While Britain is a sporting nation, we have little experience of some sports. As everyone knows, ticketing for these Games was a challenging process, not simply because of the crushing demand, but also because we had to sell tickets to sports that nobody had ever really seen. Take handball. The reality was that we had never sold a single ticket to a handball match in this country. Ever. And, with the early group matches being staged in the copper box, we had 5,000 seats to sell for every session. Amazingly, they sold. And within a few days the athletes were calling the copper box 'The Box That Rocks'. When I went to watch Hungary play South Korea, the noise was crushing. It was the same for volleyball and badminton.

At every venue you went to the noise was deafening. This is what took the federations by surprise. Every president I spoke to told me the same thing: 'Nobody has ever given us these kind of crowds.' It wasn't just about numbers. The British crowds were enthusiastic and, more than that, respectful. This wasn't a question of team GB or nothing. I remember on Super Saturday when Greg Rutherford had basically already got a big chunk of that long jump gold medal around his neck, but was a nail-biting two jumps away from possessing the crown, the British crowd still cheered the remaining athletes down the runway, both Americans, both good jumpers, who could have been lifted by their support. The generosity of spirit among British fans was genuinely uplifting, whether in the stadia or in their hundreds and thousands on the streets.

In the triathlon, while the open-water swimming is fantastic, it's hard to follow – it's not an obvious crowd participation sport. In the cycling phase, the riders come past so quickly, individual competitors are hard to identify, but once you were down to that little group of five in the final stages of the run, everyone in the crowd knew what was happening. They were on the other side of the lake from the tribune, but the ticketed seats were nothing compared to the thousands who flocked into Hyde Park that morning to watch this fraternal battle. I will never forget the wall of sound that hit Alistair and Jonathan Brownlee as they ran along the south side of the Serpentine. Two brothers battling it out for Olympic gold – it's hard to imagine anything more dramatic, particularly when you think what it must have meant for that family. Then one of them getting his 15 second penalty for going too early on the bike and, in order to come back into contention, running himself to exhaustion and onto an intravenous drip – delaying the presentation.

I was involved in just one presentation ceremony – the one for Jessica Ennis. It had a particular resonance for me because of

Sheffield, of course, and I've known Jess for a long time. I presented her with her gold medal in Berlin when she won in 2009, and her silver in Daegu in 2011. And on that day in South Korea I told her that I had already laid claim to one presentation at the London Games – the only one – and that would be the women's heptathlon, because she would win it. I reminded her of that when I handed her her flowers on 4 August 2012. And that was so good, not simply because she is so talented or so madly normal, but she's going to be such an enormous magnet for young girls to take up sport.

In many respects, it was the women's Games. The Princess Royal, at the end of the first week, said, 'Well, thank goodness, the women have kept you all afloat,' and she was right. Lizzie Armitstead's battling silver medal in the cycling started the ball rolling. Heather Stanning and Helen Glover in the coxless pairs brought Team GB its first gold of the Games, and the first ever won by GB women rowers. Two days later Katherine Grainger and Anna Watkins led the double sculls from start to finish. Then Katherine Copeland and Sophie Hosking in the lightweight sculls made it a hat trick.

Nicola Adams's gold, achieved with precision and delicacy, has secured the status of women's boxing in the UK. If anyone doubted that women should be in the ring, she's changed that now forever. In another kind of ring you had our equestrians – Zara Phillips, who didn't even know she had made the team until a few weeks before, and Charlotte Dujardin, who entranced us all with her gold-winning individual dressage. And the women's hockey team, coming back and beating New Zealand for the bronze medal, showed just what character they possessed.

As for my own sport, on any indices of assessment the standout performance was David Rudisha's scintillating 800m where he broke his own world record, the most definitive piece of front running I have ever seen. Usain Bolt was good – and a wonderful showman – but Rudisha was magnificent. And Mo Farah's second gold in the 5000m, when he had barely recovered from the 10,000m a week before, showed the power of the crowd to pull you over the line. But there were so many exceptional performances I feel it's invidious even to begin to name them.

When asked what I personally took away from London 2012, it was in many ways much simpler than compiling a list of golden moments. It was new friendships. Tessa Jowell and I come from opposite sides of the political divide and we would probably never have met had it not been for her crusading zeal in bringing the Games to London. Risking the ire of the politically correct, you'd go tiger shooting with Tessa. I call her Mary Poppins with a stiletto. At the outset, as secretary of state for media, culture and sport in the last Labour government, when she received the policy paper from her civil servants – the advice being not to bid for the 2012 Games – she went straight to Downing Street and basically said to Tony Blair, 'What are you? A man or a mouse?' By his own admission, Blair got bullied into bidding for the Games. And then she lay down in the road when Gordon Brown was being slow about signing off the budget. She's brave, she can be very emotional in a good way, and at every step she was fully committed. In the 2012 Queen's birthday honours, she was made a Dame of the British Empire, the female equivalent of a knight. And she deserves it. Ever since I've known her she's been working for our international legacy programme, International Inspiration, using the power of sport to enrich children's lives, doing time on what we called the Magic Bus, delivering equipment to local communities in India. And all this in her downtime, the moment parliament went into recess. She is simply one of the nicest people I have ever met, and I am lucky enough to count her now among my closest friends.

Until my involvement with London 2012, the majority of my friendships were forged at university between the ages of 18 and 23. Now a whole new roster has come along, including Keith Mills,

Paul Deighton and Hugh Robertson, the Conservative minister for sport, whom I didn't know when I was involved in politics as he was elected by his Kent constituency in 2001. And in what other walk of life would I count Danny Boyle among my friends? These friendships are now rock solid and lifelong.

No chairman and CEO have ever made it through from beginning to end of an Olympics as Paul and I have done. It has helped that neither of us takes life too seriously. We both had the ability to close the door and laugh about the bizarre world we were living in, while trying hard not to be rude to people too often. Neither of us care about being universally liked. Paul's role was to drive the organisation while mine was to protect him from all those things that might have stopped that happening. Above all, Paul and I were a team. From the outset, I told him, 'If ever your job becomes untenable, then I go, too.'

The most important thing a chairman can do is to allow smart people to flourish, and by accepting responsibility for the things that go wrong as well as the things that go right. It goes back to my father and what he said after the disastrous 800m final in Moscow. 'It's not "we win, you lose". It doesn't work like that.' That was the attitude I took with the LOCOG team. And, as far as I know, we are unique in the annals of Olympic history. Every one of our directors – whether it was Sport or the General Counsel – made it through from their appointment to the closing ceremony, and I can honestly say that I have never worked with a more focused or passionate group of people. It's quite possible that I never will again.

Another happy surprise was Boris Johnson, who was superb. At key moments in the process he proved as staunch a defender as Tessa had been a few years earlier. Boris came into the mayoralty with a few preconceived notions of what the IOC was about, as well as a healthy nervousness of the nature of *grands projets* – understandable from his point of view given that the Games were initially in the stewardship of a Labour government. But he soon grasped both the enormity of the project and its importance to London, as did Jeremy Hunt, Tessa Jowell's successor as secretary at state, who, with Hugh Robertson, skilfully shepherded the project within government, crucially – and essentially – maintaining the bi-partisan approach. As luck would have it, Jeremy is also my local MP.

Behind Boris's public persona lies a razor-sharp brain, and a keen sense of humour that, on occasion, had me twitching nervously on public platforms, challenging us not to collapse into laughter. There will be few experiences in the future that will offer the sheer fun of one of Boris's press conferences, when he could casually throw away the script, and the press were as likely to receive a tutorial in Latin or Greek as an explanation of the Olympic route network. And while the IOC were decidedly nervous of him at first, he's now considered one of the family.

Writing these last few paragraphs just days after the curtain has come down on the Paralympic Games, it's too soon to know whether my ultimate goal – that London 2012 could inspire and excite our young people into sport and into healthier and happier lives – will be fulfilled. But I am optimistic.

The extraordinary performance of Team GB set the tone. We could have sold all the tickets, we could have had a great atmosphere in the stadium and other venues, but we needed home-town results to truly capture the imagination. And the fact that they amassed twenty-nine gold medals between them was beyond the headiest expectations. They gave us a host of indelible memories, and it is those moments that will inspire the next generation. Above all else, our future sportsmen and women need role models, just as John Sherwood inspired that 12-year-old boy in Sheffield all those years ago.

Gymnastics has made household names of Louis Smith and Kristian Thomas, who dazzled with his high-flying floor routine, and of course Beth Tweddle, a great servant to British sport, who was absolutely key in taking the Olympic message to the north west. For Greg Searle to win bronze in the men's eight at the age of 40, all of twenty years after he won an Olympic rowing title in Barcelona, was an astonishing achievement in such a brutal endurance sport. As for Bradley Wiggins, topping his Tour de France victory with Olympic gold was the stuff of boyhood fantasies.

With so much spectacular sport in so many different venues, it was impossible for me to watch more than a fraction of it – that pleasure will have to wait until I sit down in front of a boxed set once the long winter evenings arrive. But being there, of course, provided an extra dimension that no TV coverage, however good, can ever fully capture. I will never forget watching Victoria Pendleton and Chris Hoy take gold. I was unprepared for the sheer intensity of the roar produced by 6,000 euphoric fans, which engulfed the Velodrome from start to finish. And I have no doubt that we have in Chris Hoy – who added three more golds to his haul – our greatest Olympian ever. His split-second judgement and decision-making were peerless.

And what can you say about Victoria Pendleton? Fiercely competitive, this talented young woman wears her heart on her sleeve and she gave us everything, from ecstasy to agony and every emotion in between. As for Jason Kenny, for so long riding in Chris Hoy's shadow, he is now the holder of two Olympic golds and I predict that at Rio he will be unstoppable. The same is true of Laura Trott – two gold medals, and still only 20.

If the opening ceremony can be said to have launched the Games, Super Saturday sent them into orbit. Not one of the 80,000 present in the stadium who watched Jess Ennis take the tape in the 800m when she didn't have to, saw Greg Rutherford's obvious bemuse-ment when he realised he had won the long jump, witnessed Mo Farah's passionate self-belief when, after 24 laps, he went to the front, accelerating all the way to the finish line, will ever forget a day of pure magic.

For Mo Farah, winning the 10,000m was the first of what would turn out to be an historic double. The Olympic 10,000m is a serious title that no Briton has ever won before, and he ran a near-perfect race, despite not having a team around him to help, resisting several early surges that could have taken the edge off his run for home. He is undoubtedly the greatest male runner Britain has ever produced.

But when it comes to drama, perhaps nothing can beat the final of the men's 10m dive, which was nail-biting stuff right up to the wire. Being poster boy for the London Games was a heavy load for such young shoulders to bear. But thanks to guts, nerve and sheer determination, Tom Daley fought his way to bronze against prodigiously talented opposition. I wish I had seen it – that combination of beauty, precision and courage makes for addictive viewing. But on that night, the last Saturday of the Games, I was preparing my speech for the closing ceremony, and so I followed the drama on the radio, no less thrilling thanks to the superb Radio 5 commentary team.

Of course, it's not just British athletes who have the power to inspire. Usain Bolt is a superb ambassador for his sport, and was perhaps the greatest single draw of the entire Games. His gold medals in the 100m and 200m and 100m relay, together with the performances of his compadres, not least Yohan Blake, reinforced the total domination of men's sprinting by Jamaica – an island of just two and a half million people.

Australia's Sally Pearson gave a phenomenal winning performance in the 100m hurdles. The USA's Allyson Felix is a sprinter of such grace she restores your faith in the purity of the sport. She runs with the lightness of a gazelle. As well as taking gold in the 100m, she was part of the 4 x 100m victorious quartet of American sprinters. This was a sublime performance from each one of them. The great skill of relay running is not about how fast you can burn up the track, but how safely you can get a baton round and they were millimetre perfect, even as they raced faster than anyone has ever run before to break the long-standing world record.

To some degree, being the chairman of an Olympic organising committee is akin to hosting a very large party. You are not there to enjoy yourself, but to see that everybody else enjoys themselves. The same will not hold true in Rio. There my role will be that of spectator and I would love to think that among those representing Britain will be some young people who were inspired by London 2012 to dedicate themselves to another four years of grind and struggle for the privilege of competing in the greatest sporting occasion known to man.

A key decision, taken early on, was our mission to explain what was going on. In the venues and in the TV coverage, a three-minute segment was screened before each event, capturing the essence of the discipline people were about to watch, be it swimming, gymnastics or track and field. Young people are excited by competition of all kinds, but this excitement will only truly impact on the impulse to take up a sport if they have at least some understanding of what they are watching. This innovation was delivered by our sports presentation unit and driven by Debbie Jevans, our director of sport, who was also responsible for the great sporting relationships behind the scenes that helped create the environment that allowed athletes to perform at their very best, including the training of the volunteers to say the right things at the right moments.

The success of the London Paralympic Games seems to have taken everybody by surprise. It shouldn't have done. This is our history. When we were bidding in Singapore, we didn't have to invent a synthetic connection. The Paralympic Games were effectively created in the National Spinal Injuries Centre in Stoke Mandeville near Aylesbury, established by Ludwig Guttmann in 1943 at the request of the British government. A Jewish neurosurgeon who arrived in Britain in 1939, having escaped Nazi Germany, he understood the potential of physical sport as a way of rehabilitating the damaged bodies and scarred ambitions of severely injured servicemen in the Second World War. It gave them both physical strength and self-respect at a time when the world seemed to have written them off.

Dr Guttmann's work was the genesis of the Paralympic movement, and I was delighted when his daughter Eva Loeffler accepted our invitation to be Mayor of the Paralympic village. On 28 July 1948, on the day the London Games started, he staged a parallel competition for wheelchair-bound former combatants. The Stoke Mandeville Games soon became an annual event and by 1960, Guttmann's achievement was recognised by the IOC and his vision of a parallel international games became a reality at the Rome Olympics in 1960.

By 2008, the Paralympic Games were no longer seen as a sideshow to the main event. In Beijing, the BBC were bombarded by phone calls and emails demanding more live coverage. In September 2011, I was in Trafalgar Square for International Paralympics Day and watched as queues of primary school children patiently, but with mounting excitement, queue for the autographs of Oscar Pistorius, David Weir, and Ellie Simmonds. We also did as much as we could to demystify the Games, focusing not on disability but on ability – the feats of strength, endurance and skill that 99 per cent of the so-called able-bodied population are unable to contemplate. As the Games approached, the public began to recognise that the Paralympics wasn't an add-on but an extension of an extraordinary summer of sport. And in some areas – notably swimming – I thought there was a better atmosphere in the Paralympics than there had been in the Games themselves, not least because we were achieving spectacular home-town results.

Those who bought tickets were not disappointed, nor were the millions who tuned in to Channel 4, who did a first rate job as our domestic broadcaster, and who – in an echo of Beijing – were soon demanding even more coverage than had originally been planned. What we witnessed proved both thrilling and humbling, giving all who watched spine-tingling moments that have already had a profound effect on public attitudes, shattering taboos, opening minds to what people can do, rather than focusing on what they can't.

In my closing speech at the Paralympic Games, I spoke of my profound admiration for the volunteers – the Games makers, 70,000 of them – who stand among the heroes of London 2012. I spoke of meeting Emily, who talked about what the Games meant for her, and what participating in wheelchair basketball meant to her. 'It has lifted the cloud of limitation,' she said. And I believe that in this country we will never think of sport in the same way, and we will never think of disability in the same way. The Paralympians have lifted the cloud of limitation.

I also spoke of another volunteer I met. The Games were just one week in and I was on the Central Line, when I spotted a man in his forties wearing the familiar purple uniform, sitting on the other side of the carriage. The pass round his neck said 'Medic'. So I asked what he was involved in. Boxing, he told me, as part of the medical team. I started to thank him for all he was doing, saying how glad I was that we had the right people in the right places.

'No,' he said, stopping me. 'I should be thanking you.' He explained that he was a consultant anaesthetist at St Mary's Paddington, working in intensive care. And on the morning of 7 July 2005, he had been on duty when victims of the terrorist attacks started to come in, in his case from Edgware Road under-ground station. Seven people died at the scene, including the bomber. But, in spite of the carnage and appalling injuries, all 38 of the injured taken to St Mary's survived. He had never forgotten the link between London's winning the Olympics, which had been announced less than 24 hours before, and this horror, which he had seen from the front line. 'So for me this is closure,' he explained. 'I didn't know whether I would be able to face it. I'm so glad I did. I have seen the worst of mankind and now I've seen the best of mankind.'

And my mind went back to the moment when the dreadful news reached us in Singapore. How we had gone from the euphoria of winning the Games the previous night to that first mention of an 'incident', followed inexorably by the unimaginable reality of what had happened – the 52 people on their way to work who died, the hundreds of injured, and the thousands of families and friends whose lives would never be the same again. Just like Andrew Hartle, I had never quite escaped the link. For me, this unexpected encounter in the familiar environment of the London tube was a seismic moment. For the first time since that terrible day, he told me, he felt proud to be British, proud to live in London. He felt that the Olympics had given us a new start. 'And we don't often get a chance to do that.'

In a few months' time, a journey that has taken very nearly a decade will come to a close. The last job LOCOG needs to do is to wind itself up. By May 2013, I, and everyone else there who helped bring the Games to London, will have moved on. But although my children consider me ancient, I'm still only in my mid-fifties. And while I may no longer hope to run faster, jump higher or be stronger, there's still a lot I want to do with my life. I'm not ready to slow down yet.

GLOSSARY

AAA

Amateur Athletics Association. Formerly governing body of the sport of athletics in England (and of Wales from 1948), the AAA was established in 1880, and is the oldest in the world. Known as 'the three As', their annual championships were considered the de facto British National championships. As Sport England, their current role focuses on community sport and the development of young athletes.

British Amateur Athletic Board

Grouping of athletics associations from England, Scotland, Wales and Northern Ireland, responsible for international selection.

British Athletic Federation

Instituted in 1991. Known as UK Athletics (UKA) since 1999. Governing body of the sport of athletics in Britain and arbiter of British records.

EAA

European Athletic Association. Founded in 1932, a spin-off from the IAAF, arbiter of European records, organiser of the European Championships and European Team Championships (formerly the Europa Cup).

English Schools

English Schools Athletics Association. Founded in 1925, to promote the enjoyment of athletics in schools, organiser of annual track and cross country championships.

IAAF
International Association of Athletics Federations (formerly the International Amateur Athletic Federation). The governing body of the sport of athletics, organiser of the World Championships and arbiter of world records. Founded in 1912.

IOC
International Olympic Committee. Organisers of the Olympic Games. Founded in 1894 by Baron Pierre de Coubertin. First Games held in Athens in 1896. Headquarters in Lausanne, Switzerland.

IOC Athletes Commission
A consultative body of the IOC, made up of active athletes whose role is to ensure their interests are protected. Instigated in 1981 by the then president Juan Antonio Samaranch during the IOC congress in Baden-Baden.

SportAccord
Until 1999, the General Association of International Sports Federations (GAISF). Founded in 1967, headquarters in Lausanne, to promote communication and cooperation between different sports federations, currently numbering 90.

UK Sports Council
Established by Harold Wilson in 1966, this represented the first attempt by government to become formally involved in sport, superseded in 1997 by UK Sport, Britain's high-performance sports agency.

CAREER STATISTICS

A complete list of the track races in which Sebastian Coe has competed since 1973

Abbreviations

pb – personal best   sf – semi final   UK – United Kingdom record
h – heat   cr – championship record   WR – World record
f – final   CR – Commonwealth record   OR – Olympic record

Date	Event	Track	Distance	Place	Time
1973 (age 15/16)					
17 Mar	AAA Indoor Youth Championships	Cosford	800m	4th	2:02.6
1 May	B. Milers' club	Stretford	800m	3rd	1:56.6 (pb)
5 May	Longwood Youth	Huddersfield	1500m	1st	4:07.4
13 May	B. Milers' Club	Crystal Palace	800m	2nd	1:56.0 (pb)
18 May	West District Schools	Sheffield	800m	1st	2:01.1
18 May	West District Schools	Sheffield	1500m	1st	4:15.4
23 May	Sheffield Selection	Sheffield	3000m	1st	8:43.7 (pb)
3 Jun	Northern League	Sheffield	1500m	3rd	4:07.5
9 Jun	York School Championships	York	3000m	1st	8:49.0
16 Jun	N. Counties Youth	Sheffield	1500m	1st	3:59.5 (pb)
7 Jul	English Schools	Bebington	3000m	1st	8:40.2 (pb)
17 Jul	S. Yorks League	Doncaster	800m	1st	1:59.7
21 Jul	City Championships	Sheffield	800m	1st	1:57.0
21 Jul	City Championships	Sheffield	1500m	1st	4:07.4
4 Aug	AAA Youth Championships	Aldersley	1500m	1st	3:55.0 (pb)
14 Aug	Stretford League	Manchester	3000m	6th	8:34.6 (pb)
9 Sep	Hallamsh Harriers Championships	Sheffield	400m	-	51.8 (pb)
15 Sep	Rotherham Festival	Rotherham	1500m	1st	3:58.0

Date	Event	Track	Distance	Place	Time
1974 (aged 16/17)					
10 April	Training run	Rotherham	800m		1:55.1 (pb)
Apr–Nov	Injured with stress fracture				
1975 (aged 17/18)					
21 Mar	Indoor Under 20 Championships	Cosford	1500m(h)	2nd	4:08.0
22 Mar	Indoor Under 20 Championships	Cosford	1500m(f)	1st	3:54.4 (pb)
13 Apr	Pye Cup	Cleckheaton	1500m	1st	3:49.7 (pb)
30 Apr	B. Milers' Club	Rawtenstall	1500m	1st	3:54.0
31 May	Yorks Senior Championships	Cleckheaton	1500m	1st	3:51.3
8 Jun	Pye Cup	Cleckheaton	800m	1st	1:53.8 (pb)
8 Jun	Pye Cup	Cleckheaton	4 x 400m	-	50.5
21 Jun	N. Counties Under 20	Gateshead	1500m	1st	3:50.8
25 Jun	Northern League	Sheffield	300m	2nd	36.2 (pb)
28 Jun	N. Counties Under 20	Blackburn	3000m	1st	8:14.8 (pb)
26 Jul	AAA Junior Championships	Kirkby	1500m(h)	1st	3:52.0
27 Jul	AAA Junior Championships	Kirkby	1500m(f)	1st	3:47.1(pb)
10 Aug	GB v. France/Spain	Warley	1500m	1st	3:50.8
22 Aug	European Junior Championships	Athens	1500m(h)	4th	3:48.8
24 Aug	European Junior Championships	Athens	1500m(f)	3rd	3:45.2 (pb)
1976 (aged 18/19)					
24 Jan	AAA Indoor Championships	Cosford	1500m	5th	3:51.0
6 Mar	Loughborough Match	Crystal Palace	4 x 800m	-	1:52.0(pb)
20 Mar	Loughborough Match	Cosford	600m relay	-	80.4
28 Mar	B. Milers' Club	Stretford	1500m	1st	3:47.4
14 Apr	H. Wilson Mile	Crystal Palace	1 mile	1st	4:07.6 (pb)
1 May	B. Milers' Club	Stretford	1 mile	1st	4:05.7 (pb)
12 May	Loughborough Match	Loughborough	800m	1st	1:53.0
16 May	Yorkshire Championships	Cleckheaton	1500m	1st	3:43.3 (pb)
19 May	Loughborough v. Borough Rd	Isleworth	800m	1st	1:53.0

Date	Event	Track	Distance	Place	Time
31 May	Inter-Counties Championships	Crystal Palace	1 mile	2nd	4:02.4 (pb)
11 Jun	Olympic Selection	Crystal Palace	1500m	7th	3:43.2 (pb)
17 Jun	Loughborough v AAA	Loughborough	800m	1st	1:50.7 (pb)
24 Jul	Heckington Sports	Heckington	1 mile	1st	4:09.1
1 Aug	Open Meeting	Nottingham	1000m	1st	2:30.0
8 Aug	B. Milers' Club	Stretford	800m	1st	1:47.7 (pb)
13 Aug	AAA Championships	Crystal Palace	1500m(h)	3rd	3:34.05
14 Aug	AAA Championships	Crystal Palace	1500m(f)	4th	3:42.67 (pb)
21 Aug	Rediffusion Games	Gateshead	1 mile	3rd	4:01.7 (pb)
30 Aug	Emsley Carr Mile	Crystal Palace	1 mile	7th	3:58.35 (pb)
14 Sep	Bell's Games	Gateshead	1 mile	2nd	4:01.5
20 Nov	Indoor Meeting	Cosford	600m	1st	1:19.7

1977 (aged 19/20)

Date	Event	Track	Distance	Place	Time
29 Jan	AAA Indoor Championships	Cosford	800m	1st	1:49.1
19 Feb	GB v. W. Germany	Dortmund	800m	1st	1:47.6 (CR)
26 Feb	GB v. France	Cosford	800m	1st	1:47.5 (CR)
12 Mar	European Indoor Championships	San Sebastian	800m(h)	1st	1:50.5
13 Mar	European Indoor Championships	San Sebastian	800m(sf)	1st	1:48.2
14 Mar	European Indoor Championships	San Sebastian	800m(f)	1st	1:46.54 (CR)
3 Jul	Dewhurst Games	Spalding	800m	1st	1:51.7
23 Jul	AAA Championships	Crystal Palace	800m	2nd	1:46.83
30 Jul	Philips Games	Gateshead	800m	2nd	1:47.4
14 Aug	Europa Cup	Helsinki	800m	4th	1:47.61
16 Aug	Ivo Van Damme	Brussels	800m	3rd	1:46.31 (pb)
24 Aug	Club Meeting	Rotherham	400m	1st	49.1
28 Aug	GB v. W. Germany	Crystal Palace	800m	1st	1:47.78
29 Aug	Emsley Carr Mile	Crystal Palace	1 mile	1st	3:57.67 (pb)
7 Sep	Courage Games	St Ives	800m	1st	1:48.1
9 Sep	Coca-Cola	Crystal Palace	800m	2nd	1:44.95 (UK)

1978 (aged 20/21)

Date	Event	Track	Distance	Place	Time
26 Apr	Loughborough Match	Crystal Palace	400m	1st	48.0(pb)
10 May	Loughborough Match	Isleworth	400m	1st	47.7(pb)
14 May	Yorkshire Championships	Cleckheaton	800m	1st	1:45.6 (cr)
1 Jun	Loughborough v. AAA	Loughborough	800m	1st	1:50.0

Date	Event	Track	Distance	Place	Time
9 Jul	Philips Games	Gateshead	800m	1st	1:46.83
15 Jul	UK Championships	Meadowbank	800m	1st	1:47.14
10 Aug	International Invitation	Viareggio	800m	1st	1:45.7
18 Aug	Ivo Van Damme	Brussels	800m	1st	1:44.25 (UK)
29 Aug	European Championships	Prague	800m(h)	1st	1:46.81
30 Aug	European Championships	Prague	800m(sf)	1st	1:47.44
31 Aug	European Championships	Prague	800m(f)	3rd	1:44.76
15 Sep	Coca-Cola	Crystal Palace	800m	1st	1:43.97 (UK)
17 Sep	McEwans Games	Gateshead	1 mile	1st	4:02.17

1979 (aged 21/22)

Date	Event	Track	Distance	Place	Time
27 Jan	AAA Indoor Championships	Cosford	3000m	1st	7:59.8 (pb)
25 Apr	Loughborough Match	Crystal Palace	400m	2nd	48.3
9 May	Loughborough Match	Loughborough	800m	1st	1:51.0
20 May	Yorkshire Championships	Cleckheaton	800m	1st	1:50.5
21 May	Yorkshire Championships	Cleckheaton	400m	1st	47.6 (pb)
23 May	Loughborough Match	Loughborough	400m	1st	47.4 (pb)
23 May	Loughborough Match	Loughborough	800m	1st	1:54.8
31 May	Loughborough v. AAA	Loughborough	800m	1st	1:47.9
16 Jun	N. Counties Championships	Stretford	800m	1st	1:46.3
30 Jun	Europa Cup Semi Final	Malmo	800m	1st	1:46.63
3 Jul	Bislett Games	Oslo	800m	1st	1:42.33 (WR)
7 Jul	International Meeting	Meisingset	800m	1st	1:54.8
13 Jul	AAA Championships	Crystal Palace	400m(h)	1st	46.95 (pb)
14 Jul	AAA Championships	Crystal Palace	400m (f)	2nd	46.87 (pb)
17 Jul	Golden Mile	Oslo	1 mile	1st	3:48.95 (WR)
29 Jul	Dewhurst Games	Spalding	600m	1st	76.5
5 Aug	Europa Cup Final	Turin	800m	1st	1:47.28
5 Aug	Europa Cup Final	Turin	4 x 400m	6th	45.5
8 Aug	International Invitation	Viareggio	800m	1st	1:45.4
15 Aug	Weltklasse	Zurich	1500m	1st	3:32.03 (WR)

Date	Event	Track	Distance	Place	Time
1980 (aged 22/23)					
23 Apr	Loughborough Match	Crystal Palace	3000m	1st	7:57.4 (pb)
7 May	Loughborough Match	Isleworth	1500m	1st	3:45.1
11 May	Yorkshire Championships	Cudworth	5000m	1st	14.06.2 (pb)
21 May	Philips Meeting	Crystal Palace	800m	1st	1:47.48
25 May	Inter-Counties Championships	Birmingham	800m(h)	1st	1:48.93
26 May	Inter-Counties Championships	Birmingham	800m(f)	1st	1:45.41
1 Jun	International Invitation	Turin	800m	1st	1:45.74
5 Jun	Loughborough v. AAA	Loughborough	800m	1st	1:45.0
7 Jun	N. Counties Champs	Hull	800m	1st	1:44.7
15 Jun	UK Championships	Crystal Palace	400m	8th	47.10
1 Jul	Bislett Games	Oslo	1000m	1st	2:13.40 (WR)
24 Jul	Olympic Games	Moscow	800m(h)	1st	1:48.44
25 Jul	Olympic Games	Moscow	800m(sf)	1st	1:46.61
26 Jul	Olympic Games	Moscow	800m(f)	2nd	1:45.85
30 Jul	Olympic Games	Moscow	1500m(h)	2nd	3:40.05
31 Jul	Olympic Games	Moscow	1500m(sf)	1st	3:39.34
1 Aug	Olympic Games	Moscow	1500m(f)	1st	3:38.40
8 Aug	Coca Cola	Crystal Palace	800m	1st	1:45.81
13 Aug	Weltklasse	Zurich	1500m	1st	3:32.19
14 Aug	International Invitation	Viareggio	800m	2nd	1:45.07
1981 (aged 23/24)					
24 Jan	AAA Indoor Championships	Cosford	3,000m	1st	7:55.2 (pb)
11 Feb	GB v. GDR (Indoor)	Cosford	800m	1st	1:46.0 (WR)
3 May	UAU Championships	Crystal Palace	400m	1st	46.9
13 May	Loughborough Match	Borough Road	400m	1st	47.4
17 May	Yorkshire Championships	Cleckheaton	800m	1st	1:46.5
3 Jun	England v. USA/Eth/Bel	Crystal Palace	800m	1st	1:44.06
3 Jun	England v. USA/Eth/Bel	Crystal Palace	4 x 400	-	45.7
7 Jun	GB v. USSR	Gateshead	4 x 400	-	46.5
10 Jun	International Invitation	Florence	800m	1st	1:41.73 (WR)

Date	Event	Track	Distance	Place	Time
5 Jul	Europa Cup Semi	Helsinki	800m	1st	1:47.57
7 Jul	International Invitation	Stockholm	1500m	1st	3:31.95 (pb)
11 Jul	Bislett Games	Oslo	1000m	1st	2:12.18 (WR)
17 Jul	GB v. USSR	Gateshead	800m	1st	1:47.47
19 Jul	Dairygate	Leicester	1000m	1st	2:17.6
31 Jul	Talbot Games	Crystal Palace	800m	1st	1:46.72
5 Aug	International Invitation	Viareggio	800m	1st	1:47.12
7 Aug	AAA Championships	Crystal Palace	800m(h)	1st	1:45.84
8 Aug	AAA Championships	Crystal Palace	800m(f)	1st	1:45.41
15 Aug	Europa Cup Final	Zagreb	800m	1st	1:47.03
19 Aug	Weltklasse	Zurich	1 mile	1st	3:48.53 (WR)
28 Aug	Golden Mile	Brussels	1 mile	1st	3:47.33 (WR)
4 Sep	World Cup	Rome	800m	1st	1:46.16

1982 (aged 24/ 25)

Date	Event	Track	Distance	Place	Time
16 May	Yorkshire Championships	Cudworth	1500m	1st	3:39.1
5 Jun	International Invitation	Bordeaux	2000m	1st	4:58.85 (pb)
4 Aug	Time Trial	Nottingham	800m	1st	1:46.5
17 Aug	International Invitation	Zurich	800m	1st	1:44.48
20 Aug	Talbot Games	Crystal Palace	800m	1st	1:45.85
22 Aug	International Invitation	Cologne	800m	1st	1:45.10
30 Aug	BAAB/Heinz Games	Crystal Palace	4 x 800	1st	(7:03.89) (WR)
			4th leg		1:44.01
6 Sep	European Championships	Athens	800m(h)	1st	1:48.66
7 Sep	European Championships	Athens	800m(sf)	1st	1:47.98
8 Sep	European Championships	Athens	800m(f)	2nd	1:46.68

1983 (aged 25/26)

Date	Event	Track	Distance	Place	Time
12 Feb	GB v. France (Indoor)	Cosford	1500m	1st	3:42.06
12 Mar	England v. USA (Indoor)	Cosford	800m	1st	1:44.91 (WR)

Date	Event	Track	Distance	Place	Time
19 Mar	GB v. Norway (Indoor)	Oslo	1000m	1st	2:18.58 (WR)
16 May	Yorkshire Championships	Cleckheaton	1500m	1st	3:45.8
5 Jun	GB v. USSR	Birmingham	1 mile	1st	4:03.37
12 Jun	Loughborough v. AAA	Loughborough	800m	1st	1:44.99
24 Jun	Permit Meeting	Paris	1500m	2nd	3:35.17
28 Jun	Permit Meeting	Oslo	800m	1st	1:43.80
15 Jul	Talbot Games	Crystal Palace	1500m	2nd	3:36.03
23 Jul	AAA Championships	Crystal Palace	1 mile	2nd	3:52.93
31 Jul	Gateshead Games	Gateshead	800m	4th	1:45.31

1984 (aged 26/27)

Date	Event	Track	Distance	Place	Time
12 May	GRE League	Wolverhampton	4 x 400m	-	-
			2nd leg	-	46.8
19 May	Middlesex Championships	Enfield	800m	1st	1:45.2
2 Jun	S. Counties Championships	Crystal Palace	1500m	1st	3:43.11
24 Jun	AAA Championships	Crystal Palace	1500m	2nd	3:39.79
28 Jun	Permit Meeting	Oslo	800m	1st	1:43.84
4 Jul	Beverly Baxter Meeting	Haringey	1 mile	1st	3:54.6
3 Aug	Olympic Games	Los Angeles	800m(h)	1st	1:45.71
4 Aug	Olympic Games	Los Angeles	800m(h)	3rd	1:46.75
5 Aug	Olympic Games	Los Angeles	800m(sf)	1st	1:45.51
6 Aug	Olympic Games	Los Angeles	800m(f)	2nd	1:43.64
9 Aug	Olympic Games	Los Angeles	1500m(h)	2nd	3:45.30
10 Aug	Olympic Games	Los Angeles	1500m(sf)	3rd	3:35.81
11 Aug	Olympic Games	Los Angeles	1500m(f)	1st	3:32.53 (OR)
19 Aug	GRE League	Haringey	1500m	1st	3:45.20
22 Aug	Weltklasse	Zurich	1500m	1st	3:32.39

1985 (aged 27/ 28)

Date	Event	Track	Distance	Place	Time
11 May	GRE League	Birmingham	800m	1st	1:49.37
18 May	Middlesex Championships	Enfield	800m	1st	1:44.0
8 Jun	Euro/Club Championships	Haringey	800m	1st	1:48.37

Date	Event	Track	Distance	Place	Time
9 Jun	Euro/Club Championships	Haringey	1500m	1st	3:47.27
16 Jun	Moorcroft Mile	Coventry	1 mile	1st	3:54.5
21 Jun	England v USA	Birmingham	800m	1st	1:46.23
19 Jul	Peugeot Talbot	Crystal Palace	800m	1st	1:44.34
27 Jul	Bislett Games	Oslo	1 mile	3rd	3:49.22
2 Aug	IAC/Coca-Cola	Crystal Palace	1 mile	2nd	3:56.89
21 Aug	Weltklasse	Zurich	1500m	2nd	3:32.13
25 Aug	Grand Prix	Cologne	800m	2nd	1:43.07

1986 (aged 28/ 29)

Date	Event	Track	Distance	Place	Time
25 Jan	AAA Indoor Championships	Cosford	3000m	3rd	7:55.58
8 Feb	GB v Hungary (Indoor)	Cosford	1500m	1st	3:45.65
8 Mar	England v USA (Indoor)	Cosford	3000m	1st	7:54.32 (pb)
10 May	GRE League	Birmingham	1500m	1st	3:45.27
17 May	Middlesex Championships	Enfield	800m	1st	1:47.9
4 Jun	Invitation	Madrid	800m	1st	1:45.66
27 Jun	Invitation	Hengelo	1500m	1st	3:34.32
1 Jul	Grand Prix	Stockholm	800m	2nd	1:44.17
11 Jul	Peugeot Talbot	Crystal Palace	800m	1st	1:44.10
16 Jul	Beverly Baxter	Haringey	1000m	1st	2:14.90
28 Jul	Commonwealth Games	Edinburgh	800m(h)	1st	1:53.13
28 Jul	Commonwealth Games	Edinburgh	800m(sf)	3rd	1:48.07
13 Aug	Weltklasse	Zurich	1500m	2nd	3:35.22
20 Aug	Invitation	Berne	1500m	1st	3:35.09
26 Aug	European Championships	Stuttgart	800m(h)	1st	1:47.64
27 Aug	European Championships	Stuttgart	800m(sf)	3rd	1:47.10
28 Aug	European Championships	Stuttgart	800m(f)	1st	1:44.50
29 Aug	European Championships	Stuttgart	1500m(h)	2nd	3:39.03
31 Aug	European Championships	Stuttgart	1500m(f)	2nd	3:41.67
7 Sep	Grand Prix	Rieti	1500m	1st	3:29.77 (pb)
12 Sep	McVities	Crystal Palace	800m	1st	1:44.28

Date	Event	Track	Distance	Place	Time
1987 (aged 29/30)					
13 Mar	England v. USA (Indoor)	Cosford	3000m	1st	7:54.33
9 May	GRE League	Portsmouth	800m	1st	1:46.18
9 May	GRE League	Portsmouth	4 x 400m	-	46.8
1988 (aged 30/31)					
13 Feb	Meadowlands Meeting (Indoor)	New Jersey	3000m	dnf	-
12 Mar	England v. USA	Cosford	3000m	2nd	8:05.80
14 May	Middlesex Championships	Enfield	800m	1st	1:48.8
19 Jun	GB v. USSR/France	Portsmouth	800m	1st	1:48.63
24 Jun	Grand Prix	Lausanne	800m	2nd	1:45.50
8 Jul	Peugeot Talbot	Crystal Palace	800m	1st	1:46.13
31 Jul	Invitation	Rapperswil	1500m	1st	3:37.74
8 Aug	AAA Championships (trials)	Birmingham	1500m(h)	5th	3:45.01
26 Aug	Grand Prix	Berlin	800m	2nd	1:47.87
28 Aug	Grand Prix	Koblenz	800m	2nd	1:43.93
31 Aug	Invitation	Rieti	1500m	3rd	3:35.72
1989 (aged 31/32)					
20 May	Middlesex Championships	Enfield	800m	1st	1:47.2
3 Jun	Euro/Club Championships	Belgrade	1500m	1st	3:51.89
24 Jun	Euro/Club Championships	Belgrade	800m	1st	1:46.60
24 Jun	Invitation	Birmingham	800m	1st	1:46.83
21 Jul	Invitation	Rovereto	800m	1st	1:45.97
2 Aug	Invitation	Viareggio	800m	1st	1:46.04
13 Aug	AAA Championships (trials)	Birmingham	1500m	1st	3.41.38
16 Aug	Weltklasse	Zurich	1500m	2nd	3:34.05
20 Aug	Grand Prix	Cologne	800m	4th	1:45.13
29 Aug	Invitation	Berne	800m	1st	1:43.38
9 Sep	World Cup	Barcelona	1500m	2nd	3:35.79
15 Sep	McVities	Crystal Palace	800m	1st	1:45.70

Date	Event	Track	Distance	Place	Time
1990 (aged 32/33)					
4 Jan	Invitation	Hobart	1000m	1st	2:21.0
14 Jan	Invitation	Sydney	800m	1st	1:47.66
29 Jan	C'wealth Games	Auckland	800m(h)	2nd	1:49.83
29 Jan	C'wealth Games	Auckland	800m(sf)	4th	1:47.67
1 Feb	C'wealth Games	Auckland	800m(f)	6th	1:47.24

INDEX